RAPE DURING
CIVIL WAR

RAPE DURING CIVIL WAR

Dara Kay Cohen

CORNELL UNIVERSITY PRESS   ITHACA AND LONDON

First published 2016 by Cornell University Press
First printing, Cornell Paperbacks, 2016
Printed in the United States of America

Library of Congress Cataloging-in-Publication Data

Names: Cohen, Dara Kay, 1979– author.
Title: Rape during civil war / Dara Kay Cohen.
Description: Ithaca ; London : Cornell University Press, 2016. |
    Includes bibliographical references and index.
Identifiers: LCCN 2016013022 | ISBN 9781501702518 (cloth : alk. paper) |
    ISBN 9781501705274 (pbk. : alk. paper)
Subjects: LCSH: Rape as a weapon of war. | Soldiers—Sexual behavior. |
    Civil war.
Classification: LCC HV6558 .C643 2016 | DDC 362.883—dc23
LC record available at http://lccn.loc.gov/2016013022

Cornell University Press strives to use environmentally responsible suppliers and materials to the fullest extent possible in the publishing of its books. Such materials include vegetable-based, low-VOC inks and acid-free papers that are recycled, totally chlorine-free, or partly composed of nonwood fibers. For further information, visit our website at www.cornellpress.cornell.edu.

Cloth printing   10 9 8 7 6 5 4 3 2 1
Paperback printing   10 9 8 7 6 5 4 3 2 1

To Barry and Layla

Contents

Tables and Figures

Tables

Figures

Acknowledgments

This book focuses on a puzzle: why do some armed groups rape while others never do? The puzzle is challenging for (at least) two reasons. First, the data on rape—perhaps more so than on almost any other form of violence—are notoriously poor, making rigorous research difficult. And second, the process of researching the topic of rape can be emotionally demanding. As I began the research for this book, it became clear that in order to understand armed groups' motivations for rape in wartime, I would need to hear directly from the members of armed groups. The process that followed—including six trips to three countries to conduct interviews and collect data—has been immensely rewarding, but it has not been easy. Some of the stories that were shared with me—both by ex-combatants and by victims of violence—are indelibly imprinted on my memory. But despite the disturbing subject matter, and the fact that some of the events described are horrifying, the tone throughout the book is analytical, mostly leaving aside outrage in the presentation of the data and the analyses. While my indignation at the terrible violence that many people have endured in the wars featured in this book certainly guided the choice of topic, the role of a social scientist is to evaluate dispassionately the evidence for competing arguments. I am first and foremost extremely grateful for the many people around the world whom I interviewed for the research in this book and who have entrusted me with the painful details of their most difficult days. My hope is that the research I have conducted will serve as a basis for activists, practitioners, scholars, and policymakers to better advocate for change in the future.

I began the process of writing this book nearly ten years ago, and I have been assisted by many friends, colleagues, students, and mentors along the way. I am deeply indebted to faculty at Stanford University for encouragement and guidance. Jim Fearon has been a wonderful teacher and mentor, and his intense engagement, challenging questions, and careful comments on many drafts of this project—both during my time at Stanford and for years after I graduated—have immeasurably strengthened my arguments and ideas. Jeremy Weinstein was the first faculty member I approached with the idea of writing on wartime rape, and his early and avid support was key in helping me to muster the courage to complete this project. Scott Sagan provided helpful comments on drafts and important advice on how to frame the research questions. I am also thankful to David Laitin, who helped me to clarify my early ideas about pursuing wartime rape as a research topic, and to Ken Schultz and Martha Crenshaw for extensive comments on various drafts.

Beyond the faculty at Stanford, I have had the unbelievable fortune of being mentored by Elisabeth Wood at Yale University. She is one of the most generous advisers imaginable and has been giving of both her time and her resources in support of this project. I am so thankful for her thoughtful advice on my work, the profession, and indeed, life in general. I am intensely grateful for the opportunity to have been (and to continue to be) a student of such an inspiring scholar and teacher.

I worked on this manuscript while serving as an assistant professor at two universities and benefited from advice and comments from many of the faculty at both institutions, including Brian Atwood, Sherry Gray, Ron Krebs, Jim Ron, Kathryn Sikkink, and Joe Soss at the University of Minnesota, and Graham Allison, Matt Baum, Bill Clark, Tarek Masoud, Quinton Mayne, Ryan Sheely, and Steve Walt at Harvard University. I am especially grateful to Michael Barnett, my former senior colleague at the Humphrey School of Public Affairs at Minnesota, who read a rough draft and offered detailed advice on how to shape the book project.

Extraordinary undergraduate and graduate students, across three universities, provided excellent research assistance in the process of gathering data and writing the case studies. Thank you to Dan Bacon, Jessie Hao, and Emma Welch at Stanford; Sean Fahnhorst, Amelia Kendall, Cardessa Luckett, and Matthew Stenberg at the University of Minnesota; and Ahsan Barkatullah, Nyasha Weinberg, and Hannah Winnink at Harvard. Matthew Valerius at Minnesota and Shelley Liu at Harvard were extremely hardworking and well organized at critical stages, and I am particularly grateful for their efforts.

I am thankful to many people who have offered ideas and comments—both in writing and through stimulating conversations—throughout the years, including Brooke Ackerly, Erin Baines, Amanda Blair, Mia Bloom, Charli Carpenter, Jeff Checkel, Kate Cronin-Furman, Christian Davenport, Alex Downes, Lynn Eden, Tanisha Fazal, Jonathan Forney, Page Fortna, Lee Ann Fujii, Scott Gates, Anita Gohdes, Joshua Goldstein, Mala Htun, Valerie Hudson, Macartan Humphreys, Mackenzie Israel-Trummel, Patrick Johnston, Stathis Kalyvas, Paul Kapur, Sabrina Karim, Matthew Kocher, Michele Leiby, Jason Lyall, Meghan Foster Lynch, Andy Mack, Bridget Marchesi, Zoe Marks, Dyan Mazurana, Rose McDermott, Alex Montgomery, Will Moore, Rebecca Neilsen, Fionnuala Ní Aoláin, Ragnhild Nordås, Bob Pape, Jeremy Pressman, Andrew Radin, Dani Reiter, Scott Sagan, Beth Simmons, Laura Sjoberg, Inger Skjaelsbæk, Alan Stam, Paul Staniland, Jessica Stanton, Scott Straus, Dawn Teele, Kai Thaler, Kimberly Theidon, and Barb Walter. I apologize to those I may have neglected to mention.

I received a large number of helpful comments on the book at various stages from participants in seminars at Brown University, Columbia University, Dartmouth College, German Institute of Global and Area Studies (GIGA), Harvard University, Hebrew University, McGill University, Northeastern University, Northwestern University, Princeton University, University of British Columbia, University of California-San Diego, University of Chicago, University of Connecticut, University of Florida, University of Michigan, University of Minnesota, University of Pennsylvania, University of Pittsburgh, University of Wisconsin-Madison, Uppsala University, and Yale University.

I had a wonderful cohort of colleagues at Stanford whose support and friendship were helpful both to this project and to getting the early stages of our professional lives started, especially Claire Adida, Rikhil Bhavnani, Eduardo Bruera, Matt Carnes, Luke Condra, Jesse Driscoll, Roy Elis, Desha Girod, Oliver Kaplan, Bethany Lacina, Nicholai Lidow, Avital Livny, Neil Malhotra, Yotam Margalit, Victor Menaldo, Natan Sachs, Jake Shapiro, and Alberto Simpser. I am especially appreciative of Jessica Weeks, whose friendship and support have influenced this project and my academic career.

I received generous financial support, without which this work would not have been possible, from the Humphrey School at the University of Minnesota and the Kennedy School at Harvard University. I also received funding for fieldwork and data collection from the National Science Foundation Doctoral Dissertation Improvement Grant (SES-0720440); the Peace Scholar Dissertation Fellowship of the United States Institute of Peace; and the Center for International Security and Cooperation (CISAC), the Freeman Spogli Institute for International Studies, and the Clayman Institute for Gender Research at Stanford University.

At Cornell University Press, Roger Haydon was enthusiastic about this book from its earliest stages and offered expert advice and humorous guidance that sharpened the final manuscript. I am grateful to the anonymous reviewers for their thoughtful feedback, to the Cornell University Press faculty board of editors for detailed questions and comments, and to Bridget Samburg for assistance with editing.

Earlier versions of some of the material in this book were previously published in "Explaining Rape during Civil War: Cross-National Evidence (1980–2009)," *American Political Science Review* 107, no. 3 (August 2013): 461–77; and "Female Combatants and the Perpetration of Violence: Wartime Rape in the Sierra Leone Civil War," *World Politics* 65, no. 3 (July 2013): 383–415. I thank the publishers of these journals for their permission to use this material.

My fieldwork was facilitated by the energetic, accomplished research assistants who also served as my interpreters during my fieldwork. I thank Violetta Conteh Moody and Amie Tholley, in Sierra Leone; Elsa Pinto and Augustinho Caet, in Timor-Leste; and Erika Murcia, in El Salvador. While dozens of people and organizations were helpful to me in conducting my fieldwork, Ibrahim Bangura of PRIDE-SL deserves special recognition for facilitating my research in Sierra Leone.

I am appreciative of the generosity of numerous scholars and researchers who shared their carefully collected quantitative and qualitative data with me: Jana Asher, Patrick Ball, Jim Fearon, Maggie Haertsch, Amelia Hoover Green, Michael Horowitz, Macartan Humphreys, Sabrina Karim, Michele Leiby, Hannah Loney, Jeffrey Pickering, and Jeremy Weinstein.

Although much of the work of an academic scholar is solitary, it would not be possible without a web of support from close friends and relatives. Megan Kaden, Melissa Sontag Broudo, and Larisa Shambaugh were all unflinching in their willingness to discuss the difficult topic of the book—and the sometimes-grueling process of writing it. I am grateful for the support of my parents, Linda and Ken, and my sister, Leah, who were curious and encouraging about this project, even agreeing to be an adoptive family to my dog, Truman, when I traveled to conduct research. My beloved grandparents Marty and Molly—who both passed away during the process of writing the book—became avid globetrotters in their later years and never tired of hearing tales about my travels overseas.

And finally, I thank my family. My daughter, Layla, whose arrival delayed the completion of this book and who learned to walk and then talk while I revised the manuscript: you inspire my work by igniting within me a sincere hope that you will grow up in a better and different—safer and more equal—world, especially for women and girls. Barry, my husband and my best friend, whose belief in me is unrelenting, and whose unqualified support of my academic pursuits—including accompanying me to Sierra Leone and Timor-Leste—knows no bounds: you are an unparalleled partner and a marvelous parent, and you help me remember the things that are most important in life. This book is for both of you.

RAPE DURING
CIVIL WAR

THE PUZZLE OF RAPE IN CIVIL WAR

The rebels finally came to Freetown when I was eighteen years old. I was hiding in a house with my family when the rebels came to the door and said that they were here to "get ladies." They grabbed me and brought me outside. They tied my arms and legs to a car, so I was lying on the street like this [stands up from her chair and spreads both her arms and her legs wide apart]. Eight men raped me, in front of my father and my whole family. I was a virgin and was very attractive. In my family, we don't talk about what happened to me. In Africa, virginity is highly prized. I will not be able to marry now.

—Freetown, Sierra Leone, August 2, 2006

During the militia attacks of 1999, there was terrible violence and many people were forced to leave their homes. My cousin is in a wheelchair. When everyone was fleeing in 1999, the family made the difficult decision to leave her behind. They would have been unable to escape if she came with them. So she was left by herself, and she was raped by the militias. She got pregnant [sighs, her eyes fill with tears]. The child is beautiful.

—Dili, Timor-Leste, July 13, 2012

Stories like these are common in countries where civil wars are characterized by the widespread rape of noncombatants. Members of the armed groups involved in the wars in Sierra Leone and Timor-Leste raped thousands of civilians. But it would be a mistake to conclude that all civil wars are marked by such terrible violence. In fact, many other recent conflicts saw no or only limited reports of rape. Of the ninety-one major civil wars that occurred between 1980 and 2012, fifty-nine had reports of significant rape during at least one year of the conflict.[1] This finding suggests that while rape is a serious problem in many wars, it is not ubiquitous in every war.[2]

Numerous powerful beliefs currently exist about the causes of wartime rape, and they have a major impact on the policies designed to prevent rape in wartime and to mitigate its consequences. Much conventional wisdom—for example, that rape is more likely in ethnic wars, or that a country's level of gender inequality

1

is correlated with wartime rape—is based on lessons drawn from the two most-studied cases of wartime rape: Rwanda and Bosnia-Herzegovina. Evidence suggests that in both of these bitter ethnic wars, rape was directed by political leaders and military commanders as part of an organized military strategy.

Even within the context of a single war, some armed groups perpetrate rape while others never do. In Sierra Leone, for instance, the majority of victims—like the one from Sierra Leone quoted above—were raped by members of the rebel factions. In contrast, during the 1999 crisis in Timor-Leste, members of state-supported militia groups perpetrated the vast majority of the rape—including the attack on the interviewee's cousin—but the rebel forces were almost never reported as perpetrators of rape. Turning to global patterns, the variation in perpetrators is made more stark: during major civil wars between 1980 and 2012, it was most common for both sides (that is, both state forces and insurgent groups) to be reported as perpetrators of rape. Perpetration by only state actors occurred with less frequency; by only insurgent actors it was relatively rare.[3]

Observers often assume that the underlying causes of all wartime rape are similar to those in Rwanda and Bosnia-Herzegovina: namely, that rape is ordered as part of military strategy, and as a tool of ethnic cleansing or genocide. In this book, I argue that many of these common assumptions are flawed. They are based on incorrect inferences, have limited explanatory power, are not supported by the best available evidence, and, perhaps most importantly, are likely to produce ineffective policies aimed at preventing rape in future wars. So, how can patterns of rape in recent civil wars best be explained? And in particular, what distinguishes armed groups that perpetrate rape on a massive scale from those that do not? Using multiple methods of research—including an original dataset of reported rape in all recent major civil wars and extensive fieldwork in three postconflict countries—I systematically examine a set of common arguments for rape in wartime, and advance a new argument, called *combatant socialization*.

Central Argument in Brief

I argue that armed groups may use wartime rape as a socialization tool when they suffer from low intragroup cohesion. Rape—and especially gang rape, or rape by multiple perpetrators—enables armed groups with forcibly recruited fighters to create bonds of loyalty and esteem from initial circumstances of fear and mistrust. Members of the group form social bonds by participating in acts of rape, and these bonds are strengthened and reproduced in the process of recounting the violence in the aftermath. The creation of cohesion is important from the perspective of the members of the armed group because cohesion provides abductees with basic needs, including protection, food, and shelter, during the chaos of conflict.

The use of kidnapping as a recruitment mechanism was surprisingly common during recent civil wars: about 29 percent of state forces reportedly used press-ganging—the term commonly used to describe abduction by states—to garner fighters, while about 22 percent of insurgent groups used abduction. As I demonstrate, groups that use these extreme forms of forced recruitment are significantly more likely to be reported as perpetrators of rape than are groups that use voluntary methods. The main goal of the analyses in this book is to understand why press-ganging and abduction can lead to the increased use of rape in wartime—a process I term combatant socialization.

Research from the fields of economics, sociology, and criminology makes it clear that violence can serve an essential purpose in organizing the structure of groups. Institutions with continuous influxes of new, random, involuntary members or recruits—such as armed groups, street gangs, and prisons—are common venues for such violence (Humphreys and Weinstein 2006; Jankowski 1991; Kaminski 2003). As Humphreys and Weinstein (2006) write, anxiety over individuals' status within groups may lead to performative violence.[4] By participating in group violence—in this case, rape—and by bragging about the individual rapes they committed, combatants signal to their new peers both their membership in the unit and their willingness to take risks to remain in the group. Rape then becomes a part of the process of hazing new recruits and of maintaining social order among existing members while also communicating norms of masculinity, virility, and strength.

A phenomenon as complex as wartime rape may have any number of conceivable causes; none of the arguments considered in this book, including combatant socialization, can fully explain every instance of wartime rape. Overall, the socialization aspects of wartime rape have been largely overlooked in previous research. While the combatant socialization argument is not the only or even the most important factor in all cases, I provide both cross-national and case study evidence that combatant socialization accounts for variation in wartime rape as well as or better than some rival explanations, including ethnic hatred and gender inequality. I also find strong support for theories of opportunity and the corrupting role of material resources for armed groups. These findings challenge common arguments and have important implications for both theory and policy.

Defining Key Terms

Before proceeding further, it is useful to clarify some key terms. Following Elisabeth Wood (2006, 308), I define rape as "the coerced (under physical force or threat of physical force against the victim or a third person) penetration of the anus or vagina by the penis or another object, or of the mouth by the penis."[5]

This book is focused exclusively on rape by combatants during intrastate conflict. It is important to note that I analyze the occurrence of *rape* specifically, not "sexual violence" more broadly defined. I focus on rape because it is arguably the most severe, may be among the most common, and is the form on which the policy community has most focused. But it is, of course, only one form of sexual violence. During wartime, victims have reported a dizzying array of sexualized violations, including sexual slavery, sexual mutilation, forced sterilization, and forced abortion. It is probable that each of these forms of sexual violence follows its own distinct logic—and these are likely quite different from the logic of rape.[6] While each of these various types of sexual violence merits its own in-depth study, they are outside of the scope of the main argument presented in this book.[7]

One reason I have focused on rape rather than on sexual violence writ large is that no clear definitions exist of what constitutes sexual violence. Scholars have employed numerous definitions of sexual violence in recent studies.[8] Most definitions include rape; however, some include nonviolent acts such as forced undressing and sexualized insults, while others include a variety of other violations that involve physical violence. In a survey of ex-combatants in Liberia, the authors included forced marriage in their definition of sexual violence (Johnson et al. 2008). In a study of gender-based violence in Timor-Leste, the authors' definition of sexual violence included a range of violations from being "forced to give/receive oral/vaginal/anal sex" to "improper sexual comments" (Hynes et al. 2004, 301). A cross-national report on wartime sexual violence between 1987 and 2007 included sexual harassment, sexual abuse, rape, gang rape, attempted rape, sexual slavery, forced pregnancy, and sex trafficking (Bastick, Grimm, and Kunz 2007, 19). Obviously, how sexual violence is defined has a significant impact on the extent to which researchers may find the phenomenon in a particular context.[9] The lack of a consensus definition of sex violence has hampered progress in its analysis, because it is difficult to compare findings across contexts when researchers use vastly different definitions.

Even the definition of rape is contested. Cultural understandings of what constitutes rape and other forms of sexual violence vary dramatically. Marital rape, for instance, is not universally recognized as such (Rozée 1993). Recent studies about men's attitudes toward rape illustrate this point. In a survey conducted in the Democratic Republic of the Congo (DRC), few male respondents recognized forcing a female partner to have sex as rape (Slegh et al. 2012). Another survey, of thousands of men in six Asian countries (Fulu et al. 2013), found that the prevalence of men who reported in engaging in acts that constitute the rape of intimate partners reached as high as 22 percent, suggesting that such violence may not be understood as wrong in some contexts and may be very widespread.[10]

Confusion over cultural understandings of rape is another reason that this study analyzes exclusively rape by armed combatants, focusing in particular on gang rape. Gang rape—especially when perpetrated in public and by strangers, as is often reported in wartime—is arguably recognized as near-universally taboo.[11] Even in regions where peacetime rape is thought to be common, scholars have noted that public gang rape is perceived as terrifying. Ingrid Samset (2011) found that peacetime rape prior to the war in the DRC—the so-called "rape capital of the world" (BBC News 2010)—was mainly committed by one perpetrator in private; however, wartime rape came as a shock to local people, in part because of its increased brutality and public nature.

What Is Known about Rape and War

While a complete overview of what scholars and researchers have learned in recent years about the incidence of rape in wartime is far too vast to recount here,[12] several key findings from the established knowledge of rape in wartime form the basis for the analysis in this book. These include the following: rape is likely to increase during periods of wartime, there exist both male and female victims and perpetrators of rape, and the most commonly reported form of rape during wartime is gang rape.

Rape Increases during Wartime

While the systematic data on wartime rape are sparse, it is generally recognized that the likelihood of rape increases during wartime (Wood 2013) and is commonly viewed as "a 'normal' accompaniment to war" (Goldstein 2001, 362). A World Bank report, for example, notes that "the incidence of rape increases often dramatically during war" (Hoeffler and Reynal-Querol 2003, 15). In at least two cross-national statistical studies, scholars have found a correlation between periods of wartime and reports of rape and other forms of sexual violence. First, in a study of sexual violence in 2003, Butler, Gluch, and Mitchell (2007) found that civil wars are positively associated with increased reports of sexual violence. Although the finding falls just short of statistical significance, the authors argue that it provides suggestive evidence that "women [become more] vulnerable during armed conflict and wartime" (679). Similarly, in an analysis of "collective rape" between 1980 and 2003, Green (2006) found a strong relationship between the presence of civil war and reports of rape; she notes that such a correlation does not hold for interstate wars, possibly due to an increased probability that civilians will be targeted during civil wars as compared to interstate wars. Rape may also be more likely because of a lack of legal and normative prohibitions, the stress of conflict, and increased contact between armed fighters and vulnerable individuals.

Both Women and Men Are Victims—and Perpetrators

In this book, I focus on female victims of wartime rape. This decision in part reflects the conventional wisdom—supported by the vast majority of evidence from research findings—that most victims of wartime rape are women (e.g., Aranburu 2012, 286). But it is also due to the enormous barriers to collecting systematic and reliable data on male victims of rape, including underreporting by male victims and the norms and practices of researchers and scholars who document sexual violations.[13] It is unfortunate that, although more data are being collected, current sources are insufficient to analyze male rape in the statistical analyses or case studies in this book.

Male rape is widely thought to be vastly underreported during wartime, due to "shame, confusion, guilt, fear and stigma" (Sivakumaran 2007, 255). In countries where homosexuality is illegal or punishable by death, underreporting is likely to be particularly problematic.[14] The available data from Sierra Leone on male rape—the best-documented of the cases explored in this book—are suggestive of underreporting by male victims. In the national victimization survey of more than 3,600 households, which is used in the Sierra Leone analysis in chapter 3, there was exactly one report of the rape of a male victim (and this report was independently confirmed by the survey's author). Similarly, in my fieldwork interviews in Sierra Leone, male rape victims were rarely reported, and then only in the form of rumors, not self-identification. This was in marked contrast to female victims, who not infrequently self-identified as rape victims. However, Human Rights Watch (HRW) (2003, 42) received a number of reports of men who were raped by the Revolutionary United Front (RUF) rebels in Sierra Leone, and the Trial Chamber for the Special Court of Sierra Leone documented the rape of men

(Sivakumaran 2010).[15] It therefore remains unclear if few men were victimized or if men did not report their violations—perhaps because, as the HRW report notes, male victims feared being perceived as homosexual. A similar dearth of data on male victims in both Timor-Leste and El Salvador prevents a detailed analysis in the case study chapters of the sexual violations men have suffered.

Another barrier to collecting systematic data on male victims is the way in which researchers design studies. Many studies of wartime rape assume men are the perpetrators and women are the victims, and as a result, most surveys of victims do not ask specific questions about the sex of the perpetrators. The absence of systematic data on male victimization suggests that pervasive gender norms prevent researchers and policymakers alike from designing robust, gender-neutral studies of wartime sexual violence. Turning again to Sierra Leone, in nearly all of the existing surveys that have focused on rape and other forms of sexual violence there—such as a widely cited study by Physicians for Human Rights (PHR) (Reis et al. 2002)—women were the only respondents and few, if any, questions were posed to respondents about male sexual victimization (Cohen 2013b). Research practices are slowly changing: a small number of recent studies have found that when men are directly asked about their experiences with violence, they may be willing to report it. In a survey from the DRC that was published in the *Journal of the American Medical Association*, researchers specifically asked men about their histories with sexual violence and found high levels of reporting. But until such research practices become more common, the incidence of male victimization will remain largely unknown—and unknowable.

A related problem is the way analysts interpret data about sexual violence when the victims are men.[16] In an analysis of a random sample of testimonies given to the Peruvian Truth and Reconciliation Commission (TRC), Michele Leiby (2012) found that the incidence of male victims of sexual violence (defined broadly to include sexual humiliation, rape, torture, mutilation, and threats) was far higher than had been reported in the official statistics of the TRC. She argues that sexual violations committed against male victims were often officially counted as incidents of "torture" rather than sexual violence. Similarly, in Sierra Leone, the TRC separated "rape" and "sexual abuse" into two distinct categories. Sexual abuse was defined as forced undressing and other types of public sexual humiliation—and the majority (61 percent) of reported victims were men. This pattern contrasted sharply with rape, of which all reported victims were women (Conibere et al. 2004, 13). In sum, while male victims still are fairly hidden in studies of wartime rape and other forms of sexual violence, much of the existing evidence suggests that women make up the majority of the victims of rape, justifying the central focus of the present analysis.

In contrast, there is increasing evidence that women may be perpetrators of wartime rape. A number of studies have documented the involvement of women as perpetrators of rape and other forms of sexual violence in a variety of conflicts, including in the DRC (Johnson et al. 2010), in Liberia (Specht 2006; Advocates for Human Rights 2009), in Haiti (Faedi Duramy 2014), in Rwanda (Jones 2002; Sharlach 1999; Wood 2009; African Rights 1995), and as part of the Abu Ghraib prison scandal (Landesman 2002; McKelvey 2007; Gourevitch and Morris 2008). But while these studies imply that women are involved in perpetrating sexual violations more often than is commonly assumed, systematic data on the relative frequency of such violence by women—and men—are not available for most conflicts. One exception is Sierra Leone, and patterns of perpetration by women, men, and mixed-sex groups are explored in chapter 3.

Gang Rape Is the Most Commonly Reported Form

By many accounts, when wartime rape is widespread, gang rape is the most commonly reported form, across numerous conflicts and time periods (e.g., Mezey 1994; Tanaka 1997; Theidon 2007). Historian Joanna Bourke (2007) argues that the prevalence of multiple perpetrators is one of the features that distinguish wartime rape from peacetime rape.[17] Peacetime rates of gang rape are typically between 5 and 20 percent in most countries, while the proportion of reported rapes with multiple perpetrators is much higher during wartime (Wood 2013, 133).[18] Case studies from numerous disciplines reveal similar patterns. During the Peruvian civil war, "gang rape was the norm" (Sharlach 2009, 452), while "gang rape was 'the standard torture mechanism'" in Chile, Argentina, and Uruguay for women viewed as dangerous to the state (Goldstein 2001, 364). Wartime gang rape is also well documented in conflicts in Bosnia-Herzegovina, Guatemala, Sierra Leone, the DRC, and Vietnam (Wood 2013).

Beyond case studies, there are not a large number of systematic, comparative studies; of those that exist, almost all find that gang rape comprises the vast majority of reported wartime rape, particularly in cases where rape is believed to have been widespread. Wood (2013) points out that victims often report high levels of gang rape in studies where they are asked specifically about the number of perpetrators. Recent surveys largely confirm the findings from earlier case studies. A nationally representative survey of numerous forms of wartime violence in Sierra Leone found that three-quarters of the reported wartime rape was gang rape (Asher 2004). In addition, a 2010 survey by the Harvard Humanitarian Initiative in the DRC found that the most common form of rape was gang rape, with 69 percent of rape victims reporting that they had been gang-raped (Kelly et al. 2011). Although such studies with specific statistics are relatively rare, available evidence does indicate that the frequency of reported gang rape increases dramatically during wartime as compared to peacetime. This pattern may be the result of reporting bias; it is possible, for example, that victims are more likely to report gang rape than single-perpetrator rape, especially when such attacks are public.[19] But the fact that the incidence of gang rape appears to increase during periods of war across such a vast range of contexts, where barriers to reporting and cultural norms vary dramatically, decreases the likelihood that the finding is spurious.

Scope of the Argument

Civil Wars versus Wars between States

This study focuses on one type of conflict: recent, major civil wars that were ongoing between 1980 and 2012.[20] Civil wars have been the most common types of conflicts since World War II. Major civil wars, in which at least one thousand people are killed as a direct result of battle—the standard measure of severity—have occurred in about one-third of all countries over the past fifty years (Blattman and Miguel 2010). Civil wars have killed far more people than have interstate wars over the same period; by one estimate, the total number of people killed as a direct result of battle between 1945 and 1999 in civil wars was five times greater than the number killed in interstate wars (Fearon and Laitin 2003). For these reasons, it is arguably more important—and certainly more urgent, from a policy perspective—to understand the dynamics of rape during civil war than it is to analyze rape during wars between states.

The arguments developed in the book may be of some utility in explaining variation in rape during interstate war, but I have limited the statistical analyses to intrastate conflict only, and the three case studies are all civil wars. This distinction also follows the major division in the field of international relations between the study of civil war and the study of wars between states. However, the study period of 1980 to 2012 excludes some well-known cases of wartime rape, such as the Red Army's march across Eastern Europe and the extensive violence against women during the 1947 partition of India. By focusing the analysis on this more recent era, I am able to use sources and methods that would otherwise be unavailable, including collecting reliable data to estimate cross-national regressions and conducting interviews with perpetrators.

The use of rape during *civil* war is a particularly interesting case within the broader study of wartime rape. Existing theories about war and rape often suggest that civil war is an unlikely context for widespread rape (e.g., Benard 1994; Hayden 2000). One scholar argues that "civil wars have generally been considered 'low-rape' wars" because rape is typically employed when the perpetrator wants to destroy a society permanently (Benard 1994, 36). Bourke (2007, 378) also maintains that sexual abuse is "easier" on the perpetrator—and therefore more likely—when the victim is seen as "racially and culturally foreign and inferior." Given that civil war commonly involves fighting among groups that ultimately seek to govern a country, and that many civil wars are not divided along ethnic lines in which one party is viewed as racially inferior, the use of rape during civil conflict is puzzling.

Rape by Armed Combatants

I analyze rape of noncombatants by members of armed groups during periods of war. This category of violence is the center of much recent policy discourse and the target of many international efforts to punish past perpetrators and to deter future ones. The focus in this book on armed groups as perpetrators is due in part to the mandate of international actors like the United Nations, which tend to concentrate on violence that directly results from war.

This does not imply, however, that rape by combatants is the most frequent form of rape in war zones. Increasing evidence shows that rape and other forms of sexual violence perpetrated by those known to the victim—and especially by intimate partners—is far more common than rape by combatants. A widely cited study based on a household survey in the DRC found that the number of women who reported sexual violence by an intimate partner was almost twice the number of women who reported rape by a nonpartner (Peterman, Palermo, and Bredenkamp 2011). Other studies confirm that intimate partner violence—both sexual and otherwise—is likely the most common form of violence experienced by women worldwide (Heise, Ellsberg, and Gottemoeller 2002). The 2012 Human Security Report also emphasized these patterns, arguing that "survey data suggest that most sexual violence in war-affected countries is *domestic*—which means it takes place primarily in the family. The most frequent perpetrators are not combatants, but husbands, other partners, household members, and relatives" (HSRP 2012, 33).[21]

Despite documentation of the frequency of rape by intimate partners and family members, issues with both conceptualization and data availability make it challenging to analyze violence by partners in this book. First, as I argue in chapter 1, rape by combatants during wartime is fundamentally different in form, brutality, and purpose than rape and sexual violence by intimate partners. Although important connections exist between wartime and partner violence—for example, scholars have examined whether returning soldiers may be more likely to abuse their partners (e.g., Newby et al. 2005)—conceptualizing wartime rape as a continuation of peacetime partner violence is of limited analytic utility (Wood 2015).[22] Indeed, scholars have found that there may be little correlation between previous experience with conflict and postconflict sexual violence; rape may become common in areas that were not affected by conflict, and vice versa (Jewkes et al. 2013). Second, while numerous excellent studies examine intimate partner violence in a variety of countries, they are limited in terms of location and scope; they are often not nationally representative and are rarely conducted on an annual basis. Reliable annual, cross-national data sources about such violence, akin to the sources used for the data on wartime rape presented later in the book, do not currently exist. Finally, while it is often assumed that rape in all forms increases during periods of war, sufficient data are not currently available to systematically test that claim; rarely are data available on rates of rape prior to the onset of conflict. For all of these reasons, I limit the following analysis to rape by combatants only.

Key Puzzles

In this book, I explore a set of key puzzles about the patterns of wartime rape. A robust explanation of why rape occurs during wartime must be able to account for each of these puzzles, and much of the remainder of the book is devoted to evaluating whether competing arguments can explain these questions.

Puzzle 1: Prevalence of Gang Rape

Why does wartime rape frequently take the form of gang rape, when gang rape is a relatively rare form of peacetime violence? The increased incidence of gang rape during periods of war suggests another reason, besides common explanations of increased opportunity or hatred of women, that rape occurs. The frequency of gang rape suggests that wartime rape can be analyzed as a form of group violence, similar to other acts of group violence such as mass killing. Viewing wartime rape as a type of group violence—explored in chapter 1—can prove fruitful in making sense of where and when rape is likely to occur.

Puzzle 2: Patterns of Perpetrators

How do we account for which armed groups are reported as perpetrators of wartime rape? Evidence from recent civil wars—the universe of cases analyzed in this book—suggests that in many cases, although they are often portrayed as monsters, the perpetrators of wartime rape are armed groups comprised of ordinary people, not sociopaths or members of highly trained militaries.[23] So why do these ordinary people, once they become members of armed groups, perpetrate rape, sometimes on a massive scale? In addition, reported perpetrators include not only men, but also women. How do we explain the involvement of female perpetrators in the rape of noncombatant victims? While many existing explanations for wartime rape are gendered, assuming a male perpetrator and a female victim, the fact that women may also participate in acts of rape raises important questions about the motivations and meanings of wartime rape. A robust explanation for wartime rape should be able to account for these complex patterns.

Puzzle 3: Lack of Evidence of Direct Orders

Wartime rape is now commonly described as a powerful, highly effective, and nearly costless "tool of war." Yet there is scant evidence from any recent civil conflict that military commanders or insurgent leaders ordered rape as part of an organized military strategy. If rape is so frequently being used as a tool or weapon of war, why is there not stronger evidence that rape is part of an official strategy?[24] To be sure, there are cases where orders or evidence of orders to rape are documented, but these cases are extraordinarily rare.[25] In addition, if rape is as "cheap" to perpetrate as the conventional wisdom suggests, why does it not happen even more often? While significant rape (cases that were coded in the highest two levels on the four-level scale presented later in the book) was reported in two-thirds of civil wars between 1980 and 2012, many current explanations would predict an even higher proportion.

In this book, I argue two related points that help to resolve these questions about orders. First, violence that is ordered by commanders as part of a strategy requires an explanation different from violence that is merely tolerated. Strategic violence implies a rational strategy directed from the top levels of the command structure. Violence that is tolerated by the command suggests that the violence originates with the soldiers themselves. Elisabeth Wood (2016) extends previous arguments, which typically divide wartime rape into two categories—either strategic or opportunistic—to create a third, intermediary category: "practice." She defines political violence as a practice as "violence that is neither ordered nor authorized but is tolerated by commanders" (2016, 1). I argue that this category of violence as a practice is likely a more common form of wartime rape than is rape as strategy. This observation has important implications for both theory and policy.

Second, rape is nowhere near as costless as the conventional wisdom suggests. In fact, numerous costs both to the armed group and to the individual perpetrator likely prevent even greater incidents of rape during wartime. Important among these costs is the threat of disease for the perpetrators, which can spread rapidly and affect their ability to perform their duties. I discuss these costs in more detail in chapter 1.

A related issue is a growing concern that analysts often assume the intended purpose of rape when studying its effects (Aranburu 2010; Cohen, Hoover Green, and Wood 2013; Eriksson Baaz and Stern 2013). For example, if rape has the effect of terrorizing civilians and displacing populations, analysts often argue that the perpetrators explicitly intended these effects as part of an overarching strategy of using rape as a weapon. However, because so few researchers have studied rape from the perspective of the perpetrators, direct evidence that combatants use rape in such rational and highly calculated ways is limited.[26]

Organization of the Book

This book is organized into three main parts: a discussion of the theoretical arguments about the determinants of wartime rape; statistical tests of hypotheses that are derived from these arguments; and a set of three in-depth case studies, based on my fieldwork interviews and analyses of subnational quantitative and qualitative data, that allow further tests of the hypotheses on the micro level.

The first chapter presents the main argument of the book: the combatant socialization argument. Beginning from the first key puzzle of wartime rape—why gang rape?—I describe how rape may be used by combatants to increase intragroup social ties where they are lacking. I focus on two important aspects of the process of combatant socialization: first, how violence can create cohesion among combatants, and second, why *sexualized* violence, in particular, is selected for cohesion building. I then distill the diverse range of arguments about the determinants of wartime rape, from a variety of disciplines and policy debates, into three sets of testable alternative explanations that I consider throughout the remainder of the book: opportunism/greed, ethnic hatred, and gender inequality. At the end of the chapter, I present a set of hypotheses and observable implications.

I then turn to the empirical strategy for the study and explain why I selected the three case studies and why I have combined quantitative statistical analyses and qualitative case studies based on my fieldwork. There are numerous research challenges and ethical concerns about conducting research on wartime rape, particularly when using field-based methods. While there exists a variety of possible sources for information on wartime rape, I argue that interviews with members of armed groups are essential to understanding the motivations of perpetrators.

I use an original dataset that captures reports of wartime rape from all ninety-one major civil wars between 1980 and 2012 to show that there is enormous variation in the patterns of wartime rape across recent civil conflicts. This variation itself challenges the conventional wisdom that rape is ubiquitous in wartime, perpetrated by all armed groups in all types of wars. In fact, while rape has occurred in the majority of recent wars, important patterns—in terms of where, when, and by whom rape has occurred—can be leveraged to better understand its causes.

After establishing that there is substantial variation in wartime rape, I examine the cross-national evidence for each of the hypotheses from the previous chapter. The most important finding uncovered by the statistical analysis is that abduction by insurgent groups and press-ganging by state forces—which I argue are proxies for low intragroup social cohesion—are strongly associated with reports of rape by insurgents and states, respectively. I also find strong support for arguments about opportunistic violence and the role of lootable resources in enabling violence. Equally as important, several powerful common explanations for rape in wartime—that rape is more likely in ethnic wars, during genocides, or in countries with marked gender inequality—are not supported by the evidence. I conclude that the combatant socialization argument explains wartime rape better than many competing alternatives.

The remaining chapters present three carefully selected case studies of civil wars from three different regions of the world—two of which were mass-rape wars, and one of which was characterized by relatively few reports of rape. In addition, of the two mass-rape wars, one is a case in which the majority of the rape was perpetrated by the rebel factions, while the other is a case in which the rape was mainly perpetrated by state-supported armed groups. In each chapter, I test the combatant socialization argument as well as the most plausible alternatives for that particular case.

I look first at the civil war in Sierra Leone (1991–2002), during which the RUF, the main rebel faction, committed the majority of the mass rape. In addition to my extensive fieldwork interviews with ex-combatants and noncombatants, the case of Sierra Leone is especially well documented, allowing for a detailed analysis of a variety of observable implications of the competing explanations. Sierra Leone is also notable as a case in which many women served as combatants in the rebel forces. Alongside the combatant socialization argument, I consider two alternative explanations for the patterns of rape in Sierra Leone: several strands of the opportunism/greed argument and—especially relevant given the participation of many female fighters—arguments about gender inequality.

In the next chapter, I examine another case of mass rape during the war in Timor-Leste (1975–1999). Although various forms of sexual violence reportedly occurred throughout the war, during the 1999 postreferendum crisis there was a massive increase in reports of rape perpetrated by state actors and their agents, local militias. Beyond the rise in reported incidents for this final year of the war, there is important variation in who perpetrated the rape during the conflict. The reported perpetrators of rape changed over time, from mostly Indonesian forces to mainly East Timorese pro-Indonesian militias. These documented patterns of rape in Timor-Leste raise important questions about how best to explain wartime rape. To do that, I evaluate the combatant socialization argument and two alternative explanations: that rape was the result of opportunity and greed, made possible because of the total chaos surrounding the period of the 1999 vote, and that rape was used as a form of revenge, either by Indonesia for Timor-Leste's vote for independence or by the local Timorese militia members themselves, who were expressing political grievances about perceived wrongs.

The last of the case study chapters analyzes the civil war in El Salvador (1980–1992), which experienced much lower levels of wartime rape than did the other two cases. The Salvadoran Armed Forces used widespread press-ganging throughout the conflict, and the Farabundo Martí National Liberation Front (FMLN) guerrilla movement, although largely voluntary, turned to abduction for a brief period. While engaging in these extreme forms of forced recruitment, both groups experienced significant problems with weak cohesion. The combatant socialization argument would predict that both groups would be at an increased likelihood for perpetrating gang rape—but there is limited evidence that either did so. Why was rape not *more* widespread during the conflict? This final case helps to test the scope conditions, or boundaries, of the combatant socialization argument and provides insight into what factors may make rape less likely to occur. In particular, intense internal ideological pressures within the FMLN, and strong external pressures from the United States on the Salvadoran Armed Forces, likely contributed to the absence of rape perpetrated by both groups.

Finally, the concluding chapter explores implications for both theory and policy. On the broadest level, the findings demonstrate that some of the conventional wisdom on the causes of rape in wartime is, at best, incomplete and, at worst, deeply flawed. Current narratives about the causes of rape too frequently focus on macro level or structural factors, such as the type of conflict or features of the country where the war is occurring, while ignoring the importance of variation at the level of the armed group. This misplaced attention can lead to erroneous conclusions about why rape happens and, ultimately, to misguided policy interventions. Through exploring the patterns of reported rape across recent civil wars—and through a detailed analysis of armed groups—the results of this study can offer lessons to policymakers, practitioners, and advocates seeking to mitigate the horrors of wartime rape.

THE LOGIC OF WARTIME RAPE

[What types of activities would the members of your group typically do together?] The group rape of women. Afterward, we would feel good and talk about it a lot, discuss it among ourselves, and laugh about it.

—RUF ex-combatant, Sierra Leone, March 29, 2008

What explains variation in the use of rape during civil conflicts? Despite the lack of clear evidence about basic patterns of wartime rape, ideas proliferate about its causes. One scholar counted more than a dozen different theories in the various literature, with explanations ranging from biology (men are evolutionarily prone to rape) to the type of war (ethnic wars create the conditions necessary for mass rape) (Wood 2009). Few of these theories are satisfying, and as I argue throughout the book, many fail to account for the remarkable variation in the forms of rape, the patterns of how rape is committed across time and space, and the identity of its perpetrators and victims.

In the first part of this chapter, I introduce an explanation of wartime rape that I call *combatant socialization*. Starting from the well-documented fact that the majority of reported wartime rape—when rape is widespread—is gang rape,[1] I argue that wartime rape may be the result of a violent socialization process that takes place among the rank and file of combatant groups, especially groups with low levels of internal social cohesion. I maintain that factions with particularly low levels of internal cohesion are those that use extreme forms of forced recruitment to garner fighters—whether abduction (by insurgents) or its equivalent, press-ganging (by states). Drawing on literature from a variety of disciplines—particularly sociology, psychology, and criminology—and across a number of related contexts, I argue that gang rape is a form of group violence that increases social cohesion and performs various functions that are essential from the perspective of the armed group. Gang rape—unlike, for example, marital rape—is arguably universally taboo; as a stigmatizing form of violence, it can help to sever ties to fighters' pasts. Gang rape is also a form of public, sexualized violence, which serves to communicate norms of masculinity, virility, and strength between fighters of both sexes. All of these are qualities of immense importance to fighters in armed groups, especially to those who have recently suffered the violence and humiliation of abduction. Finally, because gang rape carries risks—sometimes grave or debilitating risks, including sexually transmitted infections (STIs)—for the perpetrator, it can help to forge ties of trust among strangers.[2]

In the second part of the chapter, I present a series of competing, existing arguments about wartime rape. I consider the most common and influential explanations and separate them into three broad sets of arguments—opportunism/greed, ethnic hatred, and gender inequality—from which I derive a set of hypotheses and observable implications that I test in subsequent chapters. The explanations for wartime rape that I include have been put forth by scholars as well as by policymakers, practitioners, and human rights advocates.[3]

Every explanation examined here can likely account for at least one case of wartime rape; indeed, detailed case studies of particular events and incidents often inform the development of more general explanations. The purpose of this chapter, however, is not to provide an exhaustive list of every possible cause of wartime rape but rather to distill those that are most prominent in both theory and policy. Of course, wartime rape may have any number of conceivable causes, and none of the arguments presented here, including combatant socialization, can fully explain every instance. In subsequent chapters, I use a number of methods—including statistical analysis and three fieldwork-based case studies—to determine which explanations find the most support across the universe of recent civil wars. In other words, which explanations for wartime rape are generalizable across contexts? Which explanations are best able to account for the central puzzles described in the introduction? The answers to these questions are essential both for scholars who analyze wartime violence and for those in the policy world working to mitigate the severity and consequences of wartime rape.

In this chapter, I first present the combatant socialization argument, along with its main assumptions and its basis in numerous fields of research. In particular—relying on the literature from psychology, sociology (especially military sociology), and political science—I address questions of how and why cohesion forms through a process of socialization. I explore puzzles about the power of social groups in perpetrating violence, including large-scale violence like genocide. I also raise two theoretical questions: First, why does violence serve to create cohesion among fighters in armed groups? Second, why is *sexual* violence selected by some groups, and what other alternatives exist for building unit cohesion? I then discuss a number of related arguments about rape and other forms of civilian abuse and explain how these arguments are distinct from combatant socialization. In the second part of the chapter, I examine the three broad sets of competing arguments that I consider throughout the remainder of the book. Table 1.2, which summarizes the main arguments and the hypotheses tested throughout the book, is presented at the conclusion of this chapter.

Combatant Socialization

The central argument of this book is that wartime rape is best understood as a form of *group violence*.[4] Through this lens, it is possible to draw on a number of related fields of study that have focused on similar types of group violence in order to address some of the more puzzling aspects of wartime rape. As outlined in the introduction, one of the most persistent puzzles of wartime rape is why gang rape is far more frequent during wartime than in peacetime. Estimates of peacetime gang rape as a proportion of all peacetime rape vary but nearly always comprise a minority of reports; one set of scholars estimates that peacetime gang rape comprises between 2 and 27 percent of all cases (Horvath and Woodhams 2013, 2). In contrast, studies of wartime rape have found that 75 percent or more of reported cases of rape are gang rape. Although many scholars have argued that wartime rape is a continuation of peacetime gender violence (e.g., Boesten and Fisher 2012), I argue instead that wartime rape is distinct from rape during peacetime in several fundamental ways. First, the increased prevalence of multiple-perpetrator rape in wartime suggests that wartime rape has a different purpose than peacetime violence. Second, evidence shows that members of armed groups who perpetrate wartime rape are different from the types of people who rape during peacetime. Third, the victims of wartime rape differ from those who are raped during peacetime, particularly in terms of their relationships to perpetrators.[5] Finally, wartime rape is frequently more brutal than peacetime rape. All of these differences mean that, although gendered forms of violence exist in both peacetime and wartime, wartime rape requires a different type of explanation than peacetime gender violence.

The need for a different explanation suggests that the focus in much of the previous literature on combatants' opportunities to commit violence—and related principal-agent explanations for rape—is incomplete. Mere opportunity cannot account for the manner in which rape is actually perpetrated—often as part of a group, and under intense social pressure to participate. Principal-agent explanations, in which leaders direct their subordinates to commit violence, are also problematic—and occasionally contradictory. Some scholars understand agents to be "overworking" when they commit sexual violations (Mitchell 2004), while others argue that principals order or encourage rape as part of a military strategy to undermine the morale of the opposition (e.g., Leiby 2009).

That mass rape is a part of military strategy (or a "tool of war") is now a widely held belief. For example, the former foreign secretary of Britain William Hague wrote in an editorial in 2012 that "more often than not [rape] is carried out not by invading armies but by one group against another: deliberately to destroy, degrade, humiliate and scar political opponents or entire ethnic and religious groups" (*Times*, October 15, 2012). Similarly, physician-turned-activist Dr. Denis Mukwege said the following during an interview about rape in the DRC:

> The most important reason [that rape is so prevalent in the DRC], among others, is that rape is used as a war strategy. When a woman is publicly raped, and so violently, not only is she traumatized, but the whole community is traumatized—her husband, her children, and the whole village. The result is often that a population will leave the village and will leave it to the armed bands who can then use the cattle and the fields. And so that's just as good a result as using weapons. (Mukwege and Ensler 2009)

Overall, however, the explanation of rape as a military strategy suffers from a lack of supporting evidence. As previously argued, rape is rarely directed by commanders—although there are notable exceptions, both in recent conflicts and in the historical record.[6] In addition, in much of the current debate, the consequences of rape are frequently conflated with its goals (Aranburu 2010; Wood 2012; Cohen, Hoover Green, and Wood 2013, 9–10; Eriksson Baaz and Stern 2013). It is indisputable that rape may have the effect of displacing a population or weakening the opposition. However, this does not necessarily imply that these outcomes were the result of an explicit strategy. Returning to the example of the DRC, in the most comprehensive studies that have been conducted with combatants, they did *not* specifically mention a strategy of using rape to take land and animals (Eriksson Baaz and Stern 2013). To determine the motivations for rape—and whether it is being used strategically—researchers must study the perpetrators themselves, a task I take up in the three case study chapters.

Abductors' Central Dilemma

Combatant groups that forcibly recruit new members—whether by abduction into an insurgency or by press-ganging into a state military—face a central dilemma: how to create a coherent group out of strangers who do not know each other and feel no loyalty toward the group of which they are now members. The process of being abducted or press-ganged is violent; it often involves beating, forced labor, and, for women, rape and other forms of sexual violence.[7] Many of those interviewed for this book reported feeling frightened and isolated when they were first abducted. The perpetration of costly, risky group violence is a means of overcoming these problems and of building trust and loyalty in such groups.

Scholars have noted that battlefield experiences, and group perpetration of atrocities such as mass killing, can forge strong ties between strangers. Gang rape, as a public, sexualized form of violence, is another such means for increasing group cohesion (e.g., Goldstein 2001). Despite its prevalence, not all rape in wartime is gang rape, and bonding among perpetrators can also occur in the aftermath of single rape—that is, in perpetrating a rape alone, and then recounting it to peers afterward. Scholars have noted that perpetrators may brag about the rapes in which they participated, in order to "revel in a sense of enhanced masculinity" (Sanday 2007, 83).

I argue that combatant groups with the lowest levels of social cohesion are those that recruit their members both randomly and through extreme force.[8] Forcibly and randomly recruited combatants, whose members initially know very little about one another, may be more likely to commit wartime gang rape than those recruits who voluntarily join a fighting force. While social cohesion has not been found to be necessary for the battlefield effectiveness of an armed group, it is nonetheless essential for the group's longevity.[9] Social cohesion may decrease the chances that abducted fighters will try to escape or turn violent against the leadership. In addition, the collective responsibility for group atrocities like gang rape can serve to further increase ties of loyalty to the group. Overall, social cohesion is especially important in combatant groups comprised of kidnapped strangers—to enable the survival of the group—and rape is a powerful means of creating this cohesion.

Though the term "socialization" has various meanings, I understand socialization to be a process through which individual actors become committed to an armed group, including learning the norms and rules of the fighting force—and especially the norms and rules regarding rape and sexualized violence. As Checkel (2015, 11) argues, the endpoint of a process of socialization is either a learned role (where the individual may not agree with the action but still performs it) or the full internalization and acceptance of the norms and rules as the "right thing to do." As applied to the use of rape by armed groups, socialization is complete when rape regularly occurs in the absence of overt orders, coercion, or threats.[10] Scholars have argued that socialization can be achieved through the mutual hatred of an enemy group, as a result of a guiding ideology shared by all members of the group, or, most relevant for this study, from a set of benefits that derives from a group activity (O'Neill 2001, 104). Gang rape illustrates this last method of socialization: benefits for the group (greater cohesion) are created through acts of group violence (gang rape).

Creating cohesion through gang rape need not be a conscious decision by the combatants or their commanders. It is unlikely that combatants themselves identify gang rape with the explicit purpose of forming social bonds, although the quotation from the RUF ex-combatant at the start of this chapter suggests that some do. Rather, combatants may perceive that regular participation in rape develops out of the dynamics of the combatant group. Wood (2016) argues that this type of violence comprises a third category of political violence, which is neither strategic nor opportunistic. She defines a "practice" as "violence which is neither ordered nor authorized but is tolerated by commanders" (1).[11] Individual combatants do not necessarily want to be integrated into the group that has just forcibly kidnapped them, but leaving the group is often not a viable option. Becoming more socially cohesive with one's peers is a means of survival for abducted fighters and a way of gaining acceptance in a violent and confusing situation. If trapped in a group of hostile strangers, individuals will often choose participation in costly group behavior over continued estrangement from their peers. The fact that rape can also carry personal risks for the perpetrators, including danger to physical health, may reinforce its utility as a costly signal of loyalty and commitment, as a particularly useful intragroup organizing device, and finally as a tool of cohesion. In sum, gang rape is a particularly efficient method of both creating and perpetuating cohesion—not just as an initial hazing mechanism but also as a sustained socialization practice once the norms and beliefs about its use are internalized.[12] The cohesive benefits of rape may be one of the central reasons that leaders of the combatant units may not be able to prevent it from occurring—or may not sincerely attempt to do so. As Wood (2016, 16) argues, commanders may view actively prohibiting violence as a practice "too costly in the short term," in terms of discipline, resources, or lessening respect for the command, often in part because they are "little troubled by the suffering of women and others targeted with rape."

In one of the few existing studies of how this process works inside armed group units—albeit in a very different, non–civil war context—Donna Winslow (1999, 429) examines the practices of "non-conventional methods for promoting unit cohesion" within the Canadian Airborne Regiment (CAR). She argues that the need for unit cohesion was especially strong in the CAR because the men had to rely on each other when jumping out of airplanes, a particularly difficult and emotionally demanding task. This extreme and unique reliance on one another may be akin to the emotional upheaval and need for survival experienced by abducted combatants. Winslow documents how the CAR engaged in a variety of degrading and sometimes sexualized rituals whose ultimate purpose, she maintains, was the creation of bonds of loyalty and friendship within the group. Winslow cites research showing that the more severe these violent rituals, the stronger the bond to the unit. Bonding within armed groups, she concludes, can sometimes take the form of inappropriate or harmful practices. Similarly, I would argue that the "need" for bonding is greater in groups that have forcibly and randomly recruited their fighters; individuals in these groups must almost immediately begin to rely on one another for basic survival despite having little foundation on which to base this trust.

Table 1.1 presents the logic of the relationship between the recruitment mechanism and violent outcomes. The argument suggests that groups that can rely on existing social ties for in-group cohesion may do so; this is a far easier method of creating a coherent group of combatants with strong internal bonds—and certainly less costly than extensive military training exercises designed to forge social ties. For example, in the early stages of the war, the Civil Defense Forces (CDF) in Sierra Leone recruited fighters mainly through social and kinship ties within individual communities, and they committed far less rape than did other armed groups. Scott Gates (2002, 115) makes a similar argument: that ethnically homogenous groups will have stronger "solidary norms," or social attachments, than other types of armed groups.[13] However, a combatant group that relies on the random abduction of strangers for its membership must turn to alternative methods for creating in-group cohesion. One of these is the use of costly group behaviors, such as gang rape; other potential methods of producing social cohesion are explored later in this chapter. This need for social bonding increases during periods of rapid recruitment of new fighters. For example, following a number of deaths from battle, particularly *fast* recruiting may intensify the causal effects of abduction; that is, when units need to build cohesion very quickly, gang rape may be particularly likely. In both the Sierra Leone and Timor-Leste case studies, periods of intensive abduction are associated with such peaks in rape.

TABLE 1.1   Combatant socialization argument: Recruitment, unit cohesion, and violent outcomes

RECRUITMENT MECHANISM		OUTCOME
Voluntary recruitment (strong social ties; high cohesion)	→	Rare acts of costly group behavior that contribute to cohesion
Weak forced recruitment— coercion/conscription (some strong social ties; medium cohesion)	→	Some acts of costly group behavior that contribute to cohesion
Extreme forced recruitment— abduction/press-ganging (weak social ties; low cohesion)	→	Frequent acts of costly group behavior that contribute to cohesion

Extreme forms of forced recruitment—abduction and press-ganging—are distinct from weaker forms, such as coercion and conscription, in at least two ways. First, and as explored in more depth in the next section, evidence suggests that abduction and press-ganging are not generally committed by bloc, unlike coercion and conscription, where groups of family or friends subsequently serve together. Second, abduction and press-ganging often involve direct violence, including beating and sexual violations. Coercion and conscription, on the other hand, more commonly involve implicit or explicit threats of violence—thus allowing fighters a degree of agency (albeit a small degree) in deciding to join. Such differences in recruitment practices prove to be highly consequential for the internal cohesion of armed groups. To draw on the previous example, as the CDF relied more heavily on abduction later in the war, the shift toward extreme forced recruitment corresponded with a predictable increase in rape.

The combatant socialization argument suggests the main testable hypothesis for this book:

> H1: Insurgent groups that depend on abduction, and states that depend on press-ganging, are more likely to perpetrate rape than groups that use more voluntary methods of recruitment.

Assumptions

The argument makes two assumptions about recruitment into armed groups. First, it takes the type of recruitment mechanism as exogenously given. How combatant groups choose recruitment mechanisms—which groups abduct fighters and which recruit them without force or coercion—remains an open question in the field. One potential explanation is proposed by Weinstein (2007), who hypothesizes that groups with initial access to material resources, who later run out of these resources to distribute, may turn to abduction as a last resort. Weinstein cites the case of Renamo's turn to abduction in Mozambique as an example. This account, however, does not satisfactorily explain other cases, such as that of Sierra Leone, a country rich in diamond resources, where groups with access to material inducements used forcible recruitment even from their earliest stages. Data from Sierra Leone show that few members of the RUF were offered material resources, such as drugs and diamonds, even during the beginning of the war, and that the vast majority of members were forcibly recruited. A different theory about forced recruitment has been offered by Beber and Blattman (2013), who explore the incentives for rebel groups to recruit child soldiers coercively. The authors argue that abducting child fighters is preferable to using more voluntary methods when the following conditions exist: children lack other options, supervision is costless, and leaders lack access to resources. However, it is not clear how the model would extend to adults, who presumably face different constraints.[14] Finally, Humphreys and Weinstein (2006) briefly suggest that forced recruitment may be more likely in cases where a rebellion begins because of the "private desires of leaders" rather than as a popular movement, for which volunteer fighters should be abundant. However, without better data on the origins of rebellions, it is difficult to test their proposition.

Second, I assume that abduction and press-ganging are *not* committed by bloc, where groups of family or friends who are abducted together subsequently serve together in military units.[15] Although no systematic data exist, this assumption is supported by findings from at least four recent studies. First, a survey of ex-combatants in Sierra Leone found that abducted combatants typically knew few others in their units (Humphreys and Weinstein 2004).[16] Second, Weinstein (2005, 612) makes a similar argument about Renamo in Mozambique: "Coercive recruitment yielded a rebel movement that lacked any coherent social bonds. The practice of abduction meant that rebel recruits represented the entire diversity of Mozambique's ethnic and religious population." Third, in her study of the socialization processes of abducted child soldiers in the Lord's Resistance Army in Uganda, Vermeij (2009, 63) states, "Most children are taken to Sudan and separated from children from their home village." She argues that this separation is designed to prevent children from escaping and to further sever their ties to their previous lives. Finally, through interviews with members of the Salvadoran Army, which used widespread press-ganging to recruit soldiers, Hoover Green (pers. comm.) found that few soldiers knew anyone in their units upon joining.

Previous research clearly supports the idea that rape can create bonds between people in social groups, and may provide psychological benefits to the perpetrators, by inducing feelings of power and victory that improve group morale (Benard 1994; Card 1996; Sanday 2007).[17] But not all armed groups turn to this form of morale-boosting socialization; rape plays an especially vital role in groups with low social cohesion whose members know very little about one another. The combatant socialization argument presented here expands on the previous literature by tracing the source of variation in group rape to the initial recruitment choices of armed groups. I turn next to the military sociology literature on how social cohesion forms and why it matters in military units.

Cohesion and Military Units

According to the military sociology literature, small groups are the foundations of armed factions. Beginning with research conducted in the aftermath of World War II, scholars have focused on the role of personal relationships within armed units as a key explanatory variable in how militaries function. One of the earliest and most influential series of studies, which focused on the German Army in World War II, emphasized the importance of the "primary group"—defined as the squad or section—rather than ideology in sustaining the army's members (Shils and Janowitz 1948). In what has now become conventional wisdom, these studies found that the combatants' main reason for fighting was a strong sense of commitment to their fellow combatants. Primary groups are "emotionally central" to the individual, and the creation of bonds among members is a major goal of military training, accomplished in part through severing previous social ties and building new loyalties (Morris 1996, 691).

In more recent research, social psychologists generally identify two main types of cohesion: social, sometimes also called interpersonal, cohesion; and task cohesion. Social cohesion is a measure of affect—in essence, how much the members of a unit like each other. Task cohesion, on the other hand, refers to the ability of the group to achieve tangible collective goals. Much of the research on cohesion in military units is concerned with whether and how social cohesion predicts military effectiveness, or a unit's propensity to win battles or to perform other complex military tasks (MacCoun 1993). As a result of the World War II–era studies of primary group cohesion, it is widely believed that social ties and effectiveness are positively correlated: in other words, greater levels of social cohesion are thought to increase the battlefield effectiveness of military units (Kier 1998; MacCoun, Kier, and Belkin 2006).[18]

However, despite the theory's popularity, research over the last few decades has found that the positive correlation between social cohesion and military effectiveness is neither simple nor straightforward. In her comprehensive review of the military cohesion literature, Elizabeth Kier (1998) argues that social cohesion is not necessarily linked to military effectiveness and that strong social cohesion may even be counterproductive to the achievement of military and organizational goals.[19] Kier maintains that the claims that primary group cohesion is the major source for combat motivation are often overstated or incorrect. Along with other scholars, she stresses that only task cohesion has been found to be correlated with effectiveness, although the direction of causation is unclear (MacCoun 1993; Kier 1998; MacCoun, Kier, and Belkin 2006).

Researchers have found that social cohesion may develop easily in some settings and can be formed arbitrarily in experimental situations (MacCoun 1993).[20] Kier (1998) further argues that social cohesion is mainly a function of situation (e.g., a sense of tradition within the group) and structure (e.g., the stability of membership or group size). Although social cohesion is not closely related to the characteristics of individual combatants, she maintains, some studies have found that the more attributes that group members shared, such as social class, age, or ethnicity, the more socially cohesive the group. Such shared attributes, however, do not seem to affect task cohesion (MacCoun 1993).

To be clear, I make no claims about the influence of rape on military effectiveness—or on task cohesion.[21] Available evidence, in fact, suggests little correlation between the social cohesion created through acts of rape and the ability of armed groups to be successful fighters in battle. By one estimate, the main rebel group in Sierra Leone—which reportedly committed the vast majority of the rape—lost almost two-thirds of the battles it fought over the course of the war.[22]

Instead, I argue that gang rape allows armed groups who forcibly and randomly recruit their fighters to create and to maintain a coherent fighting group in the most basic of senses: to produce social bonds where they are lacking, to increase trust among people who may otherwise be predisposed to fighting each other, and to create a sense of collective responsibility that reduces attempts at desertions or mutinies and allows the armed group to endure. Given what is known about task cohesion, it is doubtful that participation in rape would increase task cohesion, which—in well-resourced militaries—is formed through careful training exercises that mimic the chaos of fighting in war. My main focus is therefore the creation of social cohesion through participation in violence.[23]

This argument is supported by military research that suggests the group perpetration of violence—including rape—enables armed units to develop social cohesion. For example, Osiel (1999, 155) argues that mass murder in World War II was a means for "securing a spectacular measure of . . . cohesion." Additionally, in his famous study of Reserve Police Battalion 101, Christopher Browning (1992) describes the cohesion that developed from both the enormous pressures the men felt to conform and their fear of being ostracized if they refused to participate in killing. In an example from a different time period—during the Argentinean counterinsurgency war (1975–1980)—one scholar cites "socially bonding torture practices" as a method used to create cohesion among groups of abducted combatants in the state forces (Robben 2006, 363).

In related work, researchers have also established that violence can serve a powerful function in organizing the structure of groups with continual influxes of new members (Humphreys and Weinstein 2008; Kaminski 2003). Scholars have shown that performing acts of brutal violence can be part of the process of integrating new members and maintaining social order among existing members. This violence is also believed to be useful in cutting ties to a combatant's previous life, making it more difficult for an individual fighter to desert, and creating a sense of loyalty to the group as well as collective responsibility for violent acts.[24] Finally, findings from the research on group cohesion indicate that social cohesion increases after "successful performance" (MacCoun 1993, 294). The effect of performance on cohesion may be stronger than the effect of cohesion on performance; in fact, research provides direct evidence that successful performance creates social cohesion. This principle undergirds the use in military exercises of group success experiences (MacCoun 1993). Group violence may provide the members of armed groups with similar positive feelings of success and collective accomplishment, and this feeling, in turn, translates into social cohesion.

Why Sexual Violence?

Given that previous research has suggested that violence in a variety of forms can produce bonds of social cohesion, why do armed groups with especially low cohesion turn to *sexualized* violence? Reasons for selecting rape over other, nonsexual forms of violence are debated in the literature, and findings from a variety of fields are suggestive—but not conclusive. Overall, this research confirms that sexual violence promotes cohesion in a number of ways.

Research shows that perpetrators both gain and maintain social status within a group during the course of a gang rape (Amir 1971; Groth and Birnbaum 1979). Many studies in psychology and sociology on gang rape find that perpetrators experience an increase in the esteem they feel for one another (Brownmiller 1975; Franklin 2004; O'Sullivan 1991; Scully 1990). Public health researchers have analyzed gang rape in the U.S. context and consistently found a relationship between sexual violence and status within groups of perpetrators. In a study of young male perpetrators of violence against women, one set of researchers found that sexualized violence is related directly to increasing "male social stature among peers" (Reed et al. 2008, 265).

Much of the recent research supports this idea that rape increases the social status of its perpetrators. In a study of juvenile gang rapists in the Netherlands, perpetrators gave a few reasons for participating, including a fear of retribution if they did not join in and a desire to fit in as part of the group. Fear of being ostracized from a group has similarly been hypothesized to be a major motivating force for the prevalence of wartime gang rape (Henry, Ward, and Hirshberg 2003). Sexual desire is often mentioned only as a secondary motivating reason for gang rape (Bijleveld et al. 2007). Scholars have found that the rewards to perpetrators include participation in a group-wide act of violence and the ability to brag about taking part in the attack (Bijleveld et al. 2007). Very few of the perpetrators reported trying to stop acts of gang rape; indeed, many later recalled the attack as "an enjoyable activity that had given them status" (Bijleveld et al. 2007, 24). In other theoretical work on gang rape, scholars have found that it is an outcome of psychological processes within the group. Scholars have noted that gang rape involves collective responsibility for a crime, the loss of individual identity and values, and the creation of cohesion and camaraderie (Henry, Ward, and Hirshberg 2003; Hauffe and Porter 2009).

Some of the research on gang rape emphasizes the homosocial (and possibly latent homosexual) aspects of participating in a sex act with male peers (Blanchard 1959). Similar arguments have been made about fraternity gang rape (Sanday 2007) and about sexual violence by street gangs in the United States (Bourgois 1996, 211).[25] But other scholars deemphasize the sexual nature of the attack, claiming instead that the bonding elements of the attack are the primary motivator (Brownmiller 1975; Groth and Birnbaum 1979; Franklin 2004; Bijleveld and Hendriks 2003). The collective act of humiliating a victim is the main source of increased bonding among the perpetrators. Several interview subjects in Sierra Leone mentioned that rape was shameful only for the victim. For example, one respondent said, "[During a gang rape] sometimes we would feel shy in front of each other, especially when the commander is around. But the sex was a humiliation to the [victims]."[26] This aspect of rape seems to be one of the most persistent, across both time and cultural contexts: rape often confers lasting shame on the victim, but rarely on the perpetrators.

A number of largely qualitative studies demonstrate the connection between social cohesion and sexual violence empirically. These studies include interviews of perpetrators—and friends of perpetrators—in several countries. One study in South Africa found that of the incidents of gang rape disclosed by participants, 76 percent were "carried out for fun, as a game or because the men were bored" (Jewkes and Sikweyiya 2013, 118); further, 41 percent of respondents reported that "they felt fine, good or closer to their friends after the rape" (119).

Beyond the case of South Africa, other research has focused the practice in Cambodia of *bauk* (literally, "plus"), which involves the group rape by men of a single female victim. Reviewing a series of studies focused on aspects of youth sexuality, a set of authors found that "male bonding is a major factor underlying the practice . . . and appears to be closely associated with peer pressure to prove their masculinity" (Wilkinson, Bearup, and Soprach 2005, 166). In interviews, young Cambodian men described the cohesion-building aspects of *bauk*: "my team and I do it like this because we need sex and want to have fun together" (162) and "we follow our friends who ask us to join. We want our friends to enjoy with us. Close friends always share things together" (164). Some also mentioned the social pressure to participate: "I know that *bauk* is not good. . . . I have a sister too . . . but my friends force me. . . . I cannot stay by myself" (163). The role of masculinity in *bauk* was also emphasized by some of the interviewees:

"[A man] wouldn't be a man if he was unable to rape her" (164). Finally, a unique ethnographic study of sexuality in Papua New Guinea had similar findings about gang rape. There, the authors of the study write, "the underlying psychosocial dynamic for socially acceptable gang rape derives from a strong emphasis on male bonding coupled with ideologies of female pollution and danger" (NSRRT and Jenkins 1994, 102).

Besides these country-specific studies, an innovative and very large survey on violence against women published in *The Lancet* inquired about motivations for rape; the study included more than ten thousand men in six Asian countries (Bangladesh, Cambodia, China, Indonesia, Sri Lanka, and Papua New Guinea) (Jewkes et al. 2013). The respondents were asked about their participation in single- and multiple-perpetrator rape as well as their motivations for doing so. Across both types of rape, the most common motivations—selected from a series of prepared statements—were entitlement ("I wanted her," "I wanted to have sex," or "I wanted to show I could do it") and entertainment ("I wanted to have fun" or "I was bored"). However, when disaggregated, the answers differed between perpetrators of single rape and gang rape. In particular, perpetrators of gang rape were more likely to mention reasons of anger and punishment ("I was angry with her" or "I wanted to punish her") as well as rape after drinking than were perpetrators of single rape (and the differences were statistically significant).[27] These findings provide additional suggestive evidence for rape as a bonding experience among perpetrators: a shared goal of punishment provided the central motivation, likely facilitated by group alcohol consumption.

Precisely *how* cohesion is created through rape is the source of some debate. Some scholars argue that norms of masculinity—especially salient in the context of armed groups—are best communicated through sexualized actions. Morris (1996, 706–7) argues that sexual violence is central to some types of all-male or mostly male groups because "rape-conducive sexual norms" are "imparted . . . inadvertently" to members of military organizations. Indeed, there are multiple examples from related contexts, including urban gangs and fraternities, that male or mostly male groups commit sexualized violence—perhaps because such violence communicates normative masculinity, strength, and virility. In their studies of fighters in the DRC, Eriksson Baaz and Stern (2009, 499) argue that military organizations contribute to "a certain heterosexual male violent masculinity" that affects all combatants, including women, and may contribute to the selection of sexualized forms of violence.

Psychological research suggests a related set of reasons for building cohesion through sexual violence. In a series of psychology studies on "precarious manhood," Vandello et al. (2008, 1326) argue that manhood is a status that is "achieved rather than . . . ascribed" and that requires visible social proof.[28]

They argue that when manhood status is threatened, strategies commonly used to restore it include dangerous physical aggression, especially public physical aggression that is "risky to enact and costly to fake" (1327).[29] The abduction or press-ganging of recruits into an armed group—a process often involving terrible abuse—is a particularly status-threatening and anxiety-provoking event. Applying the findings above to the case of forcibly recruited combatants, it might be especially important to this population to restore some semblance of manhood and social status through public acts of risky violence. While the Vandello et al. studies do not consider sexual violence in particular, their research can help explain how sexualized public displays of aggression may be considered by the fighters—albeit subconsciously—central for communicating messages about masculinity in the aftermath of the trauma of their own abduction and press-ganging. As Franklin (2004, 31) writes,

> Participants in . . . group rapes usually recall feeling positive emotions at the time. During the assault, there is a drug-like high produced by the excitement and danger. Afterwards, there is a feeling of closeness and camaraderie, a sense of bonding produced by communal transgression. But there may also be an enormous, collective sigh of relief, in that they have survived this public test with their masculinity intact. In other words, underneath the experienced veneer of camaraderie and warmth is a desperate struggle to achieve dominance, maintain status, or even to get through the ordeal with one's masculinity intact.

Others have argued that rape is selected because it creates intense shame for the victim, perhaps more so than other forms of violence. Quoting psychologist Inger Skjelsbæk, Alison (2007, 81) writes, "Sexual violence is 'preferred' . . . because 'this is the form of violence which most clearly communicates masculinisation and feminisation.'" Eriksson Baaz and Stern (2009, 498) summarize the previous work on why violence is sexualized as suggesting "a complex web of contributing factors" that include the perpetuation of cycles of violence by those who feel victimized, along with opportunity, the disintegration of social norms and sexual desire. Why sexual violence is chosen thus remains uncertain, but these previous studies point to potential answers.

Rape Is More Costly than Previously Recognized

One aspect of rape that has been overlooked in much of the previous research—and that may help explain why it is selected over other forms of violence—is the risk that rape carries for perpetrators. Most scholars view rape as a costless form of violence for the perpetrator, in both peacetime and wartime contexts. For example, in a study involving interviews of over one hundred convicted rapists in U.S. prisons, one scholar concluded that "rape is a low-risk, high-reward act," because rapists reported little fear of being reported or caught (Scully 1990, 137). Similarly, some scholars maintain that rape is a weapon particularly well suited for conflict. Bloom (1999) notes that no expensive or advanced technology is required to perpetrate rape. In addition, Bloom argues that because combatants typically know that, until recently, rape has not been prosecuted as a crime against humanity, rape may be as effective as mass murder but without the same risk of postwar prosecution. Mass rape is considered by some as a useful mechanism by which to clear a population from contested territory, while also lacking the threat of provoking international outrage, since rape is viewed as a "lesser crime" than lethal violence (e.g., Bloom 1999).

Such views are also apparent in the policy and advocacy discourse. As part of the November 2012 launch of a large policy initiative aimed at ending rape in war, William Hague stated that "rape and sexual violence is used as a deliberate weapon of war . . . to humiliate, scar and destroy whole ethnic groups or religious or political opponents, *cheaply*, silently and devastatingly" (emphasis added).[30] Activist Eve Ensler, in an interview on NPR (Mukwege and Ensler 2009) about rape in the DRC, said that "rape is a very cheap method of warfare. You don't have to buy scud missiles or hand grenades. You just send soldiers in, and they take care of communities."

However, evidence suggests instead that rape is *especially costly* when compared to other forms of violence. If rape were as easy, cheap, and effective as the discourse often implies, then it should occur even more often than it does. Rape is an intimate form of violence; it requires that the perpetrator use his or her body as the weapon or, in the case of object rape, have very close contact with the victim—features that introduce risks to both individuals and armed groups. In one of the first studies of group rape, Amir (1971) recognized risk taking as one of the central elements in the group-bonding process. I argue that wartime rape is costly for perpetrators for at least three reasons: the risk of disease, the time it takes to perpetrate, and its emotional toll. I consider each of these costs in turn.

First, and most significantly, rape is known to be the cause of the rampant spread of sexually transmitted infections in conflict zones. Scholars regularly note that STIs may adversely affect the health of victims of wartime rape (e.g., Keen 2005, 45; Ghobarah, Huth, and Russett 2003). Villagers I interviewed in Sierra Leone frequently described how rape victims experienced abdominal pain, swollen stomachs, "bad water" (a local term for vaginal discharge), itching, bleeding, and the inability to conceive, as well as mental health consequences.[31] Additionally, some scholars have claimed that through campaigns of rape, infected combatants may purposely spread HIV/AIDS to victims as a form of biological warfare. Mullins (2009) reports that infected men raped women during the Rwandan genocide with the explicit intention of giving victims the fatal disease. More recently, there are reports from the DRC that HIV/AIDS has been deliberately spread through rape (UN Human Rights 2009). However, whether STIs are in fact used as intentional biological weapons—and if so, how frequently—has not yet been established conclusively.

Only one of the ex-combatant interviewees in Sierra Leone reported concern about contracting HIV/AIDS, perhaps because the rate of AIDS appears to be relatively low in the country, or because life expectancy is so short in Sierra Leone—even absent the war—that a disease with devastating consequences in the long term is simply not a sufficient deterrent.[32] "Fighters didn't care about AIDS," reported one ex-combatant.[33] Others confirmed this: "Not a lot of fighters knew about AIDS," and "no one was thinking about AIDS."[34] However, HIV/AIDS is a major problem in many countries, and concerns over contracting the disease likely vary widely.

Despite the focus on the health consequences for rape victims, there is silence regarding the effects of STIs on the perpetrators of rape in modern wars.[35] Interviews with ex-combatants in Sierra Leone revealed the high physical costs of participating in rape. Respondents reported that gonorrhea and syphilis were common during the war, infecting both perpetrators and victims of rape. Sexually transmitted infection was not trivial, considering the illnesses made it difficult for combatants to fight effectively. Because the combatants were based in the jungle, with little or no access to antibiotics, the diseases quickly worsened, often rendering those infected unable to urinate, or even to walk or to run.[36] To treat people infected with STIs (as well as other common illnesses, like malaria and typhoid), the combatants would seek out pharmacies in the towns they raided to steal antibiotics and would also kidnap doctors and nurses who could care for the sick.[37] Contracting an STI could also be fatal. Commanders sometimes faced difficult decisions about what to do with fighters who were stricken with severe STIs. A former RUF commander reported that he was forced to kill two men sick with gonorrhea when his unit had to flee an area. He was concerned that the men would be tortured and killed by the army if they were left behind, and there was no way to carry them along.[38] Similar stories were also shared by others.

Thus, STIs were not only costly to the individual combatant, but a price incurred by the group as a whole, limiting the fighting ability of combatants and requiring groups to bear the burden of caring for the sick. Many of the fighters in Sierra Leone shared concerns over contracting diseases as a result of rape, as discussed at length in chapter 4. In interviews, the fighters accurately identified syphilis and gonorrhea both by name and by their relevant symptoms. For instance, one former fighter in Sierra Leone described the symptoms of STIs as follows: "the body drops down and you feel not active; sometimes they [those fighters affected] would notice a pain in the urethra after only three or four days."[39] A rebel commander said that as many as ten of his men had suffered from STIs: "They had pain and itching in their [genitals]; it hurt to urinate and there was a lot of pus."[40] Another said, "You would know that you are sick within two or three days."[41] The medical literature confirms these reports; symptoms of gonorrhea in men appear within one to fourteen days of exposure and include pus and pain in the testicles and lower abdomen. Syphilis involves flu-like symptoms, sometimes as little as two weeks after contracting the disease.[42]

Because of the short time period between contracting gonorrhea or syphilis and the onset of extremely unpleasant symptoms, fighters in Sierra Leone were aware of the costs of participating in rape as well as the direct relationship between rape and illness. Based on my interviews, there is no doubt that the combatants knew they were getting sick as a consequence of rape. One respondent noted that the incidence of sexually transmitted infections led his peers to target younger women and girls: "One solution [to the problem of STIs] was to not rape anyone above twenty years old—if women have already been used by others, you are more likely to get [sick]."[43] Therefore, as in other wars throughout history, the possibility of a disease epidemic among the fighters was a major potential cost to those engaging in rape on a mass scale.

While ex-combatants reported concern over contracting STIs after the war had ended, they may not have cared about such risks during the conflict. Combatants, after all, face far more serious threats than STIs in the midst of war. Evidence from other civil wars, however, suggests that fighters do evaluate the risks associated with rape. In a study by the Harvard Humanitarian Initiative (HHI) of sexual violence in the DRC, researchers found in interviews with *current* fighters in the Mai Mai militia that combatants expressed concern over contracting STIs, including HIV/AIDS, if they were to participate in rape. One respondent said, "The consequences for those who have committed rape can be mostly to get contaminated by diseases." The researchers summarized the fighters' views on STIs as a "form of unavoidable punishment that would result even if one were not formally 'caught' raping" (HHI 2009, 40). A second example of armed groups weighing the costs of sexually transmitted disease during the course of a conflict is the Lord's Resistance Army (LRA) in Uganda. Annan et al. (2009) argue that the loss of a high-ranking LRA commander to AIDS early in the conflict led the rebel leader Joseph Kony to create strict rules prohibiting the rape of noncombatants in order to limit the spread of STIs to fighters. Thus, there is mounting evidence that armed groups carefully consider the costs of rape for the perpetrators, especially in terms of the effects on the health of fighters. This may be one reason why rape is not even more common during wartime.

Beyond the risks of disease, there are two additional potential costs from the perpetrators' perspective. The first is that rape is relatively costly in terms of time. It is more complicated to carry out rape than to commit other types of violence and torture, such as using guns to kill or machetes to amputate. Furthermore, a gang rape takes much longer to complete than does a single-perpetrator rape (Porter and Alison 2006). Several former child soldiers shared stories of having to stand guard while fellow soldiers participated in rape, in order to warn their superiors if enemy combatants approached the area.[44] Gang rape is therefore comparatively inefficient as a form of violence. This is supported by the interview evidence: ex-combatants reported that rape was often perpetrated in the aftermath of fighting, not as part of the active violence of fighting.

Finally, because of the close physical contact required, rape carries the potential of emotional hardship for the perpetrator that other types of violence arguably do not. In particular, intimate violence is thought to be especially traumatizing to the perpetrator. For example, historians argue that the gas chambers during the Holocaust were developed in response to the trauma endured by the armed units charged with the horrific task of mass shootings in Russia (Marrus 1987, 50). While acts of gang rape are later recalled with enjoyment by some perpetrators (Bijleveld et al. 2007, 24), others feel that they were forced by peer pressure to participate and are haunted by their acts (Houge 2008). Carpenter (2006) argues that forced participation in rape is experienced as a form of psychological torture by the perpetrator. Of course, all intimate violence involves close contact with victims, but only rape requires the body itself to be used as a weapon; this level of intimacy has been found to be especially disturbing for perpetrators of gang rape. These feelings may help explain, in part, the use of objects in wartime rape. Research shows some perpetrators of gang rape find the act to be nonerotic; they do not ejaculate, and they use objects instead of their bodies to rape the victim (Brownmiller 1975; Groth and Birnbaum 1979; O'Sullivan 1991).

Disease, time costs, and the emotional toll—as well as numerous other group-level costs that I have not considered in depth, such as alienating or enraging civilian populations (Gottschall 2004) or attracting international condemnation—would all seem to indicate that wartime rape is a counterproductive, or irrational, form of wartime violence for both the individual and the group.[45] These costs pose a significant challenge to the conventional wisdom that rape is easy and costless. But if rape is so costly, why don't commanders try to prevent it?

Evidence from my interviews suggests that commanders were concerned with the costs of rape, which can partly explain why they did not actively encourage or order it. But in general, commanders also did not discourage rape, because of its utility in forming a group identity within their factions.

Research on the rationality of seemingly counterproductive violence can help to make sense of why, if rape is costly, wartime rape still occurs, and on such a large scale. Three related arguments about seemingly irrational violence by armed groups are useful here. First, gang rape can be viewed as a form of "coupled violence," in which the violence being committed is not essential to the aims of the war. The violence may, in fact, be counterproductive to explicitly military goals, but it is in line with the goal of seeking other goods desirable to combatants (Hovil and Werker 2005). Hovil and Werker draw on Berman's (2003) research on religious extremism to illustrate their argument. Berman finds that seemingly counterproductive forms of religious violence are not so counterproductive after all, and that extremist violence reduces defection and increases group loyalty. Similarly, gang rape may not advance military goals and may appear counterproductive to the strategic goals of the perpetrating group by, for example, terrorizing the civilian population. However, gang rape is committed with the (likely subconscious) goal of creating social bonds among members of an armed group, a paramount aim in armed groups made up of strangers.

A second related logic may be found in Fearon (1995), who notes that, in the war in the former Yugoslavia, Serbian combatants exhumed bodies in Croatian ancestral cemeteries and machine-gunned the remains of the corpses. Such an act raises questions about why combatants would incur costs to themselves, such as wasting ammunition and spending time performing the unpleasant task of desecrating graves, when there is no tangible military or strategic benefit. Fearon (1995, 4) argues that the graves were culturally very important to the Croats, and "Serb gunners knew this, of course, knew that the Croats knew it, and knew that the Croats knew that they knew it." Thus intimidation and humiliation were the "goods" that combatants in this case were seeking, for the larger purpose of persuading moderates on both sides that coexistence would not be possible after the conflict.

Finally, a third mechanism may be found in a rational choice model of cults and religions (Iannaccone 1992). In this model, costly and potentially stigmatizing behaviors for the individual may be beneficial to the group. Iannaccone argues that this situation creates a free-rider problem—that is, individual members of a group may be tempted to abstain from the costly behavior if they feel they can continue to benefit from membership in the group. The group can overcome this problem by penalizing alternative behaviors. In the case of wartime rape, the group pressure created through public acts of gang rape, closely observed by other group members, raises the cost of not participating. Thus, even in the absence of direct orders to rape, many combatants will feel compelled to participate. Stigmatizing behaviors are chosen specifically *because* they increase group participation. Gang rape is stigmatizing behavior. It is costly to the individual, requires participation in a group practice, and in turn—as research has clearly established—increases group solidarity.

Gang Rape and Perpetrator Motivations

The research on gang rape, even in peacetime conditions, is sparse, and the behavior of and interactions among perpetrators of gang rape have received little scholarly attention; in fact, one scholar noted that gang rape may be the least-studied violent crime (Franklin 2004). Research on perpetrators' motivations in wartime rape is particularly spare. One set of scholars called this a "theoretical vacuum" in the literature (Henry, Ward, and Hirshberg 2003, 535), while a new edited volume on the general theme of gang rape noted that the research is "still in its infancy" (Horvath and Woodhams 2013, 286). Current research on perpetrators of gang rape tends to be highly descriptive, often comparing features of single-offender and group rape, including the location of the attack, the ages of the victims and perpetrators, the presence or absence of physical violence, and the degree of resistance by the victim (e.g., Hauffe and Porter 2009; Porter and Alison 2006; Ullman 2007). Researchers have found that perpetrators of group rape are often younger than lone perpetrators and that group rape is typically more violent than rape committed by a single offender (Bijleveld and Hendriks 2003; Gidycz and Koss 1990). In a study of perpetrators of peacetime gang rape, there was little evidence of explicit premeditation of the attack, beyond simply agreeing that the group was to have sex with a victim. In a few studies, researchers have analyzed the interactions between perpetrators and victims (e.g., Hauffe and Porter 2009). The behavior and interactions of perpetrators of gang rape with one another, on the other hand, have received little scholarly attention. While a small number of studies compare various aspects of gang rape and single-perpetrator rape, relatively few *theories* exist to explain group rape.

In one of the earliest and most influential studies of the subject, Amir (1971) introduced a sociology-based theory of group rape.[46] Amir maintains that sexual identity inevitably becomes a source of anxiety in young males, especially in cultures lacking explicit rites of passage to adulthood. Group rape, he argues, serves as a rite of passage in which aggression and humiliation are key features. Gang rape enables the perpetrators to establish status and reputations of toughness within the group. Amir argues that engaging in gang rape occurs only occasionally in such groups, and particularly during periods when the status of members of the group is being questioned or threatened. Amir writes that gang rape can assist in "solidify[ing] the status claims of a member as well as the cohesiveness of the whole group" (1971, 185).

Gang rape is notable for its performance aspects. Research indicates that perpetrators of gang rape often watch one another and organize an order of participation. Researchers believe that the intended "audience" of the performance is the other perpetrators, with the victim serving as a "vehicle" for the perpetrators (e.g., Sanday 2007; Holmstrom and Burgess 1980; Theidon 2007). In a study of crack-dealing gangs in East Harlem, one anthropologist described the performance elements of gang rape, where the perpetrators recounted manipulating their bodies so that the other members could better see the rape (Bourgois 1996, 211). Others report similar findings: perpetrators use the victim as a "vehicle for interacting with other men" (Groth and Birnbaum 1979, 115), and the perpetrators who watch the rape are "the public" for whom it is performed (Bijleveld et al. 2007, 28); some even argue that gang rape is a form of "cultural theater" (Franklin 2004, 25).

Studies of gang rape in the context of U.S. college fraternities and street gangs may offer contexts suitable for understanding acts of wartime sexual violence. In fact, researchers of fraternity gang rape have made explicit connections between college fraternities and military organizations (Martin and Hummer 1989). In Peggy Reeves Sanday's (2007) study of the phenomenon of gang rape on college campuses, she too notes that one result of gang rape is a bonding among men, especially in male-segregated institutions. In other similar environments, researchers have argued that there is a strong social pressure to engage in acts of gang rape. Bourgois (1996, 208) writes that, among drug gangs in East Harlem, nonparticipation in gang rape meant being excluded from a "violent male ritual." Others report that perpetrators feel they will be mocked, or labeled a homosexual, if they fail to participate (Bourke 2007, 376).

Perhaps most significantly, the social processes found in group rape contrast starkly to those in rape committed by a lone perpetrator. Single-offender rape is more often believed to be the result of personal sexual desire than is gang rape (Hauffe and Porter 2009). Additionally, the role of the victim varies in these two types of assault. Whereas victims of gang rape are, as previously described, more often considered a vehicle for creating esteem and social bonds among perpetrators, the victim in lone-perpetrator rapes is seen as a sexual outlet (Hauffe and Porter 2009; Bijleveld et al. 2007). Similarly, in the criminological literature, perpetrators of gang rape are viewed as fundamentally different from perpetrators of single rape. Gang rapists are believed to be less pathological than are single rapists (Bijleveld and Hendriks 2003; Brownmiller 1975); the difference can be attributed to the fact that pressures from a group can cause individuals to behave in ways that they never would if they were alone (Groth and Birnbaum 1979; Porter and Alison 2006; Franklin 2004). This is supported by the finding that perpetrators of group rape are far less likely to have previously committed sexual offenses than are lone perpetrators (Bijleveld and Hendriks 2003). Indeed, criminologists see co-offenders of gang rape as having more in common with groups who commit other types of violence than with perpetrators of single rape (Bijleveld et al. 2007), suggesting that ordinary civilians—like abducted combatants—are far more likely to perpetrate gang rape than to rape alone.

The differences identified between lone perpetrators and group perpetrators help explain acts of wartime gang rape, particularly those perpetrated by groups of forcibly recruited combatants. Forced combatants are not carefully selected for their propensity to commit violence; rather, they are randomly pulled out of their communities and made to join fighting forces. Malamuth (1996, 276) cites instances in which ordinary men participated in wartime rape and other forms of coercive sex, including the conflicts in Bosnia and the case of comfort women forced into sexual slavery by the Japanese during World War II. These findings help make sense of how seemingly typical men (and women) can commit rape on a massive scale during wartime when they might refrain from such behavior in peacetime, an unresolved question in the literature (Mezey 1994; Henry, Ward, and Hirshberg 2003).

Group Violence

The notion that "ordinary men" commit atrocities in groups that they might not commit alone has been the subject of significant interest in the fields of psychology, sociology, anthropology, and history.[47] A wealth of literature from these disciplines addresses the role that ordinary people have played in genocides; this research is useful for understanding group violence more broadly, including group rape. These studies explore a difficult question: Why are people who otherwise have strong moral inhibitions against violence willing to participate in the execution of terrible atrocities during wartime?

Much of the earlier literature reflects on experiences during the Holocaust. In his seminal study, Browning (1992) describes how most members of Reserve Police Battalion 101 were horrified by their task of mass murder, and yet they perpetrated the killings nonetheless—not because they feared being punished if they refrained (indeed, Browning documents cases in which some refused to participate with little consequence), but because of group pressures not to shirk their duties. Some have argued that the majority of those who participated in the Holocaust were simply sadists who derived great pleasure from carrying out their brutal jobs. However, Kelman and Hamilton (1989) argue that while some Nazi officials and concentration camp commanders could probably be described as such, dark psychological explanations are inadequate for explaining events like the Holocaust, during which so many of the perpetrators had little direct contact with the victims. Likewise, in her analysis of Adolf Eichmann and his role in the Holocaust, Arendt (1963, 253) highlights the "terrible and terrifying" normality of many perpetrators.

Building on this earlier work, more recent literature explores group violence during the Rwandan genocide. Much of it rejects the idea that the genocide was motivated on the individual level by ethnic hatred, focusing instead on the intense social pressures to participate in the killing. For example, Straus (2006, 119) argues that the demographic characteristics of the *genocidaires* were nearly identical to those of the adult male Hutu population, leading him to conclude that "Rwanda's perpetrators were ordinary in all but the crimes they committed." Fujii (2009, 19), like Straus, emphasizes the ordinariness of the perpetrators, arguing that "local ties and group dynamics" motivated people to join in the genocide. The dynamics explored in both studies are remarkably similar to the descriptions of pressures to participate in gang rape that I heard in my own research.

More broadly, cutting-edge psychological research finds that individuals—members of violent groups, such as rebel groups and national militaries—must initially overcome an innate hesitation to commit violence, and especially violence that is physically close, such as rape (Littman and Paluck 2015). Once this hesitation is overcome, whether through training that simulates battle or simply through force or pressure to commit violence, violent behavior then tends to lead to more violence. This occurs through one of several processes: desensitization, moral disengagement, or other forms of "dissonance reduction" that allow individuals to justify committing violence they once found repugnant (87–88, 94). In addition, violence serves to strengthen "identification"—or cohesion—with the broader group, by providing "new and peripheral members . . . recognition, respect and status" (90). Psychological studies have also revealed that individuals who suffer in order to join groups are more likely to experience cohesion with group members than those who have not suffered. Members of the LRA in Uganda reported higher cohesion with the group when they had perpetrated acts of violence against relatives and friends (93). Overall, evidence shows that the psychological process is a cycle of violence and group identification (89): "When individuals identify with groups that use violence to achieve their political, economic, or social goals, they will be motivated to comply with the group's violent standards, whether or not the violence is condoned by the broader society and, to some extent, regardless of the individual's own views."

Scope of the Argument

What Alternatives Exist for Socialization and Cohesion Building?

That some armed groups turn to sexual violence to build cohesion begs the question of whether plausible alternatives for socialization and cohesion building might exist—and under what conditions these alternatives might be selected over sexual violence. The research on what Paul Kenny (2011, 2) calls "organizational socialization," or "the process by which the self-concept of the individual becomes inseparable from his membership of the organization," suggests a number of potential pathways to cohesion building within military units. Kenny sorts these pathways into three main types: (1) training exercises, especially boot camp drills; (2) a shared sense of the burden to face external threats and stressful events; and (3) rituals, including the recruitment process, hazing, and initiation rites. Using a paired case comparison of the Wehrmacht in World War II—generally viewed as a case of strong social cohesion—and the US Army in the Vietnam War—a case of weak social cohesion—Kenny concludes that intensive training is necessary but not sufficient in producing cohesion. Indeed, he finds that unit-level rituals may create cohesion within small groups while contributing to an overall disintegration of the broader military organization. Other studies focused on similar pathways have found that group experiences of stress are among the more important cohesion-building processes (e.g., Bartone et al. 2002).

This research has several implications for the present study. First, armed groups that forcibly recruit their fighters are unlikely to engage in intensive and costly boot camp training exercises (which are exactly the types of exercises known to build both task and social cohesion). As Kenny (2011) argues, boot camp training is not intended to enhance military skills, which are developed during combat training, but rather to indoctrinate and to instill the importance of following orders. As is described in the El Salvador case study, the Armed Forces of El Salvador offered cursory combat training, but made no investments in boot camp training. I argue that this choice in how to expend resources made the Armed Forces more likely to turn to violence to create cohesion. In general, and in the absence of intensive boot camp drilling, weaker, less organized, and less resourced armed groups typically turn to other activities to break ties to the past and build cohesion among group members.

Second, shared stressful experiences can create bonds. Battle itself may serve as such a shared experience, but many modern civil wars are not particularly battle heavy. As Collier and Hoeffler (2007, 717) write of recent civil wars, "Poorly equipped and organized armies may often not engage in direct battles with the opposing forces."[48] They argue that this is one reason why the number of deaths caused directly by battle may be only a small percentage of the total number of people who die during modern civil wars. Given the paucity of battles, armed groups are forced to build and maintain social cohesion through other activities of their own making. In addition, research suggests that it is important that fighters view the burdens of combat as shared by commanders. In the Vietnam War, perceptions that officers had it easier than the rank-and-file soldiers were deeply corrosive to cohesion (Kenny 2011).

Third, rituals are crucial for forging social ties, especially in small groups. Kenny (2011, 14) argues that "the recruitment process and the initiation stage have a highly significant impact on identity formation." He cites ritual killing among the child combatants in the LRA in Uganda as an example. But rituals are not limited to initiation rites or coerced violence; they can include strict dress codes, graduation ceremonies, or more mundane tasks (Kenny 2011, 18). In my interviews, members of armed groups in Sierra Leone and of the militias in Timor-Leste reported similar rituals. One former militia member in Timor-Leste described the bloodletting initiation rite of a militia group called Aitarak: "The members of groups like Aitarak would each cut their hands and put the blood in a cup for all to drink. There was a swearing ceremony."[49] Participation in acts of gang rape can also be seen as a ritualized method of increasing cohesion. Why the rituals sometimes become violent, and why this violence becomes sexualized, are critical questions that must, again, draw on the research about the importance of public violent acts that demonstrate masculinity.

In sum, several alternative methods for building cohesion exist within armed groups. Previous research implies at least two conditions under which such alternatives to sexual violence might be selected: first, when groups are well resourced and can invest in basic training exercises, and second, when groups experience frequent battles or other stressful experiences shared by commanders and fighters alike. The frequency of rape in modern civil wars—particularly by groups that abduct and press-gang their fighters[50]—may be the result of armed groups that do not invest heavily in basic training and do not typically fight many battles. Instead, violent rituals, both sexual and otherwise, are used to fill the void. As is explored later in the chapter on El Salvador, at least two other factors serve to weaken the appeal of sexualized violence for cohesion building: ideological pressures from within the group, usually arising from political beliefs about the legitimate uses of violence; and political pressures from outside the group, such as strong preferences against sexual violence by an external sponsor.

How Does the Practice Begin?

The argument presented thus far raises the question of how a combatant group begins to employ rape. A definitive answer is elusive, yet the process may be elucidated by research on individual propensity toward rape and the essential role of leadership in group rape.

A selection mechanism may initially be at work. Because of the nontrivial proportion of men who may want to rape, the existence of these "bad apples" in every armed group likely means that some incidents of rape are committed by every armed group in every conflict. Indeed, a much-cited study of "normal" men's inherent desire to rape is based on a set of surveys in the early 1980s of college-aged men in Canada and the United States (Malamuth 1981). Respondents were asked to report the likelihood that they "personally would rape, if they could be assured of not being caught or punished." Answers were given on a 5-point scale, with 1 being "not at all likely" and 5 being "very likely." Researchers found that about 35 percent of the men answered somewhere in the 2-to-5 range; that is, they would be more than "not at all likely" to rape (140). Feminist scholars have long argued that men who rape are usually ordinary people—not, on average, mentally ill or pathological. Rather, such scholars typically maintain that there exists a male proclivity to rape, although its source—whether social pressures (e.g., Sanday) or biology (e.g., Brownmiller)—is a point of much debate.

In addition to the likely presence of at least some "bad apples" in small armed group units, research on gang rape suggests that leadership plays a major role. One study of thirty-nine incidents involving convictions for multiple-perpetrator rape found that in nearly every case, there was a clear leader who either ordered or modeled the behavior to the others in the group. Further, leadership—defined as providing the initial idea for the attack, selecting the target, or being the first to commit the sexual act—was especially strong in larger groups of perpetrators (i.e., three to five people) (Porter and Alison 2001). Leaders are typically the most "delinquent" of the group, with greater emotional problems than so-called followers, and are believed to be more likely than followers to reoffend (Woodhams et al. 2012, 731). A leader typically reports acting "out of a need to prove his leadership—and by implication his masculinity—to the others . . . [while followers] feel enormous pressure to live up to [the leader's] expectations" (Franklin 2004, 31).

Although this research provides a basis for the idea that a small percentage of fighters may actively seek to rape noncombatants, and also that these fighters may become leaders in initiating incidents of gang rape in small groups, it is only in some cases that rape becomes a widespread practice of an armed group. Rape may then spread across armed groups as the groups experience an influx of new recruits, due perhaps to an explicit decision to grow the size of the group, or to replace fighters who have been lost to battle, disease, or desertion. I examine these dynamics in the case study chapters.

Related Arguments

The combatant socialization argument is distinct in important ways from three other, related explanations of the roots of wartime violence. First, the argument differs from more general theories of rape as "male bonding" for two key reasons. Theories of male bonding, obviously, apply specifically to men and are predicated on the idea that men form friendships with one another through voluntary acts of misogynist, sexualized violence in male-only groups (Sanday 2007). However, bonding through acts of rape is not exclusive to male perpetrators, nor are the acts necessarily founded on enjoyment or sexual gratification. Scholars who advocate this perspective often also argue that men behave differently in sex-segregated environments, such as military units, than they would in mixed-gender contexts. One of the central findings of anthropologist Peggy Reeves Sanday, in her early study of rape-prone societies (1981) and in her later work on gang rape on college campuses (2007), is that men in all-male environments are far more likely to engage in sexual violence against women than are those in more gender-equal environments. Related to this argument is the idea that the presence of women in all-male groups mitigates the violent behavior of men by changing the ways in which men relate to one another. Claudia Card (1996) hypothesizes that the involvement of women in combat and leadership roles would render gang rape highly unusual.[51]

The combatant socialization argument does not assume that most perpetrators of rape—whether male or female—independently desire to participate in such violence, at least not for reasons of sexual gratification; this position is supported in large part through interviews in the case studies. Interviews with ex-combatants, some of whom expressed intense regret as they recounted their stories, support the idea that perpetrators of gang rape are ordinary people who would likely not perpetrate rape on their own. One ex-combatant in Sierra Leone relayed a story of raping a woman, which he described as "an act of someone with no conscience." He concluded with something of an apology: "I beg for people to take us back as sons and brothers because what we did to them was really, really terrible."[52] As previously described, earlier feminist literature on rape also often argues that all men harbor an implicit desire to rape women (e.g., Brownmiller 1975).[53] Theories of rape as male bonding, however, cannot explain variation—why some groups of men commit rape and others do not, why women also participate, or why such a high proportion of wartime rape is gang rape, as opposed to single-perpetrator rape.

Second, the combatant socialization argument is distinct from a theory of civilian abuse advanced by Macartan Humphreys and Jeremy Weinstein (2006). Humphreys and Weinstein also emphasize that the lack of social cohesion is an essential factor in the commission of civilian abuses, and they find a strong negative relationship between the "density of social ties" (i.e., whether a recruit knew friends, family members, or community leaders in his or her faction) and the level of civilian abuse. A mechanism they hypothesize is that social ties may serve a policing function. Knowing other people in the unit, they argue, made it more difficult to "defect," or to misbehave in a manner costly to the group.

I concur with the basic premise that an absence of social ties has an effect on violence perpetrated against civilians, and I build on this previous work to explain variation in *forms* of violence rather than *levels* of violence. I argue that the selection of particular types of (sexual) violence serves a deeper purpose for the armed group. Humphreys and Weinstein's (2006) mechanism does not explain why some forms of violence are selected over others; in other words, why rape or amputation and not just looting? In their conclusion, Humphreys and Weinstein suggest that other mechanisms besides the policing function may be at work including "uncertainty over the relative status of different members within the organization [that] may result in individuals performing violent acts to establish their position within the organization" (444). The combatant socialization argument expands on this alternative mechanism.

A final related argument centers on the importance of norms of violence in armed groups. The norms around the use and nonuse of violence that are communicated by leaders of armed groups, along with the norms that individual fighters may espouse, interact in ways that can help explain the use of wartime rape. Elisabeth Wood (2008; 2009; 2012) presents a theoretical framework for understanding how the norms of the leaders and the fighters can either reduce or encourage the likelihood of rape and other forms of sexual violence. Wood argues that individual combatants' beliefs, leadership strategy, small group dynamics, and military hierarchy can all contribute to the content and diffusion of norms of violence within a fighting unit. Wood maintains that the use of rape depends on the armed group's norms and values, mediated by the strength of the group's institutions such as socialization and discipline.[54] Based on detailed case studies, Wood hypothesizes that groups will not use rape if they have an effective command structure that prohibits rape or when they are dependent upon a civilian population.[55] While not disputing the argument that group norms are vital in understanding the variation in rape during war, a question remains open: from where do these norms arise? My argument helps to resolve this question by locating the origin of group norms in the recruitment choices of the armed groups.

Competing Explanations for Wartime Rape

The disparate literatures on the causes of wartime rape can be divided into three broad categories: opportunism/greed, ethnic hatred, and gender inequality. Far from being exhaustive, these arguments represent the most salient testable theories across a vast range of literatures, and each yields a unique set of observable implications that can be explored on both the macro and micro levels. I later test these explanations, using a cross-national dataset of all recent major civil wars, to determine their generalizability; then, I utilize detailed case studies to establish whether these explanations find support in particular cases.

Opportunism/Greed

The most common argument made for why rape occurs during wartime centers on the idea that war affords men an unprecedented opportunity to rape. There are several variations on this theme. First, some observers view rape as a "natural," unavoidable outcome of war. War, and the breakdown of the state that may accompany conflict, results in a lawless chaos; it destroys the social norms, institutions, and legal prohibitions that exist in peacetime, which in turn unleashes the latent desire of at least some men to commit rape (e.g., Goldstein 2001; Eriksson Baaz and Stern 2009). This perspective has been articulated in previous research during interviews with former fighters. For example, a former child soldier who fought with the Sierra Leone Army said, "I liked it in the army because we could do anything we liked to do. When some civilian had something I liked, I just took it without him doing anything to me. We used to rape women. Anything I wanted to do [I did]. I was free" (Peters and Richards 1998, 194). In another study, a former captive of the RUF rebel group in Sierra Leone explained rape as a result of the absence of constraints: "In normal circumstances [the members of the RUF] would restrain themselves. But they would rather experiment with their sexual freedom and they were not under any form of governance or rules" (Keen 2005, 44).

Conflicts marked by high levels of rape from all factions are frequently cited as evidence for this perspective. Reported perpetrators of rape in the ongoing war in the failed state of the DRC include nearly every possible type of actor, including the armed forces, the national police, the rebel forces, and civilians, both male and female (Evans 2007; Johnson et al. 2010). More broadly, there is an expectation that young men, carrying weapons and possibly intoxicated or drugged, will inevitably rape women. This view is captured in a reporter's description of the wartime violence in Liberia: "Rape is common because of the number of drugged and drunk young men roaming the countryside with guns" (Wax 2003). One former combatant whom I interviewed in Sierra Leone said, "Guns and war—these gave men the feeling that they could rape with impunity."[56]

According to opportunism/greed arguments, male combatants commit rape for private motivations—namely, sexual gratification—rather than for any sort of military strategy or group purpose.[57] From this perspective, rape is understood as a costless activity and often considered a form of "consumption," similar to looting. Men, in this view, have an inherent desire for sex with women that goes unfulfilled during their duties as fighters. Rape, then, may be the result of a lack of access to sex that would normally take place within combatants' peacetime relationships with their wives and girlfriends.

Indeed, ex-combatants and others I interviewed in both Sierra Leone and Timor-Leste frequently named sexual gratification as one of the reasons for widespread rape. As one ex-combatant in Sierra Leone reported, "The rebels used rape because they did not have girlfriends in the bush."[58] Another former fighter in Sierra Leone stated, "The men needed to ejaculate; as long as [the victims] were female, the fighters didn't care."[59] A former rebel commander in Timor-Leste described the rape by pro-Indonesia militias: "The militias were capturing women for sexual satisfaction. Sometimes they were killed afterwards, sometimes they were released."[60] An NGO worker also reported that at least some of the rape perpetrated by the militias in Timor-Leste was the result of private motivations: "The militia would have 'support the referendum' parties, and they would pressure the village chief to provide music. They would drink and have a party and sometimes rape the local women."[61] Finally, a Timorese victims' rights advocate, when asked if the militia-perpetrated rape was directly ordered by the Indonesian military, replied, "It was a chaotic situation. Some individual men in that situation have a personal motivation to commit rape. And some men will take advantage of that opportunity."[62]

The uncontrollable need for sexual fulfillment undergirds central assumptions made by some about the causes of wartime rape, particularly regarding access to sex for soldiers. Part of the role of comfort women enslaved for Japan's army was reportedly to prevent the rape of civilians, mitigating the risk of public outrage and the spread of disease (Goldstein 2001; Wood 2009). Additionally, a common story told about the widespread rape in the DRC is that the poorly paid fighters lack the ability to pay for sex workers. A news article featuring an interview with a Congolese army colonel stated that, because fighters have "almost no money, soldiers and deserters are tempted to rape because they are isolated deep in the forest, and cannot afford wives or prostitutes" (Murdock 2011).[63]

A related version of the opportunism/greed argument has also been offered by scholars using a principal-agent model to explain excess violence—that is, violence beyond the sanctioned killing of enemy combatants—by armed actors (e.g., Mitchell 2004; Butler, Gluch, and Mitchell 2007; Leiby 2011).[64] As Neil Mitchell (2004, 50) argues, killing during wartime may at times occur by accident, but "rape is not done by mistake." Mitchell maintains that rape is a singular type of violence, and the presence of rape can be used as a "universal barometer" (181) to understand the nature of control that a commander exerts. The perpetration of rape by armed actors, he maintains, indicates that a commander cannot or will not control his fighters, while a lack of rape suggests a commander in control. In Mitchell's view, rape by combatants is both "selfish" and "nonstrategic" and, critically, costless from the perspective of the commander. The sum of these strands of the opportunism/greed argument suggests a testable hypothesis:

> H2: Rape by state actors and by insurgents is more likely during periods of state collapse, when peacetime barriers against rape have disintegrated.

In addition, state actors may be more likely to rape when military professionalism is particularly weak. National militaries that are poorly resourced and poorly trained may provide fewer checks on the behavior of soldiers and may be more likely to engage in the abuse of civilians. Ouédraogo (2014) writes that weak military professionalism was the proximate cause of an episode of rape and other violence perpetrated in 2011 by members of the military in Burkina Faso. This perspective offers a related hypothesis:

> H3: Rape by state actors is more likely when military professionalism is low.

A second influential set of arguments about opportunism/greed focuses on a selection mechanism, or the types of people who want to join armed groups. Mueller (2000) argues that a small number of criminal types caused the violence during the wars in the former Yugoslavia and Rwanda. These bands of people, whom Mueller describes in turn as "criminal and hooligan opportunists" (42) and "common, opportunistic, sadistic . . . marauders," (43) are organized together to commit crimes during the context of war (ethnic war, in these cases, but the theory is not limited to ethnic war). According to Mueller, the gangs are loosely organized by political elites who use coercive violence for political ends. The people who behave violently are understood to be rough types who enjoy violence, and the war provides an excellent excuse to do so without the usual constraints of peacetime. Research on rape in peacetime contexts lends credence to the notion of a selection mechanism. For example, in studies of college fraternities, scholars have suggested a selection mechanism as a reason that fraternities and sports teams seem more likely to engage in gang rape than do other types of campus organizations; they argue that certain types of sexually aggressive men are more likely to join fraternities or sports team (O'Sullivan 1991). One potential cause of wartime rape, then, is that some armed groups attract people who seek to rape.

Jeremy Weinstein (2007) proposes a related explanation, arguing that civilian abuse, broadly defined, is more likely when insurgent groups have access to material resources, including contraband or external funding.[65] The theory suggests two mechanisms for why resources may lead to violence. The first involves *recruitment*: Weinstein argues that insurgent groups with access to material resources attract "opportunistic joiners" (103), or those with shorter time horizons and less commitment to the long-term goals of the group, in contrast to groups that rely on ideology alone to recruit fighters. In practice, this means that groups with material resources attract more violence-prone recruits and, as a result, will be more likely to commit civilian abuses on a mass scale.

A second mechanism is about *accountability*: the availability of material resources enables insurgent groups to be unaccountable to the civilian population, which in turn leads to exploitative violence, including looting and sexual violence. In other words, the more combatants rely on the civilian population for material support, the less likely they may be to abuse them. Of course, the likelihood of rape and other forms of abuse may lessen as the reliance by combatant groups on civilians increases—for all forms of support, not only material support. Some groups actively cultivate civilian support for a variety of reasons. But material support is one of the most crucial forms, and most observable ways, by which a civilian population can assist an armed group. In the case studies discussed later, I briefly consider this explanation of needing or wanting civilian support as one potential reason for the absence of civilian abuse on the part of some armed groups. In short, regardless of the mechanism, Weinstein (2007) argues that the availability of material resources is a powerful predictor of whether civilian abuses will occur.

Insurgents may be more likely to rape in conflicts where insurgencies are fueled by "economic endowments," especially those that are easily converted into selective incentives to entice new recruits (Weinstein 2005, 599), such as contrabands like drugs or diamonds, or external support from a diaspora.[66] Together, these arguments suggest a fourth hypothesis:

> H4: Rape by insurgents is more likely in conflicts where insurgent groups rely on material resources.

Violence against civilians, according to these scholars, is an unfortunate consequence of selecting or attracting fighters who are abusive and unaccountable to the noncombatant population; it is not an instrumental means to an end. The forms of violence used by armed groups, including rape, are selected by individual fighters due to personal preferences.

Ethnic Hatred

One of the most frequently cited environments for extreme violence, including widespread rape, is ethnic war (e.g., Horowitz 1985; Bloom 1999; Plümper and Neumayer 2006). These scholars argue that, because they "engage intense emotions and a sense of existential threat," ethnic conflicts are likely to be more violent than non-ethnic conflicts (Fearon 2006, 862). For example, Plümper and Neumayer (2006, 735) write that "reports of systematic rapes and rape-related murder of women, forced impregnation and forced abortion are particularly abundant during ethnic wars." Further, they theorize that rape plays a key role in humiliating the ethnic opponent in a war. In addition, Alison (2007, 79) argues that rape in wartime rarely occurs "indiscriminately"; rather, especially in the context of modern ethnic wars, "rape is intentionally committed by specific men against specific women." Conventional wisdom in the policy and advocacy arenas, seemingly based on high-profile cases such as the wars in Bosnia-Herzegovina and Rwanda, concurs that ethnic wars are especially likely to be conflicts with widespread rape. An Amnesty International representative quoted in a BBC article on wartime rape illustrates this point: "Rape is often used in ethnic conflicts as a way for attackers to perpetuate their social control and redraw ethnic boundaries" (Smith-Spark 2004).

The mechanism for the hypothesis is that combatants rape to symbolically demonstrate ethnic loathing or dominance over their ethnic opponents. In this way, rape may form a fundamental, and rational, part of combatant groups' strategies in war: namely, to intimidate other, competing, ethnically opposed combatant groups (e.g., Bastick, Grimm, and Kunz 2007). Drawing on lessons learned from well-documented conflicts, NGOs and human rights advocates who are seeking prosecutions for rape as a war crime commonly hold this view. Human rights advocacy organizations tend to argue that rape during conflict is the result of its terrible power—particularly during ethnic wars—as a "weapon" or as part of a "strategy of war."[67] From this perspective, wartime rape is an organized, top-down phenomenon, explicitly ordered—rather than tolerated—by commanders to terrorize ethnic opponents. Scholars have suggested that rape may be selected as a form of violence due to its ability to instill grave fear in populations. This fear is at least partly founded on the presumed stigma that rape may place on a victim and the victim's family (Benard 1994; Card 1996).[68] This argument suggests the following hypothesis:

> H5: Ethnic wars are more likely than non-ethnic wars to be associated with higher conflict-wide levels of wartime rape.

The ethnic hatred argument includes two additional variations. First, some have argued specifically that rape is more likely to feature in genocidal wars than in ethnic wars more broadly. These observers view rape as a "central technique" (Mullins 2009, 15) in the technology of genocide in such conflicts as those in the former Yugoslavia, Rwanda, and Darfur. Second, drawing on previous work by Catharine MacKinnon (1993), feminist scholars refer to a category of "genocidal rape." Lisa Sharlach (2000, 89) argues that rape—even if the victim is not killed—should fall under the UN definition of genocide in the 1948 genocide convention, which includes "causing serious bodily or mental harm to members of the group and/or deliberately inflicting on the group conditions of life calculated to bring about its physical destruction in whole or in part." Sharlach maintains that the physical and psychological harms inflicted on a rape victim, and on the victim's ethnic group in the form of mass trauma, are a type of genocidal violence. Scholars also argue that genocidal rape—typically but not always perpetrated by the state—may occur in different forms: rape may occur immediately prior to the lethal violence of the genocide, either as a form of lethal violence itself (i.e., a victim may be raped until she or he dies) (Rittner and Roth 2012) or as a way of inflicting devastating long-term physical or psychological trauma (e.g., victims may be physically unable to or emotionally incapable of having children after a rape) (Koo 2002).[69] This suggests another hypothesis:

> H6: States or insurgents that perpetrate genocide are more likely to commit wartime rape than those who do not.

Of course, not all genocides involve mass rape. In some cases, sexual contact with an ethnic other was understood to be polluting to the perpetrator. For example, sexual relationships with Jews during the Holocaust were strictly forbidden as a form of *Rassenschande* (race defilement), although more recent research has revealed reports of rapes of Jewish women, as well as forced sterilization and forced prostitution (Hedgepeth and Saidel 2010). Scott Straus (2006) hypothesizes that genocidal violence may be more likely when ethnic groups are well integrated into societies, through proximity and intermarriage.[70] Elisabeth Wood (2009), extending this hypothesis to sexual violence, argues that wartime rape may be more likely in cases where ethnic groups are uninhibited by racial pollution norms and perceive each other as potential sexual and marital partners. One explanation for the lack of rape in the current Israeli-Palestinian conflict is that the members of the Israel Defense Forces do not generally view Palestinians as potential sexual or marital partners (Nitsan 2012).[71]

A second variation of the ethnic hatred argument is that rape can be used in a campaign of ethnic cleansing, or forced expulsion, during secessionist wars.[72] Rape can be a method of ensuring that an ethnic population will flee a disputed territory, guaranteeing that displaced people will not return, and "sexually contaminating" women of a given ethnicity (e.g., Bloom 1999; Sharlach 2000; Farr 2009.)[73] Of course, rape can be used as a tactic of intimidation in nonethnic wars as well. One scholar speculates that secessionist wars, in which a country is partitioned into new states, are more likely to feature rape as a tool for increasing hatred between warring groups—essentially, as a method of enforcing the idea that "life together is finished" (Hayden 2000, 32).[74] This argument suggests the following hypothesis, with applications to both nonethnic and ethnic wars:

> H7: Wars with secessionist aims, and especially those that involve ethnic cleansing, are more likely to involve insurgent-perpetrated rape.

Gender Inequality

Feminist scholars have identified, both implicitly and explicitly, a causal relationship between gender inequality and wartime rape (e.g., Hansen 2001; Koo 2002). In addition, a common contention, especially in the human rights advocacy community, holds that wartime rape is more likely in countries where women have fewer political and legal rights. For example, a Human Rights Watch report asserts that "women's subordinate and unequal status in peacetime renders them predictably at risk for sexual violence in times of war" (Jefferson 2004). Others have argued that rape may be more likely when women are gaining rights and men may feel threatened (Baron and Straus 1989). A 2011 news article describes a series of brutal rapes of women in northeastern India that illustrates this logic; many of the victims were young, educated women with jobs, while most of the perpetrators were conservative, uneducated, and offended by the newfound freedoms of the victims (*New York Times*, March 26, 2011). However, most arguments about the relationship between gender inequality and wartime rape predict a correlation between the relative lack of women's rights and widespread rape.

Scholarship on the status of women and the use of rape during war focuses in particular on the symbolic meaning of rape and the role that gender inequality may play in facilitating a culture that accepts or encourages violence against women. These scholars typically view rape as an act of violence by the men in a society directed toward the women in the society (or toward the men who control a particular group of women). According to this perspective, rape is a violation—unrelated to on-the-ground wartime strategy—that allows men to inflict psychological harm on women and their communities (e.g., Seifert 1996; Benard 1994; Green 2006). Rape is selected as a type of violence because it is shameful not only for the victim, but also for her husband and male relatives, who are seen to have failed to protect the victim (Bastick, Grimm, and Kunz 2007). Women may become victims because of their symbolic roles as mothers, and as "bearers of honour" (Bastick, Grimm, and Kunz 2007, 14) particularly in ethnic conflicts, or simply because they make easy targets. Some argue that gender inequality creates social norms that encourage violence and aggression against women, including wartime rape (e.g., Baron and Straus 1989; MacKinnon 2006). Similarly, Peggy Reeves Sanday (1981) argues that rape-prone societies are ones that tend to be heavily segregated by sex, and in which the social contributions of women are not highly valued. Others maintain that wartime worsens existing gender inequality, making women especially vulnerable to violence (Farr 2009). Scholars have established that gender inequality is strongly associated with civil war onset (Caprioli 2005; Fearon 2010), but have not investigated whether gender inequality is correlated with specific forms of violence once conflict has begun, including rape. The gender inequality arguments imply the final hypothesis:

> H8: *Conflicts in countries with greater gender inequality are more likely to be correlated with higher conflict-wide levels of wartime rape.*

Each of these arguments has unique observable implications that I test, using both macro- and micro-level data, in subsequent chapters. The observable implications are summarized in table 1.2.

TABLE 1.2 Wartime rape: Arguments, hypotheses, and observable implications

ARGUMENTS	HYPOTHESES	OBSERVABLE IMPLICATIONS	
		MACRO LEVEL	*MICRO LEVEL*
Combatant socialization	*H1:* Extreme forced recruitment → state- and insurgent-perpetrated rape	Rape is more likely by armed groups engaged in extreme forms of forced recruitment	− Rape is more likely to perpetrated by armed groups engaged in extreme forms of forced recruitment (i.e. press-ganging by states; abduction by insurgents) − Reports that rape is cohesive, not divisive − Rape is not directly ordered by commanders − Perpetrators of both sexes
Opportunism/ greed	*H2:* State collapse → state- and insurgent-perpetrated rape	Rape is more likely when state collapse is more severe	− Rape covaries with looting/ property crime − Reports that rape is due to lack of access to sexual partners − Rape is viewed by commanders as costless or as a reward for fighters − Victims are same demographic as peacetime spouses/sexual partners
	H3: Low military professionalism → state-perpetrated rape	Rape is more likely when national militaries are poorly resourced and poorly trained	− Rape is more likely to be perpetrated by branches of the national military with poorer funding and training (non-elite units)
	H4: Material resources → insurgent-perpetrated rape	Rape is more likely when insurgents funded by contraband or external sources	− Rape is more likely to perpetrated by insurgent groups funded by contraband or external sources (e.g. diaspora communities)
Ethnic hatred	*H5:* Ethnic wars → conflict-wide rape	Rape is more likely in ethnic wars	− Victims are frequently raped by perpetrators of a different ethnicity − Rape is more prevalent in regions where the population has a different ethnicity than combatants − Evidence of rape being used as a targeted or collective form of punishment − Rape is ordered by commanders
	H6: Perpetrators of genocide → state- and insurgent-perpetrated rape	Rape is more likely during periods of genocide	− Victims are frequently raped by perpetrators of a different ethnicity − Reports of victims being raped and then killed

		OBSERVABLE IMPLICATIONS	
ARGUMENTS	HYPOTHESES	*MACRO LEVEL*	*MICRO LEVEL*
	H7: Secessionist aims/ ethnic cleansing → insurgent-perpetrated rape	Rape is more likely during wars with secessionist aims, or those with campaigns of ethnic cleansing	– Rape reported during campaigns of forced displacement
Gender inequality	*H8:* Greater gender inequality → conflict-wide rape	Rape is more likely in countries with more pronounced gender inequality	– Armed groups that demonstrate a commitment to gender equality (recruiting and arming female fighters; ideology) are less likely to rape

In this chapter, I have presented an argument about combatant socialization—the main argument of the book—as well as its theoretical foundations in a number of disciplines. I have also discussed the three competing sets of arguments I will consider in the subsequent chapters: opportunism/greed, ethnic hatred, and gender inequality. In the next chapter, I turn to testing the macro-level implications of the arguments on a cross-national sample of major civil wars.

RESEARCH STRATEGY, CROSS-NATIONAL EVIDENCE (1980–2009), AND STATISTICAL TESTS

Research Strategy

The process of researching wartime rape is fraught with a variety of challenges. In this study, I use multiple research methods to examine the incidence of war-time rape. I rely on two main sources of data: an original cross-national dataset of wartime rape during all recent major civil wars (1980–2012),[1] and qualitative evidence gathered during fieldwork interviews with both ex-combatants and noncombatants about their first-hand experiences with violence during the civil wars in their countries. The overarching goal of the research strategy is to present a general argument to account for variation in the occurrence of rape during civil wars. The cross-national evidence has two purposes. First, the data can demonstrate that there is indeed substantial variation—in where, when, and by whom rape has been perpetrated—that can be exploited to develop a robust argument about the root causes of rape. Second, the data can establish whether statistically significant associations between important factors exist for a universe of cases. However, the statistical analyses cannot determine the direction of the relationship, or whether one variable seems to be causing another, nor can they explain how the mechanisms linking important factors may take shape on the ground. The qualitative interviews, presented in the three case studies later in the book, are necessary for tracing the main mechanisms of competing arguments on the micro level. Both types of data are used to evaluate the evidence for as many of the macro- and micro-level observable implications as possible—including temporal correlations between different forms of violence, the patterns of both victims and perpetrators in each war, and the descriptions that former combatants themselves offered about rape—in order to determine which arguments have the most support.[2]

In this chapter, I first discuss the qualitative and quantitative methodologies employed in this study and examine some of the difficulties inherent in conducting research on rape.[3] I then turn to the quantitative analysis to test the general predictions of the hypotheses presented at the end of chapter 1.

Qualitative Interviews

The main purpose of the interviews with ex-combatants is to elucidate how members of armed groups understand rape in the context of war. The central argument of the book—that gang rape helps to create social bonds within groups of abducted combatants—is inherently difficult to test. The process of forming such bonds through sexual violence is largely internal to individuals and may be mostly subconscious. It is also difficult to discuss, and perhaps particularly so with a researcher. In interviews, therefore, my questions were aimed at understanding the social processes around wartime rape—why it happened, how the perpetrators felt about the violence when it was happening, how they recalled the violence in its aftermath, and how witnessing or participating in such violence changed their views of their peers or themselves. The statements highlighted in each of the case study chapters are key pieces of evidence. These often describe rape as unordered violence that was frequently viewed as a form of recreation (rather than part of a war fighting strategy) and as central to creating bonds of loyalty and consolidating norms around masculinity and virility.

Importance of the Perpetrators' Perspectives

A great deal of the existing research on wartime rape—much of it based on interviews and testimonies—is from the perspectives of victims and witnesses. Most scholars interested in this field of study are intent on recording and understanding the experiences of women, who likely make up the vast majority of victims of wartime rape. With few exceptions (e.g., Eriksson Baaz and Stern 2013), the stories are rarely told from the perspectives of perpetrators, for reasons personal, practical, and theoretical. For example, some researchers find interviewing perpetrators of rape too difficult and do not trust their ability to retain scholarly objectivity in the process (Houge 2008). Many of the authors of the few existing studies focused on wartime perpetrators refrained from conducting interviews of their own, relying instead on evidence such as testimonies from perpetrators drawn from court documents.[4] Human rights organizations that document violations have also tended to focus almost exclusively on victims, collecting detailed interviews of the people who have experienced violence—and rightly so, given organizational objectives.

While victim-focused research is essential for raising awareness of human rights violations and providing evidence for war crimes prosecutions, these data are less useful for understanding *why* rape is used by armed groups during wartime. Instead, perpetrators' motives are often extrapolated from patterns of violence. For instance, one human rights organization—in a report focused on sexual violence in Sierra Leone—stated that an observed pattern of an increase in rape following victories over contested territory indicated that insurgents were using rape to "[reward] themselves . . . [and] to assert their domination over the population" (Taylor 2003, 26–27). These motivations for rape, however, appear to have been assumed from victims' reports; no interviews with fighters are cited as support.[5]

Complicating matters is the fact that first-hand documentary sources detailing explicitly the motivations and goals of wartime rape, including tangible evidence of orders to rape, are exceptionally rare (Gottschall 2004).[6] One infamous exception, along with the others mentioned in the introduction, is the so-called Brana Plan, which has been widely interpreted as a policy of rape against women in the Bosnian conflict. According to the minutes of a 1991 meeting of Yugoslav army officers, a plan was developed by the army's special services—which included experts in psychological warfare—suggesting a campaign of sexual violence for the purpose of spreading terror and clearing a population from contested territory. The most important excerpt from the plan is this: "Our analysis of the behavior of the Muslim communities demonstrates that the morale, will, and bellicose nature of their groups can be undermined only if we aim our action at the point where the religious and social structure is most fragile. We refer to the women, especially adolescents, and to the children. Decisive intervention on these social figures would spread confusion . . . , thus causing first of all fear and then panic, leading to a probable [Muslim] retreat from the territories involved in war activity" (quoted in Allen 1996, 57). Even in this case the evidence is not a smoking gun; the strategy of targeting vulnerable groups stops short of an explicit policy of rape. In general, this type of evidence from the command of an armed group is very unusual.[7]

Given these challenges, interviews with perpetrators are very important in understanding the motivations for wartime rape. Wood (2006) considers interviews with combatants one of the most important reasons for conducting fieldwork, due to the lack of otherwise available resources from which to gather such information. More broadly, recent micro-level research on civil war violence has increasingly relied on interview evidence, both alone and in combination with quantitative data (e.g., Straus 2006; Wood 2003; Weinstein 2007).[8] I draw extensively on original interviews with perpetrators in the subsequent chapters.[9] Although I used different strategies for contacting ex-combatants in each of the case studies (as described in each chapter), I was never explicit about the topic of my study, nor about my main focus of interest: namely, rape. Instead, I told potential interviewees that I was interested in speaking with former fighters about their experiences with violence during the war. The interviews were mainly oral histories, with each ex-combatant telling me the story of how they joined the group and what they (and their peers) did as a member. I never asked explicitly about rape, but if the interviewee broached the topic, I asked followup questions; I found that this technique often yielded detailed reflections. Finally, although the interviews are not representative, as is described in each case study, I interviewed people from as many of the armed groups as possible and attempted to include different types of fighters—men and women, adult fighters and former child soldiers, rank and file and commanders. More on the methodology of the interviews appears in the case chapters as well as in the appendix.

Case Selection

The three case studies presented in chapters 3, 4, and 5 represent different types of wars, involving different cultural/religious contexts and distinct backgrounds of violence. I selected these cases after I had collected the original dataset for the project and after I had developed the initial idea for a theory about the role of combatant socialization in fostering wartime rape, drawing on the literature on gang rape and other group violence discussed in chapter 1. The war in Sierra Leone took place in a Muslim-majority country, under conditions (for some of the war years) of complete state failure. At times, numerous armed groups were fighting both the state and one another. The main rebel faction—funded by contraband—aimed to overthrow the central government. Although the war was marked by terrible violence, there were no episodes of mass killing, nor did the violence comprise a genocide or politicide. In contrast, during the civil war in El Salvador, there was one major rebel group facing the state: an umbrella organization with a united leadership, guided by Marxist ideals and liberation theology. In El Salvador, the state did not experience a total collapse during the war years. Episodes of mass killing, understood to be part of a genocide/politicide, occurred during the early years of the war. Finally, the war in Timor-Leste—a Catholic-majority country, like El Salvador—lasted nearly twenty-five years, or about twice as long as the other two cases. The central aim of the rebel group was autonomy from Indonesia, a goal that differed from those in the other two wars. The war in Timor-Leste was also characterized by both mass killing and genocide/politicide.

Most essential for the purposes of the present analysis, the three cases reflect variation both in terms of the magnitude of wartime rape and the types of perpetrators. Specifically, the conflicts in Sierra Leone and Timor-Leste exhibited relatively high levels of wartime rape, while the civil war in El Salvador experienced a relatively low level. Additionally, the main perpetrators of rape in Sierra Leone were insurgents, while in Timor-Leste and El Salvador the rape was mainly committed by state actors and their auxiliaries. In addition, all three wars were nonethnic conflicts (or at the very least, are all considered less than unambiguously ethnic conflicts, as classified by Fearon and Laitin [2015]). The choice to focus on nonethnic wars was intended to test "hard" cases for current arguments, some of which hypothesize that ethnic hatreds best explain variation in wartime rape. As is presented later in the chapter, I find that neither ethnic war, secessionist war, ethnic cleansing, nor genocide is systematically positively associated with rape during civil war during the study period. The case selection therefore helps to explain conflicts where ethnic tensions cannot be a plausible cause of wartime rape. Finally, the cases were selected as representatives of three different geographic regions around the globe, in order to reflect the reality that wartime rape is not limited to particular areas of the world.

I present a summary of these important sources of variation in table 2.1.

TABLE 2.1 Case-study selection justification

CONFLICT	LEVEL OF WARTIME RAPE	PERPETRATORS	ETHNIC CONFLICT?	GEOGRAPHIC REGION
Sierra Leone	High	Mostly insurgents (and some state)	Mixed/ambiguous	Sub-Saharan Africa
Timor-Leste	High	Mostly government (and some state-backed local militias)	Mixed/ambiguous	Asia
El Salvador	Low	State only	No	Latin America

Description of Quantitative Data

Data and Measurement

The universe of cases in the dataset includes all ninety-one major civil wars that took place between 1980 and 2012, as defined by the Fearon and Laitin 2015 dataset—an update of the widely cited Fearon and Laitin 2003 dataset.[10] Each war included in the study meets the following definition of a large-scale civil war: the conflict featured (1) fighting between state actors and nonstate groups who sought to control either a government or a region, or who sought to change state policies, (2) the deaths of at least one thousand people over the course of the conflict, with an annual average of at least one hundred, and (3) at least one hundred deaths caused by each side of the conflict (Fearon and Laitin 2003, 76). While some controversy exists over what wars are coded as "civil war," (including the case of Timor-Leste, as discussed in chapter 5), the dataset includes the largest and most deadly conflicts of the past three decades. The wars included in the study are listed in table 2.2.

MEASURING RAPE DURING CIVIL WAR

Collecting reliable data on rape—a form of violence that is often associated with shame for the victims and may leave no visible scars—is not a straightforward task. Numerous scholars across a variety of disciplines have written richly detailed case studies of wars involving what is believed to be widespread rape, including Bangladesh, Bosnia-Herzegovina, Darfur, Iraq, Peru, Rwanda, and World War II (e.g., Bloom 1999; Chang 1997; Hedgepeth and Saidel 2010; Leiby 2009; Sharlach 2000; Wood 2009). These previous studies provide important information about a handful of cases, but they do not systematically collect relevant variables of interest.

Several additional scholars have created datasets and informal lists—based mostly on news coverage and occasional reports by human rights groups—of incidents of wartime rape and other forms of sexual violence that occurred during the last few decades (e.g., Green 2006; Bastick, Grimm, and Kunz 2007; Farr 2009). The cases included in four of these previous studies are summarized in table 2.3. I use these four studies as a check on the dataset I have created, and I find there is close agreement; the footnote to the table details the differences.

Because there were no comprehensive, cross-national data on wartime rape, I collected an original dataset. I use coding procedures similar to those used in Butler, Gluch, and Mitchell's (2007) article on state-directed sexual violence. The Butler et al. coding scheme is in turn based on the widely used Political Terror Scale (PTS) (Gibney, Cornett, and Wood 2015), a five-point measure of the level

TABLE 2.2 Major civil wars active between 1980 and 2012

COUNTRY	CASE NAME	WAR YEARS
Afghanistan	Mujahedeen	1978–92
Afghanistan	Taliban	1992–2001
Afghanistan	Taliban II	2003–
Algeria	FIS, GIA, GSPC	1992–
Angola	UNITA	1975–2002
Angola	FLEC (Cabinda)	1992–2004
Azerbaijan	Nagorno-Karabagh	1992–94
Bangladesh	Chittagong Hills	1976–97
Bosnia Herz.	Rep. Srpska/Croats	1992–95
Burma	CPB, Karens, etc.	1948–
Burundi	Org. massacres, both sides	1988–88
Burundi	Hutu groups v. govt	1993–2006
Cambodia	Khmer Rouge, FUNCINPEC, etc.	1978–98
Chad	FROLINAT, various	1965–
Chad	FARF, other rebels in South	1992–98
China	Xinjiang	1990–98
Colombia	FARC, ELN, etc.	1963–
Congo/Brazzaville	Factional fighting	1997–99
Croatia	Krajina	1992–95
Dem. Rep. Congo/Zaire	AFDL (Kabila)	1996–97
Dem. Rep. Congo/Zaire	RCD, etc. v. govt	1998–
El Salvador	FMLN	1979–92
Ethiopia	Eritrea, Tigray, etc.	1962–92
Ethiopia	Oromo Lib. Front	1992–
Georgia	Abkhazia	1992–94
Guatemala	URNG, various	1968–96
Guinea Bissau	Mil. Faction	1998–99
Haiti	Mil. Coup	1991–95
India	N. East rebels	1978–
India	Sikhs	1982–93
India	Naxalites	1988–
India	Kashmir	1989–
Indonesia	OPM (West Papua)	1965–85
Indonesia	E. Timor	1975–99
Indonesia	GAM I (Aceh)	1989–91
Indonesia	GAM II (Aceh)	1999–2005
Iran	KDPI (Kurds)	1979–93
Iran	MEK	1980–1982
Iran	PJAK	2004–
Iraq	KDP, PUK (Kurds)	1974–93
Iraq	Shia uprising	1991–91
Iraq	Sunni and Shia rebels	2004–
Israel	Palestinian insurgents	1949–
Ivory Coast	anti-Gbagbo	2002–07
Lebanon	various militias	1975–90
Liberia	NPFL (Taylor), INPFL (Johnson)	1989–96
Liberia	LURD	2000–03
Libya	NTC	2011
Mali	Tuaregs	1989–94
Morocco	Polisario	1975–88

COUNTRY	CASE NAME	WAR YEARS
Mozambique	RENAMO	1976–92
Nepal	CPN-M/UPF (Maoists)	1997–2006
Nicaragua	Contras	1981–88
Nigeria	NVPDF, MEND	2004–
Nigeria	Boko Haram	2009–
Pakistan	MQM:Sindhis v. Mohajirs	1992–99
Pakistan	Baluchistan	2004–
Pakistan	Taliban	2004–
Papua New Guinea	BRA (Bougainville)	1988–98
Peru	Sendero Luminoso	1981–99
Philippines	NPA	1969–
Philippines	MNLF, MILF	1970–
Russia	Chechnya	1994–96
Russia	Chechnya II	1999–
Rwanda	RPF, genocide	1990–2002
Senegal	MFDC (Casamance)	1989–
Sierra Leone	RUF, AFRC, etc.	1991–2000
Somalia	SSDF, SNM (Isaaqs)	1981–91
Somalia	post-Barre	1991–
South Africa	Namibia	1980–1988
South Africa	ANC, PAC, Azapo	1983–94
Sri Lanka	LTTE, etc.	1983–2009
Sri Lanka	JVP II	1987–89
Sudan	SPLA, etc.	1983–2005
Sudan	Darfur (SLA, JEM, etc.)	2003–
Syria	Muslim Brothers	1979–1982
Syria	FSA	2011–
Tajikistan	UTO	1992–97
Thailand	Hill Tribes, CPT	1966–81
Thailand	Pattani	2004–
Turkey	Militia-ized party politics	1977–80
Turkey	PKK	1984–
Uganda	NRA, etc.	1981–88
Uganda	LRA, West Nile, etc.	1987–
United Kingdom	IRA	1969–98
Yemen	South Yemen	1994–94
Yemen	al-Houthi rebels	2004–
Yemen Peop. Rep.	Faction of Socialist Party	1986–87
Yugoslavia	Croatia/Krajina	1991–91
Yugoslavia	UCK	1998–99
Zimbabwe	Ndebele guerillas	1983–87

Source: Data on civil wars and case names are from Fearon and Laitin 2015.

and degree of physical-integrity rights violations. I extend the Butler et al. measure by coding reports of rape by state actors *and* rebel groups, instead of only state security forces, and by coding all years from 1980 to 2012, instead of just 2003.

Based on the US State Department's Country Reports on Human Rights Practices,[11] and with the assistance of a team of student research assistants, I coded both state and nonstate perpetrators of rape, by armed group type, for the years 1980 to 2012, in all countries that had experienced a large-scale civil war. The unit of analysis is the *actor type-conflict-year* (e.g., rebel forces in Sierra Leone in 1995).[12] I used a four-point scale that reflects the magnitude of reported rape by each actor type

TABLE 2.3   Cases included in previous cross-national studies of wartime rape and sexual violence

"COLLECTIVE RAPE" (1980–2003) GREEN 2006[1]	SEXUAL VIOLENCE IN ARMED CONFLICT (1987–2007) BASTICK ET AL. 2007[2]	VIOLENCE AGAINST WOMEN IN CONFLICT (1997–2000) UN REPORT 2001[3]	"EXTREME WAR RAPE" IN RECENT CIVIL WARS FARR 2009[4]
Afghanistan	Afghanistan	Afghanistan	Afghanistan
Algeria	Algeria	Burundi	Algeria
Angola	Angola	Colombia	Angola
Argentina	Azerbaijan	Dem. Rep. Congo	Bosnia Herzegovina
Azerbaijan	Bosnia Herzegovina	East Timor	Burundi
Bangladesh	Myanmar/Burma	India	Cambodia
Bosnia Herz.	Burundi	Indonesia	Chad
Burundi	Cambodia	Myanmar/Burma	Colombia
Chile	Central African Republic	Russia (Chechnya)	Cote d'Ivoire
Dem. Rep. Congo	Chad	Serbia (Kosovo)	Dem. Rep. Congo
El Salvador	Colombia	Sierra Leone	East Timor
Guatemala	Cote d'Ivoire	Sri Lanka	Guatemala
Haiti	Croatia		Haiti
India	Dem. Rep. Congo		Iraq
Indonesia	East Timor		Liberia
Kenya	El Salvador		Myanmar/Burma
Kuwait	Eritrea		Nepal
Liberia	Ethiopia		Peru
Mozambique	Georgia		Russia (Chechnya)
Myanmar/Burma	Guatemala		Rwanda
Nicaragua	Guinea-Bissau		Serbia (Kosovo)
Nigeria	Haiti		Sierra Leone
Peru	India		Somalia
Philippines	Indonesia		Sri Lanka
Republic of Congo	Iraq		Sudan
Russia (Chechnya)	Israel/Palestinian		Tajikistan
Rwanda	Territories		Uganda
Serbia (Kosovo)	Kuwait		
Sierra Leone	Liberia		
Solomon Islands	Mozambique		
Somalia	Nepal		
Sri Lanka	Nicaragua		
Sudan	Papua New Guinea		
Turkey	Peru		
Uganda	Philippines		
Uruguay	Republic of Congo		
Zimbabwe			

"COLLECTIVE RAPE" (1980–2003) GREEN 2006[1]	SEXUAL VIOLENCE IN ARMED CONFLICT (1987–2007) BASTICK ET AL. 2007[2]	VIOLENCE AGAINST WOMEN IN CONFLICT (1997–2000) UN REPORT 2001[3]	"EXTREME WAR RAPE" IN RECENT CIVIL WARS FARR 2009[4]
Russian Federation (Chechnya)			
Rwanda			
Serbia (Kosovo)			
Sierra Leone			
Solomon Islands			
Somalia			
Sri Lanka			
Sudan			
Tajikistan			
Turkey			
Uganda			
United States (Guantanamo detainees)			
Zimbabwe			

[1] This list includes many cases that I code as having reports of wartime rape; however, the Green (2006) data are not limited to wartime, so it is difficult to make a direct comparison with my data.

[2] Two cases in this report differ from my dataset: Azerbaijan, which I code as having no reports of wartime rape, and Yemen, which I code as having incidents of rape in the al-Houthi war (2004–ongoing). For Azerbaijan, the authors note that documentary evidence of rape is thin. Based on their description of the conflicts, Bastick et al. (2007) did not include the al-Houthi war in Yemen in their report.

[3] All of these countries are coded in my dataset as having reports of rape. These countries are case studies in the UN report, which notes that this list is neither exhaustive nor representative. Each case study specifically mentions rape perpetrated against noncombatants. The original list also included Japan, which reflected developments with regard to justice on the issue of comfort women.

[4] Farr (2009) codes one case, Cambodia, as an example of "extreme war rape"; I coded it as having little wartime rape. This discrepancy may be because my coding begins in 1980, and so does not account for the first two years of the Cambodian conflict.

in each conflict-year. Table 2.4 displays a summary of the coding rules for the scale, which ranges from 0 to 3. The scale, of course, is a measure by the State Department of the *reporting* of rape. A coding of 0, therefore, indicates not that no rape at all occurred in a particular conflict, but rather that the State Department received no reports of its occurrence. Still, it is doubtful that a conflict with no reports of rape might in fact be a case of widespread rape. Even in cases of countries with no or limited diplomatic relations with the United States during the study period, such as Myanmar, I coded reports of significant conflict-related rape.

In the coding rules, a coding of 0, 1, or 2 is based solely on the description of the magnitude of the reported rape, as is shown in table 2.4. The highest level of rape, 3, is reserved for those conflict-years that are described in the most dire terms in the source document. These terms include phrases that are used in the policy discourse as synonyms for "severe" but are imprecise in a social science context.

TABLE 2.4   Level of wartime rape: Summary of coding rules

LEVEL OF RAPE	CODING RULES
3	Rape likely related to civil war and • was described as "massive" or on a "massive scale," or • was "systematic," used as a "means of intimidation," an "instrument of control and punishment," a "weapon," a "tactic to terrorize the populace," a "terror tactic," a "tool of war" AND was described with any of the terms that qualify for a coding of 2 (e.g., "common")
2	Rape likely related to civil war, but did not meet the requirements for a 3 coding, and • was described as "widespread," "common," "commonplace," "extensive," "frequent," "often," "innumerable," "persistent," "recurring," a "pattern," a "common pattern," or a "spree," or • occurred "commonly," "frequently," in "large numbers," "periodically," "regularly," "routinely," "widely," or on a "number of occasions," or • there were "many" or "numerous" instances, or • was "systematic," used as a "means of intimidation," an "instrument of control and punishment," a "weapon," a "tactic to terrorize the populace," a "terror tactic," a "tool of war" AND WAS NOT described with any of the other terms that qualify for a coding of 2
1	Rape likely related to civil war, but did not meet requirements for a 2 or 3 coding, and there were "isolated reports," "some reports," or "reports," or "there continued to be reports"
0	No mention of rape likely related to civil war

In particular, some of these terms describe the *intention* of the rape rather than its magnitude (e.g., "weapon of war"). To avoid coding those conflicts where *only* the intention was described in the source but not the magnitude, the rule requires the following: that to be coded as a 3, the description of rape must contain an intention term *and additionally* contain at least one term that would qualify for a coding of 2.[13] The Sierra Leone report from 1999, for example, describes rape as a "terror tactic" and notes that "rebels committed numerous egregious abuses, including . . . rape." The description of the intent of the violence as a "terror tactic," combined with the term "numerous," which qualifies for a coding of 2, triggers a coding of 3 for this conflict-year.[14]

Unlike cross-national data on battle deaths, the four-point scale of wartime rape does not include the number of reported violations (or reported victims) per conflict-year. Accurate counts of acts of rape or of the numbers of victims are only rarely available, and only for a small number of cases. In addition, it is difficult to define what one incident of rape might include. For example, interviews during my fieldwork revealed a great deal of variation both in the number of perpetrators (which ranged from a single person to many perpetrators) and in the frequency of rape (some victims had been raped once, while others had been raped hundreds of times over a period of months). A four-point scale of violence is less precise than a count of incidents, but also less likely to suffer from a number of potential biases that would plague an incident- or event-based dataset. The four-point scale of wartime rape, while not fine-grained, allows for inferences about the *relative magnitude of rape* across conflicts and enables the first series of systematic tests of hypotheses about rape across a universe of cases.

Although the argument presented in this book is focused on gang rape, the dataset I collected includes reports of *all* conflict-related rape, not only reports of gang rape. This is because the State Department reports are often not detailed about the forms of rape, beyond a description of the intensity. However, in cases where gang rape was specifically reported, I found that such reports are correlated with the reported intensity of wartime rape.[15] In addition, while the combatant socialization argument centers mainly on gang rape, scholars have found that bragging to peers in the aftermath of single-perpetrator rape may also form social cohesion.[16] Therefore, the data on rape includes reports of both gang rape and single-perpetrator rape, reflecting the range of possible perpetrator combinations.

LIMITATIONS OF THE DATA

While the data are important for developing a better understanding the patterns of wartime rape, three limitations should be noted. First, although the data are drawn from the same source—the US State Department's Country Reports on Human Rights Practices—over a period of time, and the source has a presumed consistency in collection methods, there may have been inconsistent interest in rape over time.[17] For example, it is plausible that after the wartime rape in Rwanda and Bosnia-Herzegovina received a great deal of attention in the mid-1990s, human rights organizations began to focus on the issue more than they had in previous years. An increase in the number and severity of reports over time—as is apparent in the data—may indicate increased interest in the issue over time, rather than an increase in the underlying incidence. As Mala Htun and Laurel Weldon (2015) write, Human Rights Watch began its women's rights program in 1989 and Amnesty International started its work on violence against women prior to the 1993 Vienna World Conference on Human Rights, suggesting that the reporting on violence against women may have become more robust after these points.[18] While some observers have claimed that increased reporting indicates that the problem of rape in wartime is worsening, others have argued that increased reporting is more likely indicative of increased interest in the problem. Based on the available cross-national data on rape and other forms of sexual violence, it is not possible to resolve these opposing interpretations; whether wartime rape is getting better over time, or getting worse, remains uncertain.[19] Figure 2.4 later in the chapter displays the temporal variation in reporting of wartime rape.

Second, there are limitations associated with how the violations are described, how the data are collected, and how the data are ultimately coded from the reports. Precise numbers of victims are rarely reported, so the coding is by necessity based on qualitative descriptors such as "isolated reports" and "widespread occurrence." Terms like "widespread"—hardly a detailed or precise description—may have different meanings in different contexts. Also, potential biases could result from both the underreporting and the overreporting of rape. Conflict zones may not allow foreign observers access to information about human rights violations, or victims may not want to speak about their experiences, especially while the war is ongoing, resulting in the underreporting of sexual violations. Alternatively, victims and NGOs may sense an advantage in emphasizing or embellishing certain forms of violence in order to receive aid or donor funds (Cohen and Hoover Green 2012).[20] Finally, numerous potential sources of error are introduced in the process of translating qualitative reports of difficult-to-measure data on human rights abuses into a quantitative dataset. Scholars have found that researchers may code violations as more serious when human rights reports are longer, regardless of the actual content of the reports (Clark and Sikkink 2013). In an effort to avoid these sources of bias, I measured intercoder reliability and checked my coding against all other available sources that examined conflicts with high levels of rape and other forms of sexual violence.

Third, some have argued that the State Department may intentionally misreport human rights violations for political reasons, or, less strategically, that the process of producing the human rights reports may be biased, especially on gender-related issues.[21] The global political climate can have an effect on what gets recorded in the annual reports, and reports on human rights abuses from allied countries may be edited to appear less severe due to political pressures (HSRP 2008).[22] However, even in cases where the United States was a strong supporter of one side in a civil conflict, I coded reports of major human rights violations by that side. For example, the government of El Salvador, to which the US government devoted enormous resources to support counterinsurgency efforts, is nonetheless accused in the State Department reports of committing serious wartime violence against detained suspected insurgents, including beating, raping, administering electric shocks, and forcing signed confessions. Alternatively, although likely far rarer, the reports may be written by activist foreign service officers who report unsubstantiated accounts of human rights violations.[23] Finally, the field offices that report to the State Department on human rights violations may vary in quality or focus, affecting the content of the reports.[24]

Given these concerns, it is fair to ask whether the State Department human rights reports can be trusted as a source for documenting cross-national variation in wartime violence. First, it should be noted that the State Department is a trusted source for data on human rights violations for a number of widely used quantitative datasets on human rights violations, including the Political Terror Scale and the CIRI Human Rights Data Project, which have both yielded many peer-reviewed publications on human rights violations. The State Department is also an important source for the WomanStats Project, a large database of information of the status of women around the world.

Despite the ubiquity of the reports as a source for quantitative studies of human rights, concerns may remain about their utility as a source of information on wartime rape in particular. I assessed the accuracy and biases of the data coded from the State Department reports in a number of ways. As previously noted, I compared the data against a number of other existing lists, all based on a wide range of sources. In addition, to further assess the quality of my State Department–based dataset, I compared an earlier version of the data (Cohen 2013a) to the coding of the Sexual Violence in Armed Conflict (SVAC) dataset (Cohen and Nordås 2014), which uses a broader definition of sexual violence, including a range of violations beyond rape. In addition, the SVAC dataset is based on two additional sources—Amnesty International (AI) and Human Rights Watch (HRW)—as well as the State Department reports.[25] There is not a perfect overlap in either conflicts or dates; my data are based on the Fearon and Laitin list of large-scale civil wars, while the SVAC project is based on UCDP/PRIO's list of interstate and intrastate wars and includes both minor and major conflicts.[26] Coding rules for rape and sexual violence also differ slightly between the two projects. The SVAC project includes coding of the specific numbers of victims if they are mentioned (e.g., "thousands" is coded as 3), whereas my data uses only qualitative descriptors (e.g., "widespread"), not numerical ones. Furthermore, although the study period in Cohen (2013) is 1980 to 2009, the SVAC study begins nine years later, covering 1989 to 2009. Nonetheless, despite these differences, there is close agreement across the datasets when comparing the highest reported levels of rape/sexual violence in the set of cases and years that overlap.[27]

In addition, I compared the coding of the highest levels of sexual violence for all actor-conflict-years for each of the three sources used for the SVAC project. If the State Department was systematically biased against reporting sexual violence, then the reporting in the other two sources should generally be more severe than that of the State Department. However, as is displayed in figures 2.1 and 2.2, during the study period, the State Department tended to report more serious sexual violence than either HRW or AI did, for both state and nonstate actor types.

In sum, these patterns suggest that, despite their limitations, the State Department reports are a comprehensive source for coding cross-national data on wartime rape and other forms of sexual violence. Most importantly, the data collected from these reports do not differ dramatically from those of the major human rights advocacy organizations, and when they do, the reports tend to

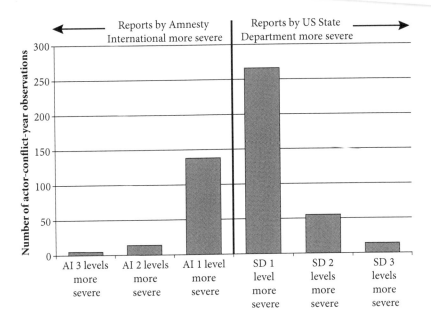

FIGURE 2.1 Comparison of reports by State Department (SD) and Amnesty International (AI) of wartime sexual violence

Source: Data are from the Sexual Violence in Armed Conflict [SVAC] dataset (Cohen and Nordås 2014). Figure designed by Amelia Hoover Green.

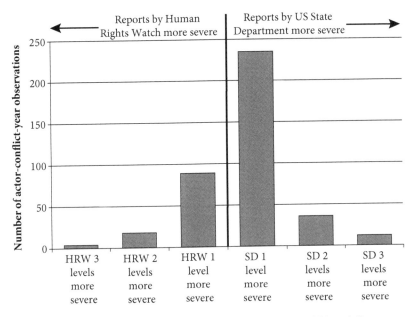

FIGURE 2.2 Comparison of reports by State Department (SD) and Human Rights Watch (HRW) of wartime sexual violence

Source: Data are from the Sexual Violence in Armed Conflict [SVAC] dataset (Cohen and Nordås 2014). Figure designed by Amelia Hoover Green.

describe violence in worse terms—suggesting that the State Department reports are unlikely to be biased *against* reporting incidents of wartime rape, at least relative to the other available sources. Thus, while recognizing that the four-point scale used in this analysis is a blunt instrument, the data make a contribution by allowing comparisons of relative levels of rape, by conflict-year and armed group type, across a universe of cases.

Variation

I collected four versions of *Wartime Rape*, the dependent variable. I coded the highest reported levels of rape perpetrated (1) by insurgent groups and (2) by state actors in each conflict-year, and I created a variable reflecting (3) the overall highest level of rape in the conflict-year, using the maximum coded level of rape by either actor type in the conflict-year. Finally, I coded a conflict-level version of the variable that reflects (4) the highest level of rape by actor type in each conflict, which is used to evaluate arguments about cross-conflict variation. Each dependent variable is used to evaluate different hypotheses, depending on the appropriate level of analysis.

These variables can be used to trace the remarkable ways in which wartime rape has varied—across space, time, perpetrator group, and other dimensions—over the last three decades. Documenting this variation is itself an essential part of the research process, because it shows that wartime rape is neither ubiquitous during war nor perpetrated by all armed groups in every conflict. In other words, the variation suggests that there is indeed a puzzle to be explained: Why does rape occur in some contexts and not others? In addition, the variation provides important historical context to recent crises. For example, by analyzing the trends in reports of rape in the Middle East region, it is clear that the spate of sexual crimes reported during the Arab Spring uprisings are atypical, at least in the context of war.[28] Finally, these patterns are also helpful in describing some of the characteristics of the wars with the most severe reported rape. While the data can be analyzed in numerous ways, I consider five important sources of variation.

VARIATION BY COUNTRY/REGION

Conventional wisdom suggests that wars in Sub-Saharan Africa are most commonly characterized by mass rape. Of the twenty-one wars that experienced the highest level of rape (coded as 3), slightly less than half (48 percent, or ten wars) were located in Sub-Saharan Africa. However, when analyzing wars with the worst level of mass rape *as a proportion of all civil wars in the region*, a distinct pattern emerges. In Sub-Saharan Africa, 32 percent of civil wars (or ten of thirty-one wars) featured the highest level of reported rape; in Eastern Europe, by contrast, 44 percent (four of the nine wars) involved the highest level of rape.

In other words, during the study period, Eastern Europe had a higher proportion of civil wars with the worst level of rape than did Sub-Saharan Africa.

When analyzing wars with the highest two levels of reported rape (coded as 2 or 3; n=55), Sub-Saharan Africa again had the largest number of wars marked by these levels (twenty-five wars), followed by Asia (eighteen), North Africa/Middle East (seven), Eastern Europe (six), and Latin America (three). Proportionally, Sub-Saharan Africa had more wars with these levels of rape than did Asia or Eastern Europe or Asia (84 percent [twenty-five of thirty-one wars], 69 percent [eighteen of twenty-six wars], and 66 percent [six of nine wars], respectively). Finally, 50 percent of the wars in Latin America (three of six wars), and 39 percent of the wars in North Africa/Middle East (seven of eighteen wars) were high-rape wars. Again, these patterns show that while the majority of the wars in Sub-Saharan Africa had reports of substantial wartime rape, about two-thirds of the wars in both Eastern Europe and Asia also had such reports.

VARIATION BY CONFLICT

There is dramatic variation by war in the severity of wartime rape. As is displayed in figure 2.3, twenty-one civil wars had at least one conflict-year with reports

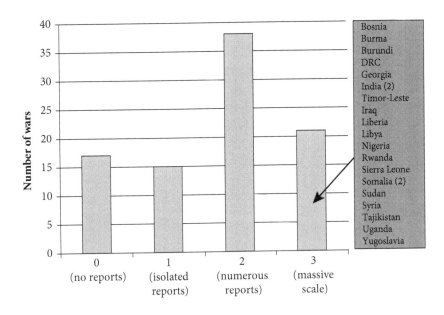

FIGURE 2.3   Distribution of highest reported level of wartime rape during civil war

Note: N=91 wars. The number 2 after India and Somalia indicates that two civil wars during the study period were coded as 3.

of massive rape (i.e., at least one conflict-year coded as 3), while thirty-eight wars were coded as having many or numerous reports of rape (i.e., at least one conflict-year coded as 2), fifteen were coded as having isolated reports (i.e., with at least one conflict-year coded as 1), and seventeen had no reports of rape (i.e., all conflict-years coded as 0). The wars with the highest levels of wartime rape include many of those previously recognized as "mass rape" wars and included in others' studies: Bosnia-Herzegovina, Burma/Myanmar, Burundi, Democratic Republic of the Congo, Georgia, India (both the Kashmir and Northeastern wars), Iraq (Kurds), Liberia (NPFL), Libya, Nigeria (NVPDF), Rwanda, Sierra Leone, Somalia (both the post-Barre and Isaaqs wars), Sudan (Darfur), Syria (FSA), Tajikistan, Timor-Leste, Uganda (LRA), and Yugoslavia (UCK).[29]

Overall, the data show that fifty-nine of the ninety-one wars in the study period, or 65 percent, involved significant rape during at least one conflict-year (i.e., a code of 2 or 3, corresponding to "numerous" or "massive" reports of rape, respectively). This variation suggests that wartime rape is a major problem in many wars—indeed, in nearly two-thirds of the major civil wars in the study period—but also that rape is not, as some have argued, a ubiquitous feature of every conflict.

VARIATION BY TYPE AND AIM OF CONFLICT

Wars with the highest levels of reported rape were more likely to be ethnic wars. Among the fifty-nine wars with the highest two levels of wartime rape (i.e., either a 2 or 3 for at least one conflict-year), 61 percent (thirty-six of fifty-nine wars) were classified as ethnic wars, and 16 percent (eight of fifty-nine wars) were nonethnic wars; the remaining fifteen wars were classified as mixed or ambiguous. This pattern has prompted some observers to claim that ethnic hatreds are a root cause of wartime rape. However, as the statistical analysis later in the chapter shows, ethnic war—and a number of other related ethnicity variables—are not associated with wartime rape. Ethnic wars are so common in this period that wars characterized by rape are not distinguished by this feature.[30]

Additionally, the ninety-one wars included in the study were categorized as having one of three fundamental aims (Fearon and Laitin 2015): the rebels targeted a takeover of the central state, the rebels sought exit or autonomy, or the goal was mixed or ambiguous. Wars with the worst two levels of rape were more likely to be wars in which the rebels aimed to take over the state than secessionist wars by which rebels sought to exit the state. Of the fifty-nine wars with the highest two levels of reported rape, 47 percent (twenty-nine wars) wars were of the first type, with rebels targeting the center, while 39 percent of these wars (twenty-two wars) had a goal of secession.

VARIATION BY PERPETRATOR GROUP TYPE

Beyond the variation apparent in a comparison of wars, countries, and regions, there is also variation *within* wars: some armed groups exercise restraint while others do not, even in the context of the same war. This micro-level variation is arguably the most important for understanding the root causes of and motivations for rape in wartime; the differences between armed groups—and how these may affect the likelihood of rape—is the focus in the three case studies presented later in the book.

As is illustrated in table 2.5, it was most common for *both* state and nonstate actors to be reported as perpetrators of rape; perpetration by state actors alone was less frequent, and rape by insurgent actors alone was relatively rare.[31] These patterns suggest a very important finding: contrary to the common perception that unruly and undisciplined rebel groups are the main abusers of human rights, it is actually state actors who are far more frequently reported as perpetrators of rape.

In addition, the evidence shows that the rape perpetrated by states often takes place in the context of prison or detention, where it is used as a means of punishment or torture. To collect data on patterns of prisoner abuse, I coded mentions of whether the victims were reported to be prisoners or detainees. I find that in the majority of cases where state forces were reported as perpetrators, descriptions included the rape of prisoners and detainees. More specifically, of the ninety-one major civil wars between 1980 and 2012, sixty-nine wars (76 percent) had reports of state perpetrators of rape; of those sixty-nine wars, fifty-nine (86 percent) included at least some reports of rape of detainees associated with the conflict. One example is from the 1991 report on Indonesia: "The use of torture to extract information from criminal suspects or witnesses is prohibited under the Indonesia Criminal Procedures Code (KUHAP). Nonetheless, credible reports of torture and mistreatment, including rape, of criminal suspects, detainees, and prisoners were frequent. This was especially true in Aceh, where there were numerous credible reports of systematic torture of suspected rebel sympathizers while in military or police custody."[32] This insight about the frequency and forms of state-perpetrated rape raises disturbing questions as to why state-perpetrated rape occurs so frequently in detention. The patterns also have important implications for policy, because research

TABLE 2.5 Frequency of perpetrator types in civil wars with reported rape

PERPETRATOR TYPE	% OF CONFLICTS (N)
Both state and insurgent actors	62% (46)
State actors only	31% (23)
Insurgent actors only	7% (5)
Total (wars with reported rape)	100% (74)

suggests that states are susceptible to naming and shaming in international campaigns (Krain 2012)—and are likely to be more sensitive to such campaigns than are nonstate actors (see also Cohen, Hoover Green, and Wood 2013). I return to some of the policy implications of these patterns in the conclusion.[33]

VARIATION BY MAJORITY RELIGION

The relatively infrequent reporting of significant levels of rape (i.e., coded as 2 or 3) in the North Africa/Middle East region—about 39 percent of wars there involved such reports, the lowest of the global regions, besides the Western region—suggests that religion may play a role in wartime rape. With the exception of Israel and Lebanon, the eighteen civil wars in this region all occurred in countries with a Muslim majority in excess of 90 percent of the population.[34] While studies have found that sexual assaults short of rape are common in the region (e.g., Replogle 2011), could it be that wars in Muslim-majority states are less likely to be characterized by large-scale rape?

The data suggest no: the proportion of widespread wartime rape in Muslim-majority states is about the same as in Muslim-minority states. Of the forty-one wars that occurred in states with a population greater than 50 percent Muslim, twenty-seven wars (about 66 percent) were coded at the highest two levels of wartime rape. Of the fifty wars in states whose populations are below 50 percent Muslim, thirty-two wars (about 64 percent) were coded at the highest two levels of wartime rape.[35]

The relatively low rates of reported mass rape in the North Africa/Middle East region are more likely to be a cultural effect than a religious one. It could be that wartime rape is less likely in countries with strict and traditional gender roles, where women often lack social mobility and may be less vulnerable to attacks during wartime.[36] Alternatively, and for the same reasons, rape may be common but reporting in these regions may be especially sparse and thus unlikely to be captured in the types of sources used to create the State Department reports. The WomanStats Project (2011) rape and sexual assault scale identifies the North Africa/Middle East region as having some of the strongest barriers—ranked as "severe" or "intense"—to reporting rape in the world. Without more complete data on rape in this region, it is not possible to resolve these two possibilities.

VARIATION OVER TIME

Figure 2.4 shows the variation in the level of reported rape over time for all of the conflict-years in the study period. The size of a circle, and the number below each circle, indicates the number of conflict-years in the study period that were coded at each of the four levels of rape in every year. The figure shows that, while wartime rape was reported in a handful of conflicts as early as 1981, reports of rape began to increase in 1988. The first cases of mass rape (coded as 3) were

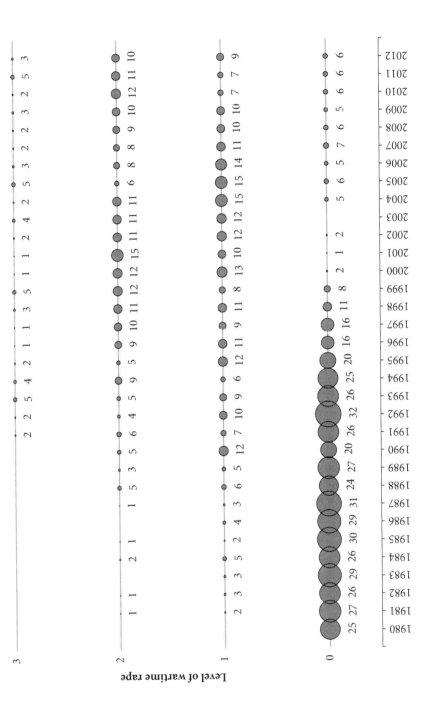

FIGURE 2.4 Reports of wartime rape over time

Note: N=1090 conflict-years. The size of each circle, and the number below it, indicates the frequency of conflict-years that were coded at each of the four levels of rape in every year in the study period.

reported in 1991, and mass rape has been reported every year thereafter, lending some support to the claim that widespread rape has increased in recent years. On the other hand, an observed increase in the severity of rape over time may indicate increased reporting or better measurement, not an increase in the underlying incidence. Due to the lack of reliable cross-national temporal data, it is not possible to know whether the underlying incidence of wartime rape is increasing or decreasing on a global scale over time. As I, and my coauthors, have maintained elsewhere (Hoover Green, Cohen, and Wood 2012), this type of variation is arguably the least important for policymakers—because whether and how the data are biased over time is uncertain, it is not possible to draw reliable conclusions about temporal patterns. Furthermore, an increasing or decreasing global pattern of rape is not especially relevant if acute crises of wartime rape are ongoing, and in desperate need of resources and international intervention.

EXPLANATORY VARIABLES

As described in chapter 1, the main explanatory variable for the combatant socialization argument is the internal social cohesion of armed groups. To directly test the argument, I would need measures of cohesion within armed groups, such as the degree of mutual respect or the strength of friendships among fighters. However, these data do not exist on a cross-national scale. Instead, I use a proxy measure for internal cohesion: the type of recruitment method that armed groups use to garner members. I argue that combatant groups that forcibly abduct random strangers through kidnapping and press-ganging suffer from low internal cohesion, whereas groups that rely on more voluntary methods are likely to have stronger internal cohesion (and are less likely to perpetrate widespread rape). While the proxy measure may not perfectly capture the strength of internal bonds, I find that recruitment methods are measurable variables that are closely tied to social cohesion. In subsequent chapters, including those drawing on interviews with the fighters, evidence suggests that groups that randomly abduct fighters tend to suffer from low social cohesion and poor morale.

RECRUITMENT AND COHESION IN INSURGENT GROUPS

Based on the State Department reports, I coded a dummy variable, *Abduction*, indicating whether specifically abduction by nonstate armed groups was reported, along with a separate measure, *Forced Recruitment*, indicating whether such groups had ever used coercive recruitment generally.[37] Examples of reporting of recruitment practices in the State Department reports include descriptions such as "The LRA regularly abducted children of both sexes for impressment into its own ranks" (coded as abduction, from Uganda) and "Guerrillas also committed human rights violations including . . . forced labor and recruitment" (coded as forced recruitment, from Guatemala).[38] Abduction was not coded as such unless it was explicitly reported, as in the Uganda example, and is thus a more restrictive measure of the more extreme form of forced recruitment.[39]

Tables 2.6 and 2.7 display a summary of the conflicts in which insurgent abduction and forced recruitment were reported, as well as a cross tabulation between conflict-level reports of insurgent-perpetrated rape and reports of abduction. The tables show that insurgents used forcible or coercive methods to recruit fighters in 46 percent of the conflicts in the study period; reports of abduction were less common, appearing in 22 percent of the conflicts. These cases are not well explained by arguments about opportunism and greed (Weinstein 2007; Mueller 2000); in such cases of forced recruitment, fighters are not choosing to join an armed group, nor are they recruited for their propensity to commit violence.

TABLE 2.6 Reports of abduction and forced recruitment by insurgent groups

WERE THERE EVER REPORTS OF ABDUCTION BY ANY INSURGENT GROUP?	WERE THERE EVER REPORTS OF FORCED RECRUITMENT BY ANY INSURGENT GROUP?
Yes in 20 conflicts (22% of total)	Yes in 42 conflicts (46% of total)
Afghanistan (Mujahideen; Taliban); Algeria (FIS); Burma; Burundi (Hutu groups); Cambodia; Colombia; DRC (RCD); El Salvador; Guatemala; Liberia (NPFL; LURD); Mozambique; Nepal; Pakistan (Taliban); Sierra Leone; Somalia (post-Barre); Sudan (SPLA); Turkey (PKK); Uganda (LRA)	Afghanistan (Mujahideen; Taliban; Taliban II); Algeria (FIS); Algeria; Angola (UNITA); Bosnia-Herzegovina; Burma; Burundi (Hutu groups); Cambodia; Chad (FROLINAT); Colombia; Croatia; DRC (RCD); El Salvador; Ethiopia (Eritrea); Guatemala; India (Naxalites); Israel; Ivory Coast; Lebanon; Liberia (NPFL; LURD); Morocco; Mozambique; Nepal; Nicaragua; Pakistan (Taliban); Peru; Philippines (MNLF; NPA); Russia; Sierra Leone; Somalia (post-Barre); South Africa (Namibia); Sri Lanka (JVP II; LTTE); Sudan (SPLA; Darfur); Tajikistan; Turkey (PKK); Uganda (LRA); Yemen (al-Houthi)

TABLE 2.7 Cross tabulation of rape and abduction by insurgents

		ABDUCTION BY INSURGENTS		
		NO	YES	TOTAL
RAPE BY INSURGENTS	NO	49% (35)	25% (5)	44% (40)
	YES	51% (36)	75% (15)	56% (51)
	TOTAL	78% (71)	22% (20)	100% (91)

RECRUITMENT AND COHESION IN NATIONAL MILITARIES

Recruitment of fighters into national militaries takes one of three forms. The first is voluntary service, and the second and third are forms of recruitment by forcible means: *conscription*, in which (usually male) citizens are required by law to serve for a specific term in the armed forces,[40] and *press-ganging* (or impressment), in which fighters are kidnapped, without notice, to serve in the state forces with no regulated terms of service and are usually not paid (or paid very little) (Mulligan and Shleifer 2005). The latter, while typically considered an antiquated practice, is surprisingly common in modern civil wars and occurred frequently in the study period.

Based on the State Department reports, I coded a dummy variable, *Press-gang*, for each conflict, indicating whether the state was ever reported to have used press-ganging. Examples of reporting on press-ganging include the following descriptions: "The Sandinista Army continued military impressment, conducting sweeps of public facilities and forcibly removing youths as young as 12" (from Nicaragua); "The military draft is applied arbitrarily, and recruits are forcibly taken off of streets and buses" (from El Salvador); and "Although a military service decree was issued and youth are being required to register, the authorities still frequently round up youth off the streets or seize them from their homes to press them into military service" (from Ethiopia).[41]

The dichotomous *Conscription* variable uses data from several sources in order to cover the study period (Horowitz and Stam 2014; Karim 2015; Pickering 2010).[42] The dummy indicates whether the state in each conflict-year used conscription to recruit its fighters. The measure varies by conflict-year, and in some cases, states switch from a volunteer army to a conscripted army (or vice versa) over the course of the war. A summary of the conflicts with reports of press-ganging and conscription by states, as well as a cross tabulation between conflict-level reports of state-perpetrated rape and press-ganging, are displayed in tables 2.8 and 2.9.

The distinction between extreme forms of recruitment, like abduction and press-ganging, and weaker forms of coercive recruitment and conscription is important because it may indicate an analytic difference between the forms of impressment and their consequences for cohesion. Because the abduction process may occur quickly, with little advance notice, and can be physically violent, it may have a different, more corrosive effect on the internal dynamics of an armed group than other, weaker forms of coercion. These forms of coercion may be more gradual, facilitated by preexisting social ties, and allow the fighter some (albeit small) degree of agency in deciding to join. If it is true that the low internal cohesion resulting from the abduction of strangers predicts wartime rape, then we should

TABLE 2.8   Reports of press-ganging and conscription by state forces

WERE THERE EVER REPORTS OF PRESS-GANGING BY THE STATE?	DID THE STATE EVER RECRUIT THROUGH CONSCRIPTION?
Yes in 26 conflicts (29% of total)	Yes in 58 conflicts (64% of total)
Afghanistan (Mujahedeen); Angola (FLEC; UNITA); Burma; Cambodia; Chad (FROLINAT; FARF); DRC (RCD); El Salvador; Ethiopia (Eritrea); Guatemala; Iraq (KDP; Shia uprising); Liberia (NPFL; LURD); Libya (NTC); Nicaragua; Russia (Chechnya II); Rwanda; Somalia (SSDF); Sudan (SPLA; Darfur); Syria (FSA); Tajikistan; Yugoslavia (Croatia/Krajina; UCK)	Afghanistan (Mujahedeen; Taliban); Algeria; Angola (FLEC; UNITA); Azerbaijan; Bosnia Herzegovina; Burma; Burundi (Hutu groups); Cambodia; Chad (FROLINAT); China; Colombia; Croatia; El Salvador; Ethiopia (Eritrea); Georgia; Guatemala; Guinea Bissau; Indonesia (Timor Leste; GAM I; GAM II; OPM); Iran (KDPI; MEK; PJAK); Iraq (KDP; Shia uprising); Israel; Ivory Coast; Liberia (LURD); Mali; Morocco; Mozambique; Nicaragua; Peru; Russia (Chechnya; Chechnya II); Rwanda; Senegal; Somalia (post-Barre; SSDF); South Africa (ANC, Namibia); Sudan (SPLA; Darfur); Syria (Muslim Brothers; FSA); Tajikistan; Thailand (Hill Tribes; Pattani); Turkey (Militia-ized party politics; PKK); Uganda (LRA); Yemen (South Yemen; al-Houthi); Yemen People's Republic (Faction of Socialist Party); Yugoslavia (Croatia/Krajina; UCK)

TABLE 2.9   Cross tabulation of rape and press-ganging by state forces

		PRESS-GANGING BY STATES		
		NO	YES	TOTAL
RAPE BY STATES	NO	29% (19)	12% (3)	24% (22)
	YES	71% (46)	88% (23)	76% (69)
	TOTAL	71% (65)	29% (26)	100% (91)

observe a stronger effect for extreme forms of recruitment—abduction and press-ganging—than for the weaker forms.

Additional Variables and Controls

Other variables used to test alternative hypotheses, and to control for additional important explanatory factors, are based on existing quantitative studies and datasets.

STATE- AND CONFLICT-LEVEL FACTORS

The extent of the breakdown of a state, or the absence of state authority, is measured with the *Magfail* variable from the Political Instability Task Force (PITF) dataset. The variable is coded on a four-point scale reflecting the magnitude of the failure of state authority, in country-years, between 1955 and 2012. A value of 1 indicates an "adverse regime change" with no significant failure of the state, 2 indicates a failure in limited parts of a country, 3 indicates failure in substantial parts of the country, and 4 indicates total state collapse. Following others (e.g., Williams and Masters 2011), I added a value of 0 to the scale to indicate no adverse changes in governance and no failure of state authority. Episodes of state collapse were relatively infrequent. In the study period, 11 percent of conflict-years (n=1090) experienced some degree of state failure: nine conflict-years (1 percent) are coded as 1, sixteen years are coded as 2 (1.5 percent), thirty years are coded as 3 (3 percent), and sixty-eight years are coded as 4 (6 percent).[43]

To measure ethnic war, I use *Ethwar* from Fearon and Laitin 2015. *Ethwar* is a three-level variable in which a value of 0 indicates the war was not ethnic and a value of 2 indicates that the war was ethnic, while a value of 1 indicates that the war was ambiguous or mixed. Seventeen (19 percent) of the conflicts in the study period were nonethnic, fifty-four (59 percent) ethnic, and twenty (22 percent) were ambiguous,

To measure the strength of the military in each state, I used the variable *Troop Quality* from Pickering 2010 and extended it to include more recent years. *Troop Quality* was calculated by dividing military expenditures by the number of military personnel from the National Material Capabilities dataset (version 4.0) of the Correlates of War Project (Sarkees and Wayman 2010). *Troop Quality* provides a measure of how well resourced—and is a proxy for how well trained—the state military was in each conflict-year. These data are only available through 2007, so subsequent years are dropped from analyses. *Troop Quality* is negatively and weakly correlated with the level of rape perpetrated by governments, lending some support to the argument that better-trained forces may be less likely to commit atrocities against noncombatants.[44]

Finally, to capture the extent of gender inequality in each state, I used *Fertility*, the fertility rate, or the number of births per woman.[45] Caprioli et al. (2009) argue that the fertility rate is the best available measure of gender inequality, because it reflects not only cultural factors, such as personal choice and the need for children, but also discrimination against women and structural inequality in the forms of lower levels of education, employment, and political power.[46] Fertility rates are available on an annual basis from the World Bank (2015a) and range from 1.2 to 9.1 for the countries in the sample.[47] Mean fertility rates are essentially the same in countries with high and low levels of wartime rape: the mean fertility rate for wars with the highest two levels of wartime rape is 4.6, as compared to a mean fertility rate of 4.7 for wars coded as 1 or 0.

INSURGENT-RELATED FACTORS

To measure the goals of the insurgent groups, as previously described, I use the variable *Aim* from Fearon and Laitin 2015. A value of 1 indicates that the rebels aimed at overtaking the center, a value of 3 indicates that the rebels aimed at exit or autonomy (that is, wars that were secessionist in nature), and a value of 2 indicates that the aim was mixed or ambiguous. In the study period, forty-six wars (51 percent) were coded as 1, thirty-four wars (37 percent) as 3, and eleven wars (12 percent) as 2.

To capture whether the insurgents relied on funding from contraband, I use the conflict-level, dichotomous *Drugs* variable from Fearon and Laitin 2015. A value of 1 indicates there was "significant contraband financing of rebels" and a value of 0 indicates there was not. Insurgents were funded by contraband in nineteen (or 21 percent) of the conflicts in the study period.[48]

For a measure of diaspora funding, I created a dummy variable, *Diaspora*, reflecting the reporting of diaspora funding from the UCDP External Support dataset (Högbladh, Pettersson, and Themnér 2011), which covers the time period from 1975 to 2009. A value of 1 indicates that an insurgent group received diaspora funding in a conflict-year, and a value of 0 indicates that it did not. In the study period, insurgents were reported to have received funding from diasporas in seventy-four conflict-years, or 7 percent of the total.

VIOLENCE-RELATED FACTORS

Genocide is coded as a dummy variable based on the Political Instability Task Force (Marshall, Gurr, and Harff 2015). The PITF is a set of genocide and politicide cases first developed by Barbara Harff (2003) with a recent update by Marshall, Gurr, and Harff (2015).[49] The PITF identified forty-three instances of genocide and politicide between 1955 and 2014. Many cases began and ended before 1980, the first year in my dataset, or did not occur during conflicts captured by the Fearon and Laitin 2015 list of civil wars. Of the forty-three cases identified, nineteen coincide with civil wars in the study period. All conflict-years that were coded by the PITF as years with genocide/politicide take the value of 1, and all other conflict-years are coded as 0. In total, 137 conflict-years in the dataset experienced genocide/politicide (all 137 years had state perpetrators; 21 years also had nonstate perpetrators), which comprise 13 percent of the conflict-years in the study period.

Because there are no existing cross-national data on ethnic cleansing, I created an approximation, *Ethnic Cleansing*, by combining two variables—*Ethnic War* and *Aim*—from Fearon and Laitin 2015. Rebel groups with a secessionist aim in the context of an ethnic war may be a reliable measure of ethnic cleansing by insurgents; no such approximation is available to measure ethnic cleansing by state actors. I coded a dummy variable, such that a value of 1 indicates ethnic-secessionist wars in which the conflict was ethnic in nature (*Ethwar* = 2) and during which the rebel groups aimed at regional autonomy (*Aim* = 3); all other conflict-years are coded as 0.[50] A total of thirty-two conflicts, or about 35 percent of the total, are coded as both ethnic and secessionist, capturing cases of possible ethnic cleansing.

One of the central assumptions in much of the current literature is that homicide covaries with nonlethal forms of violence against civilians (e.g., Weinstein 2007; Kalyvas 2006.) To account for whether wars with more rape are simply wars with more lethal violence, I control for the lethality of the conflict. Because there are no ideal cross-national measures of lethal violence against only civilians, I use several measures of wartime deaths. First, scholars commonly use battle deaths (a measure that includes both soldiers and civilians) as a proxy because of the high correlation with civilian deaths (e.g., Weinstein 2007, 306). *Battle Deaths* estimates vary by conflict-year (UCDP 2015); I used the "best" estimate when one was available, and the low estimate in cases when one was not. There were no death estimates of any type for 202 conflict-years, almost 20 percent of the dataset.[51] To avoid losing such a large number of observations, I include *Battle Deaths* in a set of robustness checks (see table 2.12) but not in the main series of regressions. As shown in table 2.13, battle deaths are positively but only weakly correlated with the overall level of wartime rape (0.07), which suggests that rape and lethal violence require different theoretical explanations.

The measure I use in the main analysis is *Kill* from the CIRI data (Cingranelli, Richards, and Clay 2014), a three-level variable that reflects extrajudicial killings by government officials and by private groups if instigated by the state. A score of 0 indicates the frequent practice of extrajudicial killings, 1 indicates the occasional practice of extrajudicial killings, and 2 indicates that such killings did not occur in a given year. For ease of interpretation, I reversed the coding so that 2 indicates killing occurred with frequency and 0 indicates that it did not occur. Because *Kill, Battle Deaths*, and *Genocide* all capture lethal violence, they are not included in the same models.[52]

CONTROLS

Some scholars have claimed that rape has gotten worse over time. Others have argued that monitoring and reporting practices are getting better, so what looks to be worsening human rights practices is at least partially an artifact of measurement (Clark and Sikkink 2013). To address these concerns, I have controlled for *Year* in all regressions; the fact that year is consistently statistically significant, and that its inclusion increases the fit of the models, suggests either that measurement is improving over time or that the problem is getting worse.

The remaining variables are from widely used datasets, including controls for *Population* (Fearon and Laitin 2015) and *Democracy* (Marshall, Gurr, and Jaggers 2014). Finally, I calculated the *Duration* of the wars, as of 2012.[53] See table 2.10 for summary statistics for the dependent and independent variables.

TABLE 2.10 Descriptive statistics for dependent and independent variables

VARIABLE	N	MEAN	STANDARD DEVIATION	MIN	MAX	VARIES BY CONFLICT-YEAR?
Rape, conflict-wide (0, 1, 2, 3)	1088	0.83	0.94	0	3	✓
Rape, insurgent perpetrators (0, 1, 2, 3)	1088	0.45	0.84	0	3	✓
Rape, state perpetrators (0, 1, 2, 3)	1088	0.64	0.84	0	3	✓
Ethnic war (0, 1, 2)	1090	1.47	0.78	0	2	
Magnitude of state failure (0, 1, 2, 3, 4)	1090	0.37	1.09	0	4	✓
Conflict aim (1, 2, 3)	1090	1.97	0.91	1	3	
Fertility rate	1090	4.66	1.84	1.17	9.12	✓
Extrajudicial killings (0, 1, 2)	954	1.60	0.59	0	2	✓
Genocide by insurgents (0, 1)	1090	0.02	0.14	0	1	✓
Ethnic cleansing (ethnic-secessionist wars) (0, 1)	1090	0.37	0.48	0	1	
Contraband funding (0, 1)	1090	0.30	0.46	0	1	
Insurgent abduction (0, 1)	1090	0.31	0.46	0	1	
Insurgent forced recruitment (0, 1)	1090	0.63	0.48	0	1	
Genocide by state (0, 1)	1090	0.13	0.33	0	1	✓
Troop quality (log) (1980–2007)	888	8.85	1.06	5.94	12.07	✓
Press-ganging by state (0,1)	1090	0.29	0.45	0	1	
Conscription by state (1980–2001) (0, 1)	1002	0.49	0.50	0	1	✓
Polity2	1051	0.96	6.14	−9	10	✓
Duration (as of 2012)	1090	23.93	15.98	1	65	
Population (log)	1062	10.37	1.54	7.08	14.03	✓
Δ GDP/capita	1072	1.18	3.61	−6.04	24.61	✓
Quality of government	576	0.41	0.20	0.04	0.98	✓
Diaspora funding (0, 1)	1013	0.07	0.26	0	1	✓
Battle deaths (log)	888	6.35	1.83	2.71	11.29	✓
Conflict intensity (1, 2)	876	1.32	0.47	1	2	✓
Women's economic rights (0, 1, 2, 3)	923	0.95	0.57	0	2	✓
Women's political rights (0, 1, 2, 3)	954	1.66	0.62	0	3	✓
Women's social rights (0, 1, 2, 3)	759	0.89	0.61	0	3	✓
Government mass killing (0, 1)	742	0.15	0.35	0	1	✓
Female labor-force participation	1060	48.87	19.75	9.8	90.8	✓
Muslim population	1090	38.78	40.40	0	99.7	

Statistical Analyses

To determine the support for each of the competing arguments, I use regression analysis to estimate the independent effect of each variable on the reported magnitude of wartime rape, controlling for potentially confounding factors. In particular, I estimate a series of ordered probit regressions on the set of all active conflict-years in the study period.[54] Ordered probit is used to model the likelihood of wartime rape falling into one of the four distinct categories. Unlike a linear model, which assumes that these categories are evenly spaced, an ordered probit regression relaxes that assumption as long as the categories are ordered rather than simply categorical. Since it is not possible to ascertain that the distance between no reports of rape and limited reports is the same as the distance between limited reports and numerous reports, or between numerous reports and reports of massive rape, an ordered probit regression is the best model choice for the dependent variable.

Table 2.11 displays the results, with models separated by the level of analysis (conflict-level, insurgent-perpetrated or state-perpetrated violence).[55] In each model, I cluster the standard errors by conflict in order to avoid overestimating the amount of information in the sample and to address the probability that conflict-years are not statistically independent of each other. I next review the evidence for each of the four main arguments—and the eight hypotheses—described in chapter 1.

Combatant Socialization

There is strong support for the combatant socialization argument (*H1*), for both insurgent- and state-perpetrated violence. The more extreme forms of forced recruitment—abduction by insurgents and press-ganging by states—are both associated with increased reports of wartime rape. For insurgent-perpetrated violence (model 2), the coefficient for abduction is positive and statistically significant at the .05 level. Similarly, for state-perpetrated violence, the coefficient for press-ganging is also positive and is statistically significant at the .01 level (model 4). The broader measure of forced recruitment by insurgents, while positive, was not statistically significant (model 3), suggesting that it is abduction in particular that is associated with increased wartime rape. Finally, conscription by national militaries is negatively associated with wartime rape, but is also not statistically significant, whether controlling for troop quality (model 5) or not (not shown).

These findings imply that extreme forms of forced recruitment by armed groups are associated with wartime rape while weaker forms are not—and, more

TABLE 2.11 Rape during civil war: Ordered probit results

	CONFLICT-LEVEL RAPE	RAPE BY INSURGENTS		RAPE BY STATE ACTORS	
	MODEL 1	MODEL 2	MODEL 3	MODEL 4	MODEL 5
Ethnic war	−0.13	0.22	0.16	−0.16	−0.16
	[0.12]	[0.16]	[0.17]	[0.13]	[0.13]
Magnitude of state failure	0.06	0.23**	0.22**	0.07	0.05
	[0.10]	[0.07]	[0.08]	[0.08]	[0.08]
Conflict aim	−0.13	−0.21	−0.16	−0.11	−0.12
	[0.11]	[0.14]	[0.15]	[0.11]	[0.11]
Fertility rate	0.10	0.08	0.11	−0.02	0.00
	[0.07]	[0.08]	[0.07]	[0.06]	[0.07]
Extrajudicial killings	0.33**				
	[0.12]				
Insurgent Groups					
Genocide by insurgents		−0.37	−0.79*		
		[0.29]	[0.33]		
Contraband		0.67**	0.80**		
		[0.23]	[0.25]		
Abduction		0.55*			
		[0.27]			
Forced recruitment			0.44		
			[0.30]		
State Groups					
Genocide by governments				0.12	0.28
				[0.24]	[0.23]
Troop quality (log)				−0.11	−0.12
				[0.08]	[0.09]
Press-ganging				0.76**	
				[0.21]	
Conscription					−0.06
					[0.16]
Controls					
Polity2	−0.01	−0.01	−0.02	0.01	−0.01
	[0.02]	[0.02]	[0.02]	[0.02]	[0.02]
Duration	−0.00	−0.01	−0.01	−0.01	−0.00
	[0.01]	[0.01]	[0.01]	[0.01]	[0.01]
Year	0.08**	0.07**	0.08**	0.09**	0.09**
	[0.01]	[0.01]	[0.01]	[0.01]	[0.01]
Population (log)	0.18**	0.07	0.08	0.24**	0.18**
	[0.07]	[0.08]	[0.08]	[0.06]	[0.06]
Cut 1	166.54**	148.57**	152.53**	173.56**	181.96**
	[17.66]	[22.66]	[21.44]	[18.91]	[20.44]
Cut 2	167.44**	149.07**	153.02**	174.62**	182.96**
	[17.67]	[22.67]	[21.46]	[18.92]	[20.44]
Cut 3	168.71**	150.03**	153.96**	175.79**	184.10**
	[17.66]	[22.69]	[21.49]	[18.93]	[20.45]
Observations	933	1,023	1,023	873	843
Pseudo R-squared	0.17	0.20	0.20	0.19	0.16

Note: Robust standard errors in parentheses. ** $p < 0.01$, * $p < 0.05$, + $p < 0.1$

broadly, that different forms of impressment have different consequences for cohesion. Because abduction is often random, occurs with little advance notice, and can be physically violent, it may have a more damaging effect on the internal cohesion of an armed group than do weaker forms of forced recruitment, such as coercion and conscription. I examine these differences in more detail in the case studies in chapters 3, 4, and 5. In general, I find that fighters report lower cohesion—and more fear and isolation upon joining—in groups that abducted their combatants.

Opportunism/Greed

The opportunism/greed argument has several hypotheses, with implications for all three levels of analysis, which are each tested in separate models. The first hypothesis (H2) is about the relationship between state failure and rape. For overall conflict-level rape, the measure of the magnitude of state collapse is positively associated with overall conflict-wide rape, but the coefficient is not statistically significant (model 1).

However, for insurgent-perpetrated violence, the magnitude of state failure is positively associated with rape (models 2 and 3) at the .01 level. The same variable is also positively associated with state-perpetrated rape, but does not reach statistical significance (models 4 and 5). These results suggest that that the anarchy of state collapse affords rebel groups the ability to rape without fear of retribution or punishment by the state, perhaps even more so than during the general chaos of wartime. The positive sign on the coefficient in models 4 and 5—while not reaching statistical significance—does suggest that state collapse may allow state armed groups a similar opportunity to "misuse the power and authority attached to their public office" (Butler, Gluch, and Mitchell 2007, 669). Butler, Gluch, and Mitchell (2007, 673) argue that sexual violence by government forces is primarily motivated by "out-of-control agents," whose principals (governments) cannot sufficiently monitor their soldiers. This is a notion echoed in some of the more recent policy discourse around "cultures of impunity."[56] Alternative measures of state collapse are tested in the robustness checks section.

The second opportunism/greed hypothesis (H3) concerns the effects of poor military professionalism on the proliferation of rape. However, although the negative sign on the coefficient is in the hypothesized direction, the variable *Troop Quality* is not significant in any specification (models 4 and 5). The conventional wisdom that rape by states should be more likely when national military forces are poorly resourced and, presumably, poorly trained does not find support in this analysis. This finding suggests that rape cannot be linked directly to a lack of resources.

Turning to the third opportunism/greed hypothesis (H4), on contraband funding for insurgencies, the main variable for insurgent contraband funding is both positive and statistically significant at the .01 level (models 2 and 3). This result shows that lootable resources, such as drugs and diamonds, are strongly associated with rape by insurgent groups. However, the sign on the variable for diaspora funding of insurgents—a key form of external support—is negative and not significant either with or without controlling for contraband funding (not shown). These findings suggest that the type of material support employed by an insurgency matters for the forms of violence they are likely to commit. Forms of support that can easily be used as a selective incentive, used to entice recruits, may be more likely to attract opportunistic fighters who are prone to violence (Weinstein 2005). Lootable resources may be more corrupting for insurgencies than diaspora support (including remittances and other types of support, such as sanctuary), perhaps because they are more easily converted into selective incentives. The negative sign on the diaspora variable may also indicate that external pressures from a diaspora movement depress the perpetration of particularly shameful atrocities like rape.

Furthermore, the results demonstrate that it is lootable resources in particular—in contrast to unaccountable sources of funding more broadly—that are associated with wartime rape. Ultimately, the recruitment mechanism (attracting "bad types" to armed groups) may be more important than the accountability mechanism (not depending on civilians for support and therefore abusing them with impunity) for explaining why such material resources are associated with an increase in rape. To further test the relative strength of these two competing mechanisms, I turn to the micro-level evidence in the case chapters, where I consider these mechanisms as alternatives to the combatant socialization argument.

Ethnic Hatred

None of the ethnic hatred hypotheses finds support in the data. First, despite the fact that the majority of wars with high levels of rape were classified as ethnic wars, *Ethnic War* is not independently associated with overall conflict-levels of rape (*H5*): the coefficient for ethnic war is neither in the hypothesized direction nor statistically significant (model 1).

In the analysis of the type of perpetrator, hypotheses for the ethnic hatred arguments for insurgent-perpetrated rape are also not supported. While the variable for ethnic war is in the predicted direction, it fails to reach statistical significance (models 2 and 3). For state actors, the relationship between ethnic war and rape is in the opposite direction of the prediction—suggesting states are more likely to commit rape in nonethnic wars—but also does not reach statistical significance.

Although the coefficient for state-perpetrated genocide (*H6*) is in the predicted direction, it does not reach statistical significance (models 5 and 6). The coefficient for insurgent-perpetrated genocide is not in the hypothesized direction and is only significant in model 3. The statistically significant coefficient indicates that in the rare cases where genocide is perpetrated by nonstate actors, genocide may actually *decrease* the likelihood of rape—perhaps because of pollution norms, whereby "sexual violence across ethnic boundaries may be understood . . . as polluting the [perpetrator]" (Wood 2008, 341).[57]

Additionally, *Aim* (*H7*) fails to reach statistical significance in any of the models and is not in the hypothesized direction. The finding suggests that rebels' secessionist aims are not strongly associated with wartime rape, casting doubt on previous speculation that separatist conflicts may increase the likelihood of rape as a tool of humiliation.[58]

Finally, the related strategy of ethnic cleansing (*H7*) is negatively associated with rape by insurgents. While this variable reaches statistical significance when included in a model with both *Ethnic War* and *Aim* (not shown), the variable's sign is not in the hypothesized direction, failing to support the idea that a systematic relationship exists between ethnic cleansing and rape.[59]

Gender Inequality

The last of the four major arguments tested in this book is about the effects of gender inequality on wartime rape (*H8*). The coefficient of the main proxy measure, *Fertility*, never reaches standard levels of statistical significance. These results suggest that—given that a war has begun—there is no apparent relationship between broad, country-level indicators of gender inequality and rape during civil war. However, as previously noted, scholars have consistently found a relationship between gender inequality and the onset of civil conflict. The insignificance of the findings in this analysis may therefore reflect the unfortunate reality that, in those countries undergoing major civil war, gender inequality is so widespread that it cannot account for variation in wartime rape.

Additional Factors and Controls

The controls for democracy and duration are nearly consistently negative—suggesting that lower levels of democracy and shorter wars are associated with rape—but insignificant. *Population* is consistently positive and significant for conflict-level rape and state-perpetrated violence. Larger populations may be more likely to experience state-perpetrated rape, echoing results from earlier studies that found evidence that, all else equal, larger states may be more likely to repress their citizens (Poe and Tate 1994). Finally, the coefficient on the variable *Year* is consistently positive and statistically significant, indicating that time is an important factor in worsening reports of rape. However, this does not settle the debate over whether rape has indeed gotten more severe over time, or whether monitoring and reporting practices are improving.

Substantive Results

Although the cross-national regression analyses show a strong and robust association between abduction, press-ganging, and rape, it is difficult to directly interpret the size of the effect in an ordered probit regression. To determine the substantive impact of abduction and press-ganging on the perpetration of rape, I calculated the likelihood of each level of rape with and without the presence of abduction by insurgents, and with and without the presence of press-ganging by states.[60] As before, I estimated ordered probit models with standard errors clustered by conflict. Figure 2.5 shows the mean predicted probabilities of insurgent-perpetrated rape at each level of the dependent variable given abduction or no abduction, holding all other variables at their means, with 95 percent confidence intervals indicated. Figure 2.6 displays the same information for state-perpetrated rape.

In all cases, it is clear that abduction and press-ganging increase the probability of wartime rape. Indeed, rebel groups that rely on abduction are about 1.7 times,

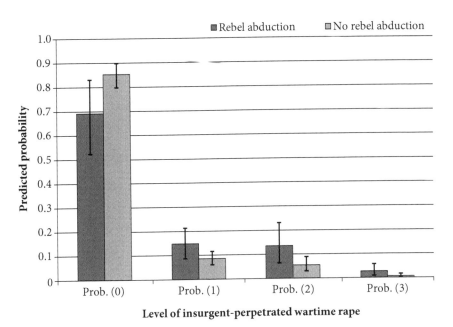

FIGURE 2.5 Probability of insurgent-perpetrated wartime rape with and without abduction

Note: Ordered probit model with standard errors clustered by conflict. Each simulation includes the following control variables: *Ethnic War, Magfail, Aim, Fertility, Genocide (by insurgents), Contraband, Polity2, Duration, Year,* and *Population (log)* (all control variables set at their mean values). The error bars represent the 95 percent confidence interval for each predicted probability value. Estimates calculated using CLARIFY. Two-tailed t-tests show that the differences in the mean predicted probabilities at levels 0, 1, and 2 are statistically significant at the 5 percent or 10 percent level. However, the difference between the mean predicted probability values for level-3 wartime rape falls just short of statistical significance (p=0.13).

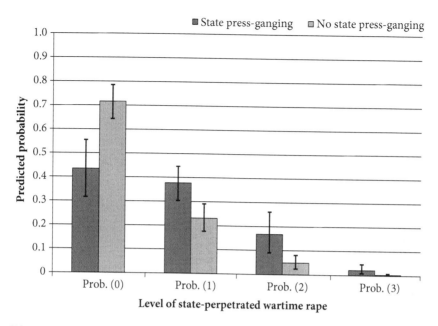

FIGURE 2.6 Probability of state-perpetrated wartime rape with and without press-ganging

Note: Ordered probit model with standard errors clustered by conflict. Each simulation includes the following control variables: *Ethnic War, Magfail, Aim, Fertility, Genocide (by state actors), Troop Quality (log), Polity2, Duration, Year,* and *Population (log)* (all control variables set at their mean values). The error bars represent the 95 percent confidence interval for each predicted probability value. Estimates calculated using CLARIFY. Two-tailed t-tests show that the differences in the mean predicted probabilities at levels 0, 1, and 2 are statistically significant at the 1 percent or 5 percent level. The difference between the mean predicted probability values for level-3 wartime rape is statistically significant at the 10 percent level.

2.5 times, and 4 times more likely to commit wartime rape at levels 1, 2, and 3, respectively, than those groups that do not abduct their fighters. State forces that rely on press-ganging are about 1.6 times, 3.4 times, and 7.2 times more likely to commit wartime rape at levels 1, 2, and 3, respectively, than those groups that do not press-gang. These findings support the hypothesis that abduction and press-ganging have a sizable effect on the likelihood of wartime rape.

Robustness Checks and Additional Tests

I carried out a series of robustness checks to allay concerns about temporal changes in data quality, to check if different aggregations of the dependent variable alter the results, and to ensure that the findings are not driven by particular variable choices, especially for some of the most difficult-to-measure concepts.[61]

To address concerns that data coded from the 1980s-era State Department Country Reports on Human Rights Practices may be of poorer quality than data from later years (e.g., HSRP 2012), I conducted separate analyses for the 1980s and the post-1980s periods. As displayed earlier in figure 2.4, fewer and less severe reports of rape were made in the 1980s than in the 1990s or the 2000s. In an analysis of each individual decade (1980s, 1990s, 2000s) I find that the main results hold for the latter two periods, but are mixed in the former. In the 1980s, the results remain robust for nonstate actors (that is, abduction remains statistically significant), but not for states; in particular, press-ganging loses statistical significance and the coefficient has a negative sign. In addition, the results remain robust for the analysis of the aggregated post-1980s years (i.e., 1990–2012) (results not shown).

To provide further assurance on the coding of the categories of wartime rape, I collapsed the dependent variable in two ways to create two dummy measures, and estimated a series of probit models, used for binary dependent variables. First, I tested a dummy of no reports versus any reported rape (a code of 0 is 0 and a code of 1 for 1, 2, and 3). Second, I tested no and low reports against higher reports (a code of 0 or 1 is a 0 and a code of 2 or 3 is a 1). In both of these sets of regression, the main results remain robust (results not shown).

Because ideal data on lethal violence are not available, I tested three other measures of conflict severity. First, I used a measure of *Battle Deaths* in place of the extrajudicial killing and genocide variables. Because of the importance of this variable in many recent studies of civilian victimization, I display the results in table 2.12. Both abduction and press-ganging remain positive and statistically significant, although abduction loses some significance (and is now at the .10 level). This important finding further confirms that abduction and press-ganging exert independent effects on wartime rape, beyond the general violence of the war.

Second, I created a dummy measure of mass killing by the state, defined as the intentional homicide of more than fifty thousand noncombatants (Valentino, Huth, and Balch-Lindsay 2004); this covers events from 1945 to 2000, so more recent years are excluded. Finally, I also used a measure of conflict intensity from the UCDP/PRIO Armed Conflict Dataset (Pettersson and Wallensteen 2015), where 1 indicates between 25 and 999 deaths in a given year and 2 indicates one thousand or more deaths in a given year. The UCDP/PRIO list of civil wars, actors, and war years do not perfectly match the list from Fearon and Laitin 2015, which resulted in a significant number of missing observations.[62] Neither of these lethal violence measures alters the central results for the main independent variables (results not shown).[63]

Gender inequality is another variable that is especially difficult to measure. I tested two alternative proxies for gender inequality. The first is a frequently

TABLE 2.12 Rape during civil war: Ordered probit results with battle deaths

	CONFLICT-LEVEL RAPE	RAPE BY INSURGENTS		RAPE BY STATE ACTORS	
	MODEL 1	MODEL 2	MODEL 3	MODEL 4	MODEL 5
Ethnic war	−0.12	0.18	0.09	−0.12	−0.09
	[0.11]	[0.18]	[0.17]	[0.13]	[0.14]
Magnitude of state failure	0.24**	0.25**	0.25**	0.06	0.03
	[0.09]	[0.08]	[0.09]	[0.09]	[0.09]
Conflict aim	−0.06	−0.13	−0.09	−0.05	−0.06
	[0.11]	[0.15]	[0.16]	[0.12]	[0.12]
Fertility rate	0.06	0.10	0.12	−0.03	−0.03
	[0.07]	[0.08]	[0.08]	[0.07]	[0.08]
Battle deaths (log)	0.10*	0.12*	0.12*	0.06	0.08+
	[0.05]	[0.05]	[0.06]	[0.05]	[0.05]
Insurgent Groups					
Contraband		0.51*	0.60*		
		[0.23]	[0.25]		
Abduction		0.51+			
		[0.28]			
Forced recruitment			0.32		
			[0.29]		
State Groups					
Troop quality (log)				−0.11	−0.12
				[0.09]	[0.09]
Press-ganging				0.70**	
				[0.21]	
Conscription					−0.03
					[0.17]
Controls					
Polity2	−0.02	−0.02	−0.02	−0.00	−0.02
	[0.02]	[0.02]	[0.02]	[0.02]	[0.02]
Duration	−0.00	−0.01	−0.01	−0.01	−0.00
	[0.01]	[0.01]	[0.01]	[0.01]	[0.01]
Year	0.09**	0.08**	0.09**	0.09**	0.09**
	[0.01]	[0.01]	[0.01]	[0.01]	[0.01]
Population (log)	0.17**	0.09	0.09	0.23**	0.17**
	[0.06]	[0.08]	[0.08]	[0.06]	[0.06]
Cut 1	177.13**	171.49**	179.43**	175.57**	180.15**
	[17.47]	[26.12]	[23.55]	[21.25]	[22.69]
Cut 2	178.04**	172.02**	179.94**	176.65**	181.19**
	[17.49]	[26.14]	[23.58]	[21.26]	[22.70]
Cut 3	179.30**	173.10**	181.00**	177.83**	182.36**
	[17.51]	[26.16]	[23.62]	[21.27]	[22.71]
Observations	830	830	830	713	691
Pseudo R−squared	0.17	0.21	0.20	0.18	0.16

Note: Robust standard errors in parentheses. ** $p < 0.01$, * $p < 0.05$, + $p < 0.1$

used gender inequality variable—the rate of female labor force participation—created using data from the World Bank (2009).[64] This proxy was not statistically significant, nor did it alter the main findings. The second proxy was a set of measures of women's rights. First, I used three separate measures of women's rights—*Political Rights*, *Social Rights*, and *Economic Rights*—from the CIRI Human Rights Dataset (Cingranelli, Richards, and Clay 2014), which are coded from the State Department human rights reports.[65] It should be noted that scholars have expressed concern that the CIRI data are more indicative of official government policy than of women's actual lived experience (Caprioli et al. 2009). The women's rights variables are insignificant and do not alter the central findings (results not shown).[66]

I also tested two alternative measures of state weakness: the change in GDP/capita from the start of the war to the current year (calculated from Fearon and Laitin 2015) and a measure of the quality of government (De Soysa and Fjelde 2010), an index variable capturing degrees of bureaucratic quality, law and order, and corruption from the International Country Risk Guide dataset. The results are similar to those of each of the proxy measures for state weakness, and the central independent variables remain significant in each (results not shown).

Finally, because some of the variables are not time-variant, I checked the results in a cross-sectional analysis. I aggregated the data to the level of the conflict and conducted a conflict-level analysis of the ninety-one wars in the study period, with the highest level of reported rape as the dependent variable. The results remain mostly robust in this more aggregate analysis. In particular, while insurgent abduction loses statistical significance, forced recruitment gains significance. Government press-ganging remain highly statistically significant (results not shown).

The statistical analyses presented in this chapter provide strong support for the central argument in this book. Most importantly, I find a consistent and significant association between extreme forms of forced recruitment—which I argue serve as proxies for low levels of intragroup social cohesion—and increased reports of wartime rape. This result is robust to the inclusion of a number of different, potentially confounding variables and remains largely consistent across a series of robustness checks. The size of the effect is quite large—specifically, abduction and press-ganging can as much as quadruple the probability of rape by insurgents and septuple the probability of rape by states. The results suggest that recruitment practices are important keys to understanding the conditions that make widespread rape possible.

The analysis also demonstrates support for other arguments. Background conditions for the war, including the degree of state failure, are associated with increased wartime rape, lending some support to the conventional wisdom about opportunism. In addition, insurgent funding that can be converted into selective incentives, such as contraband, may be especially corrupting—and could be associated with those armed groups attracting a particularly "bad type" of fighter, one who is more likely to abuse, and to rape, civilians. Further, the results show that wars with more lethal violence are not simply wars with more rape. Several analyses reveal that forced recruitment has an independent and significant association with wartime rape, apart from the broader lethal violence of the war.

Equally as important, I find no support for a number of the most powerful conventional wisdoms about the root causes of rape. Across the set of recent major civil wars, none of the ethnic hatred variables, nor the variables capturing measures of gender inequality, are in the hypothesized direction *and* statistically significant. Although ethnic hatreds and gender inequality may be connected to other aspects of the conflict—for example, making wars more likely to begin— once wars have started, these factors do not serve to explain why widespread rape occurs in some wars but not others

However, while these analyses show a strong correlation between recruitment mechanism and wartime rape, there are two caveats to keep in mind. First, although I argue that forced recruitment is a reliable proxy for internal group cohesion, there are other factors—such as norms—that may be causing both forced recruitment *and* higher levels of rape. For example, Elisabeth Wood (e.g., 2012) has argued that norms around violence, and the ways the internal hierarchy enforces these norms through institutions like disciplinary practices, are essential for understanding variation in the use and nonuse of sexual violence. Through examining the mechanism on the micro level in detailed case studies— and especially drawing on interviews with fighters—I find that groups that randomly abduct fighters tend to suffer from low social cohesion and poor morale, critical evidence in support of the idea that abduction is a plausible proxy.

Second, and on a related note, it may be the case that the relationships revealed by this analysis are not causal, or perhaps do not flow in the direction that the main argument predicts. It is possible, for instance, that armed groups that perpetrate rape have alienated the civilian population and, unable to recruit voluntary members, are therefore forced to abduct. If this were the case, then the statistical findings would be identical, but the reason for the correlation between abduction and rape would be the reverse of that implied by combatant socialization argument. In this case, rape by armed groups may be driving away volunteers and forcing them to abduct recruits, rather than abduction making rape useful in building cohesion. To address these types of identification issues, I have controlled for numerous plausible omitted variables and employed several proxies for some of the more difficult-to-measure variables. Concerns about endogeneity,

TABLE 2.13 Correlation matrix

	RAPE (CONFLICT)	RAPE (INSURGENT)	RAPE (STATE)	ETHNIC WAR	STATE FAILURE	CONFLICT AIM	FERTILITY RATE	EXTRA-JUDICIAL KILLINGS	GENOCIDE: INSURGENTS	CONTRA-BAND FUNDING	INSURGENT ABDUCTION	GENOCIDE: STATE	TROOP QUALITY (LOG)	PRESS-GANGING BY THE STATE	BATTLE DEATHS (LOG)
Rape (conflict)	1														
Rape (insurgent)	0.73	1													
Rape (state)	0.83	0.38	1												
Ethnic war	-0.02	0.01	-0.02	1											
State failure	0.14	0.25	-0.02	0.04	1										
Conflict aim	-0.09	-0.13	-0.04	0.48	-0.17	1									
Fertility rate	-0.02	0.1	-0.07	0.01	0.25	-0.41	1								
Extrajudicial killings	0.21	0.14	0.23	-0.12	0.08	-0.13	0.08	1							
Genocide by insurgents	-0.05	0	-0.05	0.1	0.03	-0.15	0.19	0.04	1						
Contraband funding	0.2	0.2	0.16	-0.27	-0.01	-0.03	-0.04	0.08	0.2	1					
Insurgent abduction	0.16	0.24	0.06	-0.37	0.07	-0.32	0.13	0.05	-0.08	0.29	1				
Genocide by state	-0.05	0.03	-0.06	-0.02	0.03	-0.07	0.23	0.13	0.37	-0.05	0.07	1			
Troop quality (log)	-0.04	-0.05	-0.05	0.06	-0.04	0.26	-0.54	-0.05	0.06	-0.04	-0.24	-0.01	1		
Press-ganging by state	0.07	0.06	0.12	-0.1	0.01	-0.26	0.36	0.13	0.2	0.1	0.16	0.32	-0.27	1	
Battle deaths (log)	0.07	0.11	0.05	-0.1	0.14	-0.23	0.14	0.22	0.17	0.12	0.12	0.31	0.01	0.14	1

or reverse causation, can also be at least partially addressed by tracing the central mechanisms on the micro level in the case study chapters—and, in particular, by analyzing the temporal patterns in reports of types of violence. In sum, the statistical analyses support the macro-level implications of several arguments, including the combatant socialization and opportunism/greed arguments. In the next three chapters of the book, I examine how the mechanism works on the micro level, as well as how the combatant socialization argument stacks up against other plausible competing arguments in specific cases.

MASS RAPE BY REBEL ACTORS
Sierra Leone (1991–2002)

> **Every man was a hot man. If one of us caught a woman, they would all want to have sex with her. We'd decide among ourselves who goes first. Those who would rather not rape were made fun of later. . . . I never heard a commander say "men must rape women."**
>
> —Interviewee 10, male RUF ex-combatant, Freetown, Sierra Leone, May 28, 2007

> **Rape was a form of entertainment. We teased each other about the proper way to do it. We would talk about it with each other, bragging. The men who refused to rape felt pressure to loot or kill more to prove themselves. Each man had his own aims; some preferred money to women.**
>
> —Interviewee 20, male SLA ex-combatant, Freetown, Sierra Leone, June 19, 2007

The eleven-year-long civil war in the West African nation of Sierra Leone is infamous for its brutal forms of violence against noncombatants, including amputation, cannibalism, rape, torture, and the use of child soldiers. While some observers argue that the widespread rape in Sierra Leone was used as a "weapon of war," interview evidence and quantitative data show instead that the use of rape was far less strategic.

This chapter focuses on three central patterns that clarify why rape became so pervasive during the conflict. First, while reports of rape by combatants occurred throughout the war, most sources indicate a spike in the occurrence of rape in the late 1990s. Second, although global patterns indicate that governments tend to be the most frequent perpetrators of rape, the opposite was true in Sierra Leone: a rebel group, the Revolutionary United Front (RUF), committed the vast majority of the rape. Finally, the reported perpetrators of rape—again, mostly members of the RUF—include both male and female combatants. These patterns raise a number of questions about rape in Sierra Leone. Why did reports of rape increase dramatically during several key years of the war? Why was the RUF the most frequently reported perpetrator? How do we explain the participation of female perpetrators?

Contrary to conventional wisdom, the evidence from Sierra Leone strongly suggests that rape was not used as part of a military strategy. The most compelling evidence is the patterns of victims and perpetrators: Overall, victims were rarely targeted according to any strategic logic. Indeed, there is no evidence that victims were routinely or systematically selected because of ethnicity, political affiliation, or economic status. In addition, the various armed groups—especially the Civil Defense Forces (CDF) and the RUF—were remarkably similar demographically (Humphreys and Weinstein 2004). The two groups were not divided along ethnic or religious lines—a division that might give rise to an ideology of hatred that could guide decisions about the use of violence.

Given that rape was likely not used as a "tool of war" in this case, I instead consider two plausible arguments about why rape became so widespread in Sierra Leone. I draw on original data collected during six months of field research in Sierra Leone, including over two hundred interviews with both ex-combatants and noncombatants, along with existing survey data from ex-combatants and victims of violence. First, I examine the micro-level implications of several strands of the opportunism/greed argument, including a close consideration of how violence varied over time. Second, I analyze the evidence for the combatant socialization argument. Ultimately, while both of these arguments find some support in the data, I argue that the patterns of violence are best explained by combatant socialization. Interviews with ex-combatants demonstrate that armed groups with low levels of internal social cohesion—specifically, groups that relied on abduction as a recruitment mechanism—used rape as a means of creating a more coherent fighting unit.

History of the War

Sierra Leone is a small coastal country of roughly five million people, bordering Liberia and Guinea.[1] A former British colony, Sierra Leone was granted independence in 1961. After a series of military coups, Sierra Leone became, for several decades, a one-party state. The civil war began in March 1991, when areas along the eastern border were attacked by rebels under the command of RUF leader Foday Sankoh, a former corporal in the Sierra Leone Army (SLA), and his ally, the Liberian rebel leader-cum-president Charles Taylor. The initial goals of the RUF included the reinstatement of multiparty elections in Sierra Leone and the overthrow of the one-party hegemon, the All People's Congress (APC). The APC, however, was riddled with corruption and was not fully supportive of the SLA's counterinsurgency efforts. Long periods without pay and resentment among SLA soldiers ultimately resulted in a 1992 coup against the APC by former soldiers.

The new regime, called the National Provisional Ruling Council (NPRC), was a military government that suspended the constitution; its central goal was to stop the rebel forces. In the mid-1990s, as the rebels began to control the diamond-rich regions in their progression across the country toward the capital city of Freetown, the NPRC contracted the mercenary firm Executive Outcomes. Peace and stability seemed imminent in 1996, when democratic elections resulted in a new civilian government and a peace accord was signed in Abidjan, Côte d'Ivoire. Civilian president Ahmad Tejan Kabbah formally institutionalized the CDF, made up of grassroots paramilitary groups armed and funded by the state to protect their home areas.

However, in 1997 a second coup by the sidelined military—now called the Armed Forces Revolutionary Council (AFRC)—prompted the exile of the newly elected government. The AFRC called for the RUF to join them in Freetown under the rule of army officer Johnny Paul Koroma. The AFRC/RUF were driven out of the capital nine months later by a Nigerian-led regional peacekeeping force that reinstated Kabbah as president. The AFRC/RUF retreated to the jungle, where they replenished their supplies with profits from the diamond exchange—the so-called "blood diamonds" (Smillie, Gberie, and Hazleton 2000). The group eventually attacked the capital city of Freetown in early 1998 in what is now known as the January 6 Invasion. Although the AFRC/RUF ultimately suffered a dramatic loss to the CDF and Nigerian-led ECOMOG troops, the two-week siege resulted in thousands of deaths and other types of violence, including some of the highest numbers of reported rape during the conflict (Smith, Gambette, and Longley 2004, 30–39).

In 1999, the Sierra Leone government and the RUF signed a peace agreement in Lomé, Togo. The fragile peace was threatened when over four hundred UN peacekeepers were abducted and held hostage by RUF commanders. The British government intervened to free the hostages, which ultimately led to the final stages of the war. The war was declared officially over in 2002 by Kabbah. By then a member of the Sierra Leone People's Party (SLPP), Kabbah won a landslide victory in the 2002 presidential election, and UN peacekeepers finally withdrew in December 2005. More recently, a round of parliamentary and presidential elections took place in Sierra Leone in the summer of 2007, during which Ernest Bai Koroma, the opposition candidate from the APC, was elected in the run-off election. In a test of postconflict democratic consolidation, Koroma was reelected for a second term in largely free and fair elections in 2012.

Data Sources and Availability

Violence during the Sierra Leone civil war is well documented. A relative wealth of information is available, both on the violence that was perpetrated, including rape, and on the characteristics of combatants. These data include testimonies given to the Sierra Leone Truth and Reconciliation Commission (TRC) that were then aggregated into a dataset (Gohdes and Ball 2010), as well as data that scholars and researchers have collected through several major survey studies, and a conflict mapping project.[2] I used a number of these sources of data to analyze patterns of violence in Sierra Leone.

Available Data Sources

I rely on multiple sources for data on violence to triangulate information, in order to mitigate the potential biases that any one source may contain. For example, surveys may underreport the incidence of rape, while testimonies given to the TRC may be biased toward reports from larger or more urban centers. Because there is no systematic method of evaluating and then controlling for these biases, drawing on numerous sources is the best way to draw reliable inferences.

I used five major data sources to determine the patterns of rape and other forms of violence in Sierra Leone.[3] First, the ABA/Benetech Sierra Leone War Crimes Documentation (SLWCD) survey (Asher et al. 2004) is a nationally representative survey conducted in 2004 of 3,631 randomly selected households in all 149 chiefdoms. The survey, which yielded reports of more than 64,700 violations, asked about eleven categories of violence, including rape,[4] and about details of the perpetrators, including the faction to which they belonged and the number and sex of the perpetrators involved in each violation. Second is a quantitative dataset (Gohdes and Ball 2010) created by the Human Rights Data Analysis Group (HRDAG) that coded details from the 7,700 narrative statements given by Sierra Leoneans to the TRC into fourteen types of violations, including rape, perpetrated between 1991 and 2000 (TRC of Sierra Leone 2004).[5] The TRC sample is not representative,[6] and the statement-takers made special efforts to visit areas that were thought to be especially affected by violence; the TRC ultimately collected testimonies from 141 of 149 chiefdoms in the country (Conibere et al. 2004). A third source for data on rape is a 2002 survey about conflict-related sexual violence conducted by Physicians for Human Rights (PHR) of 991 internally displaced women from 1,048 households in three internally displaced persons (IDP) camps in Freetown, Port Loko, and Kenema (Reis et al. 2002). A fourth source for data on violence is a quantitative dataset (Bellows and Miguel 2009) that coded and aggregated the details of the hundreds of incidents described in the No Peace without Justice (NPWJ) Conflict Mapping Project (Smith, Gambette, and Longley 2004). The NPWJ project resulted in a 550-page narrative report detailing approximately 5,500 incidents of violence that occurred across all chiefdoms during the years of the war. The data were collected through a combination of interviews—with about four hundred key informants—and information from open source material (Smith, Gambette, and Longley 2004, 6–7). The final source I use, for data on the demographics of the combatant groups, is an innovative, nationally representative survey of ex-combatants from all factions (Humphreys and Weinstein 2004).

Interviews

In addition to the macro-level patterns drawn from existing data sources, this case study draws on a large number of original interviews I conducted with ex-combatants and noncombatants. Over the course of three research trips between 2006 and 2008, during a total of six months, I interviewed 206 people, including 34 male and female ex-combatants from the RUF rebels, members of the state forces (the SLA and the AFRC) and the CDF, as well as villagers and chiefs in rural and urban areas, and government and NGO workers.

As in each of my fieldwork sites, I never explicitly revealed that the focus of my research was wartime rape. However, the topic of rape was commonly broached in interviews and focus groups. Unlike interviews conducted for this project in Timor-Leste and El Salvador, interviewees in Sierra Leone were quite open about their experiences. While cultural differences may account for some of this variation, it is also possible that the shame and stigma of rape may shift on a broader social level, especially when it occurs on a massive scale over a long period of time, and in a context that includes many other forms of widespread violence. In cases like Sierra Leone, with large numbers of victims, the shame associated with being a rape victim—or being related to one—may be mitigated. This observation is reflected in studies that found, in contexts where rape was widespread, some victims of rape are especially forthcoming to researchers about their experiences (Taylor 2003).

I used two separate methods to recruit interviewees in Sierra Leone, depending on their status as an ex-combatant or a noncombatant. For ex-combatants, most interviews were conducted in Freetown, at the offices of PRIDE (Post-conflict Reintegration Initiative for Development and Empowerment), a local NGO. All but one of the ex-combatant interviews were conducted with just me and a translator (from Krio to English), and each interview typically lasted between one and two hours. The NGO arranged interviewees for me, drawing on its extensive network. I also recruited interviewees through informal networks of taxi drivers in Freetown, many of whom were rumored to be RUF ex-combatants. I made every effort to interview as diverse a combatant population as possible—male and female combatants, former child fighters and adult combatants, former rebels and former members of the national military, rank-and-file fighters and commanders. Although the sample is not representative, potential biases are mitigated in part by the diversity of the respondents. As with nearly all the interviews included in the book, the interviews were conducted on the condition of anonymity.

To interview noncombatants, I visited both larger strategic towns and randomly selected villages to get a sense of variation in the occurrence of rape by region and by which faction had been in control for the majority of the war.[7] In contrast to the ex-combatant interviews, I mainly relied on a focus group format. In each village, when my translator and I arrived, we met with the chief of the village to explain our research. In every case, the chiefs welcomed us to their village and gave us permission to conduct our work. I sought to interview six women in each village, although in practice the number ranged between four and ten. I requested specifically to speak with women who had remained in the village over the course of the war (i.e., had not fled to the capital city of Freetown or the neighboring countries of Guinea or Liberia) and who had "suffered from violence" during the war; I intentionally kept this latter description vague rather than asking to interview victims and survivors of sexual violence. The women of the village then determined the willing and appropriate candidates among themselves. Each focus group usually lasted between 1½ and 2½ hours and was conducted in a quiet, private place, such as an empty classroom or house. In each case, the focus group discussion was concerned mainly with the facts of the violence in that village—how many major attacks there had been, details about who came to attack the village, and the types of violence that the participants had witnessed or heard about. After the group interview, I conducted a separate, private interview with the chief in each village. The purpose of these chief interviews was to confirm the events of the war and to collect additional data about the village and how the war had changed it.

Wartime Rape during the Sierra Leone Conflict
Overall Patterns of Violence and Rape

The violence of the war occurred in three main phases—reports of violence peaked in 1991, 1995, and 1998/1999; this temporal pattern is reflected in multiple data sources (Gohdes 2010). Violence also tended to move across the country over the course of the war. In the earliest phase, violence was centered in the eastern and southern regions of the country, owing to the fact that the war started on the border with Liberia. In the second phase, violence occurred mainly in the South, and in the last period of the war, violence occurred mostly in the western and northern areas (Conibere et al. 2004).

All available evidence confirms that rape was widespread during the war in Sierra Leone, although sources differ on the extent.[8] Respondents to the SLWCD survey reported an estimated 31,759 incidents of rape over the course of the war.[9] In addition, the PHR survey found that 8.4 percent of respondents (84 of 991)—all residents in IDP camps—reported incidents of rape (Reis et al. 2002, 48).

However, IDP camp residents are among the most vulnerable segments of the population, and they likely experienced violence, including rape, at a higher rate than the rest of the population.

Turning to another data source, 626 incidents of rape against 591 victims were reported to the TRC, comprising about 1.6 percent of all reported violations and 3.9 percent of all reported victims. By way of comparison, 4,514 incidents of killing (11.2 percent of violations) and 378 incidents of amputation (0.9 percent of the violations) were reported (TRC of Sierra Leone 2004). Figure 3.1 displays the TRC data on reported killing and reported rape over time. Notably, peaks in killing and peaks in rape are not contemporaneous. While the two forms of violence may appear to be closely correlated, the peak in reported number of killings occurred in the first year of the war, 1991, while the peak in reported rape occurred toward the end of the war, in 1999. This is important evidence that killing requires a different explanation than does rape and that more lethal violence does not necessarily imply more violence of other types. In addition, while the general shapes of the trend lines are similar, the temporal variation in numbers of killings is much more marked than are swings in the numbers of rapes.

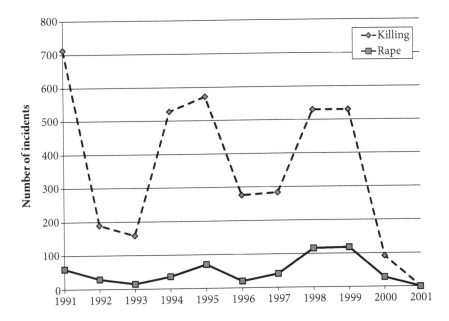

FIGURE 3.1 Wartime rape and killing over time

Note: This figure uses data from the TRC (Gohdes and Ball 2010). The killing and rape data are both categories of the variable *Violt*. For killing, 641 additional incidents have no associated date; for rape, 92 additional incidents have no associated date.

Rape was reported in each year of the war, with large increases during two of the most intense years of the conflict. The temporal patterns from the three main data sources, as shown in figure 3.2, show that rape was high at the start of the war, and then gradually decreased in frequency though 1993, which had the lowest number of reported rapes. Reports then increased again, with two peaks: one in 1995 and the second in 1998/1999. Indeed, two of the sources (TRC and SLWCD) reveal dramatic spikes in reported rape in 1998 and 1999, two of the key years of the war.[10] While the NPWJ data follow the same basic trends, the peak year for reports of rape is 1995, followed by a second peak in 1998. These patterns are also confirmed by the PHR survey, which found that 67 percent of the sexual violence, which includes rape, occurred between 1997 and 1999 (Reis et al. 2002, 48). This period encompasses the January 6, 1999, invasion of Freetown, when the AFRC/RUF attacked the capital city and ultimately suffered a dramatic loss. According to the SLWCD survey, as is shown in table 3.1 and

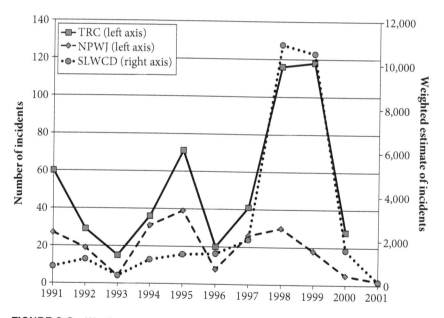

FIGURE 3.2 Wartime rape over time

Note: The TRC data shown here include 626 incidents of rape by all perpetrators; 92 of these cannot be plotted due to missing values for date. The TRC data include incidents from 1991 to 2000. The NPWJ data shown here contain 213 incidents of rape by all perpetrators; 4 of these cannot be plotted due to missing values for date. The SLWCD data shown here contain an estimated 31,759 incidents (calculated using the sampling weights) of rape by all perpetrators. However, 407 of these cannot be plotted due to missing values for date.

later discussed in more detail, rape was reported in every district and province in Sierra Leone, in areas populated by all of the major ethnic groups.

Several patterns emerge as to the nature of rape perpetrated by combatants and the forms that rape took. First, multiple sources suggest that gang rape was common during the war. As stated in the introduction, one of the central puzzles of wartime rape is the "radically higher proportion" of gang rape relative to peacetime (e.g., Bourke 2007, 377). Sierra Leone is no exception. Of the reported rape in the SLWCD survey, 76 percent was rape by multiple perpetrators, while in the PHR survey, 33 percent of rape victims (thirty-one of ninety-four) reported that they were gang-raped, with a mean of about three perpetrators per incident.[11] Fieldwork interviews with victims and witnesses confirm that gang rape happened regularly and was frequently a public event, committed in view of other combatants, family members, and villagers.[12]

A second type of reported rape was rape with objects, such as sticks and bottles. The PHR survey found that rape with objects was reported by 4 percent of those respondents who reported sexual assault. Neither the TRC nor the SLWCD survey collected or coded data on rape with objects. However, interviews with both ex-combatants and victims revealed that this form of rape occurred with some frequency, and for a variety of reasons. One ex-combatant reported, "The women selected for rape were the ones who were childless, virgins and young women. Those who refused to be raped were raped with sticks as punishment."[13] Another former fighter described a

TABLE 3.1 Geographic distribution of reported wartime rape by district, province, and majority ethnic group

DISTRICT	PROVINCE	MAJORITY ETHNIC GROUP IN PROVINCE	NUMBER OF ESTIMATED RAPES	PERCENTAGE OF TOTAL REPORTED RAPE (%)
Kono	Eastern	Mende	6,140	19
Port Loko	Northern	Temne	5,276	17
West. Area	Western	Krio/Temne	4,609	15
Bombali	Northern	Temne	4,359	14
Koinadugu	Northern	Temne	2,491	8
Kailahun	Eastern	Mende	1,999	6
Tonkolili	Northern	Temne	1,407	4
Kenema	Eastern	Mende	1,315	4
Bo	Southern	Mende	1,156	4
Kambia	Northern	Temne	985	3
Moyamba	Southern	Mende	558	2
Pujehun	Southern	Mende	384	1
Bonthe	Southern	Mende	188	1
Missing			891	3
Total			31,758	100

Note: All values calculated from Asher et al. 2004.

terrible attack on one victim: "One time the commander was not allowed to enjoy the sex, so he killed the woman, cut out her vagina and put it on a stick for the rebels to laugh at."[14] A former sexual slave, held captive by the RUF, said, "Rape is a rebellion act; it is a way to destroy people. I saw women get raped with sticks."[15] Another said, "Some men used sticks because ten or fifteen men had already had sex with a woman."[16] Another former fighter stated that he had witnessed "rape with sticks, which is rape without having to defy African traditions."[17] Finally, there were reports that "female RUF would rape with bottles and sticks."[18] Although object rape is likely not committed for reasons of sexual gratification, respondents identified a range of reasons for its use: as an act of punishment or extreme brutality, as a way to protect the fighters from defying cultural taboos or possibly contracting a disease, and as a form of participation that did not require an erect penis, thereby enabling female perpetrators, or male perpetrators who were not sexually aroused.

Third, rape, for the most part, was not targeted at categories of victims, including particular ethnic groups or the economic or social elite. As shown in table 3.1, the distribution of the violations over geographic space does not reveal systematic ethnic targeting by perpetrators of rape.[19] The districts of Kono, Port Loko, Freetown, and Bombali were the most affected, with each experiencing between 14 percent and 19 percent of the total reported rape; these districts are located across three of the major geographic and ethnic divides in the Northern and Eastern provinces and the Western Area of the country. In addition, the Mende-majority areas experienced about 35 percent of the reported rape, compared to about 46 percent in the Temne-majority areas (excluding the Western Area, where the capital city is located and where there is no ethnic majority; Asher et al. 2004). The TRC data largely confirm these patterns and reveal that the number of reported rapes among northern ethnicities, of which the majority are Temne, was essentially equal to the number reported by southern ethnicities, of which the majority are Mende (Conibere et al. 2004).

Evidence from interviews with noncombatants underscores this point. Villagers reported the fact that the combatants spoke a plethora of the local languages, which signaled that the war was not ethnic in nature. As one woman said, "When the rebels came, they were speaking Mende, Krio, Temne, and Fula—that was the first sign to me that this war was not tribal."[20] Additionally, instead of emphasizing that acts of violence were committed by people unlike themselves, the villagers did not hesitate to point out that some of the people who harmed them spoke their own language and were their co-ethnics.[21] Finally, evidence from the ex-combatant survey found that the armed factions were not generally divided along ethnic or religious lines (Humphreys and Weinstein 2004).

In addition, any desire to attack the economic elite was confounded by the fact that the economic elite in Sierra Leone are relatively not very wealthy, and their wealth is mainly land-based.[22] Villages in Sierra Leone—a country consistently ranked at the bottom of the UNDP Human Development Index[23] during the war—comprise mainly subsistence farmers (Bellows and Miguel 2006). In larger towns, where a clearer distinction exists between the elite and ordinary residents, ex-combatants relayed several stories about Lebanese women, part of wealthy families involved in the diamond trade, who were specifically targeted for rape. Nonetheless, some interviewees reported that these women were targeted not because of their political beliefs or their economic status per se, but because of their lighter skin color.[24] Overall, such attacks were rare, and there appears to be no general pattern of targeting the economic elite.

Finally, there is limited evidence that social elite, such as village chiefs, were selected for violence and public humiliation (e.g., Keen 2005, 60). However, in none of the towns or villages included in the study did respondents report that the wives and daughters of chiefs were targeted for rape. There are a few reports of women being selected for rape for revenge for prewar slights, but again, these are not part of a larger pattern.[25] In my interviews, neither villagers nor ex-combatants reported in interviews that combatants targeted particular types of victims. For instance, villagers rarely described combatants seeking out specific villagers.[26] In fact, there was often little verbal exchange between villagers and combatants. Presumably, if rape was directed at specific victims, orders regarding whom to choose and what types of violence to inflict would come from the leaders of armed groups. Yet in interviews with ex-combatants, I found no evidence that combatants were encouraged to select particular victims. Anecdotal reports from NGOs such as Human Rights Watch and PHR also support this assertion (Wood 2006, 337n41). Finally, few of the many acts of violence described in the conflict mapping project concern punitive acts of violence against specific victims (Smith, Gambette, and Longley 2004).

Perpetrator Patterns

Overall, the civil war involved a large number of combatants. It is estimated that more than eighty thousand people served in one or more of the factions over the course of the war (Humphreys and Weinstein 2008). As previously noted, while the ex-combatant survey found that the armed factions were remarkable in their demographic heterogeneity, there was significant variation across the groups in terms of participation by sex: female combatants were overwhelmingly part of the RUF—and, as discussed later, took part in a significant proportion of the violence (Humphreys and Weinstein 2004).

Although numerous factions were involved in the conflict, and various categories of rape perpetrators were reported (e.g., incidents of rape by the Guinean Armed Forces reported to the TRC), the majority of rape victims, across all sources, identified their perpetrators as members of one of the three main armed groups: the RUF, the SLA/AFRC, and the CDF. I review the evidence and patterns of reported rape by each of these groups next, in order to test the competing arguments presented later in the chapter.

Rape by the Revolutionary United Front

The RUF was reported as the main perpetrator of rape across all available sources. In the SLWCD survey, about 85 percent of respondents who were raped reported that their attackers were either RUF or simply "rebels." Of the 626 cases of rape reported to the TRC, 440 cases, or 70 percent of the total, were perpetrated by the RUF.[27] In the PHR survey, 60 percent of the respondents who identified the faction of the perpetrator reported that the RUF had raped them (Reis et al. 2002). Of the 213 incidents of rape included in the NPWJ conflict mapping project, 87 percent (186 of 213) were perpetrated by the RUF (Bellows and Miguel 2009). Finally, in my interviews, the RUF, or "rebels," were implicated in nearly every incident of rape that was reported.

It may be argued that victims have difficulty in correctly identifying the faction of their perpetrators during the fog of war. Almost universally, the respondents I interviewed reported that the combatants who came to their village were wearing both military and civilian clothing, spoke a variety of languages, and rarely directly identified themselves as part of a particular group or faction. The villagers repeatedly and consistently called such combatants "rebels." However, it is admittedly unclear how, or whether, they knew that the combatants were attached to a particular faction. It is widely reported that the RUF sometimes wore military uniforms when perpetrating atrocities, and interviews with former SLA members indicated that members of the military would at times dress as rebels when committing atrocities.[28] The task of determining perpetrators of particular crimes is extraordinarily difficult; ultimately, it is impossible to know whether witnesses are correct in their reported identifications.

Nonetheless, there is remarkable consistency across a variety of sources that the RUF committed a vastly disproportionate amount of the violence in general, and of the rape in particular. The finding that the RUF committed the majority of the rape is not merely an artifact of the number of combatants in the RUF. Indeed, among the population of demobilized fighters, only about one-third of these, or about twenty-four thousand people, were RUF combatants. According to combatant demobilization data, the CDF was the largest armed group, with about 50 percent of the total combatants (Humphreys and Weinstein 2004). If reporting on violence was simply a matter of which faction was largest, the CDF should be the most frequently reported perpetrator.

Finally, the temporal patterns of reported rape by the RUF are shown in figure 3.3, with a separate line indicating the reports from each data source. The SLWCD data (on the right y-axis) show rape occurring at steadily lower rates until 1998/1999, when there is an enormous peak. The TRC data (on the left

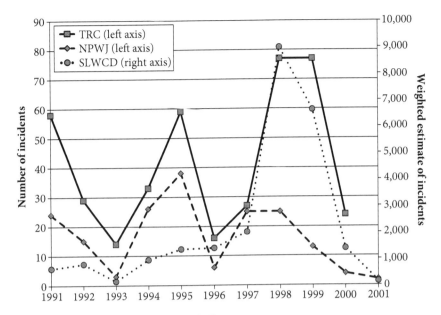

FIGURE 3.3 Wartime rape by the RUF

Note: The TRC data shown here includes reports for rape perpetrated by the RUF and "rebels." There are 477 total incidents; of these, 414 incidents were plotted, as others were missing values for date. The NPWJ data shown here includes reports for rape perpetrated by the RUF/AFRC, the RUF/NPFL, and the RUF. There are 185 total incidents; 4 of these were not plotted due to missing values for date. The SLWCD data shown here includes reports for rape perpetrated by the RUF and "rebels." There are 24,467 estimated total incidents. If a reported rape was attributed to two perpetrator groups, the weighted estimate was split equally between the groups.

y-axis) show that reports of rape by the RUF were characterized by three peaks: early in the war, in 1995, and—the highest peak—in 1998/1999. The NPWJ data (also on the left y-axis) follow roughly similar trends, with peaks in reported rape by the RUF in 1991, 1995, and 1997/1998. While none of these data sources can be considered definitive, the similarity of basic patterns across the sources suggests that the peak years for rape by the RUF include 1998 and 1999.

Rape by the Sierra Leone Army/Armed Forces Revolutionary Council

The SLA was a party to the war from the beginning, but the coup in May 1997 shifted the allegiance of the national army. The AFRC included the postcoup soldiers who had briefly formed a government but ultimately fled the capital. As a result, the TRC data treat the AFRC as a separate armed group, active only after May 25, 1997, in the third phase of the war.[29] In the TRC data, a total of eighty-six incidents of rape, or about 14 percent of the total reported incidents, were perpetrated by the SLA, the AFRC, or the SLA/AFRC. Twenty incidents of rape by the SLA were reported prior to the May 25, 1997, coup, with the earliest reports dating back to 1991. An additional sixty incidents were reportedly perpetrated by the AFRC after the coup, with another six incidents occurring sometime during 1997 with no known month.

In the NPWJ data, only 8 percent of the incidents of rape (18 of 213) were perpetrated by the SLA or AFRC, with reports spread evenly throughout the course of the war.[30] Finally, in the SLWCD survey, about 25 percent of the reported violations were committed by groups that included either the SLA or the AFRC, with the vast majority reported in 1998 and 1999.[31] Figure 3.4 shows the temporal trends in reported rape by the SLA/AFRC. Both the TRC and SLWCD data show peaks in the late 1990s. NPWJ data follow a different pattern, but the sample is too small to draw conclusions about trends.

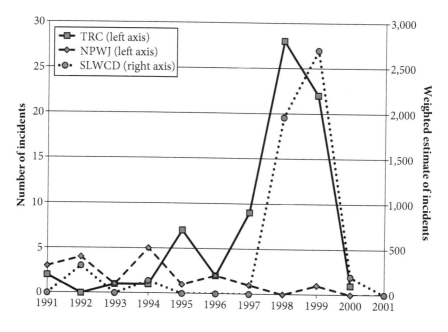

FIGURE 3.4   Wartime rape by the SLA/AFRC

Note: The TRC data shown here include reports of rape that victims said were perpetrated by the SLA, AFRC, and the "Army." There are eighty-six total incidents; of these, seventy-three incidents were plotted, as thirteen incidents were missing values for date. The NPWJ data shown here include reports of rape perpetrated by the SLA and the AFRC. There are eighteen total incidents, and all are displayed. The SLWCD data include reports of rape by the SLA and AFRC. There are 5,286 estimated total incidents. If a reported rape was attributed to two perpetrator groups, the weighted estimate was split equally between the groups.

Rape by the Civil Defense Forces

Two patterns of rape by the CDF are apparent across the main data sources. First, only a small percentage of the overall rape was reportedly perpetrated by the CDF, and second, as is displayed in figure 3.5, rape by the CDF was reported almost entirely in the final phase of the conflict. In the SLWCD survey, less than 1 percent of the reported violations were committed by the CDF—all in 1997. In the TRC data, the CDF was reported as the perpetrator in 25 incidents, or about 4 percent of the total. For those incidents that included information on the year of the violation, all but three were reported in 1998/1999, with the earliest reported incident in 1995. Finally, in the NPWJ data, the CDF (or Kamajors, who comprised the majority of the CDF) were reported as perpetrators in only about 3 percent (7 of 213) of the incidents of rape, all in 1998–1999.

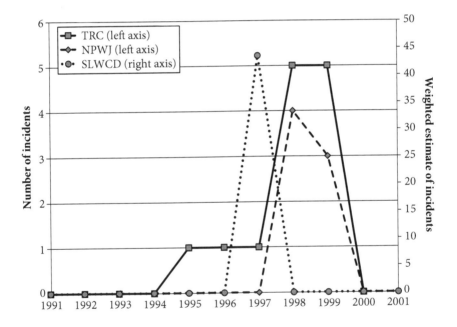

FIGURE 3.5   Wartime rape by the CDF

Note: The TRC data shown here include reports of rape perpetrated by the CDF. There are twenty-five total incidents, but only thirteen were plotted due to missing values for date. The NPWJ data shown here include reports of rape perpetrated by the CDF, CDF/Kamajors, and Kamajor/Gbethis/Ecomog/SLA. There are seven total incidents, and all are displayed. The SLWCD data include reports of rape by the CDF. There are forty-four estimated total incidents. If a reported rape was attributed to two perpetrator groups, the weighted estimate was split equally between the groups.

Overall, then, the CDF refrained from rape until the final years of the war, when their behavior suddenly changed. The stark turnaround in the perpetration of rape by this group provides a crucial test of the competing arguments, discussed in the next section.

What Explains the Patterns of Wartime Rape in Sierra Leone? Weighing the Evidence

I next examine the support for the two most plausible explanations of rape in Sierra Leone: one about opportunism and greed, in which combatants perpetrate rape for private gains, and one about combatant socialization, where fighters perpetrate rape for group-related goals rather than purely personal reasons. Using the wealth of available evidence, I evaluate whether the two arguments can account for the observed patterns of victims, perpetrators, and temporal trends.

Opportunism/Greed

The two main strands of the opportunism/greed argument—state collapse and material resources—suggest numerous micro-level observable implications, as discussed in chapter 1. I first describe the two strands and then turn to the question of whether they are supported by the evidence.

At its center, the state collapse hypothesis is concerned with the erosion of peacetime institutions, norms, and legal prohibitions, creating an opportunity for members of armed groups to perpetrate rape with impunity. The primary implication is that this should be especially true for fighters in the state military, who should be least likely to expect to suffer consequences for violations against civilians—particularly for crimes of opportunity—during periods when the state is at its weakest.

A second, related implication of the state collapse hypothesis is that reports of looting should be correlated with reports of rape. In the literature on wartime violence, both rape and looting are frequently considered crimes of opportunity (e.g., Hoover Green 2011) and may be viewed by the fighters as payment or reward for their service.[32] Indeed, scholars tend to treat rape as a private good, akin to other personal gains garnered by combatants, such as drugs, food, and guns (e.g., Mitchell 2004; Butler, Gluch, and Mitchell 2007). If the same motives undergird both rape and looting, we should expect to observe close temporal variation in reports of rape and looting.

Finally, the hypothesis about state collapse suggests that combatants view rape as a form of sex or, more ominously, have an explicit desire to perpetrate rape for the purpose of obtaining sexual gratification.[33] Consequently, we should expect rape to be targeted at women who would be appropriate sexual partners in peacetime. Proponents of these types of arguments argue that because rape victims are commonly comprised of women at their "peak physical attractiveness" (Gottschall 2004, 134), rape is fundamentally rooted in male sexual desire.

The second major opportunism hypothesis is focused on how access to material resources affects armed groups' relationships with civilians. As described in chapter 1, initial access to available material resources determines the types of individuals who "elect to participate" (Weinstein 2007, 7), those who "signed up" (Mueller 2000, 59), or who were otherwise "urged," "promised," and "enticed" by group leaders (49). According to this logic, access to resources can ultimately predict whether the group engages in abuses, including rape.

In the case of material resource–based arguments, there are two main mechanisms, as outlined in chapter 1, each with distinct observable outcomes. First, the recruitment mechanism suggests that groups with access to external resources will use these to attract voluntary fighters, who are in turn likely to be the types of combatants who seek to perpetrate rape. We should observe, in other words, that fighters who *volunteer* to join well-resourced armed groups are more likely to rape than those who are abducted. Second, and similar to the previous arguments, the accountability mechanism implies that armed groups supported by external resources—and thus freed from dependency on civilians—will be more likely to perpetrate, and more likely to tolerate, opportunistic crimes, including rape.

Support for the Argument

Overall, opportunism/greed appears to explain at least part of the observed patterns of violence. While there is not support for all of the observable implications, there is evidence to support many of them. First, if rape were correlated with state collapse, the lawless nature of war would afford the opportunity to commit such atrocities to every armed group—and, arguably, to government forces in particular. Opportunity, of course, was not constant for all units within the SLA and the RUF—especially given that the SLA had higher levels of internal discipline and training than did the RUF—nor was opportunity constant over time. However, the broad patterns of perpetration suggest that opportunity is not the final word in terms of why rape was widespread in Sierra Leone. In Sierra Leone, evidence suggests that the RUF—not the government forces—took disproportionate advantage of opportunity. State breakdown, while perhaps part of the background conditions, cannot on its own explain the patterns of violence.

Second, a frequent contention in the literature is that rape is but one form of opportunistic violence; looting is another common form. The reports of incidents of rape and looting from the TRC are displayed in figure 3.6. Although looting occurred with far more frequency than did rape, the peaks in both types of violations are fairly similar. Overall, using data aggregated to the level of the year, looting is highly correlated with rape, at .97 and .87 in the TRC data and SLWCD data (the latter is not shown in the figure), respectively. These patterns offer some support to the opportunism hypothesis. However, as I argue later, the argument does not help to explain why peaks in rape occur toward the end of the conflict. Overall, while it may be argued that the patterns of different forms of violence closely tracked one another, the interview evidence discussed later in the chapter helps to further parse which factors may be driving others.

Third, patterns of victimization across several data sources show that most victims were of the age that would have made them socially appropriate peacetime sexual partners. One proxy measurement for social acceptability of sex with young girls is the mean age of first marriage for women, which one prewar survey found to be 15.7 years in Sierra Leone (Dow 1971). The majority of reported victims were adult women, with a mean age around twenty-one (in the TRC data) and twenty-two (in the SLWCD data)—well above the mean age of first marriage. The range of reported victim ages, however, is quite large: of the rapes reported

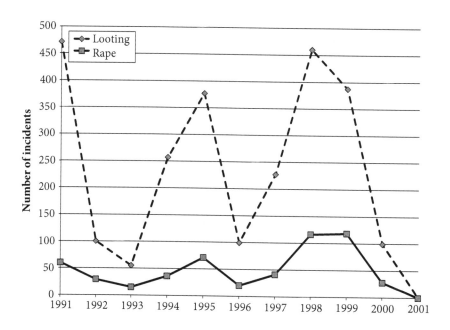

FIGURE 3.6 Wartime rape and looting over time

Note: This figure uses data from the TRC only (Gohdes and Ball 2010). The looting and rape data are both categories of the variable *Violt*.

to the SLWCD survey, for example, the youngest victim was three years old and the oldest was sixty-nine.[34] While it is commonly reported that victims who were very young were "targeted" by perpetrators (e.g., Taylor 2003, 28), there is little evidence that this was the case. Because a very large proportion of the population in Sierra Leone was comprised of young people at the time of the conflict—about 40 percent of the female population in 1995 was age fourteen or younger—the fact that 25 percent of the rape victims reported to the TRC were thirteen years old or younger actually suggests that girls are *underrepresented* among victims. Similarly, data from the SLWCD survey found that about 43 percent of reported rape victims were adults between the ages of twenty and thirty-four, while this age group comprised only 24 percent of the population.[35] Adult women, then, are *overrepresented* among victims, and could arguably be said to have been targeted for rape. In addition, interviews with some ex-combatants support the idea that rape happened, at least in part, because of a male desire to commit rape. About 25 percent of the ex-combatants I interviewed (eight of thirty-four) specifically mentioned the desire for sex as one reason for the widespread wartime rape. These patterns do not mean that younger girls were never targeted for rape by individual perpetrators, but the data do not necessarily show a systematic pattern of this.

Turning to evidence for the material resources hypothesis, there is little support for the recruitment mechanism, in which violent types of individuals choose to join violent groups. The evidence suggests that potential recruits had little ability to *decide* to join the RUF. In particular, the vast majority of combatants in the RUF—the most violent group, and the group that perpetrated the most rape—were abducted. Survey data reveal that 87 percent of the RUF ex-combatants reported having been abducted into its ranks, while very few members of the RUF (9 percent) reported having joined because they agreed with its political goals, and even fewer cited the possibility of "living better" as a reason (Humphreys and Weinstein 2004). Interview evidence also reflects this pattern: none of the RUF ex-combatants I interviewed stated that they had joined on their own accord. While it may be the case that some respondents were not being truthful about their decision to join, the general pattern—that the vast majority of the RUF fighters had been abducted—is likely still true.

Additionally, there is scant evidence that the RUF sought particularly violent types of recruits, or those who may have been looking to gain access to sex. In their analysis of the Sierra Leone case, Humphreys and Weinstein (2004, 27) consider "access to women (or men) for marriage or sex" as a potential incentive for fighters to join armed groups; these findings are also echoed by others (e.g., Marks 2013b). Humphreys and Weinstein find that 25 percent of RUF fighters reported having received "wives" during their time with the group and infer that "access to women" may have been part of the incentive structure to entice combatants to join.[36] However, the same data also show that very few men were "told they would get women" if they were to join a group; only 1.4 percent of the male RUF combatants reported having been offered women.[37] Thus, while it may be the case that access to women was recognized by combatants as an implicit incentive to join, such access was infrequently offered as an explicit incentive by the leadership to recruit particular types. Instead, the RUF kidnapped available able-bodied people to serve in their ranks. In doing so, they cast an extremely wide net in gathering new members. Bellows and Miguel describe violence within villages—including abduction—as "close to random at the household level."[38]

Temporal patterns in abduction do not support the recruitment mechanism either.[39] To the extent that there were volunteers to the RUF, they most likely joined in the early initial stages of the organization, when it is most plausible that recruits were attracted by material incentives.[40] If contraband predicts the use of rape, we should observe that the incidence of rape was highest at the beginning of the war, when these "opportunistic joiners" comprised the ranks of the RUF.[41] However, the incidence of rape was relatively low during the early years of the war, indicating again that the rape was not mainly perpetrated by the volunteers. Furthermore, some interview respondents who self-reported having been abducted into a fighting faction also self-reported that they had perpetrated rape.

Taken all together, evidence shows that rape was not committed only by "opportunistic joiners"; rather, rape was committed by both volunteers *and* abductees. Thus, even if the recruitment mechanism can help to explain violent behavior on the part of the volunteers, they represent only a small proportion of the perpetrators.[42] In sum, it is unlikely that the promise of rape attracted combatants to join the RUF, or that the group carefully selected a particular type of recruit who was seeking chances to rape.

Lastly, general patterns across armed groups do seem to support the accountability mechanism. The armed group with the greatest access to diamond resources—the RUF—was far more abusive overall than the CDF, which, at the opposite end of the spectrum, both grew out of and was heavily supported by civilians. The accountability mechanism also finds support in the temporal trends. As described below, as the CDF moved away from their home bases over time, they tended to perpetrate more violations. These trends suggest a pattern of armed groups becoming more abusive the less they need to rely on civilian support (or conversely, a pattern of less abuse when groups need to cultivate civilian support).

Despite this support for the opportunism/greed argument, several patterns among victims and perpetrators suggest that opportunism does not tell the entire story. First, a substantial number of the reported victims were too young to be considered socially acceptable sexual partners in peacetime. For example, SLWCD survey data show that 20 percent of reported victims were between the ages of ten and fourteen. Additionally, although a relatively small proportion of victims were over the age of thirty-five, if rape were driven only by the sexual desires of young men, we should not necessarily expect to see victims as old as sixty-nine—the oldest victim in the SLWCD survey.

However, opportunism cannot fully explain patterns of perpetration— neither the temporal patterns, those in the form of rape nor the identity of perpetrators. As displayed in the previous figures, rape was reported throughout the war in Sierra Leone, but especially during the late 1990s. Arguments about opportunism are relatively static; that is, they generally predict a steady rate of rape throughout the war and have difficulty accounting for sudden increases in incidents—absent a shock that increases opportunity, such as increased access to civilians. Thus, while opportunism/greed can help to explain some of the background conditions and motivations, it fails to help make sense of the timing of wartime rape.

Opportunism alone also cannot account for the massive reporting of gang rape, as opposed to single-perpetrator rape. Nor can opportunism explain the use of objects in rape, or the extreme violence that often accompanies rape. Finally, as explored in detail below, a substantial number of reports of rape by groups of RUF fighters included women as perpetrators. The presence of women at least partially undermines arguments that wartime rape is fundamentally about opportunities to seek sexual gratification.[43] Women rarely perpetrate sexual crimes, especially alone.

Combatant Socialization

The combatant socialization argument suggests that groups with low levels of internal cohesion will turn to gang rape as a means by which to socially bind its members. The argument helps to explain why the most common form of rape is gang rape. Rape was often reportedly public, and evidence from interviews with victims confirms that gang rape was frequently witnessed by other combatants and by family members or villagers. This is important, because for rape to have a bonding function, the violence must be observable to other perpetrators.

Based on the available data, several other observable implications of the combatant socialization argument can be identified: (1) a correlation exists between the frequency of abduction by an armed group and the perpetration of rape by that group; (2) fighters describe rape as cohesive and not divisive; (3) rape, while perhaps tolerated by the command, was not explicitly ordered, and thus fighters could refuse to participate; and (4) abducted fighters of both sexes perpetrated rape for socialization purposes.

In order to examine the support for the argument, I first briefly review the recruitment practices of each of the three major armed groups over the period of the conflict and then turn to the observable implications.

Recruitment by the Revolutionary United Front

While reports of abduction were tied to all factions over the course of the war, the RUF abducted fighters most often. RUF combatants "typically knew nobody in their factions" (Humphreys and Weinstein 2004, 24). Only 12 percent of RUF members reported having been recruited by a friend, relative, or community member. These data lead Humphreys and Weinstein (2004, 2) to conclude that the RUF was a group of "mutual strangers."

In my interviews, many respondents described their process of joining the RUF as terribly violent. One recruit recalled, "I was captured by the RUF while fleeing with my brothers and sister. My sister was raped—outside, on the ground, at only twelve years old. They wanted to kill all three of us, but I offered myself if they let the others go."[44] Another said, "The rebels came in the evening. They asked my mother for water and money. She refused to give them money, so they beat her and then stabbed me in the leg. They taught me that day to shoot a gun and made me kill someone in my village."[45] Finally, another described being abducted as a teenager:

> I was fifteen when the rebels came in 1992. At the time, I thought that the war was a joke. I thought that rebels had tails like animals because I had never seen a rebel. They came to our village at six o'clock in the morning, shooting and killing and burning houses. My family ran to the next town, where we had peace for only five days, until the rebels attacked that town. My older brother tried to run and they shot him as an example. I didn't recognize any of the rebels, but they all spoke Krio. They captured me and told me that I was a freedom fighter now.[46]

These disturbing descriptions highlight the fear that abductees felt when they were first captured, often in the aftermath of experiencing or witnessing extreme violence for the first times in their lives. The stories also demonstrate just how severe the problem of low cohesion must have been as new abductees joined the group.

The RUF engaged in two major periods of recruitment—one in the early 1990s (1991–1992) and another in the late 1990s (1996–1998) (Humphreys and Weinstein 2004, 22). The RUF may have abducted so many fighters due to the nature of the war itself; 95 percent of all battles involved the RUF as one of the fighting factions, yet the RUF is coded as losing almost half of the battles they fought over the course of the war.[47] Those periods of heavy recruitment, not coincidentally, were characterized by numerous battle losses for the RUF; for example, between 1996 and 1998, the RUF lost seventy-eight battles (compared to forty-three wins). Both the relatively larger number of battles and the high proportion of losses suggest that the RUF had the need to recruit new members. Further, after such losses, the RUF often needed to recruit new fighters quickly to replenish the ranks. While rapid abduction campaigns may have solved the problem of membership, they exacerbated the problem of low cohesion, thereby intensifying the causal effects of forced recruitment on rape.

It is notable that the RUF abducted the vast majority of its recruits even during the earliest years of the war. However, there is some temporal variation within the RUF recruitment patterns: 78 percent of fighters who reported joining in 1991 said they were abducted, compared with a high of 94 percent of those fighters whose first year with the RUF was 1998 (Humphreys and Weinstein 2004).

Recruitment by the Sierra Leone Army/Armed Forces Revolutionary Council

In contrast to practices of the RUF, 52 percent of the SLA and 62 percent of the AFRC were recruited by a relative, friend, or community member, while only 24 percent of the SLA and 27 percent of the AFRC did not know others in their unit. Also unlike the RUF, the SLA recruited members consistently throughout the war, with few notable periods of increased recruitment (Humphreys and Weinstein 2004). The AFRC, on the other hand, recruited most of its members in the final years of the 1990s; this was, after all, when the group was formed.

Recruitment by the Civilian Defense Forces

Unlike the RUF, 77 percent of the CDF reported having been recruited by a friend, relative, or a community member, and CDF recruits usually served in units with friends and family members. Only 7 percent of recruits reported that they knew no one in their unit, and only 2 percent reported that they had been forcibly recruited into their unit (Humphreys and Weinstein 2004). Nearly two-thirds of recruits reported joining the CDF because they believed in the political aims of the group, which they mainly described as "defending the community" and "bringing peace" (Humphreys and Weinstein 2004, 25).[48] The CDF engaged in an increased recruitment drive in the last years of the war, starting around January 1999 (IRIN 1999).

Support for the Argument

The main observable implication is covariation of reports of abduction and rape by armed group over time. In general, as shown in figure 3.7, reports of abduction and reports of rape are correlated over time. There is a clear association between the two spikes in rape in the late 1990s and the number of reported incidents of abduction across the available data sources. If the composition of the group changed little over time, there would be diminishing marginal effectiveness of gang rape. But there were periods of increased need for new fighters due to the nature of the war, particularly after episodes of intense fighting, due to deaths and desertions. The loss of fighters and the subsequent abduction and integration of new recruits may be one reason why the AFRC/RUF invasion of the capital city of Freetown in January 1999 resulted in so many reports of gang rape.

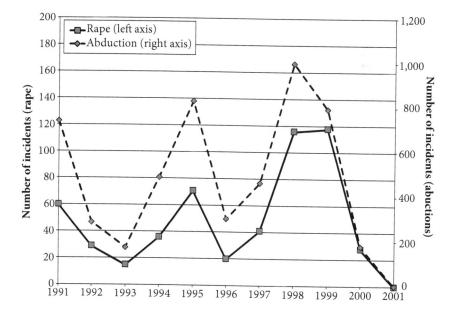

FIGURE 3.7   Wartime rape and abduction over time

Note: This figure uses data from the TRC only (Gohdes and Ball 2010). The looting and rape data are both categories of the variable Violt.

The pattern of violence committed by the CDF is further evidence of an association between abduction and rape. In the later years of the war, the individual units that comprised the CDF gradually expanded beyond defending their home chiefdoms, and the units moved into other regions and joined with other fighting forces. As they moved, they began to forcibly recruit new members—and the levels of violence committed by the CDF, including rape, increased. The NPWJ report explicitly notes this pattern, arguing that a cause of the increase in atrocities by the CDF was that the "new" recruits, who were forced to join, committed more atrocities than the "old" recruits, who had been carefully selected by their chiefs (Smith, Gambette, and Longley 2004, 54). Similarly, an IRIN (1999) report notes that after the mass recruitment drive of 1999, newly-initiated [recruits] . . . have been becoming increasingly unruly." The CDF grew rapidly during recruitment drives, and commanders reported being unsure as to how many fighters were under their supervision (Forney 2015). This suggests that abducting large numbers of fighters—and doing so very quickly—resulted in a marked loss of internal cohesion. The patterns provide support for an additional observable implication of the combatant socialization argument: as the CDF began rapidly abducting recruits, the group's propensity to commit wartime rape increased accordingly.[49]

A second observable implication is that rape should be a form of violence that creates social bonds between fighters, not something that causes divisiveness within the unit. Interviews with fighters provide abundant detail indicating that rape fostered cohesion, rather than division within the group. Respondents confirmed that rebels would often discuss their sexual prowess with one another, recounting the number of women they had raped during a particular raid. One ex-combatant stated, "The rebels felt pleased that they were having so much sex, and we would brag to each other about enjoying it so much."[50] Many fighters reported that rape was an act they viewed as "fun" or "entertainment."[51] An RUF ex-combatant said, "[After raping] we would make fun by saying, 'That girl was sweet.'"[52] "[During the war] it was a 'jungle system' and watching each other was fun, in a way," said a different fighter, while another noted, "We would watch each other and joke about how some guys were not doing it correctly."[53] Finally, one combatant confirmed, "The entire unit watches. Everyone laughs and is jubilating. It is a sign of celebration."[54] Notably, these descriptions stand in marked contrast to those of other forms of group violence, including killing. Acts of lethal violence were never recalled with pleasure, nor described as enjoyable.

There is also evidence that gang rape served to reinforce the hierarchy of the armed group, which was a means of consolidating the structure of the unit. As previous research on gang rape—discussed in chapter 1—indicates, the order of perpetrators in a gang rape often holds symbolic importance. A former member of the RUF explained that the commanders would commonly be the first perpetrators and the members of the Small Boys Units (SBUs) would go last.[55] For some members of the SBUs, rape during the war was their first sexual experience.[56] An ex-combatant described how boys as young as nine and ten years old would rape women in an effort to emulate their older peers.[57] The participation of some commanders in rape may suggest that such violence was implicitly ordered.[58] Yet, as discussed in more detail below, interviewees report that refusing to participate was possible, and often had no severe consequences—other than the loss of social standing among peers.

Many ex-combatants reported admiration, as opposed to disgust, for those who had perpetrated many rapes. In interviews, they described a culture in which those who had raped many women obtained a sort of legendary status among their peers. One interviewee spoke with awe about a fellow combatant who had raped hundreds of women: "Men bragged about sex in private conversations. The men who raped the most were the toughest—it meant you were the biggest man; one man said that he had raped over two hundred women."[59] Ex-combatants reported that those who participated in rape in Sierra Leone were seen to be more courageous, valiant, and brave than their peers. Those who committed rape were respected by their peers as "big men"—essentially, strong and virile warriors with tough attitudes. Overall, these interviews provide ample evidence that rape was a cohesive activity, underscoring again that gang rape can be an effective method of increasing esteem and social ties between perpetrators.

One measure of military unit cohesion is whether veterans stay in touch after the war. Based on the survey of ex-combatants in Sierra Leone, members of the RUF were *more* likely to stay in touch with friends from their faction after the war than were members of the CDF (Humphreys and Weinstein 2004, 41). This finding is especially interesting because, as previously discussed, CDF members were overwhelmingly recruited into their units by friends or relatives and thus might be expected to be more likely to remain in touch after the war. Evidence of enduring postwar friendships is also evidence that, despite most having been abducted into their units, the RUF combatants formed tight social bonds with their fellow fighters. These bonds were likely strengthened by their postwar experiences of stigma—compared to the experiences of CDF fighters, who largely returned home after the war.

A third observable implication is that rape was rarely directly ordered by the command; instead, ex-combatants reported that rape was innovated from the bottom up. In interviews, few of the rank-and-file ex-combatants reported ever having heard orders given to commit rape.[60] More specifically, of the thirty-four ex-combatants interviewed, about three-quarters said that they had never seen or heard a commander give an order to rape—a revealing finding, because this admission seemingly runs counter to the fighters' self-interest. In addition, only a small number of the unit commanders admitted that they had ever ordered their men to rape. One former RUF fighter said that his "commanders never ordered their men to rape, but they knew it was happening, and they did it themselves."[61] Rape was reportedly treated as a "private issue," outside the purview of direct war strategy.[62] One ex-combatant related an incident in which one of his unit members was ordered to be killed because he had a severe case of gonorrhea and had become a burden to the unit. The commander became angry about having to sacrifice one of his men and lectured the unit that their "purpose is to fight, not to have sex."[63] This statement demonstrates that the commander considered fighting and rape as different goals and underscores that rape was not a part of the military strategy. Finally, as previously noted, new RUF recruits—unlike most recent additions to the other armed groups—arrived in their units completely unvouched for. Members of the RUF, therefore, turned to rape as a means of easing their entry into the group atmosphere. One former RUF commander said succinctly, "The new guys never wanted to rape, but they were mocked a bit and treated like they were not serious rebels—and, after a few months, they got acclimated to the rape."[64] Notably, the finding that there were so few orders to rape stands in contrast to common explanations of rape in Sierra Leone.[65] Many have argued, for example, that rape was part of an organized top-down military strategy and political campaign, a "weapon of war" specifically designed, at least in part, to "dominate and degrade not only the victim but also her community" (Taylor 2003, 4).[66]

Counter to this narrative are reports that some combatants could, and did, refuse to participate in rape. Men who balked at the idea of rape reported being derided by their peers.[67] A former child soldier who had been forced to rape his sister made the decision never to rape anyone again; he recalled that this decision prompted the other members of his unit to give him the nickname "Savior."[68] Another ex-combatant reported, "Some men chose not to rape, and they were teased. We would ask them, 'Maybe you are a homosexual?'"[69] The social pressure to commit rape made it difficult to refuse and still be accepted by combatant peers. However, unlike other violations of group norms, refusal to rape did not result in being killed for defying an order, further reinforcing the notion that rape was not part of an overarching military strategy.

A fourth and final observable implication is that we should expect—or at least not be surprised by—perpetrators of both sexes in cases where women are also abducted as fighters. The RUF was the armed group that committed the most rape and had the largest proportion of female fighters (24 percent, according to Humphreys and Weinstein 2004, 14).[70] Of the gang rape reported in the SLWCD survey, 74 percent was committed by male-only groups. Mixed-sex perpetrator groups committed 25 percent of the gang rape (which comprise 19 percent of the total—combined gang and single-perpetrator—reported rape). In other words, the survey data indicate that women participated in one in four of the reported incidents of gang rape in Sierra Leone, which was nearly one in five of the total reported incidents of rape.[71]

The participation of women in gang rape took a variety of forms. First, women in the RUF acted as liaisons to locate potential victims and also held down victims during rapes.[72] One woman said in an interview, "Women would tell the men that 'I found a beautiful woman for you.' We would help capture her and hold her down. We would sometimes be rewarded with looted jewelry."[73] Seeking potential victims was seen as a way for the combatants to pursue intergroup acceptance as part of an organized process among combatants.[74] Other interviewees described similar scenes: "Women fighters would hold down unarmed women for men to rape."[75] Although there are no systematic data on the nature of women's participation in gang rape, restraining the victim likely comprises the majority of the reports in the SLWCD survey.

Beyond holding victims down, some also reported witnessing female combatants actively raping other women with objects. "Women rebels would often be involved in rapes—some of the women RUF would hold onto the victims' hands, some women RUF would rape the women with bottles and with sticks. The RUF women did not feel any mercy for the women [victims]."[76] When asked whether the women in the RUF empathized with their victims, the response from female combatants was a resounding no. "Women fighters were under the influence of drugs, so they did not even think about mercy for women being raped," one ex-combatant said.[77] The participation of women in gang rape is powerful evidence for the combatant socialization argument.[78] In a study of female fighters in Sierra Leone, Chris Coulter (2008) writes that her interviewees—almost all of whom had been abducted—reported that their motivations for becoming armed soldiers included survival, control, fear, prestige, and access to resources. These same motivations help to explain women's involvement in gang rape; the women wanted to be seen as contributing members of the unit and as part of the larger group. Women may also have believed that participating in the rape of other women reduced their own chance of being targeted for rape, both on the front and in camp; this was not mentioned in interviews, however. Overall, evidence for a cohesive function of rape is bolstered by the involvement of women, who comprised a substantial proportion of RUF combatants.

By any standard, rape during the Sierra Leone civil war was widespread. Although the case of Sierra Leone is frequently viewed as an example of rape used as a "weapon of war," evidence instead suggests that rape was not employed as part of any overt, rational military strategy. There is little evidence that rape was ordered and few discernible patterns in the victims targeted. Instead, the richly detailed available data show that the observed variation in rape—patterns in perpetrators and victims, and across space and time—can be partially explained by arguments about opportunism and greed. Looting and rape were closely correlated, and some combatants reported that rape was due, at least in part, to a desire for sexual gratification. However, opportunism arguments fail to explain the full range of changing dynamics of violence, and especially why peaks in reported rape occurred toward the end of the conflict period.

The most compelling evidence suggests that rape during the war in Sierra Leone was part of a socialization process for the lower-ranking members of the RUF—a combatant group, composed mainly of strangers, that had a much lower level of internal cohesion than the other fighting factions. Abduction and rape are closely associated over time, and the armed group made up almost entirely of abducted fighters perpetrated a vastly disproportionate amount of the reported rape. Interview evidence shows that rape was rarely ordered directly, that fighters could choose not to participate, and that it served a cohesive function for the fighters, both men and women.

MASS RAPE BY STATE ACTORS
Timor-Leste (1975–1999)

> The militia people were forced to join. They were ordinary people, ordinary farmers. Then they became a part of a militia group and they had to burn houses and to kill people for the first time. . . . I heard reports of sexual violence. It mostly happened in the western part of the country. . . . The reports were usually of gang rape, more than one perpetrator. It seemed like the boss would go first.
>
> —Director of local NGO, Kupang, West Timor, August 2, 2012

> They raped girls in their own houses. I didn't see the militiamen rape the girls but they told me they had done this. They used to tell us about what they did when they went on operation. The militiamen told us very proudly how lucky they were to have raped girls and killed and eaten animals.
>
> —Former child soldier, quoted in the UNICEF report *East Timorese Children Involved in Armed Conflict*, 2001

Waves of terrible violence—perpetrated by both the Indonesian military and pro-Indonesian militia groups—characterized the war in Timor-Leste, which spanned almost twenty-five years (1975–1999).[1] This chapter explores three notable patterns in the dynamics of rape during the conflict in Timor-Leste. First, the reported rape was most severe during the final year of the conflict, shifting in both frequency and form relative to earlier periods of the war.[2] Based on testimonies given to the truth and reconciliation commission, the Commission for Reception, Truth, and Reconciliation (known by its Portuguese acronym CAVR), about 25 percent of the reported rape for the entire war occurred in 1999 alone. One scholar writes that "untold numbers of women and girls" were raped in this period (Nevins 2005, 5). Additional evidence that suggests there was a spike in rape in 1999 is the estimated fertility rate for Timor-Leste (World Bank 2015a). The highest estimated fertility rate in Timor-Leste between 1960 and 2011 (7.11 births per woman) occurred in 2000, a year after the 1999 violence. Because periods of extreme social dislocation are not typically associated with increased fertility rates, an increase in rape may be one reason for this pattern.

Second, beyond temporal patterns, variation can be seen in who perpetrated the rape during the conflict. The identity of reported perpetrators changed over time, from mainly Indonesian forces during much of the war, to mainly East Timorese pro-Indonesian militias in 1999. On the other hand, the East Timorese insurgency was reported to have committed far less violence against noncombatants and almost none of the wartime rape.

Finally, the purpose of the violence shifted over time as well. While earlier rape was reportedly targeted against certain groups of victims—particularly, supporters of the insurgency—rape in 1999 is generally described as random or indiscriminate.[3] Thus, in at least these three ways, the conflict-related rape in 1999 marked a dramatic change in patterns of rape from earlier in the war.

Based on these patterns of variation, I explore two vexing puzzles about rape during the Timor-Leste war. First, why did the worst period of the reported rape occur during the 1999 postreferendum crisis? Second, why did the militia forces, comprised almost entirely of East Timorese, commit such brutal acts of rape against their own compatriots before and, especially, after the 1999 referendum? In other words, why was the worst reported rape of the conflict perpetrated by Timorese against other Timorese?

I consider four explanations for these puzzles, one a variation of the opportunism/greed argument and the others variations on the ethnic hatred argument.[4] In the first argument, many observers maintain that the members of the pro-Indonesia militias were, simply put, criminals, thugs, and thieves, who embraced the opportunity presented by the enormous chaos of the referendum period. The argument suggests that these groups of men—the dregs of Timorese society—took advantage of the chance to seek personal gratification on an individual basis. According to this view, rape was initiated by the militia forces themselves for private reasons—perhaps encouraged, and certainly tolerated, by the Indonesian military command, but not directly ordered as part of a military campaign or strategy.

A second argument is that rape and other violence committed against Timorese was indirectly the result of the secessionist aims of the rebels. In this view, the violence by Indonesian-supported forces was perpetrated as revenge for the outcome of the referendum. Indonesia was humiliated by the outcome of the vote, in which they lost a long and painful fight over the status of Timor-Leste, and the Timorese militias were assembled together and then ordered by the Indonesian military to destroy the country. The "militarization" or "Timorization" of the conflict served as cover for the Indonesians (Thaler 2012), and the East Timorese fighters who comprised the militias were mere puppets for the regime. This strategy of using local fighters for plausible deniability has roots throughout the conflict, including the cooperation of many Timorese with the Indonesians in exchange for pay or looting opportunities. Some observers report that, among its orders aimed at exacting revenge, the Indonesian military directly ordered the rape of East Timorese women. In this view, rape was part of the violence of retribution, perhaps meant to sever ties with the people of Timor-Leste, or to reassert Indonesian dominance despite the loss of formal control (Thaler 2012). A third related explanation is centered on the use of Timor-Leste as an example to deter other potential challengers to the Indonesian state.

A fourth explanation is a bottom-up one: the militia members were not puppets of the Indonesian military but were themselves concerned about the postindependence phase. In this view, while the militias were supported and perhaps encouraged by the military, they had their own independent justifications for exacting violence or revenge on other Timorese. These included retribution for previous violence as well as fear and anxiety about what the future might hold for them and their families. There is evidence in the empirical record for all of these explanations, including statements by the former militia fighters themselves.

In this chapter, I explore these plausible explanations as alternatives to the combatant socialization argument. I find that while the opportunism argument mostly fails to explain the patterns of violence, both the revenge/secessionist and the combatant socialization arguments can help resolve critical puzzles. It is evident, as proponents of the revenge arguments have maintained, that the violence in 1999 was encouraged and supported, both directly and indirectly, by the Indonesian military. However, the first revenge argument—that Indonesia used the militias for violence—cannot fully explain why scant evidence exists of direct orders to commit violence, including rape; nor is it clear that violence in general was directed against specific targets. The second revenge argument—that the roots of the violence are in the militias themselves—can better account for these puzzles. In addition, the combatant socialization argument can help to explain why the perpetrators of the violence changed over time, from the foreign military to local people, as did the nature and form of the rape.

History of the War

Located just north of Australia, Timor-Leste is a small island nation on the eastern half of the island of Timor; the western half of the island is part of Indonesia.[5] A neglected colony of Portugal for over four hundred years, it is one of two Roman Catholic–majority countries in Asia (the other is the Philippines). When the 1974 Carnation Revolution brought about the decolonization of all of Portugal's colonies, Timor-Leste was suddenly faced with a power vacuum. Once Portugal withdrew, in 1975, Timor-Leste experienced a brief and deadly two-week-long civil war, orchestrated in part through covert operations by Indonesia. Three main groups struggled to establish a power base and international political recognition under the already-present threat of Indonesian invasion: Fretilin (Frente Revolucionária de Timor-Leste Independente, or the Revolutionary Front for an Independent Timor), UDT (União Democrática Timorense, or the Timorese Independent Union), and Apodeti (Associação Popular Democratica Timorense, or Timorese Popular Democratic Association). The three groups differed in their ideas of what was best for the future; UDT and Apodeti supported some degree of integration with Portugal and Indonesia, respectively, while Fretilin advocated full independence. Fretilin, the early victor, raced to declare Timor-Leste's independence. The UDT leaders, who had faced fierce violence from Fretilin, then escaped to West Timor and formally requested that Indonesia support their cause (Myrttinen 2009; Rees 2004).[6]

Timor-Leste was independent for only nine days before Indonesia launched a massive invasion—by land, over the border with West Timor, as well as by sea and air. The half-island was annexed and declared the twenty-seventh province of Indonesia in July 1976, a move that was officially recognized by Australia and the United States but never formally recognized by the United Nations. The subsequent occupation of Timor-Leste by Indonesia lasted twenty-four years, until a UN-backed referendum for independence was held in 1999. Falintil (Forças Armadas da Libertação Nacional de Timor-Leste, or the Armed Forces for the National Liberation of East Timor), the guerrilla force and military arm of Fretilin, was the main pro-independence insurgent group that fought against the Indonesian forces from 1975 to 1999. The resistance movement was divided into three main fronts: fighters based in the jungle, an urban clandestine movement that supported the fighters, and a political movement that sought attention and funds from international solidarity groups.[7]

The occupation period included the institution of a new official language, Bahasa Indonesia, and a state program to populate Timor-Leste with Indonesians. Both of these programs, combined with rumors of a system of forced sterilization, later fueled arguments for viewing the Indonesian violence in Timor-Leste as genocide. While ruling through brutal force, the Indonesian occupation nonetheless featured significant investments in developing Timor-Leste, both economic and social, including increasing the local literacy rate and building a large number of schools (Myrttinen 2009).[8]

The central reason for the initial Indonesian invasion was ostensibly to prevent a communist victory in Timor-Leste. Indonesian fears about the future of an independent Timor-Leste were centered on the possibility that either China or the Soviet Union would attempt to use Timor-Leste as a base for operations in the region. Another reason for the Indonesian interest in Timor-Leste was a concern that other groups on other islands in the Indonesian archipelago would similarly declare independence, causing massive destabilization of the Indonesian state. Indonesia claimed that the East Timorese desire for independence was undermined by the purported ethnic similarity of the East Timorese population to that of West Timor, as well as its proximity to Indonesia.[9] Cold War concerns, both strategic and economic, including the recent US loss in the Vietnam War and regional oil agreements, undergirded the US and Australian support of the initial invasion (Thaler 2012). The true extent of communist elements in the Timor-Leste guerrilla groups were likely limited and, in any case, were concentrated in the earliest stages of the conflict.

Indonesian military leaders were initially convinced that establishing control over Timor-Leste would be quick work. However, the resistance proved difficult to quell, which is especially impressive considering the asymmetry of the two warring factions. The Indonesian military received military and political support from the United States and Australia, among others, and was armed with American-, British-, and Australian-supplied weapons, which it used in aerial and naval attacks.[10] Despite these advantages, Indonesia failed to win the counterinsurgency war. Some have attributed this failure to the fact that ongoing unrest in other regions of the country prevented Indonesia from committing a sufficient number of fighters to the cause; by one estimate, the number of Indonesian troops in Timor-Leste ranged from fifteen thousand to thirty thousand (Lutz and Lutz 2013). The guerrilla movement, on the other hand, was only lightly armed, with weapons left over from the Portuguese era. Its leaders were tortured and then jailed outside of the country, and many of its fighters spent years isolated in the jungles of Timor-Leste. One local researcher described the "gun scarcity," noting that "most [fighters] did not have a gun. You had to prove yourself to receive a gun by killing one Indonesian soldier."[11]

Some observers attribute Indonesia's decision to continue fighting for a quarter of a century to the perception that the credibility of the Indonesian military was tied to victory in Timor-Leste (CAVR 2005, chap. 4; Walter 2009).[12] The Indonesian counterinsurgency operation in Timor-Leste was marked by widespread atrocities, including homicide, disappearances, and sexual violence, as well as a devastating famine caused by forced displacement to the coasts and the abandonment of farmland in the late 1970s and early 1980s. The earliest years of the fighting were especially violent and included the so-called "fence of legs" operation, in 1981, in which Indonesian forces marched East Timorese as human shields in front of armed soldiers in order to expel hidden guerrillas from the forest. Infamous events during the war include the 1991

Santa Cruz cemetery massacre, in which Indonesian troops shot approximately one hundred unarmed mourners and students at a funeral for an insurgent in Dili. The massacre reignited local East Timorese opposition to the Indonesian occupation. International journalists, in the country for a cancelled UN event, filmed the massacre, providing powerful visual evidence of the Indonesian brutality in Timor-Leste and bringing renewed—although short-lived—vigor to the international solidarity movement. In 1992, Xanana Gusmão, the leader of the insurgency and an outspoken opponent of the Indonesian occupation, was captured and subsequently jailed in Jakarta; he continued to lead the resistance from prison (Gusmão 2003). In 1996, the Nobel Peace Prize was awarded to two prominent pro-independence activists, José Ramos-Horta, who would later become president, and Bishop Carlos Belo, the head of the Timor-Leste Catholic Church.

Estimates of the number of dead as a result of the war have ranged from 50,000 to 200,000. However, the Human Rights Data Analysis Group (HRDAG), serving as the statistical experts for the CAVR, estimated the number of dead to be about 102,800. The death toll includes 18,600 people who were directly killed or disappeared, with the remainder dying from starvation—including as a result of the famine in the early 1980s, or from disease—as an indirect result of the conflict (Silva and Ball 2006). Considering the population of Timor-Leste was less than 1,000,000 at the time, a death toll of 100,000 represents 10 percent of the total population. Some scholars have classified the killing in Timor-Leste as a genocide by Indonesia (e.g., Thaler 2012), while others argue that the lethal violence does not meet international legal definitions of genocide, particularly because much of the killing surrounding the 1999 crisis was perpetrated by Timorese on fellow countrymen—even if Indonesia can be regarded as ultimately responsible for arming and encouraging the militias (e.g., Saul 2001). In political science research, the killings are classified as both a genocide and politicide, or "mass murders of political opponents by agents of the state" (Marshall, Gurr, and Harff 2015, 16).

The horrific violence Indonesia perpetrated in Timor-Leste had been seen in previous episodes of violence, in 1965 and 1966, throughout Indonesia—including Bali (Robinson 1995)—and in contemporaneous violence in Irian Jaya, Jakarta, Aceh, and Papua New Guinea (Thaler 2012).[13] Based on interviews with scholars and academics in Indonesia about why Indonesian president Suharto used such extreme brutality in Timor-Leste, Jessica Stanton (2009, 161–62) argues that because Suharto was a military dictator, his position depended on the use of brutal tactics, and he was able to ignore domestic calls against violence against civilians in Timor-Leste and elsewhere.

Crisis of 1999

Despite the earlier mass violence and battles, not much of an active war remained by the late 1990s. In these later years, Falintil was "weak militarily . . . [and] sought only to survive as a symbol against Indonesian authority and to provoke military crackdowns" (Barter 2013, 83). Some observers report that by the late 1990s, there were as few as three hundred guerrilla fighters still in the jungle. The war continued, according to one former US State Department official I interviewed, mainly because it was politically and economically beneficial to both the Indonesian military and the guerrilla leadership. The official, who was familiar with the politics of Jakarta and Dili in the late 1990s, said,

> By the end of the occupation, there was an unofficial cease-fire between the Indonesians and Falintil. You have to remember that, at the time, it was not even clear that Indonesia would hold together after May 1998. No one wanted to be the last guy killed in a failed war. By 1999, there were only about three hundred hardcore fighters left in Falintil, and only about three hundred weapons. We would go to briefings for foreign officials held by the Indonesians—at the time, we thought this was all propaganda—but they would tell us there were a few hundred weapons and only a few hundred fighters left. Now we know that was true. . . . By the 1990s, [Timor-Leste] was a pretty normalized place. There were activists who were detained and tortured, but for most people, life was pretty normal. As late as 1998, very few people had any hope it would ever change. During the last part of the 1990s, this was really a phony war. The resistance and the Indonesian military had a symbiotic relationship. For the Indonesian military, the war was very lucrative in terms of the money they received. And for the resistance, they were able to maintain the façade of the guerrilla war. In reality, the resistance was allowed to operate, even in Dili, with the [Indonesian military's] acquiescence.[14]

This all began to change in 1998. Following large public protests in June of that year in response to poor economic conditions and widespread human rights abuses, Suharto left office and was replaced by B. J. Habibie. Habibie quickly came under enormous international and domestic pressure to democratize and to institute reforms to address the consequences of the previous oppressive regime, in Timor-Leste and Indonesia.[15] Major international actors, including the United Nations, the European Union, the United States, and Australia, began public and private campaigns urging Habibie to propose a solution for Timor-Leste. Soon thereafter, the Indonesian government agreed to alter its policies in Timor-Leste and—in a remarkable change from the past—admitted to past abuses of civilians and sought to negotiate with the insurgency.[16] Indonesia announced that a handful of political prisoners would be released and proposed that Timor-Leste be given "special status" within Indonesia.[17] In addition, the Indonesian military began withdrawing its uniformed troops from some parts of the country.[18]

The announcement prompted large pro-Indonesia militia groups, supported by the Indonesian military and armed with crude weapons such as machetes and Molotov cocktails, to form in late 1998 and early 1999. The militias, of which there were initially about two dozen different groups, were comprised mainly of East Timorese (Robinson 2006, 24). While each local militia had its own leaders, and there was some variation in the extent of violence each of the groups perpetrated, all of the militia groups shared similar political goals and, by 1999, can be usefully viewed as part of a single military organization (Robinson 2006, 24). Following standard practice, I refer to these groups collectively as "militias" rather than specifying each individual group.[19]

In early 1999, Indonesia agreed to consider independence for Timor-Leste if the people rejected an autonomy status. This decision led to a period of fighting, which included the April 1999 Liquiça massacre, in which dozens of people seeking refuge in a church were killed, as well as two other prominent massacres of civilians, in Bobonaro District and Dili (Robinson 2006). In May 1999, Indonesia and Portugal agreed to allow a vote on the future of Timor-Leste, which the UN guaranteed it would oversee. Portugal, as the former colonial power, and Indonesia signed an agreement in May 1999, under the auspices of the UN, stipulating that the government of Indonesia was responsible for maintaining peace and security during voting. The referendum took place on August 30, 1999. Despite violence prior to the vote, nearly the entirety of the East Timorese electorate voted (98.6 percent), with 78.5 percent of the voters opting for independence from Indonesia and 21.5 percent voting to remain an autonomous province of Indonesia.

The vote, and the announcement of its results on September 4, was followed by several weeks of some of the worst violence in the history of this period. Following the referendum, Indonesia declared a state of martial law in Timor-Leste, and the militias and Indonesian forces pursued a devastating scorched earth policy as they retreated, causing massive upset in their wake. Notably, much of the postreferendum violence was reportedly committed by East Timorese members of the pro-Indonesia militia groups. An estimated fifteen hundred people were killed and hundreds of thousands were forcibly displaced to West Timor. Other violence included torture, house burning, disappearances, and rape (Robinson 2006). The CAVR (2005) estimates that over half of the population was forcibly displaced and 70 percent of the country's infrastructure destroyed, including the slaughter of farm animals and the razing of buildings. UNAMET (the UN

Mission in East Timor) was subjected to threats of violence and was unable to mitigate the chaos, eventually evacuating its representatives from the country.[20]

The first representatives from an international intervention force, led by Australia, arrived on September 20. After nearly a month of unrelenting violence, the last of the Indonesian troops departed in November 1999. Parliamentary and presidential elections followed soon after, and Timor-Leste officially became a nation on May 20, 2002. While low-level internal conflict in Timor-Leste continued, including a brief return to violence in mid-2006 and again in 2008, the country experienced peaceful presidential and parliamentary elections in 2012. The UN ended its official military mission in Timor-Leste in December 2012.[21]

A Civil War?

The nature of the conflict is Timor-Leste is a matter of some debate, both legally and academically. From an international law perspective, Indonesia at least initially viewed its annexation of Timor-Leste as the twenty-seventh province of the country as legitimate (Swaine 2011, 80). Others viewed it as an international conflict between Portugal, the most recent ruling colonial power, and Indonesia. The status of the conflict was complicated by the fact that Portugal had recognized Timor-Leste's independence prior to the arrival of Indonesian forces, implying instead that the conflict was between two sovereign countries—Indonesia and an independent Timor-Leste. The UN Security Council condemned the "invasion" of Timor-Leste by Indonesia. Many scholars see the fighting as the result of an illegitimate occupation of Timor-Leste by Indonesia and consider the "narrative of civil war" (Drexler 2013, 76) to be a flawed one.

Political scientists, on the other hand, generally include the conflict in Timor-Leste in studies of civil wars. The Uppsala Conflict Data Program Conflict Encyclopedia codes the war as "intrastate"—a civil war within Indonesia—until 1999, when the violence is coded as "one-sided," that is, perpetrated and supported by the Indonesian military.[22] Fearon and Laitin (2003)—who present an earlier version of the civil war data I used as a basis for the quantitative portions of this book—address the coding of Timor-Leste directly: "If a state seeks to incorporate and govern territory that is not a recognized state, we consider it a 'civil war' only if the fighting continues after the state begins to govern the territory (thus, Indonesia/Timor-Leste 1975, yes . . .)" (76n4). The conflict in Timor-Leste is therefore included in the lists of civil wars by Fearon and Laitin (2003, 2015) as well as many others (e.g., Walter 2009 includes Timor-Leste in a study of reputation and civil war). However, some scholars do exclude the case from their civil war studies (Ross 2004).

A related debate concerns whether the fighting was mostly between Indonesian and Timorese forces or—especially in 1999—between different Timorese factions. It is commonly accepted that the initial (1974) and the more recent (2006 and onward) stages of the conflict in Timor-Leste were and are between strictly East Timorese factions. To call the intervening years a civil war, particularly those between 1975 and 1999, remains controversial. There is ample evidence that the Indonesian military took steps to disguise its involvement in the East Timorese conflict. The CAVR (2005, chap. 3) reports that the Indonesian forces removed their insignia from the invading machinery and purchased weapons that were difficult to trace back to Indonesia. Some observers state that the subterfuge, along with the subsequent claim that the East Timorese were fighting each other, formed part of Indonesia's justification for its continued presence in Timor-Leste. Throughout the conflict, the Indonesian forces also recruited, trained, armed, and encouraged violence by the East Timorese militias. For example, the Indonesian military began training and arming East Timorese in West Timor as early as 1974, preparing for the initial invasion (CAVR 2005, chap. 4). In sum, while acknowledging the political sensitivities of the period from 1975 to 1999, I follow standard coding conventions in the political science literature and consider the conflict in Timor-Leste to be a civil war.

Data Sources and Availability

Timor-Leste is a particularly challenging case to study, due to numerous complicating factors: (1) the written historical record is very limited, (2) the empirical evidence for the war has been collected and analyzed largely by solidarity movement advocates and activists with deep sympathies toward the guerrilla faction, (3) interviews—particularly with those who supported the Indonesian regime during the conflict years—are difficult to arrange for reasons both political and logistical, and (4) the local culture—especially around issues of rape and sexual violence—is extremely private. It is therefore crucial to consider carefully the data used to draw conclusions as well as the possible biases of sources.

If El Salvador is a case where the (albeit relatively more limited) extent of rape is ignored in many accounts of the war despite evidence to the contrary, Timor-Leste suffers from the opposite problem. The conflict in Timor-Leste is widely recognized as having experienced massive wartime rape, with one observer estimating that "tens of thousands of women were sexually assaulted by soldiers during [the] twenty-four years of occupation" (Dunn 2003, 292).[23] Despite dire descriptions of rape, one finds a frustrating lack of direct empirical evidence of its occurrence.[24] There are several reasons for this. First, a pervasive "culture of

silence" around issues of rape and sexual violence has made gathering data difficult. Second, a limited documentary record exists on violations of all types for the
entire period of the Indonesian occupation. Indeed, there are few records from
that period in general, and the country was mainly closed off to journalists and
foreigners, with the exceptions of rare official visits and individuals smuggled in
by activists and guerrilla fighters during the war. Despite these challenges, a small
number of data collection efforts have gathered detailed information on wartime
rape in Timor-Leste. In this chapter, I draw on the available quantitative and
qualitative data, mainly from the CAVR (2005) truth and reconciliation project. I
supplement these data with my own fieldwork interviews of about fifty people—
including a set of relatively rare interviews with former militia fighters—as well
as other secondary sources.

Culture of Silence

The difficulty in collecting systematic data on the prevalence of rape and other
forms of sexual violence in Timor-Leste is due in part to what the CAVR (2005,
chap. 7.7, 5) terms the pervasive "culture of silence" around the issue, which
prevents victims from being willing to discuss their violations. Mason (2005,
746–47) ascribes the culture of silence to the "complex relationship between
gender, religion and tradition" in Timor-Leste. This has resulted in, for example,
some women being blamed for their attacks (because they supposedly did not do
enough to thwart them) and victims' fears of being perceived as sex workers. More
generally, analysts have noted a lack of social trust, both of other Timorese and of
foreigners. The militarization of Timor-Leste—including local-level informants
who monitored and shared intelligence with the Indonesian military over the
course of the occupation—turned neighbor against neighbor. One scholar noted
that many of the torture victims she interviewed were arrested because they had
been reported by another East Timorese (Stanley 2009, 82). Subsequent scholarship on transitional justice has argued that the long-term consequences of living
under the Indonesian occupation, including pervasive social distrust, prevented
and discouraged people from being entirely forthcoming in the CAVR investigation process (Drexler 2013).

A general sentiment of secrecy was apparent in my interviews as well. As one
former guerrilla stated, "Many people here do not talk about being raped by
the Indonesians."[25] Interviewees report that few attempts were made to document sexual violations by the Indonesian military during the 1975–1998 period of the occupation; in part, this was because documenting such violations
may have required reporting them to local authorities, who were connected
to the Indonesian government. Women recall being fearful of officially reporting

the sexual violence they suffered, instead preferring to deal with the violence against them in more traditional settings (Swaine 2011, 128.) The culture of silence around rape was so pervasive that few women shared their stories with each other as even this was seen as too risky. As one Timorese activist recalled, she had heard reports of rape infrequently while a child during the conflict: "Growing up, sometimes we would hear stories about rape, but only rarely. . . . Women were not brave enough to report to the police. It was not safe. Women did not even have the courage to report to each other."[26]

The fear of reporting rape has remained, even long into the postconflict period. Local women have had few opportunities to speak publicly about sexual violence, with the exception of a public hearing focused on women that was part of the CAVR's public outreach (Harris-Rimmer 2009). One member of a local women's organization recalled how difficult it was to provide services to rape victims in the aftermath of the 1999 violence, even in settings that seemed safe and private. The victims of rape were able only to cry, unable to share any details of their attacks. She said, "The raped women are different even from other women whose families were killed. They can speak, but it is difficult. The women who were raped literally cannot speak."[27] Another local women's activist recalled the difficulty in gathering information after years of working in local communities:

> At first, there were not many reports to share with the [Serious Crimes Unit of the UN] because the women were afraid to talk. [We] had to invest in building trust over a long time. We helped with basic needs, stayed in the villages. Only then could we start to gather their stories. Some are still coming forward, only now, after ten years. . . . Even after we held the public hearing, more women came forward."[28]

The culture of silence has also hampered efforts to gather systematic data on the *forms* of sexual violations. Again, the same local activist said, "It was so difficult to collect the details. We would use soft language and euphemisms, so we still do not really understand the forms of the sexual violence."[29] As a result, many accounts of Timorese experiences during the war mention mass rape and other forms of sexual violence in the litany of abuses suffered by civilians, but few analyses explore the details or patterns of any one form of violence.

Available Data Sources

Organized data collection efforts began in vain after the period of violence in 1999. Timor-Leste was, for the first time in nearly three decades, entirely open to foreigners, and as the UN moved to create a new government, the international community began to focus intently on issues of violence. As donor funds poured in to the country, the interests of the international community shaped the priorities of the local organizations. A former head of a large local women's organization explained that as international organizations began to direct funds to local organizations to gather evidence about the 1999 violence, her organization started to work on the problem of rape. "[After the referendum violence, our organization] had a lot of donor funds and no clear plan. We started focusing on 1999 because donors were so interested in the most recent violence. The issue of women was very popular at the time with NGOs. Several units at the UN were focused on the issue of rape. Local organizations did not pay much attention to this issue until that time."[30] The effect was a major increase in data collection activities, with several projects that gathered retrospective data on people's experiences with violence. In this chapter, I draw on two of these sources, as I explain below.

The largest data collection effort was coordinated by the CAVR, which began its work in January 2002 and published its final report in late 2005. These data were gathered from three main sources. First, the CAVR sought, collected, and analyzed nearly eight thousand testimonies given directly to the commission. These testimonies were from victims who had been willing to come forward to share their stories, from all parts of the country, and they include descriptions of violence against thousands more victims. Second, the CAVR data include information coded from details collected by Fokupers, a large local women's rights NGO that created a database using information gathered during the counseling sessions it provided to victims of the 1999 violence. Finally, the CAVR used data provided by Amnesty International, the main international human rights NGO focused on the situation in Timor-Leste during the conflict period.

The CAVR report has special significance in Timor-Leste as the most comprehensive historical record in the country. The final report, nearly 2,500 pages long, recounts the entire history of the country beginning centuries ago. Notably, the CAVR report includes a 118-page chapter devoted exclusively to sexual violence. The data on sexual violence for the CAVR was analyzed and an anonymized version later shared with me by HRDAG, the statistical consultants for the CAVR. Because the CAVR data are the most comprehensive available evidence on rape and other forms of sexual violence in Timor-Leste, they form the basis of the analysis in this chapter. The data are not, however, a representative sample, and so any patterns that derive from the data must be interpreted with caution.

The CAVR, using numerous best practices for gathering data on sexual violence, collected 853 reports of "sexually-based violations" against 657 victims, which comprise 1.4 percent of the total reported violations (Silva and Ball 2006, 46).[31]

"Sexually-based violations" include rape, sexual slavery, and a third category that includes sexual torture, public sexual humiliation, and sexual harassment. The CAVR collected only 393 reports of rape (of which 3 involved male victims[32]), although its purview extended over a twenty-four-year period, the entirety of the Indonesian occupation. (By contrast, and as further evidence of the culture of silence, the TRC in Sierra Leone collected testimonies on almost twice as many incidents of wartime rape [a total of 626] during a conflict that was half the duration.)[33] The Fokupers data includes 84 reports of rape from the 1999 violence.[34] The Amnesty International data, which covers 1985 to 1999, had 12 reports of rape, for a total of 489 reports of rape across the three sources in the CAVR data. It is not known if each case of reported rape is unique, as it is possible that some cases were reported more than once.

Apart from the work of the CAVR, one other targeted effort was made to collect systematic data on wartime rape using survey methodology.[35] In 2002, the Timor-Leste Gender-Based Violence Survey, a random-sample survey of women on the topic of sexual and gender-based violence, was fielded by the Reproductive Health for Refugees Consortium and the International Rescue Committee. The survey also used many best practices, but was conducted in only two of the thirteen districts of Timor-Leste (Dili and Aileu, both in the western half of the country). One-quarter of survey respondents reported at least one incident of "sexual violence"—defined quite broadly[36]—by a perpetrator outside the family during the 1999 crisis (Hynes et al. 2003, 16). However, nearly 96 percent of the reports of sexual violence were of "improper sexual comments," and no respondents reported rape during the 1999 crisis (Hynes et al. 2003, table 4.3). This is remarkable, given that rape is thought to have been so widespread during the 1999 crisis. Again, this may reflect the pervasive culture of silence.[37]

In addition to retrospective data, data from various sources during the period of the occupation have been gathered by scholars. These include statements from East Timorese who escaped, letters smuggled out of the country, reports by human rights activists, and press releases issued by Fretilin, the political wing of the insurgency. One such source, collected by Hannah Loney (2015), is a list of reports from *Timor Information Service,* a Melbourne-based solidarity newsletter that was published between 1975 and 1983. During this period, Fretilin's minister of communications used an illegal radio link to transmit information about the occupation from mountainous regions of Timor-Leste to activists near Darwin, Australia. The radio broadcasts were then transcribed and published in the *Timor Information Service* newsletter. According to Loney's database, approximately a dozen reports in the newsletter contained information about rape, women being "violated," and women being subjected to "immoral sexual acts" by the Indonesian forces during this early period of the occupation. The newsletter also includes more specific descriptions, such as the following, from a radio transmission in February 1976: "The Indonesian invaders are organising parties where women and little girls are forced to dance completely naked and [are] violated." These transmissions provide additional context to the sexual violations, but are limited in their utility for more systematic analysis because there are so few reports. In addition, several interviewees, including local and international human rights activists, urged caution in analyzing information about Indonesian violence provided by the guerrilla movement. As one former Australian diplomat put it, "I can say that there is one unequivocal fact and that is that there was a huge propaganda campaign built up by the resistance and their international supporters. There is nothing wrong with that; you would expect that to be the case. But truth is a victim of all of that."[38]

Finally, others have attempted to extrapolate information about the extent of wartime rape from indirect evidence, including the large number of "orphans" in Timor-Leste, many of whom scholars believe are abandoned children who resulted from rape (Williams and Lamont 1999; Harris-Rimmer 2007).[39] However, findings from my interviews suggest that these abandoned children were not typically products of rape by the Indonesian military, but rather the children born to women in (or associated with) Falintil. Interviewees reported that children born of rape were, in fact, very rarely abandoned and were usually raised by their mothers. A local feminist researcher said, "The mothers of babies born of rape kept their babies. . . . They feel that this was their sacrifice to liberate our nation. It is related to our [Catholic] religion."[40] A former Falintil fighter said, "Many children were born of rape by the Indonesians. . . . They were not abandoned by their mothers, but you can tell by their skin color that they had Indonesian fathers."[41] Further, a director of a local women's organization said, "Women's families would take care of the babies [born of rape]. This is characteristic of Timorese women, especially rural women. They would never abandon their kids. It was very painful for the women to raise these children. Typically, the parents of a woman would recognize that it is not her fault. The immediate family—not the husband, but the parents—would help to raise the child."[42] A pair of human rights researchers, who also said that they had not heard reports of the abandonment of children born of rape, emphasized that women keeping unwanted children was true historically as well: "Even babies born of rape by the Japanese [during World War II] were accepted by their communities. . . . There are traditional reception mechanisms for unwanted babies."[43] Rather than children born of rape, the orphans may have been the abandoned children of Falintil fighters born in the jungle, said one local historian: "If a baby was born [to fighters], the woman had to throw it away or give it to others to take. . . . Other children were taken by the military, or were thrown away close to a church."[44] These interviews all suggest that the number of children abandoned to orphanages—even if such data were available—is not a reliable indicator of the extent of rape.

Despite these significant data challenges, reports of frequent rape abound in the scholarship on violence in Timor-Leste. Many sources, including data collected by the US State Department, suggest that the extent of rape in Timor-Leste was staggering during the 1999 crisis. These sources also include a number of interviews with former combatants, including a set of interviews with child soldiers abducted into the militias, collected by UNICEF and quoted later in the chapter.

Interviews

The case study draws on original interviews with fifty-three people—some of whom were interviewed multiple times—that I conducted during fieldwork in Timor-Leste and in West Timor, Indonesia, in January and February 2008 and in June, July, and August 2012. Interviews were conducted in English, Tetun, Indonesian, and/or Portuguese, with the assistance of several local translators. These fifty-three interviews include in-depth interviews with nine former guerrilla fighters and eight former militia fighters. I also interviewed a large swath of knowledgeable experts on the history of the occupation and the violence of the 1999 crisis, including representatives from local NGOs in Timor-Leste and West Timor that focused on women's issues, human rights, and the rights of political prisoners and refugees; local and international academics, all experts on the conflict in a variety of disciplines; a former leader of and a former researcher at the CAVR; local politicians and journalists; UN employees, including those involved in prosecutions related to the 1999 violence; international NGO workers; church leaders; and former diplomats from both the United States and Australia. As in all of the case studies, all interviews were conducted on the condition of anonymity.

My fieldwork in 2008 was ill timed in terms of political unrest.[45] However, my timing in 2012 was fortuitous. I arrived just before a parliamentary election. As a result, former guerrilla fighters—many of whom are now involved in local politics—were very willing to speak with me and were proud of the time they had spent supporting the insurgency. Although interviews were all anonymous, several former members of Falintil expressed the desire for me to reveal their names. As one former Falintil fighter said, "My name does not need to be a secret—we are an independent country now."[46] In sharp contrast, it is difficult to locate anyone in current-day Timor-Leste who will speak of their previous support for Indonesia or their involvement with Indonesian forces or the militias.[47]

The former militia members I interviewed were all living in settlements in West Timor, and I traveled across the border to Atambua (close to the border with Timor-Leste, roughly in the center of the island) and Kupang, the provincial capital (about ten hours' drive by bus from the border and on the far western coast of the island), to conduct interviews there. The interviews were arranged by a local NGO that advocates for the rights of East Timorese refugees in West Timor and assists those wanting to return to Timor-Leste. The challenges inherent in interviewing ex-militia are reflected in how few studies of the groups have ever been done. In one of the rare analyses that feature interviews with ex-militia in Timor-Leste (Myrttinen 2009), the author notes that the social stigma of being identified as a former militia member and fear of possible prosecution made finding interview subjects particularly difficult. Locating interview subjects in Indonesian West Timor, on the other hand, was relatively easy, as the ex-militia who still live there are likely to be the particularly hardcore members and tend to live in communities composed mainly of refugees from Timor-Leste. In addition, although some of the ex-militia have been indicted for war crimes by the UN—including some of the men I interviewed—they are generally not fearful of being extradited to Timor-Leste for trial and were willing to talk about their experiences.[48] However, the logistics of traveling from Timor-Leste through West Timor are onerous—requiring multiple visas, and traveling over poor roads using a local bus system—presenting numerous challenges to international researchers. The unfortunate consequence is that the militia groups that were active in 1999 are understudied, and poorly understood, by conflict scholars.[49]

Wartime Rape during the Timor-Leste Conflict

Overall Patterns of Violence and Rape

Violence, both lethal and nonlethal, occurred in three main periods during the conflict and is broadly categorized as follows: first, a period of intense violence including the invasion (1975) and early years of the conflict (1976–1983), then a long period of consolidation or normalization (1984–1998) with low levels of violence,[50] and finally, a massive spike in violence surrounding the 1999 referendum (Silva and Ball 2006, 2, 53). Both lethal and nonlethal violations were most intense in the first and third periods.[51] An analysis of the spatial variation in reported violence revealed a shift over time, with the majority of the reported fatal and nonfatal violations, including rape, occurring initially in the western region, close to the border with West Timor, then moving eastward after 1975. The majority of the reported fatal and nonfatal violence in 1999, including rape, occurred in the western region (Silva and Ball 2006, 53); 81 percent of the rape reported to the CAVR occurred in western districts of Timor-Leste or in West Timor. Silva and Ball (2006) argue that these temporal and spatial patterns support the hypothesis that populations closer to the border were subjected to violence as the militias and military forces withdrew from Timor-Leste toward West Timor.

Rape reportedly occurred in every year of the conflict and in every district, according to the CAVR. However, there is large variation in the intensity of reported rape over time. Approximately half of the rape reported to the CAVR occurred between 1975 and 1984, about 25 percent between 1985 and 1998, during the consolidation period, and the remaining 25 percent in 1999 (CAVR 2005, chap. 7.7). The 1999 crisis thus exhibited a marked increase in the rate of rape.

Victims and perpetrators of rape also followed particular patterns. Testimonies collected by the CAVR include reports of rapes of women in nearly all age categories, but the age range most frequently reported—as well as the highest population-based rate—were women between fifteen and twenty-four years old (Silva and Ball 2006, 64).

Perpetrators of sexual violations (including but not limited to rape) between 1975 and 1998 were mostly reported to be Indonesian forces: 61 percent of sexual violations perpetrated prior to 1999 were reportedly perpetrated by the Indonesian military and police forces. This stands in sharp contrast to 1999, when fully 66 percent of reported sexual violations were perpetrated by Timorese militias acting alone, without Indonesian forces (Silva and Ball 2006, 102). These patterns from the CAVR data are echoed in other sources as well. The Timor-Leste Gender-Based Violence Survey, for example, found respondents most often identified the militia as the perpetrators of the "most serious incident of violence" that they had experienced during the crisis (79.6 percent of reported incidents) (Hynes et al. 2004, 306).

Figure 4.1 displays the patterns of reported rape by the three main armed groups over the period of the occupation. The figure shows that the insurgency was almost never reported as a perpetrator of rape, while the Indonesian military was reported as a perpetrator at low levels throughout the war, with a small peak in 1982 and another in 1999.

In sum, the overall patterns of rape in the Timor-Leste conflict, which are analyzed in more detail below for each of the main actors, show three major trends. First, the reported rape was most severe during the 1999 crisis, shifting in both frequency and form relative to the earlier periods of the war. Second, the reported perpetrators of rape changed over time, from mainly Indonesian forces to mainly Timorese militias. Finally, as is evident in the next section, the purpose of the violence shifted over time as well. While earlier rape was reportedly targeted against certain groups of victims, rape in 1999 is generally described as "indiscriminate"

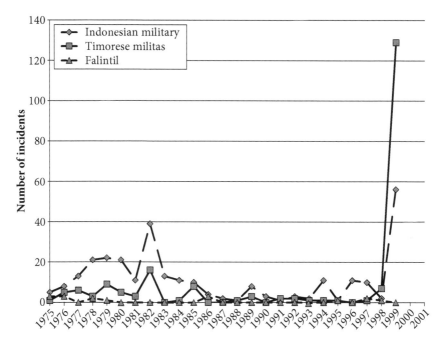

FIGURE 4.1 Wartime rape over time

Note: Data are from CAVR dataset. There are 489 total reported incidents of rape with 511 total perpetrators (some incidents have multiple perpetrators).

(e.g., UCDP Conflict Encyclopedia) and "random, often opportunistic" (Stanley 2009, 81).[52] Thus, in at least these three ways, the conflict-related rape in 1999 marked a dramatic change from rape reported earlier in the war. I consider which explanations can best account for these patterns later in the chapter, but first I turn to a more detailed exploration of the patterns of rape by each of the three main actor groups: the Indonesian military, the Timorese militias, and the Falintil guerrillas.

Rape by the Indonesian Military

Rape and other forms of sexual violence perpetrated by the Indonesian military[53] reportedly occurred with regularity throughout the war.[54] There is a general recognition that rape was used as part of "a tool of state terrorism . . . designed to break the resistance, . . . subdu[e] the population and destroy . . . local culture" (Lutz and Lutz 2013, 105). However, there are few primary or secondary sources on wartime rape committed prior to the violence of 1999.[55] The vast majority of the media coverage of rape in Timor-Leste occurred after the 1999 violence and thus is of limited utility in providing context for the earlier periods.

The existing evidence, drawn mainly from the CAVR (2005) report, suggests that rape perpetrated by the Indonesian military occurred at relatively low levels during the first two periods of the war and was targeted at certain victims. There was, however, an increase in reports of rape in 1982 (chap. 7.7, 16, 22), coincident with an increase in arbitrary detention; much of the rape reportedly occurred during interrogations. A small number of rapes were reported each year until 1998, perhaps because the military had decreased daily contact with civilians during the consolidation period (chap. 7.7, 22). Then, a large spike in reports of rape occurred around the time of the referendum, beginning in April 1999.

The reported rape by the military during the conflict's first two periods generally followed two distinct patterns: in detention as a form of torture, and as a form of proxy violence, targeted at supporters and relatives of members of the resistance.[56] First, the Indonesian military used rape as a form of torture and punishment during questioning; in fact, sexual assault reportedly took place in dedicated "rape houses" during interrogations (Mason 2005, 744).[57] In the State Department data used in the cross-national portion of this book, wartime rape by the Indonesian military was reported in 1993 and 1994 and again from 1996 to 1999. The prevalence of rape for all of these years except for 1999 was reported to be limited (and is coded as 1) and was reported entirely in the context of violence against detainees and as a method of torture.

Interviewees described the ways in which rape was used as a form of torture, against both the victims and the other witnesses to the violence. A former Falintil supporter, whose involvement in the resistance was to serve as a guide and translator for foreigners and journalists who had secretly entered the country, described his experience witnessing gang rape as a form of torture:

> By 1997, I was involved in every protest in Dili. I was captured and tortured by the Indonesians. They put a snake in my face, they burned cigarettes on my arms, they used electric shocks on my arms, they cut my arms with razors. . . . One day they brought in a female friend of mine. They gang-raped her in front of me. She was very brave. She said to me, "This is a consequence of fighting for independence. Don't you give them any space to get in." I was forced to watch the gang rape. I tried to close my eyes, but they threatened to cut off my eyelids unless I watched. I never saw my friend again. She was likely killed.[58]

Sexualized torture was not limited to female victims. Acts of male rape are described in the CAVR report, mainly in the context of torture (CAVR 2005, chap. 7.7, 16). One activist said that she was aware of sexual torture against male detainees. She said, "I heard rumors that male prisoners were forced to have sex with dogs, and that they would use electricity on their genitals."[59] Anecdotal reports also include the public castration and killing of a relative of Fretilin President Nicolau Lobato (Carey 2003, 34).

Myrttinen (2009) argues that a striking similarity exists between the forms of violence, both sexual and otherwise, employed by the Indonesian military and the violence used by states in counterinsurgency wars in Latin America. Indeed, the use of rape as a form of torture, along with the public display of brutalized bodies (Robinson 2006, 53), are reminiscent of the methods employed by the Armed Forced in El Salvador, described in chapter 5.

The second pattern of rape by the Indonesian military was as a form of proxy violence. The military was reported to have raped relatives of guerrillas as a form of revenge, or in an attempt to force guerrilla fighters to come out of hiding (Powell 2001). A Falintil ex-combatant described how rape was targeted against the female relatives of fighters, often left without male protection, in order to try to break the resistance: "One of the tactics the Indonesians used was sexual violence. The fighters were far away from their wives and their families. [Rape] was psychological warfare to make the guerrillas surrender."[60] The rape in the period before 1999 was often described as targeted. A researcher for the CAVR was struck by the organization of this violence: "In the cases of perpetration by the Indonesian military, there were specific targets. Women were sometimes the 'replacement victim'—maybe the wife of a guerrilla, if the husband could not be found. The Indonesians would attack the families—it was systematic."[61] Other interviewees concurred, describing rape by the Indonesians as "a strategy to weaken the fight against the Indonesians" and as "mental torture against people in the resistance."[62]

In addition, there is a growing awareness of so-called survival sex by East Timorese women, who sought relationships with Indonesians in order to protect themselves and their families.[63] East Timorese women who engaged with members of the Indonesian military were also reportedly subjected to threats of proxy violence. A former political leader in Timor-Leste, whose position required that he work closely with Indonesian political and military elites, was invited to a "party" hosted by the Indonesian army. He described his interaction with the local women who also attended:

> When the Indonesian army came from Jakarta, they would go to a village and ask for young girls. Once I was invited to a party at 11:00 p.m. There was a band with music and they told one of those girls to come dance with me. My wife was out of town and they thought I was that kind of man. The girls kept approaching me, one after another. They told me

to choose one—I am sorry to use this language—to be my partner for the night. I told them that I was tired and that I must go to sleep—it was midnight! One of those girls came to see me after in my office. She was brave. She said that the girls had to go to these parties every time someone came from the jungle. If the girls refused, the military men told them, "Don't forget, we know you have a relative in the jungle."[64]

As argued earlier, while ample evidence suggests that rape was as a form of torture and proxy violence throughout the occupation period, it was only in 1999 that the level of rape became widespread. This dynamic is explored in more detail in the next section.

Rape by the Pro-Indonesia Militias

Pro-Indonesia militias existed in various forms long before the 1999 crisis, although older histories of the 1999 crisis commonly viewed the militias either as having spontaneously formed in late 1998 or as having been created by Indonesia in late 1998 (Robinson 2001). However, scholarship in the last several years typically understands the militias as part of a larger Indonesian strategy to "Timorize" (Thaler 2012) the conflict, that is, to involve East Timorese in the occupation process and the violence of the conflict.[65]

Rape was reportedly perpetrated by "auxiliaries" of the Indonesian military throughout the period of the occupation, including East Timorese members of pro-Indonesia support groups (CAVR 2005, chap. 7.7, 9, 77). In contrast to earlier periods, violence by the militias around the period of the referendum was most often described as indiscriminate and brutal, performed with simple weapons like machetes, and directed at noncombatants. In addition to the massacres and the beating and maiming of civilians perpetrated by militias, rape by militias is said to have "plagued" Timor-Leste in the aftermath of the referendum (Powell 2001). A UN worker described the rape in 1999 in Timor-Leste as "much more random than in Bosnia," without any targeting of particular classes of victims.[66] A local scholar described the rape that year as "separate and different from the rest of the period" and stated that, following the referendum, there was "true chaos, a frenzy."[67]

Beyond the seeming randomness of the rape in 1999, evidence suggests that it was also different in form from previous periods. The CAVR report includes a handful of descriptions of gang rape from the period between 1975 and 1998, but does not suggest that gang rapes were widespread.[68] However, available evidence from 1999, including my interviews, suggests an increase in the incidence of gang rape. For example, among the reports of rape from 1999 collected by Fokupers, "more than half of the . . . victims were raped repeatedly, or by more than one attacker" (Robinson 2006, 33). In addition, an Indonesian activist involved in the solidarity movement in West Timor said that he heard frequent reports of rape by the militia and that most of the reports were of gang rape.[69]

Finally, in addition to the attacks that took place in Timor-Leste, sexual violations continued to occur as the population was displaced to West Timor. Rape and sexual slavery by the militias were also reported in the refugee camps in West Timor, described mainly as the result of opportunity (Swaine 2011).

Rape by Falintil

Rape by the guerrillas was rarely reported in Timor-Leste during the period from 1975 to 1999. The CAVR received only six reports of rape by Falintil over the entire duration of the war. Interviews with ex-guerrillas revealed that the rape of civilians was strictly prohibited. "We were told to respect all women, including the villagers," said one.[70] "Rapists were threatened with death," said a former combatant.[71]

In the few cases of rape by Falintil that were reported, the motivation for the rape was not political, but personal. A researcher for the CAVR described rape by Falintil as a crime of opportunity:

> In terms of sexual violence by Falintil, there were very few reports of perpetration of rape. It was not widespread. The cases by Falintil were based on individual motivation, and were very isolated. . . . The Falintil victims were members of the clandestine movement. . . . The women were not targeted because they were of a different political affiliation. The victim in the [village name] case had provided meals, had delivered letters. So it was a crime of opportunity, and maybe of biological need. Often the victims of Falintil knew the perpetrators.[72]

There were a variety of reasons for the prohibition of rape by the Falintil, and for the strong sexual norms regulating even consensual sexuality by the fighters. One justification was strategic: it is difficult to maintain the secrecy necessary for a guerrilla movement with a large number of children. "Rape might have resulted in pregnancy, and that would have given away the position of the Falintil fighters," said a former fighter.[73] But Falintil engendered strong norms that served to regulate sexual relations; these extended beyond strategy to more general beliefs about the dangers of female sexuality. Sexual relationships were discouraged and were believed to be linked to failure in battle (Mason 2005, 746). One former fighter described the local belief in *biru*—a talisman that protected the fighters. It worked, they believed, only if the fighters avoided sex with women:

> Guerrillas sacrificed getting married and having children. It was very difficult. The general rule did not prohibit fighters from getting married. But there was the issue of *biru*—you need *biru* to defend yourself. It is a physical object to protect you; it is a sort of magic. If you had sex or got married, this would destroy the power of the *biru*. So there was not a general rule, but a tradition to avoid these things.[74]

Beliefs about gender equality made for complex relations between the men and women involved in Falintil. Although fighters were taught to protect women rather than abuse them, the guerrilla movement was not reported to be an easy place for women. Women were involved in the movement—particularly in the clandestine branch—but were not treated as equals and were not issued weapons. A local researcher said that gender equality within the movement actually worsened over time, as resources became more constrained.[75]

More broadly, violence against civilians by Falintil was rare. The group tried to minimize civilian casualties and is not believed to have targeted noncombatants. A former *clandestina* who delivered food and medicines to the fighters said that the guerrilla fighters would not rape civilians, or supporters like her, because the fighters depended on their assistance to survive: "I never had a negative experience with Falintil fighters. . . . They [understood that they] must respect us and they must not violate us as women. If they did that, we would be afraid to return again."[76]

There were a few exceptions, including reports that some guerrillas resorted to looting, stealing, and, in some cases, killing villagers for food and supplies in the early years of the conflict, prior to 1991 (Cristalis and Scott 2005, 40). The CAVR found that Falintil had committed violence of various types against supporters or collaborators of the Indonesians. Indeed, having experienced violence at the hands of Falintil was cited as a reason for joining the militia forces by several fighters I interviewed. In recent years, some local politicians and activists have called for a more balanced history of the conflict and a more realistic account of the atrocities. A former member of parliament (MP) insisted, "Not all of the resistance was all glorious. . . . The good needs to be balanced along with the bad." She went on to describe an incident where the president was publicly pressed during a parliamentary session about the relative of another MP:

> Widows are still looking for the disappeared. Once, when Gusmão came to Parliament to discuss the budget, a female MP stood up and interrupted him and shouted, "What happened to my husband? I know that

you know!" There are so many missing people who have been forgotten. It is not only the famous people who died.[77]

What Explains the Patterns of Wartime Rape in Timor-Leste? Weighing the Evidence

Here, I analyze the available evidence in support of each of the three competing arguments. The first is about opportunism and greed, in which the militia violence in 1999 is viewed as spontaneous and unorganized. The second argument concerns revenge and has several distinct logics: the militia violence was directed and ordered by the Indonesian military in retaliation for the secessionist aims of the insurgency; the militia violence was directed by Indonesia as part of a signaling strategy to discourage other regions from attempting independence; and the militia violence was motivated by the militias' own political grievances, albeit with material support provided by the Indonesian military. Finally, I consider combatant socialization, in which militia fighters committed rape not as part of a political strategy, but because of the structural needs and constraints of the groups themselves. I consider the extent of the support for each of these arguments, as well as the ability of each to explain the changing dynamics of rape over time, in terms of perpetrators, patterns, and forms of the violence.[78]

Opportunism/Greed

Some observers have argued that the growth of the militias in 1999 was somewhat spontaneous. They argue that the militia members were enraged and surprised by the outcome of the referendum, and the Indonesian military lost control over the security situation in Timor-Leste.[79] Some scholars argue that Habibie, the Indonesian president, had agreed to the referendum without consulting the military (Lutz and Lutz 2013, 108). In addition, an opportunism argument is the one most typically espoused by the Indonesian government (Robinson 2001). As quoted in newspapers at the time, a general in the Indonesian army blamed the referendum violence on cultural norms, stating that murders and arsons were "part of the *amok* culture of Indonesian society" (Robinson 2001, 275).

The increase in rape during the crisis can be explained by a combination of opportunity, lawlessness, and culture. Members of the militia may have sensed that there were few repercussions for committing sexual violence. The argument is reminiscent of descriptions of "wanton and senseless" violence (Kalyvas 1999) that many who observe acts of indiscriminate violence use in the face of seemingly inexplicable events. Some argue that militias formed with neither assistance nor support from the Indonesian government, while others argue that Indonesia facilitated the violence without directly ordering it. The men who joined the militias are seen as violent thugs, lacking any overriding political goals, who acted spontaneously and were not closely directed from the top. According to some reports, rape occurred when women and girls were left behind when men fled to escape (Powell 2001; Robinson 2006), implying again that rape was, at least in part, the result of opportunity.

Support for the Argument

Some of my interviews, including those with militia fighters, support this argument, specifically citing opportunism as the main driver of the violence and emphasizing that the violence was not ordered. A former militia fighter, when asked why there was an increase in rape in 1999, answered, "It depended on the man, on the individual. Some men don't kill women or children, and some do not rape. But sometimes other men took advantage of the war to rape. It was not an order."[80] Another militia fighter concurred, saying that the choice to perpetrate rape was a personal one: "Rape . . . was based on the morality of each person. I am a man. Sometimes I might look at a woman. . . . When a man has power, sometimes he feels that he can do anything he wants."[81]

A former Falintil commander, who also said that the violence was not ordered, described the chaos during the crisis:

> In 1999, the Timorese were killing each other, stealing from each other, and raping each other. The Indonesian military was behind it, but they were not directly committing these acts. Most of the men in the militia did not have a political view or a point. They were being paid by the Indonesian military, but they had no morality. There were general directives for the militia to capture people and rape people—but it was not ordered directly. . . . The militias were capturing women for sexual satisfaction. Sometimes they were killed afterwards, sometimes they were released.[82]

An advocate for the rights of East Timorese victims of violence blamed at least some of the violence in 1999 on the types of people who joined the militias: "It was a chaotic situation. Some individual men in that situation have a personal motivation to commit rape. And some men will take advantage of that opportunity."[83] A former militia leader who had been involved in pro-Indonesia groups since 1974 described what he perceived as the differences between the "older" fighters and those militia who fought in 1999:

[How were the young men in 1999 different from those fighting in 1974?] There were huge differences. In 1974, we respected the orders from our commanders. Compare this to the 1999 militias: those young men did not respect people, they did not follow orders. They killed and destroyed civilians. . . . The militias in 1999 mixed their personal problems with the violence of the war. They took advantage of the opportunity.[84]

Other observers shared this view, maintaining that the people committing the violence were criminal types: "They were just emptying the prisons, bringing in really bad elements. . . . In Dili, they just seemed to round up local thugs."[85] A former State Department official highlighted that some of the violence was based on old local rivalries:

The violence in 1999 was more random than not. At the time, everything looked like it was either pro-Indonesia or pro-independence, but really things were much more complicated than that, especially on a local level. There was also opportunistic violence, and people were acting on conflicts that have existed since the Portuguese era.[86]

A researcher who had served on the CAVR concurred: "There were also personal conflicts, so the men had an excuse to commit violence because of the crisis."[87] The personal motivations of some of the militia fighters suggest that their acts of violence reflected local-level conflicts rather than larger political goals.

Finally, the spatial patterns of violence may support opportunism to an extent. The violence was most concentrated on the border with West Timor, an area with the least Falintil support and a low level of overall guerrilla presence—presumably enabling the militias to engage in more extensive violence against civilians than if they had been actively engaged in fighting other factions.

Despite some evidence that opportunity might have played a role in the violence, an argument about opportunism cannot account for certain notable features. First, the violence was far more extensive and brutal than mere opportunity would suggest. An observable implication of the opportunism argument is that the violence should be personally enriching to the perpetrator. Despite many accounts of looting and stealing, opportunism is unable to account for the astonishing extent of the violence, including the burning of crops and the leveling of houses and buildings. The extent of the damage and violence is more suggestive of a scorched earth campaign than of an unruly group of criminals, even those motivated by anger or desperation.

Second, an opportunism argument that focuses on the spontaneous formation of militias in 1999 ignores the long history of militia violence in Indonesia and Timor-Leste. The border districts in which violence was most extreme were the same locations where ties to Indonesia were historically strongest—and where the logistics of coordination with the TNI (Tentara Nasional Indonesia, or the Indonesian National Army) were most straightforward (Robinson 2006, 55). The documentary record of government support for the militias is extensive, including communications about sharing weapons and records of payment for some members of the militia leadership (Robinson 2006). The extent of the brutality and the likelihood of at least some top-down coordination of the violence both suggest that opportunity does not explain the patterns. Notably, few militia members emphasized opportunism in their discussions of the violence, even when describing the violence of other militia groups.

Scholars have largely discredited the opportunism argument, although it is still the official position of Indonesia. More broadly, critiques that modern civil wars are waged by thugs without political motivations are common in analyses of "new" civil wars. As Kalyvas (2001) argues, modern histories of civil wars frequently ignore combatants' own justifications for fighting, instead relying on the accounts of elites and diplomats to explain the dynamics of the conflict.

Revenge

A second competing argument—and one much more widely accepted than the first—is that the Indonesian military organized and directly ordered the violence by militias as part of a carefully planned act of revenge. In this case, the 1999 violence, including rape, is viewed as part of a top-down policy organized by political and military elites. Many recent analyses argue this, stating that the militias were "created and controlled by the Indonesian army . . . [as] part of a well-orchestrated plan," serving "as a mere smokescreen for the Indonesian military" (Robinson 2001, 275; Nevins 2002, 624). Still others have argued that the militias in Timor-Leste were "essentially death squads created to terrorize pro-independence forces" (Barter 2013, 76).

The increase in rape in 1999 is often understood as part of the violence of retribution by Indonesia, ordered by the top command. The purpose of the rape, in this view, was to humiliate and terrorize the population and, as part of a scorched earth campaign, to force people to flee the country. Others argue that the militias served an essential purpose in presenting to the Indonesian public a plausible political reason for the Indonesian withdrawal from Timor-Leste. An Indonesian human rights lawyer based in Dili said, "We grew up thinking of Timor-Leste as the twenty-seventh province. So the militias in 1999 were used for the Indonesian audience."[88]

A related revenge argument is that violence, including rape, was part of a signaling logic on the part of the Indonesian state, intended to demonstrate to other potential secessionist groups that declaring independence would be extremely costly. Walter (2009) argues that Indonesia's concern about its reputation under-girded the 1999 violence, the purpose of which was to deter challengers in other troubled areas, such as Aceh, Ambon, and West Papua.

A third and final argument is a bottom-up logic that concerns the motivations of the men who joined the militia groups, rather than the broader Indonesian state. In this view, the members of militia groups were motivated by political grievances—in particular, anger and fear at what an independent Timor-Leste might mean for them and their families. The militia members in this view were not thugs; rather, they were enacting violence as part of a campaign of revenge over the loss of their political dream of unity with Indonesia.

Support for the Argument

The motivation of revenge was a common feature in interviews, including inter-views with some of those who had served in the militia forces. Former Falintil fighters explained that the desire for revenge had led to a planned military cam-paign to punish the East Timorese. One fighter likened the violence to the after-math of a bitter end to a romantic relationship:

> [Why did the 1999 violence happen?] Indonesia had always expected Timor-Leste to lose the fight, but then Indonesia lost. The destruction of Timor-Leste by the Indonesians was not a surprise. It is like a rela-tionship between a man and a woman. If you are dating someone and they want to get married and you do not, they will leave you and they will be very angry when they leave. They will try to take everything from you. We like to say that the only thing the Indonesians left behind in Timor-Leste was the asphalt.[89]

Another former Falintil fighter felt that the military had planned the violence due to immense frustration at losing the war: "Habibie had no control over the military. At the middle rank, they were frustrated, tired, sick. The militia violence was the result of planning and pent up frustration."[90] Other observers agreed, and they emphasized that shame was another component of the desire for revenge:

> Strategically and politically, Indonesia had lost. Indonesia had con-ventional weapons and Timor-Leste only had old guns from the Por-tuguese. Indonesia felt a lot of shame. It is a big country and behind Indonesia was also Australia and the United States, but they still lost.[91]

The documentary record strongly supports the revenge argument—especially that the violence was supported, both directly and indirectly, by Indonesia. For example, many observers note that the Indonesian forces reportedly committed violence alongside the militia, both in and out of uniform (Robinson 2006). A former State Department official said, "There were also some Indonesian soldiers who pretended to be militia as well, fighting alongside them."[92] A former local political leader said that he was struck by how many unfamiliar people—including people from other islands in Indonesia—he saw in a video of a militia rally: "I saw a video of the speech that Eurico Guterres [a militia leader] gave. If you look into the faces of the people—they were not Timorese from here. They were from Alor, Flores, West Timor. Many of those people—they were not Timorese."[93]

In addition, rumors of drug use are widespread, particularly that the Indonesian forces distributed drugs to East Timorese fighters for the purpose of facilitating violence (e.g., Dunn 2001). Many interviewees mentioned these drugs, thought to be amphetamines—called *anjing gila*, or "mad dog"—as a cause for the militia violence, perhaps because their use helps to resolve the troubling problem of how Timorese could possibly have committed such terrible violence against each other. One local feminist researcher said,

> Indonesia used drugs for the Timorese to kill each other. The drugs were pills. . . . I saw the men after they had taken these drugs. If you were a woman, then they would rape you, they would abuse you. The militias were very drunk and then they also had these drugs. They would just wait in the streets for the prey to come. There were many stories of rapes. In Ermera, there was a story about a seventeen-year-old girl who was raped by her cousin who did not recognize her. The militias had asked her where her father was hiding and they eventually killed her. My sister-in-law was killed along with her six children. It is not normal to do this! It is because of the *anjing gila* pills. The pills were distributed by Indonesia.

A former militia leader specifically blamed the increase in rape at least in part on the use of drugs by the militia fighters:

> Rape happened because some men have no morals, no education. And they took drugs. The Indonesian army gave them cocaine and marijuana. We didn't even know about drugs like cocaine in 1974! . . . They would take the drugs in groups. They would mix the drugs with wine and other alcohol and then drink it. They might snort cocaine in Western countries but here they drink it![94]

Finally, a former politician rejects the opportunism argument in favor of a revenge argument, tracing the source of the fighting back to the Indonesian military: "The militias' motivations cannot be excused as drugs or money. . . . The lethal instruments, the drugs and the money all point to a chain of command."[95]

But while substantial evidence exists of Indonesian support for the militias, was militia violence—including rape—actually ordered? Writing on the violence during the crisis, Robinson (2006) and Boyle (2009) argue that the violence in 1999 was targeted. Robinson's (2006, 41–42) strongest evidence is that no international staff of the UN mission were killed, which he understands to be the result not of luck but of careful planning. Boyle (2009, 227) cites defectors, who claim that the militias sought to "liquidate all the senior pro-independence people— and their parents, sons, daughters and grandchildren." Some interview evidence supports these views. A victims' rights advocate shared his own experience of being kidnapped, pointing out how the violence was supported by the military: "I myself was kidnapped by a drunk militia—a child, really. But he had a Special Forces man behind him. So we could not see the direct orders from the regime to commit the violence, we could only see the militia committing the violence."[96]

However, few of the militia I interviewed reported direct orders to kill, and none suggested that orders were given to rape. One former militia fighter said that while there was an expectation that certain people should be killed, there were no such direct orders: "People committed violence to save their lives. If you were told to kill someone, and they were still alive the next day, then you could be killed. There were no orders that were formal."[97] This type of implicit order fits well with Wood's (2016) typology of political violence, in which strategic violence—violence that is purposefully adopted by the organization—may be either ordered or authorized. In this view, in order for the Indonesian military to escape increased international scrutiny, orders had to be implicit and militias had to be employed rather than regular forces. The militia fighter noted that lethal violence was different than rape: "There were no specific orders for rape. . . . Rape was an individual act. Sometimes, before killing the men, the women were raped, but this was not specifically ordered. Rape happened because of personal decisions, just to satisfy biological needs."[98]

Many observers believe that the massive extent of reported rape suggests that it must have been directed by the Indonesian forces. Myrtinnen (2009, 120) states that sexual violence was "used as a weapon of war," and that the militias and the security forces were responsible for "thousands" of rapes. Robinson (2006), who writes that certain victims were targeted for rape, examines in detail two cases where the victims were associated with the insurgency. In addition, activists I interviewed insist that the rape was not just opportunistic, but part of a larger campaign. One local researcher said,

> The violence was ordered by the high command. If the victim is a woman, you must rape her first, then kill her. If you do not kill her, then she will testify. . . . [What makes you think that rape was ordered?] When the militias would attack, they would look for the men. Once

the men were gone, there would be rape and abuse, rape and abuse. This is what I learned from the survivors.[99]

Finally, a former CAVR researcher maintained that orders to rape must have existed, because of the patterns of victims: "The militias' motivations were to create fear. They were ordered to rape. There is no evidence of this, but most victims were related to the resistance, and it was the same pattern during the Indonesian occupation."[100]

Moving from the motivations of Indonesia to the goals of the local East Timorese members of the militias, there is also evidence that the violence resulted from their own desires for revenge or protection. While there is certainly reason to think that the former militia members I interviewed were biased, they offered coherent justifications for turning to violence in 1999. For some, one reason was that felt they had little choice:

> At the time, we were faced with a dilemma. Indonesia suspected us of being pro-independence and Falintil suspected us of being pro-autonomy. We had to make a firm decision, and we let Indonesia know what we believed by asking them for guns. I personally asked them for the guns, and then we got many new members. The commander was killed by Fretilin, so I became in charge of the group. Indonesia gave us the guns because were being attacked and we needed to defend ourselves.[101]

A former Falintil fighter said the motivations for violence in 1999 were based in anger about the results of the referendum and in what the fighters felt they had personally lost: "Most of the militias had a problem—a political or social problem—that was their reason for fighting. They knew if the Indonesians left, they were not going to get positions in the new country, so they were very agitated."[102] Another described his painful childhood as the son of an Indonesian official. He traced the roots of his decision to fight in 1999 to the beatings and violence he had endured as a child:

> I was attacked once by the Fretilin fighters. They cut my nose and my upper arm [shows scars]. I was targeted because my father was serving Indonesia. We became targets for the pro-independence [movement]. . . . I wanted to go to university but I could not because of the preparation for the referendum. So I continued with the militia. I became a commander of the militia.[103]

Others stated that they had truly believed the referendum would result in integration and were devastated when their side lost the vote:

> I joined because I believed that the autonomy side would win. . . . In 1999, I took a car by force. I burned some houses as part of a group. But I never killed. I took food from people, but I would only steal from houses that were abandoned. We took whatever we could find—evens cars and computers—and we burned anything we could not carry. We were frustrated.[104]

Perhaps most critically, many of the former militia members I interviewed disliked being portrayed as thugs or puppets of the Indonesian regime. In contrast, they noted that supporters of Indonesia included both "moderates and radicals. The moderates wanted to analyze the pros and cons, and the radicals believed, dead or alive, we fight for autonomy."[105] A former local political leader flatly rejected the notion that militia members were all criminals: "Militias were not all bad men. Some of them had their houses burned by Falintil and they had lost everything."[106] Interviews with former militia members confirm that some joined the militia forces for political reasons. One former militia fighter expressed a belief that East Timorese and Indonesians are the same people—a belief that motivated him to reject independence: "The Portuguese came to colonize us, but we did not want colonization. We fought the Japanese and we fought the Portuguese. But we are the same as Indonesians. We are one island, and we have the same skin."[107]

Finally, several interviewees reported that they supported an independent Timor-Leste in the long term but felt that the state was unlikely to succeed without an interim period of transition: "Really, the objective of the two sides was the same. We thought we needed ten to fifteen years before independence."[108] Another echoed this sentiment:

> I voted in the referendum for autonomy. I felt that we needed to allow the Timorese people time to prepare for their independence. My long-term goal was always independence, but autonomy was best in the short term. The Timorese needed a better education. I thought that this could take maybe up to ten years and then we could request independence.[109]

Despite the evidence in favor of a revenge argument to explain rape in Timor-Leste, several observable implications are not apparent in the evidence. First, many assume—incorrectly—that for rape to occur on a massive scale, it must be ordered. As argued earlier in the book, the fact that there are many reports of rape does not necessarily imply that the rape was directed from the top. Absent evidence of direct orders—whether from documents or interviews with victims or militia—support for this claim is weak.

Second, while some observers point to the fact that many victims were associated with the resistance or with the pro-independence movement, this description fits most people in Timor-Leste at the time. Nearly 80 percent of the country voted in favor of independence, and given the size of the country, it is likely that most people had relatives who were associated in some way with the resistance over the course of the occupation. Thus, although evidence suggests that specific victims were targeted in certain cases—as with politically motivated assassinations—the vast majority of the violence from 1999 appears to have been random and carried out against ordinary men and women. Again, this a departure from the pattern of violence in earlier years of the occupation.[110]

In addition, multiple sources confirm that the worst violence surrounding the 1999 crisis took place in the western regions of the country—the areas containing the largest numbers of pro-integration sympathizers. As Boyle (2009, 227) writes, "the western districts of East Timor—comprising Suai, Maliana, Ainara, and Ermera—were widely perceived to be sympathetic to Indonesia for their language, cultural, and trade ties with villages across the border in West Timor . . . [and] were also rumored to be willing to secede and join West Timor to remain part of Indonesia." If this is indeed true, then the direction of militia violence against these regions subverts the goal of exacting revenge on supporters of independence. Had revenge been the main goal, the violence should have been most severe in the country's eastern regions, where the longtime Falintil strongholds were located.[111]

The revenge argument also requires that the militias were highly disciplined forces, capable of directing violence against specific targets, as ordered by the Indonesian command. However, the record shows that militias were far from highly disciplined; rather, their violence is often described as a "frenzy," and many witnesses report that they often appeared to be drunk or on drugs.[112] The fact that no foreign members of the UN mission were killed—despite several near misses—would therefore seem to be a coincidence rather than the result of a highly disciplined force. In addition, there is no "smoking gun," no direct evidence of orders; Robinson (2006, 67) carefully analyzes six military documents related to the militia violence and notes that none provides "definitive proof of direct high level official involvement."

Finally, if rape and other violence were part of a top-down signaling logic linked to Indonesia's reputation, the severe violence of 1999 should have been clearly and publicly claimed by Indonesia. After all, this was the first time in decades that foreigners had been allowed entry to the country, and the increase in violence supports Walter's (2009, 152) hypothesis that leaders concerned with their reputations should "seek out" publicity. However, as with earlier incidents of violence that had leaked into the international media, Indonesian forces took great pains to disguise the full extent of their involvement in the violence, instead arming and supporting local militias.[113] If publicizing violence and creating fear were the goal, there would have been no need to arm local militias.

Combatant Socialization

The combatant socialization argument suggests that armed groups that abduct their fighters are more likely to commit acts of rape—especially gang rape—than are groups that recruit members through more voluntary means. Several observable implications of the argument are crucial: first, that a correlation exists between the frequency of extreme recruitment methods and the perpetration of rape; second, that the rape by groups with abducted members takes the form of gang rape and is not necessarily targeted against specific groups; and third, that groups that use extreme forced recruitment struggle with internal cohesion, which violence—and especially sexual violence—helps them to resolve.

In order to examine the support for the argument, I first briefly review the recruitment practices of each of the major armed factions over the period of conflict in Timor-Leste; I then turn to the particular observable implications.

Recruitment by the Indonesian Armed Forces

The Indonesian military divided its forces into two categories: organic forces, which were recruited and stationed locally; and nonorganic forces, which were recruited and used across the country, such as the strategic reserve units (Myrttinen 2009). Throughout the entire study period, the Indonesian military recruited its Indonesian fighters through a system of conscription. In reports from the US State Department, as well as a news search in LexisNexis, I found no reports of large-scale press-ganging of Indonesian fighters by the Indonesian military.

However, during most of the conflict, the military used press-ganging to recruit East Timorese—though mostly for forced labor, rather than to serve as combatants.[114] The CAVR collected testimonies that reflect about 2,100 incidents of forced recruitment, affecting about two thousand different victims (Silva and Ball 2006, 46). In general, forced recruitment mainly affected adult men; for every act of forced recruitment against a female victim, the CAVR documented about 12 against male victims (Silva and Ball 2006, 55). However, there are reports of children being forcibly recruited, including young women who were forced to perform domestic tasks (CAVR 2005). A Fretilin radio message from March 1978, later transcribed in the *Timor Information Service* (1978, 15) newsletter, describes East Timorese being forced to serve as human shields: "Captured

Timorese women and children and old men are being forced to march in front of the Indonesian troops as they advance. Any civilians refusing to do so are immediately killed."

Throughout the period of the occupation, the Indonesian forces implemented a system of forced labor called TBO (Tenaga Bantuan Operasi, or Operation Assistance Force). The TBO recruits were mainly used in support roles, for example, carrying supplies and serving as scouts and spies (CAVR 2005, chap. 7.5, 30). Increased incidents of forced recruitment occurred mostly during two periods, according to the CAVR (2005) data. The first was in 1981, in conjunction with the "fence of legs" operation, during which the Indonesian forces press-ganged tens of thousands of civilians to participate in a forced march designed to expel guerrilla fighters out of the jungle (chap. 7.5, 35). Notably, very few of the abducted East Timorese were armed prior to 1999, and most reportedly performed acts of forced labor rather than serving as combatants.[115] However, this changed during the second period of increased forced recruitment, around the time of the referendum, during which militia members were abducted through "systematic forced recruitment" (chap. 7.5, 5) and were armed to serve as fighters.

Recruitment by the Pro-Indonesian Militias

Militias have existed in some form—and in much smaller numbers—in Timor-Leste since the time of Portuguese colonization, but starting in mid-1998 a substantial number of pro-Indonesian militias were established or revitalized. East Timorese joined these groups in large numbers; estimates of the number of militia members range from eight to twelve thousand (Myrttinen 2009) to thirteen to twenty thousand (Boyle 2009). The Indonesian armed forces financed the militias, and the army, the police, and some military units trained them (Robinson 2006; Myrttinen 2009).

In most descriptions of their recruitment, the majority of militia fighters were forced to join, frequently through abduction and coercion. The militia recruitment process is explicitly referred to as "press-ganging" in some reports (e.g., Powell 2001). Additionally, multiple sources confirm that militia fighters were recruited through a system of conscription at the village level, in which militia commanders were "given recruitment targets for each village" (Stanley 2009). In a testimony given to the CAVR, one militia fighter explained that he had joined after his name was submitted by the leader of his village. Each village head had been asked to provide the names of fifty young men to be recruited as militia (CAVR 2005, chap. 7.3, 132). An activist who works with former militia in West Timor said that many of those who were forced to join militias were ordinary men without military experience, not trained fighters.[116] Coercion or the threat of violence was a central recruitment method, and joining the militias was viewed as a way for those living in areas where the local administration was openly pro-Indonesian to avoid violent retribution (Myrttinen 2009). A victims' rights advocate said that some joined because they were afraid: "People at the time were very scared, and they joined the militias to save their lives."[117] Scholarly authors concur that a "considerable number . . . joined under duress" (Robinson 2001, 277). Even so, few Timorese today empathize with the abducted militia fighters. As one victims' rights advocate emphasized, "These were bad people, even if they were forced to fight. They would shoot babies and pregnant women dead."[118]

However, not all militia fighters were abducted or coerced. Some accounts characterize militia members as criminals, power-hungry thugs, and even sociopaths, drawn mainly from the lower classes, who were attracted to the militias for money or prestige (Robinson 2001; Myrttinen 2009). Few analyses recognize the fact that at least some militia fighters joined voluntarily. Politically motivated, these fighters had support from those who opposed independence; in the words of Myrttinen (2009, 114), the militias were the "legitimate voice" of those who favored integration with Indonesia. Those who willingly joined the militias did so for a variety of reasons. Stanley (2009, 81) writes that "a fair number of East Timorese chose to join the militias—to enact revenge for Fretilin-led violence in the 1980s, to gain power through the carrying of arms, or to show support to the regime in which their family had done well." A former militia fighter expressed exactly this type of motivation for joining the Aitarak militia, the largest and most feared of the various militia groups, based in the capital city of Dili: "I decided to join because I was a civil servant. Indonesia was a good government and the Indonesians I knew were good men."[119]

Myrttinen maintains that the "hard core" militia members, including those who had served with the Indonesian military or in the police forces and those who had business relationships with Indonesia, often joined because they perceived political, economic, and social benefits to integration with Indonesia. Some joined because they had been targeted by Falintil fighters in the earlier period of fighting. Other volunteers, less committed to the cause of integration, were attracted to the militias because of promises of a salary or other goods, as well as a belief that joining the militia might provide them and their families some protection from the militia violence. A former researcher for the CAVR said, "The men joined in order to feel more secure, and to receive money and food."[120] The militias also attracted some fighters with the offer of social prestige. As one researcher recalled, "The militias were the image of cool masculinity. They were armed, trained, they had motorcycles and sunglasses. They looked like rock stars in the news media."[121] In contrast to the conventional view of militia members, some interviewees described their militia involvement as an act of Indonesian and Timorese patriotism, seeing themselves as political actors (see also Myrttinen 2009). In sum, although the vast majority of the militia fighters were ordinary men who were forced to join, more recent research reveals that a small—and frequently ignored—minority joined voluntarily.

Recruitment by Falintil

Recruitment into the guerrilla forces was generally voluntary, in contrast to recruitment by the militias; the available sources contain very few reports that Falintil forcibly recruited its members. The CAVR documented only 122 acts of forced recruitment by resistance fighters between 1974 and 1999, comprising about 6 percent of the total reports of forced recruitment by all parties (Silva and Ball 2006, 92). One former Falintil fighter recalled "many very young volunteers" and added, "My decision to join came from my heart."[122] He had also served as a recruiter for Falintil later in his career, and he described meeting with groups of people to convince them of the justice of the cause. "We mainly recruited through word of mouth," he said. Another former Falintil fighter said that he had volunteered to fight at the age of seventeen, along with his brother and a friend, and they had all served in the same unit.[123] Besides the armed guerrillas, the fighters were aided by volunteer noncombatants in the other two fronts of the resistance—the *clandestinos* based in the cities, who helped the guerrillas with logistical support and supplies, and the international political movement.

Support for the Argument

The central observable implication of the combatant socialization argument is that reports of forced recruitment should be correlated with reports of rape. As shown previously, in figure 4.1, the most notable pattern is that of the militias, who were consistently reported as perpetrators of rape at lower levels of frequency than the military—until 1999, when they were reportedly the perpetrators of the largest spike in rape during the conflict. Figure 4.2 shows data for the militia groups only, for sexual violations and forced recruitment over time. The two types of violence follow largely similar patterns, both experiencing a series of small peaks between 1975 and the early 1980s. The figures also clearly demonstrate a key pattern: the most severe period for both violations, by far, was in 1999, when both types of violence experienced a massive spike relative to earlier periods.

A related implication is that rape should mainly be perpetrated by groups with low social cohesion, and especially by those groups reported to abduct new members. The argument can help resolve why reports of rape were fairly

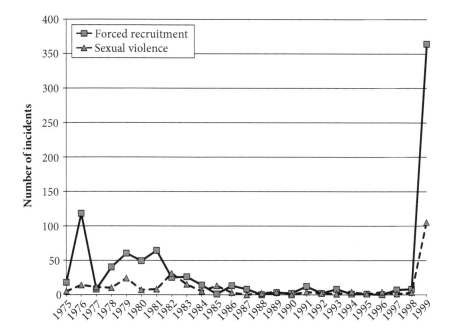

FIGURE 4.2 Wartime rape and forced recruitment by militias

Note: Data are from CAVR dataset. Militias perpetrated a total of 364 incidents of forced recruitment and 105 incidents of sexual violations.

infrequent in the first two periods of the conflict, when the Indonesian military was not abducting local people to serve as fighters. In addition, as the argument predicts, the guerrillas—comprised almost entirely of volunteer fighters—were rarely reported as perpetrators of rape in any period of the conflict.

A second observable implication is that the rape by groups with abducted fighters takes the form of gang rape and is not necessarily targeted against specific groups. The pattern of targeting and form was presented in the previous sections—rape was reportedly indiscriminate, gang rape likely increased during the 1999 crisis, and combatants who had largely been abducted were the main perpetrators.

A third implication is that armed groups that used methods of extreme forced recruitment struggled with internal cohesion, which sexual violence helped them to resolve. Interviews with former militia fighters, and those who worked with them, reveal the poor internal cohesion of the militia groups in 1999. One broad pattern is the engagement of militias in a large recruitment campaign around the period of the referendum, resulting in a sizable influx of new members. A human rights researcher noted that these new recruits were younger and inexperienced:

"The people who were recruited to the militias in 1999 included many new people. The leadership was older. Eurico Guterres [the leader of the Aitarak militia], for example, was recruited in the early 1990s. Many of the followers in 1999 were unemployed youths. They were mostly unemployed men."[124] Journalist Mark Landler, writing in 1999 about the refugees fleeing the violence, noted that "the militia groups often force[d] young people to join their ranks" (*New York Times*, September 16, 1999). A detailed report on the use of child soldiers in Timor-Leste noted that the militias formed around the period of the referendum "needed numbers in order to fulfill their aims in a very short time, and therefore once adult recruit pools were exhausted, they used youth to fill their ranks" (Barry 2001, 16). Further, the report identified that "there was a massive recruitment drive in the [western] region and many youth who were under-18 were forced to join the militia" (Barry 2001, 17). This type of fast, large-scale forced recruitment seems to be particularly associated with group rape in the context of conflict.

A former member of Aitarak, the militia based in Dili that is said to have committed a large proportion of the violence, including two of the most prominent massacres, recalled in an interview that the militia comprised many different types of people, few of whom had known each other before joining: "The average fighter was between seventeen and fifty years old. The men came from all different districts, different political parties. There were high school graduates, a few university graduates, and many illiterate people."[125] A former militia fighter from a different part of the country saw sharp differences between Aitarak and his own militia: "The members of my militia knew each other. But Aitarak was different—the people did not know each other. The majority of the men did not know each other before they joined."[126] Another former militia fighter said that many new recruits had been abducted and then integrated into his group: "Many new people joined the militia in 1999. Many of the people were enemies before they joined. . . . Some were also forced to join my group."[127] Thus, the groups using abduction to garner fighters were composed of members who often did not know or trust one another.

It may be asked why socialization is necessary in armed groups that are expected to be fairly short-lived, like the militias in Timor-Leste. The answer may be that even groups that expect to exist for only a short time need to function as a group in order to accomplish their goals. In addition, the chaos and the mass displacement of the war meant that Timorese social networks were dispersed, and the future uncertain. It was not clear to the fighters at the time how short-lived the militias would be, or even, prior to the referendum, what the outcome of the vote would be.

Even if militia members did recognize that their involvement would be relatively brief, the groups invested in rituals to integrate new members. Several fighters described ceremonies meant to initiate the new membership, including a blood-drinking ritual. As one former militia leader described, "We had a blood-drinking swearing-in ceremony. During the ceremony, we encouraged the members to obey the rules. We also swore that we would take care of their families if they got killed."[128] Threats were also commonly attached to leaving the militia. When asked how new recruits were made part of the group, one militia member replied, "We would provide an orientation to explain the objectives of the group. There were no swearing rituals but we gave a threat: if you are a part of us, you must stay with us. You can run away but we will find you and we will kill you."[129]

Because few former militia fighters admitted that their particular unit perpetrated rape—unlike in Sierra Leone—there is no direct interview evidence from my fieldwork that rape served as a cohesion-building activity. Instead, some interviews that others have conducted offer suggestive evidence of the mechanism. A UNICEF (2001) study of child soldiers in East Asia and the Pacific features interviews with thirteen former fighters, many of whom had served with the militias in the 1999 crisis in Timor-Leste. Excerpts from these interviews indicate that rape was perpetrated in groups and seemed to serve as an initiation rite meant to integrate young boys into the groups. One boy said that participating in gang rape was one of his first acts of violence upon joining the militia (Barry 2001, 63), and he described a subculture of celebrating sexual violence:

> The first time they took me from my house we had to rape a woman and then kill anything we could find, like animals and people. . . . They threatened me and told me that I had to kill people and rape women. . . . If we did a good job we received money or rice and would be given better jobs. Many of our commanders were. The first commander because he killed many people and raped many women—he was a bad man and we were afraid of him. (Barry 2001, 65)

Another interviewee, quoted at the start of this chapter, described a similar atmosphere, in which rape was a topic to brag about and a form of violence to be celebrated.

In addition to these reports by witnesses and perpetrators of rape, indirect evidence, such as the communities of former militia fighters who now live together in West Timor, certainly suggests that serving in the militias created a sense of cohesion, even among fighters who joined involuntarily. While living in exile may itself create a sense of community among the former fighters, it is also plausible that bonds of cohesion began to form in the process of violent socialization amid the chaos of the 1999 crisis. Estimates of the number of East Timorese living in West Timor vary dramatically; however, when the UNHCR (UN High Commissioner for Refugees) ended its mission in 2002, the agency estimated that about

28,000 people remained—approximately 10 percent of the estimated 250,000 people displaced as a result of the 1999 violence (ICG 2011).

Rape occurred throughout Indonesia's occupation of Timor-Leste, yet it appears that, prior to 1999, it was mainly a targeted form of violence, used by military forces against supporters of the resistance. The nature of rape changed abruptly in 1999. Militia fighters, not Indonesian forces, were the primary perpetrators; the violence was far more indiscriminate; and an increase occurred in reports of gang rape. What explains the patterns of rape in Timor-Leste?

At least four plausible arguments explain the spike in violence during the 1999 crisis in Timor-Leste: first, an opportunism argument, in which local criminal types took advantage of the chaos of the referendum period to act on their personal motivations; second, a revenge argument, in which the violence, including rape, was ordered by the Indonesian military as part of an organized scorched earth military campaign or as an example to other potential challengers or, third, was organized from the bottom up because of the militias' political grievances; and fourth, a combatant socialization argument, in which members of the militias were neither thugs nor puppets, but rather ordinary men—largely forced to join the militia groups—who participated in rape in order to create cohesive armed units.

Each of these arguments finds some support in the evidentiary record. The opportunism/greed argument can help to explain the motivations of some of the voluntary members of the militias. The revenge argument can best account for the evidence that the Indonesian military provided support and weapons to the local militia fighters. The combatant socialization argument, however, can resolve the puzzling questions posed at the beginning of the chapter. The argument suggests the worst period of the reported rape occurred during the 1999 post-referendum crisis—and was perpetrated by Timorese against other Timorese—at least in part because most militia members had been abducted into the groups. The argument can also help to explain why the nature of rape changed in 1999, as compared to the rest of the conflict, and why the rape increased in severity and became less targeted.

LESS FREQUENT RAPE IN WARTIME
El Salvador (1980–1992)

> Sometimes, when we arrived in some places, the soldiers in my unit would violate the women. Like when they'd see a woman alone, carrying water. Mostly, it was gang rape, in front of the other soldiers—but not in front of the *campesinos* or the commander. . . . I maybe saw one rape per year in my unit.

—Former Armed Forces soldier, San Salvador, March 31, 2009

> The FMLN [Farabundo Martí National Liberation Front] had strict rules regarding the interactions with the community. We must offer cash for food and animals. If a civilian was killed on purpose, the punishment was for the guerrilla to be killed. I never heard of a rape by the Resistencia Nacional or any other FMLN organization. To rape would have been to act like a dog.

—Former Resistencia Nacional commander, San Salvador, April 7, 2009

El Salvador, the smallest country in the Americas, endured a twelve-year civil war (1980–1992) between a leftist opposition group and a strict authoritarian regime—a war characterized by brutal violence and torture. An estimated seventy-five thousand people were killed during the war, most during the first four years (Wood 2003).[1] The Salvadoran government forces (hereafter referred to as the Armed Forces)[2] committed the vast majority of the violence against noncombatants, particularly in the form of massacres and indiscriminate bombing in the early part of the war, and engaged in the widespread torture of guerrillas or suspected guerrillas in detention centers and prisons. On the other hand, the opposition group, known as the FMLN (Frente Farabundo Martí para la Liberación Nacional, or Farabundo Martí National Liberation Front), was very selective in its use of violence; it had a "policy of protecting, rather than brutalizing, civilians . . . [and] would strive to evacuate civilians prior to the military arrival and escort them to safety" (Viterna 2013, 112).[3]

While the conflict was marked by terrible lethal violence, rape was far less frequent as compared to the other two cases in this book. Nearly all available evidence shows that rape in the Salvadoran civil war was relatively limited in both scope and scale—and markedly so when compared with the cases of mass rape in Sierra Leone and Timor-Leste. Rapes were reported during the conflict, yet, overall, the rape of civilians by the armed actors was relatively infrequent—and when rape did occur, it was perpetrated by the Armed Forces, not the rebel group.[4]

Although rape was more limited in El Salvador than in other conflicts, what best explains when and why it did occur? In this chapter, as in the other case studies, I consider two plausible arguments: opportunism/greed and the combatant socialization argument. I find that although opportunism can help to clarify some of the patterns of reported rape, critical observable implications of the combatant socialization argument are also apparent in the evidence; the broad patterns of variation in both recruitment practices and rape largely support the argument. Specifically, the FMLN was a voluntary group that almost never used forced recruitment and, as the argument would predict, committed very little rape. The Armed Forces used press-ganging and—again, as predicted—perpetrated rape, including gang rape. More precisely, the army, which press-ganged the majority of its fighters, was the subgroup of the Armed Forces that was most frequently reported as a perpetrator of rape and gang rape. Other observable implications of the combatant socialization argument are also evident in the case study. First, several sources note the low levels of unit cohesion within the Armed Forces that resulted from press-ganging. In addition, little evidence exists that the state gave orders to perpetrate rape, with a few notable exceptions.

However, the limited scale of rape in the Salvadoran conflict raises two intriguing puzzles, which allow for an analysis of the scope conditions—or constraints on the generalizability—of the central argument presented in this book. The resolution of these puzzles illuminate what distinguishes the conflict in El Salvador—and particularly the armed groups engaged in the war—from the wars and armed groups in Sierra Leone and Timor-Leste. The puzzles, simply put, are as follows. First, given that the Armed Forces reportedly used press-ganging with frequency, why was rape not *more* widespread and more public, outside of the context of detention? Second, the FMLN had a system of recruitment that was entirely voluntary—except for one brief period in 1984 when it abducted fighters (a practice it quickly abandoned). While the combatant socialization argument suggests that the FMLN would be likely to engage in rape during this short period of abduction, there is little evidence that it did. How was the FMLN so successful in its prevention of the rape of civilians, even when the group turned briefly to recruitment by abduction? I explore the answers to these puzzles in depth at the end of the chapter.

History of the War

Although the Salvadoran civil war began in 1980, the underlying causes of the conflict existed for decades prior.[5] As early as the 1930s, the Salvadoran government had suppressed a peasant uprising orchestrated by the Communist Party, killing thousands. For many years, a small economic elite controlled the majority of the farmable land, effectively creating a large class of rural, landless peasants. Due in large part to collusion between the economic elite and the military, extreme poverty and political disenfranchisement were widespread in the years leading up to the war.

Slowly, secret guerilla organizations began to foment in the capital of San Salvador and in some rural areas. Combined with the influence of liberation theology in the Roman Catholic Church, and its focus on issues of social justice, support for these movements gradually grew. By the late 1970s, a nonviolent mass movement driven by church activists and liberation theology had become broadly popular. At the same time, several violent groups with Marxist and/or Leninist political leanings were also established, and these groups staged large public demonstrations. Facing the prospect of civil war in El Salvador with a communist insurgency at the height of the Cold War, the United States established ongoing support for the Salvadoran military. The Carter administration provided five million dollars in military aid, and over the next twelve years, presidents Reagan and, later, George H. W. Bush continued to send millions of dollars in aid—and hundreds of military advisors—to support counterinsurgency efforts in El Salvador.

In October 1980, five separate left-wing groups seeking to overthrow the state merged to form an umbrella guerilla organization, the FMLN. Cuba had pressured the groups to unite, as a condition for the receipt of weapons, and—notwithstanding some internal differences in strategy and ideology—the FMLN emerged as a unified insurgency against the Armed Forces. Besides Cuba, a number of international sources provided financial and material support, including Russia, Nicaragua, and Vietnam (Bracamonte and Spencer 1995).

Although the FMLN focused on large military targets early on, the insurgents' strategy changed over the course of the conflict. Between 1981 and 1984, and with large numbers of combatants and supporters, the FMLN fought—and was sometimes victorious—against the Armed Forces in conventional military battles. However, US pressure on the Salvadoran government to reduce the violence, combined with increased military support from the United States, particularly in the form of air power, forced the FMLN to change tactics. The FMLN then shifted into a "classic guerilla insurgency," employing smaller, more mobile units (Peceny and Stanley 2010, 69). As a former FMLN commander said in an interview, "The FMLN was reduced to little terrorist groups."[6]

At this time, FMLN tactics centered on economic sabotage, including the destruction of power and telephone lines, bridges, and cotton crops, and on guerilla tactics, including the use of mines and snipers. A former Armed Forces soldier said that the FMLN sometimes poisoned rivers near where the army was stationed, to prevent the soldiers from drinking.[7] The FMLN also kidnapped people and held them for ransom to raise money; some have condemned this as terrorism, but the FMLN argued that such tactics were necessary in order to "recoup . . . wealth for the people" (Montgomery 1992, 118). At this stage, the number of FMLN fighters decreased to about six thousand combatants (Peceny and Stanley 2010). Between 1984 and 1989, under intense pressure from the United States, human rights abuses by the government—at least, those that were large in scale or perpetrated in public—decreased dramatically, but did not cease entirely. Killing was replaced by more private and difficult-to-detect forms of violence, such as imprisonment and torture (Stanley 1996, 3).[8]

November 1989 saw a turning point in the conflict. The FMLN conducted a massive occupation of parts of San Salvador, including some wealthy neighborhoods, and of other major cities and carried out attacks on military bases. The government responded by bombing residential neighborhoods in which insurgents were suspected of hiding. Although the FMLN had had some public support in launching the clandestine attacks, its support was not widespread enough for a large-scale fight, and the group's attack was ultimately a failure. During the fighting, the Armed Forces assassinated six Jesuit priests, their housekeeper, and her daughter at the University of Central America.[9] The killings outraged political leaders in the United States, who launched a congressional investigation into the murders. The scandal—and the end of the Cold War—helped to build support for the reduction of US aid to the Salvadoran government and ultimately hastened the end of the war. Peace accords were signed in Mexico in January 1992. A negotiated settlement with the FMLN featured the opening of El Salvador's party system to an FMLN political party, as well as the creation of more democratic institutions, such as a civilian police force that included both former insurgents and former members of the state forces.

The conflict has been broadly hailed as a counterinsurgency success. The right-wing political party—ARENA (Alianza Republicana Nacionalista, or the Nationalist Republican Alliance)—won the three presidential elections that followed the end of the war. However, scholars have cast doubt on the efficacy of the counterinsurgency's strategy, assigning more importance to other factors, such as the changing economic interests of El Salvador's elite and the end of the Cold War (Peceny and Stanley 2010). Although some researchers have argued that "there is no question that the FMLN did not win the war" (Bracamonte and Spencer 1995, xiv-xv), the FMLN as a political party eventually won the support

of the Salvadoran people. In 2009, and again in 2014, the FMLN candidate won
El Salvador's presidential election.

Data Sources and Availability

Only a small number of primary documents catalog information on rape and
other forms of sexual violence in El Salvador, and very few secondary analyses
are devoted to the issue of wartime sexual violence (Isikozlu and Millard 2010).
In this case study, in addition to available secondary sources, including books,
academic articles, news stories, and policy reports, I rely on three major primary
sources for data.

First, I use data collected by the Commission on the Truth for El Salvador,
known by its Spanish acronym CVES (Comisión de la Verdad para El Salvador)
(1993). The CVES was the first truth commission of its kind—sponsored, funded,
and staffed entirely by members of the United Nations. It was created as part of
the peace accords between the Salvadoran government and the guerrillas, and
its central mandate was to investigate "serious acts of violence" (Hayner 1994).[10]
The CVES established offices in the capital city and in each department in the
country and collected testimonies from those who elected to offer them.[11] The
CVES ultimately collected two thousand testimonies that described twenty-two
thousand separate acts of violence against more than seven thousand victims.
Of these reported acts of violence, 95 percent were perpetrated by the Armed
Forces (CVES 1993, 35–36).[12] Based on these testimonies, the commission determined that there was "no evidence of orders or a policy of rape" (Leiby 2012, 9)
and therefore did not investigate wartime sexual violations as acts of political
violence. Instead, the CVES considered rape and other forms of sexual violence
to be interpersonal crimes, committed for private, non-conflict-related reasons
(Tombs 2006; Leiby 2012).[13]

Along with its official final report, the CVES also created an unpublished
data annex that lists victims of various types of violence, including rape.[14] The
annex includes reports of rape made directly to the CVES, as well as an additional
set of cases that the commission collected "indirectly" from local groups and
human rights organizations (Wood 2009).[15] The records of the CVES, including
the full texts of the testimonies of victims, which will provide greater context to
the reports of rape, are sealed until 2042—fifty years after the conclusion of the
commission.

Overall, the findings of the CVES confirmed what Salvadorans had "long
accepted as true" (Hayner 1994, 599), naming more than forty perpetrators of
violence, mostly officers in the Salvador military. However, only days after the

final report was published, the legislature voted to create an amnesty for all perpetrators of war crimes. This move, which was not opposed by members of the FMLN (Call 2003), prevented further investigation or prosecution for any crimes committed by the state or by the insurgents during the conflict.[16] The amnesty has also meant the absence of another potentially rich source for information on violence in El Salvador: no court cases have held perpetrators to account—and as a result, no court documents exist that detail wartime abuses, including rape.

A second primary data source is the information on human rights violations gathered by two Christian legal aid organizations, Socorro Jurídico and Tutela Legal.[17] Leiby (2012) examined a sample of about eight thousand intake forms from these organizations that recorded details of human rights abuses from witnesses and survivors of violence and their families over the course of the war. The frequency of rape in this large cache of documents was very low; Leiby found that sexual violations of all types represent only 1 percent of the reported violations recorded in these documents, with remarkably few cases of rape: only twenty-nine reports of rape and gang rape, including three reports of male victims.[18]

A third and final source of data is the Comisión de Derechos Humanos de El Salvador (CDHES), an NGO that collected about nine thousand testimonies from interviews with survivors (Hoover Green 2011). The data used in analyses later in this chapter represent a combination of these three major sources— data coded from reports to the CVES, the two legal aid organizations, and the CDHES—aggregated into one large dataset (Hoover Green 2014).

Interviews

In addition to primary source data on violations, this chapter draws on a set of in-depth interviews I conducted during fieldwork in El Salvador in March and April 2009. I interviewed a total of eleven people: one current and one former member of the Salvadoran Armed Forces, both of whom had fought during the conflict; four former guerrillas, including commanders and high-level leaders of the FMLN; representatives from four different NGOs active in human rights advocacy during the conflict; and a local journalist with extensive knowledge of the conflict. Interviews were conducted mostly in Spanish, with the help of a local translator. The interviews are not a representative or large sample, but I sought perspectives from a variety of different parties involved in the conflict. Interviewees were located with the assistance of experts, scholars, and local contacts. As in the other fieldwork sites, all interviews were conducted on the condition of anonymity.

Biases in the Data

The data on rape from El Salvador present a number of challenges. This war is older than the other two included in this book, and both qualitative and quantitative sources of data are relatively sparse. Because the CVES was the first truth commission of its type, the detailed statistical appendices that have become commonly available in more recent TRC archives were not created in this case. Scholars have also expressed concern about urban biases in the data collections by the two Christian legal aid agencies (Leiby 2011) and the CDHES (Hoover Green 2011), all of which were located in the capital city of San Salvador and therefore less likely to have received reports of violence occurring in rural regions. Interviewees in El Salvador had to rely on older memories than did those in the other cases, adding to the difficulty of conducting fieldwork about events in the distant past. This is especially true because the worst of the violence occurred in the first years of the war, in the early 1980s.

In addition, human rights activists at the time of the war—both in El Salvador and around the world—were not especially attuned to rape, which had yet to become the major global issue that it is today. While the torture of prisoners and detainees was well known during the war, rape as a particular means of torture was not a focus of advocacy groups during the conflict. Instead, these groups concentrated on the search for the "disappeared" and issues of state violence and repression more broadly defined. Indeed, Rubio (2007) writes that in cases where victims of rape had been killed, officials typically recorded the rape only in cases where it was believed to have been a direct cause of the death. That said, there were several prominent cases of rape during the conflict, including the case of four US churchwomen (described later in the chapter), so it is clear that activists were not entirely unaware of the issue.

Rape may be underreported in El Salvador for a number of social and cultural reasons. Much as in Timor-Leste, a cultural silence exists around issues of sexual violence that likely affects reporting. The population in El Salvador is conservative, largely rural, and deeply religious, and reporting of rape was—and still is—quite shameful for the victims. Rubio (2007) writes that rape survivors were unlikely to report due to stigma and shame, especially those who were married. Several of the people I interviewed agreed. "Women will talk about the torture—everything but the rape they endured," said one activist.[19] "No one wants to talk about sexual violence in El Salvador," confirmed another human rights worker.[20] Rural women were especially unwilling to report rape by Salvadoran soldiers—either to the police (Aron et al. 1991; Rubio 2007) or to human rights organizations, which were based in the capital.

The discomfort experienced by Salvadorans when speaking about rape is discernible in the reports and testimonies collected during the conflict. When rape is described, the reports from victims and witnesses rely heavily on euphemisms. In her review of testimonies given during the war, Leiby (2012, 41) finds frequent use of vague verbs such as "take," "abuse," "harass," and "bother," which, she argues, are all used to suggest occurrences of rape. Underreporting of—and lack of attention to—rape continued into the postwar period, affecting retrospective studies of wartime violence. A former female fighter in the FMLN acknowledged, "After the war, women began to organize, but not around the issue of rape."[21] Nonetheless, women have spoken out publicly about their attacks in a few cases. For example, one woman, demanding justice, spoke on national television about having been gang-raped by soldiers (Aron et al. 1991). But such public statements about wartime rape are a rare exception.

Overall, even given all of the biases that may lead to underreporting, it remains unlikely that rape was widespread or occurred on a massive scale in the El Salvador conflict.[22] Across nearly all available data sources—many of which were collected at the time of the conflict, and are thus unaffected by memory—rape was reported only in very small numbers.

Wartime Rape during the El Salvador Conflict

Overall Patterns of Violence and Rape

The vast majority of the violence in the war in El Salvador was perpetrated in its earliest years; 75 percent of the reports of violence collected by the CVES (1993, 37) occurred in the first four years of the war. During these years, the Armed Forces, along with government death squads, killed thousands of left-wing supporters, guerrillas, and suspected guerrillas and suppressed political demonstrations by civilians. The violence, which occurred at a feverish pace during the early years—by one estimate, killing over one thousand people per month for over two years—was intended to quell any potential uprisings and effectively put a stop to nonviolent forms of political protest (Peceny and Stanley 2010). Results of the state's violence were often made public, with tortured bodies and body parts left at bus stops, on buses, and on the sides of roads (Stanley 1996; Wood 2003). Danner (1994, 25) describes horrific scenes of "mutilated corpses" that were left in public, including "women's genitals [that] were torn and bloody, bespeaking repeated rape." The lethal violence in this period was largely indiscriminate, with the government making little effort to distinguish between insurgents and the vast network of their supporters.

During these early years, the state perpetrated several pivotal violent events. In 1980 the Salvadoran government assassinated Archbishop Oscar Romero, an outspoken advocate for human rights in El Salvador. Also in 1980, five members of the Salvadoran National Guard abducted, raped, and murdered four US churchwomen, including three nuns and a church volunteer, apparently under direct orders. During the infamous massacre at El Mozote, in December 1981, approximately eight hundred rural people were killed by state forces, who reportedly raped women beforehand. Despite eyewitness testimony of the rapes and lethal violence from a survivor, both the US and Salvadoran governments denied for years that the massacre had taken place. Exhumations of hundreds of bodies in 1992 finally confirmed the veracity of the murders.[23]

In contrast to the Salvadoran government, the FMLN was far more targeted in its violent acts. The FMLN limited violence against civilians to the punishment of suspected informants and the coerced requisition of food (Wood 2000). A former FMLN commander admitted that, at times, a fine line existed between voluntary and coerced support of the guerillas. "You might feel yourself robbed if twenty-five armed people showed up at your door asking for food. But there was a lot of concern that the civilians did not perceive the guerillas as repressive."[24] The forms of FMLN violence reported to the CVES included only deaths, disappearances, and forced recruitment (CVES 1993, 37). As opposed to the strategy of large-scale indiscriminate violence used by the Armed Forces, the insurgency engaged in the selective killing of civilians who collaborated with the state. For example, under a campaign to assassinate members of pro-government paramilitary organizations, the FMLN killed over one thousand people in 1980 alone (Stanley 1996, 2). The group also killed civilians accidentally, in bombings directed at military targets (Wood 2009, 152).

As previously discussed, most evidence suggests that rape was infrequent.[25] Some sources report that other forms of sexual violence—especially as a form of torture in detention—were more common. A unique study (CDHES 1986)— cited by Stemple (2011) and Leiby (2011; 2012, 27), among others—was conducted over an eight-month period by a group of human rights activists who were also political prisoners. The study cataloged details of the dozens of types of violence and abuse that the 434 male prisoners detained in the same prison had suffered. Although 76 percent of the prisoners surveyed by the activists had experienced some form of sexual violence, fewer than 1 percent had been subjected specifically to rape, while 15 percent had been threatened with rape. As Leiby (2011) argues, other forms of sexual violence, such as sexual humiliation, was likely a frequent aspect of torture of male victims.[26]

Rape by the Armed Forces

Nearly all of the rape reported during the war in El Salvador was perpetrated by the Armed Forces. Both rape and gang rape by the Armed Forces were reported, although gang rape was reported less frequently than single-perpetrator rape (Leiby 2011, 218). Evidence collected by Leiby (2011, 234) from the two Christian legal aid organizations suggests that, among the various groups that comprise the Armed Forces, it was largely members of the army, the National Police, and the National Guard that perpetrated rape. Notably, the army was most commonly reported to have committed gang rape.[27] Scholars commonly cite two patterns of rape by the Armed Forces in El Salvador: rape as a form of torture against political detainees, used to gather intelligence on the guerrillas; and the rape of rural women prior to massacres, committed as part of scorched earth campaigns or to compel cooperation with the state (e.g., Isikozlu and Millard 2010; Leiby 2011; Rubio 2007).

The first pattern appears to have been the most common. Rape as a form of torture by the Armed Forces took place mainly in the context of prisons and other state facilities as part of the violence against suspected insurgents and supporters (Rubio 2007). Some scholars write that all or nearly all female political prisoners were raped, while others argue that rape was common but not universal (Aron et al. 1991).[28] The extent of rape in detention is difficult to determine, because of the generally poor level of detail in available documents and nonexistent systematic data.

It is notable that in my dataset, coded from the State Department reports, *all* cases of reported rape are in the context of detention, against captives and prisoners of the state. In terms of temporal variation, the State Department reports reflect low levels of government-perpetrated sexual violence in 1984 and again in every year from 1986 to 1991. The first instance of reported rape reads as follows:

> The Catholic Church's human rights office, Tutela Legal, asserts that while the number of cases of torture has significantly declined, the methods are more refined with use of electric shock, psychological torture and other techniques that do not leave marks. There have been repeated accusations of rape by captors.[29]

In most of the later years, rape was reported to have occurred in "some instances" or in "isolated instances" in the context of prisoner abuse. Rape is mentioned only once in 1991: a representative of COMADRES, an advocacy group for the families of the disappeared, reported that she was raped during an interrogation by the National Police.

Although the precise extent of rape as a form of torture is unknown, there are detailed qualitative reports of the torture endured by prisoners, both male and female (e.g., Stanley 1996; Tombs 2006; Leiby 2011). "During the war, when people were tortured, rape was just part of the torture," said a representative from a human rights organization. "Victims who came to us had been kidnapped, raped, beaten with fists, sometimes beaten with weapons, had received electric shocks, had hoods filled with dust secured to their heads, were put under water."[30] A representative from a prominent human rights organization estimated that the organization helped secure medical treatment for about 3,000 women and 250 men who were raped during the war. The representative also reported that this organization assisted victims of gang rape, anal rape, and rape with sticks and bottles. However, even in the context of prison torture, there is little evidence that rape was directly ordered; rather, "it was used at the discretion of the torturer" (Isikozlu and Millard 2010, 32).

In addition to the rape during detention of suspected insurgents, human rights activists, and critics of the government, a related pattern suggests that their family members were also targeted for rape. One human rights advocate who was an activist during the war recalled that of the women who founded a prominent organization, "all of their daughters were raped. . . . This was dangerous work during the war."[31] She reported a horrifying scene after her own daughter had been taken by the Salvadoran government: "My daughter was captured by the National Guard. We found her weeks later. She had no teeth and no fingernails, and she was pregnant."[32]

The second pattern of rape by the Armed Forces that is commonly cited by scholars is its occurrence during massacres in rural areas. El Mozote is the best-known example of such atrocities. One of the only survivors of the El Mozote massacre, Rufina Amaya, reported that government soldiers raped the female villagers before killing both the women and the men (Danner 1994).[33] Rape as part of mass killing in rural areas may have been part of a (failed) government campaign of spectacular violence intended to undermine civilian support of the guerrillas. Mark Danner (1994, 146), author of a book on the El Mozote massacre, describes Monterrosa, the military commander believed to have ordered the massacre, thus: "he understood that you do this as cruelly, as brutally as possible; you rape, impale, whatever to show them the cost." Other scholars note several massacres that involved rape and then killing. Leiby (2011), for example, cites two cases—in 1980 and 1981—where reports of killing and rape were concurrent. Viterna (2013, 30) writes of a November 1983 massacre by the Armed Forces, survivors of which reported that "soldiers raped young girls before killing them." But despite the pattern of rape during mass killing that features prominently in the secondary literature, details of other specific examples of this pattern are rare.

Rape by the FMLN

There are almost no reports, across all sources of data, of rape by the FMLN against civilians. Of the 450 cases recorded in the CVES annexes, none was reportedly perpetrated by the guerrillas. Similarly, of the 409 cases of sexual violence in the Hoover Green (2014) data, only one is a case of rape by the FMLN. Leiby's (2011) dataset from the Christian aid organizations includes only four reports of sexual violence (however, none of these incidents is rape; three are cases of forced "girlfriending" and one is a case of the forced undressing of a male soldier). During more than two years of ethnographic fieldwork in El Salvador, Wood (2009), who was studying violence in general, nonetheless received no reports of sexual violence by the FMLN. Indeed, only 3 percent of respondents in Hoover Green's (2011, 257) survey of FMLN ex-combatants had ever witnessed or even heard about sexual violence by guerrillas against civilians. A representative from a large human rights organization that had collected thousands of testimonies of violence said in an interview that the organization never received a report of rape by the FMLN.[34] Other scholars allow that a very small number of incidents may have occurred. For example, Isikozlu and Millard (2010, 33) note "some instances of rape" of civilians by the FMLN, but describe them as "purely opportunistic" rather than part of an organized campaign. Rubio (2007) suggests that among the small number of cases, rape by the FMLN was more common toward the end of the war, when the insurgency was weakened and more focused on survival than on controlling the behavior of its combatants. In sum, the evidence shows that the use of rape against civilians by the FMLN was remarkably limited.[35]

How did the FMLN successfully prevent the rape of civilians during the conflict in El Salvador? First, the group had strict rules—and harsh punishments—for fighters who raped civilians. In such cases, the FMLN policy was to execute the perpetrator. "Rape was considered an unacceptable attack; our most important capital was the trust of the civilian population," said a former FMLN commander. "Still, the punishment was not always enforced."[36] A high-level female former FMLN fighter said that she was aware of only one case where a guerilla was accused of raping a civilian, and the perpetrator was executed.[37] The female fighters interviewed by Viterna (2013, 154–55) also emphasized that all fighters knew that rape was punishable by death. One essential prevention factor, then, was a strong command and control combined with strictly and regularly enforced rules about sexual behavior.[38]

A second reason is that the FMLN leveraged its reputation as a protector (of women from rape by the Armed Forces) as a central recruitment tool. Rape—or, more specifically, the fear of being raped by the Salvadoran Armed

Forces—served as a primary motivation for women and their families to join the guerrillas (Isikozlu and Millard 2010; Viterna 2013). Indeed, Viterna (2013, 53, 91) writes that FMLN recruiters, who were mostly women themselves, implied that women could be protected from "certain rape by the Armed Forces" by joining the guerrillas, and that "guerrilla camps were the only places . . . where their sexual integrity would be protected." Against the backdrop of a conservative, religious culture that prized women's sexual purity, these promises proved compelling to many women who volunteered. The FMLN portrayed themselves as collective defenders of the weakest Salvadorans, in contrast to the Armed Forces, "an all-male army that raped women, tortured children and cut unborn babies out of pregnant women's bodies" (204).

The FMLN recruited women as members through the strategic use of fear: the fear of rape by the Armed Forces, and, to a lesser extent, by Honduran soldiers if women tried to flee across the border to refugee camps.[39] Viterna (2013) argues that the intense fear of rape—and the protection offered to women by the guerrillas—was intentionally selected as a recruitment narrative (rather than, say, an ideological or political narrative) because it was the most likely to appeal to otherwise reluctant young women.[40] Situating itself as the guardian of women's sexual purity earned the FMLN deep loyalty from these recruits. The narratives about rape, while successful as propaganda and as a recruitment tool, unfortunately serve to further obscure the evidence about real patterns and perpetrators of rape in El Salvador. The intense fear of rape by the Armed Forces is not matched by strong evidence that the Armed Forces actually perpetrated rape on a massive scale.[41]

What Explains the Patterns of Wartime Rape in El Salvador? Weighing the Evidence

As in the other case studies, I next analyze the available evidence in support of the two competing arguments. The first one is about opportunism and greed, in which members of the Armed Forces committed acts of rape for personal—rather than strategic—reasons. The second is about combatant socialization, in which soldiers perpetrated rape as part of the process of building intragroup cohesion.[42] I explore the extent of the support for each of these arguments, as well as the ability of each to explain the patterns of reports of rape. Because the case of El Salvador offers an opportunity to examine the scope of the combatant socialization argument, I also delve into some of the limits of the argument, as illustrated by the particulars of this case.

Opportunism/Greed

An opportunism argument would suggest that combatants perpetrate rape when they are seeking private fulfillment. In her analysis of the Salvadoran civil war, Hoover Green (2011) analyzes rape and property crimes (defined as theft, extortion, and destruction) together as crimes of opportunity, suggesting that these forms of violence follow a similar logic.

Support for the Argument

Some of my interviews provide evidence in support of the opportunism argument. A former Armed Forces soldier admitted that some members of his unit had perpetrated the rape of civilians and said that this rape happened in places where command was weakest—in geographically distant areas, and away from the watchful gaze of commanders. Rural women were particularly vulnerable: "Most rapes happened away from the capital, because the rural people are more humble; those women were scared to report rape." The soldier stated that he never heard of orders to rape and that soldiers, if caught raping, would be arrested and sent to detention centers.[43] Leiby's (2011, 217) analysis of the eight thousand reports collected by the Christian legal aid societies also reveals that many reported incidents of sexual violence, including rape, took place in private spaces, including the victims' farms and fields. Descriptions such as these are strong evidence that (in at least some cases) rape was perpetrated not as part of a military strategy, but in secret and likely for self-interested reasons.

However, the opportunism argument also has limits. Whether rape follows the same logic as looting is an empirical question that can be answered in part by analyzing temporal trends. Are the two forms of violence correlated over time? Figure 5.1 displays reports of property crimes (Hoover Green 2014), defined as theft, looting, and extortion. The data show 1,462 reports of property crimes over the course of the conflict; the Armed Forces—and especially the army—perpetrated all but one of them.[44] As is clear in the figure, reports of property crimes do not appear to be closely correlated with reports of rape. In particular, the peak year for reports of rape is 1980, early in the war, while peak years for property crimes were 1989 and 1991, toward the end of the war. In addition, the general trends show a broad decrease in rape over the course of the conflict, but a broad increase in reports of property crime (with the exceptions of a brief peak in 1981 and a precipitous decline in 1992). These temporal trends, while only a very rough test of the opportunism argument, fail to support the notion that rape is merely the result of opportunism or greed.

FIGURE 5.1 Wartime sexual violence and property crimes by the Armed Forces
Source: Data are from Hoover Green (2014).

In addition, as Leiby (2011) argues, patterns in the reports of rape suggest a different logic. Nearly half of the reported acts of sexual violence in her dataset took place in state-run facilities where commanding officers were commonly present, and reported victims were not random in terms of their political affiliations. Many victims of sexual violence were associated with the FMLN, human rights organizations, and unions. That said, the reports of the Christian legal aid societies are likely biased toward just these types of victims—politically active and urban youth (and their families) were probably most likely to file reports. While Leiby argues that these patterns suggest a larger strategy of sexual violence as a weapon of war, I find insufficient evidence to establish that *rape*, at least, was used as a strategic weapon on a large scale.[45]

Combatant Socialization

Before analyzing the evidence for the combatant socialization argument, I first discuss the recruitment practices of the Armed Forces and the FMLN. Both the Armed Forces and the FMLN drew their recruits largely from the same pool of people; thus, any differences in the violence wielded by each group are due to organizational attributes rather than distinct populations.

Recruitment by the Armed Forces

The available evidence indicates that the Armed Forces regularly engaged in forced recruitment, including press-ganging. The proportion of fighters who were forced to fight is unclear, and likely varies among the subgroups that comprised the Armed Forces, but the numbers are clearly substantial.[46] A 1989 *New York Times* article reported that the Salvadoran Armed Forces was composed of about 20 percent forced recruits. The article estimated that twelve thousand fighters per year were press-ganged, of a total of fifty-seven thousand fighters in the military as a whole (Gruson 1989). Other estimates place the percentage of forced fighters even higher in the army, at 60 percent of the total (Chavez 1983), or even "most" of the army (Cabezas 1990). Finally, Viterna (2013, 31) writes that "many" of the Salvadoran Armed Forces were boys and young men who were "forcefully conscripted by the state."

A number of sources describe the process of press-ganging by the Armed Forces. According to the State Department reports, the Armed Forces arbitrarily applied the draft and forcibly abducted new recruits from buses and streets.[47] Other sources contain reports of people being taken by force directly out of school classrooms, cinemas, and restaurants (Gruson 1989; Chavez 1983). In an interview, a former *cabo* in the Salvadoran army described his own experience: "I was seventeen when I joined. My 'process of recruitment' was that I was arrested in the street by the army, and my family had no idea where I was."[48] Based on her interviews with former fighters, Hoover Green (2011, 193) writes that "state ex-combatants described their initial recruitment using verbs like 'taken' and 'stolen'; they frequently described the next thing that happened, after the initial contact with soldiers, as being 'thrown in (a) jail.'"

Recruitment by the FMLN

In sharp contrast to the case of the Armed Forces, "the vast majority of FMLN interviewees reported joining the organization voluntarily" (Hoover Green 2011, 191–92; Wood 2003). The extreme repression of the insurgent movement and the human rights abuses by the Armed Forces spurred sustained popular support and sympathy for the guerrilla movement that lasted even after the government ceased its large-scale human rights abuses later in the 1980s (Wood 2000; Peceny and Stanley 2010). The role of government violence in attracting fighters to the FMLN was echoed in interviews. "The National Guard and the National Police were killing people and persecuting students and intellectuals; the government repression was a big help in our recruitment," said one former FMLN commander.[49] By the mid-1980s, the FMLN had attracted thousands of volunteer fighters. An estimated ten thousand volunteered as combatants, including some who received guerilla training in Cuba and Eastern Europe. Beyond the fighters themselves, the FMLN guerrillas had a vast support network; many civilians actively aided the insurgents with food, shelter, and intelligence (Wood 2000, 2003; Peceny and Stanley 2010).

Experts on the conflict find that most fighters in the FMLN, especially in the war's earlier years, were recruited through friends and family (Bracamonte and Spencer 1995). Notably, the FMLN recruited both men and women as fighters. Approximately 30 percent of the thirteen thousand demobilized combatants were women (Viterna 2013), who participated as combatants, cooks, and providers of food, clothing, and medicine and helped with deliveries of babies and care of newborns among the guerrillas (Ibanez 2001). Some women also held leadership roles as commanders and political liaisons. A small number of all-female units fought against all-male units in combat, although the extent of women's involvement in combat may have been exaggerated for propaganda purposes (Viterna 2013, 209).

While participation in the FMLN was largely voluntary, things changed for a brief but exceptional period. For several months in late 1983 and early 1984, two subgroups of the FMLN—the ERP and the FPL—abducted teenaged fighters at gunpoint in Morazán Department and forced them to join (Wood 2003, 157; Viterna 2013, 71; Hoover Green 2011). The 1984 State Department report reads, "The guerrillas launched a systematic forced recruitment campaign in the spring, in which some 1,500 young people of both sexes were abducted."[50]

Experts generally concur that the main reason for this brief turn to abduction was desperation. Simply put, the FMLN needed more recruits to keep pace with Armed Forces recruitment drives (Viterna 2013, 71–72), which increased military membership six-fold—from ten thousand to sixty thousand—between 1979 and 1987 (Hoover Green 2013, 160). In an interview, a former leader of the FLMN said the ERP's decision to recruit by force had been very controversial within the FMLN. "The ERP decided . . . if the army is doing it, why can't we? All hell broke out in the FMLN after that, and forced recruitment was publicly condemned."[51] A high-ranking leader of the FMLN said, "It is true that in some areas recruitment was forced, but this was stopped. We did it the same way the army was doing it: just enter a village and take the youth at gunpoint."[52] An officer in the military recalled, "If a bus was stopped by guerillas and if you had a military ID, those people were captured and forced to join the guerillas."[53]

Abduction of recruits was halted after only a few months. A former leader of the FMLN stated that it was stopped because it was not strategically advantageous. "It did not make sense to force people to stay [with the FMLN]. . . . The people who were forced would desert or refuse to fight. Our only advantage over regular forces, who were all recruited by force, was political will."[54] Guerillas interviewed by the *New York Times* expressed similar sentiments (Gruson 1989). Negative publicity and the flight of families from areas where the practice was occurring may have also contributed to the reversal (Wood 2003).[55]

With the exception of this brief foray into violent abduction, the FMLN rarely used such extreme forms of forced recruitment. However, weaker forms of force—mainly coercion—were somewhat common. Such coercion included "frequently [telling] individuals that they had no choice but to join the insurgency" (Viterna 2013, 112). Hoover Green (2011, 192) similarly notes that boys joined the FMLN to avoid the otherwise-inevitable press-ganging by the Armed Forces. These coercive methods of recruitment were employed by the guerillas to keep up necessary levels of force strength (Bracamonte and Spencer 1995, 22) and were tailored to the type of recruit. Viterna (2013) documented that men and women were told different coercive narratives that preyed on the salient fears of each. In particular, FMLN recruiters warned men that they risked being abducted or killed by the state forces if they didn't join the guerrillas, while—as previously described—women were reminded of the threat of rape by the Armed Forces.

Support for the Argument

Two main observable implications of the argument are testable with the available evidence. First, if the combatant socialization argument is correct, there should be a correlation between extreme recruitment methods like abduction and press-ganging and the perpetration of rape by the armed group. Second, we should observe that groups using methods of extreme forced recruitment struggled with internal cohesion—a situation they attempted to resolve through the use of violence, and especially gang rape. I examine each of these in turn.

First, rape and forced recruitment should follow similar temporal patterns. The broad patterns on the macro level largely support the predictions of the combatant socialization argument: the Armed Forces used press-ganging and perpetrated the most rape, including gang rape, while FMLN membership was almost entirely voluntary and reports of rape by the FMLN were very rare. The best available data on recruitment come from Leiby's (2011) dataset, coded from the eight thousand testimonies given to two Christian legal aid organizations, which includes information on reports of forced recruitment and acts of kidnapping/informal detention.[56] These data contain only one report of forced recruitment by the FMLN, in 1984.[57] In contrast, there are about 9,300 reports of forced recruitment and kidnapping/informal detention by the Armed Forces. While not every incident of informal detention or kidnapping resulted in press-ganging the victim to join the Armed Forces, Leiby excluded from these counts any incident where the victim was reported to have been disappeared, killed, or formally detained. Thus, it is possible that the reported kidnappings correspond to press-ganged fighters. Figure 5.2 shows the reported incidents of rape and forced recruitment and kidnapping by the Armed Forces over time, using data from Leiby (2012) and Hoover Green (2014) (note that the figure features two y-axes with different scales). Although these data should be interpreted with some caution, the general patterns provide suggestive evidence for the combatant socialization argument: specifically, both forms of violence peaked in 1980, and only a small number of reports of both types were made from 1984 onward. However, 1983 is anomalous, with relatively high reports of kidnapping and low reports of rape.

Recruitment patterns from the subgroups within the Armed Forces also support the predictions of the combatant socialization argument. Throughout this analysis, I have treated the Armed Forces as a unitary actor. But Leiby (2011) disaggregated reports of rape by the subgroups within the Armed Forces, and she found that reported incidents of rape were mainly perpetrated by the army, the National Guard, and the National Police, with the army committing the vast majority of the reported gang rape.[58] This pattern may be due in part to the

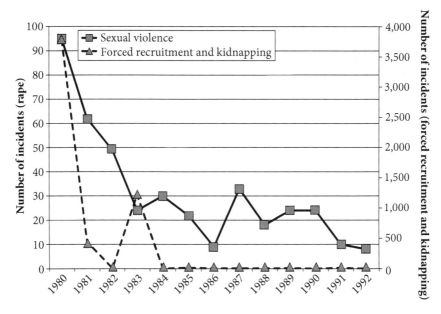

FIGURE 5.2 Wartime sexual violence and forced recruitment/kidnapping by the Armed Forces

Source: Data are from Hoover Green 2014 and Leiby 2012.

army's size. The army, which contained 13,500 people at the beginning of the conflict, had four times the population of the next largest subgroup, the National Guard (Leiby 2011, 234). Notably, however, and essential for the combatant socialization argument, the army is also the subgroup of the Armed Forces that most frequently abducted its fighters. Other groups in the security forces, including the National Guard and National Police, were more elite squads, composed of those with both army experience and literacy skills (Hoover Green 2011, 160). These basic patterns provide additional evidence for the combatant socialization argument.[59]

However, two puzzles about the case of El Salvador suggest some limitations to the argument. The first puzzle is about the FMLN, and the brief period from late 1983 to early 1984 in which guerrilla subgroups engaged in abduction in one area of the country. We would expect this to be a period when those units of the FMLN were experiencing low internal cohesion. In fact, scholars have found that the abducted recruits did experience low cohesion; the abductees refused to fight or ran away. Viterna (2013, 72) writes that when the FMLN used forced recruitment, it found that the "forced recruits were reportedly poor soldiers who defected at the earliest moment possible." Indeed, this lack of loyalty to the group was one of the principal reasons the practice was abandoned. The combatant socialization argument predicts that the result of this decreased internal cohesion would increase the likelihood that the FMLN would perpetrate rape. However, reports of rape by the FMLN did not increase during these years or in that location. Why not? How did the FMLN solve the problem of low cohesion without resorting to group violence such as gang rape?

A second puzzle arises from the Armed Forces. The Armed Forces, as previously described, engaged in widespread press-ganging. Evidence from several sources suggests that the group suffered from serious issues of low cohesion. Scholars have written, for example, that the armed units often lacked cohesiveness" and had "poor morale" (Peceny and Stanley 2010, 77; Gruson 1989). An interview with a former army soldier supports these generalizations; he stated that his service with the Armed Forces was marked by "inhuman" treatment, constant humiliation, and fear and mistrust of other soldiers.[60]

Beyond press-ganging, two other reasons explain the lack of cohesion. First, despite (or perhaps because of) the large sums of military aid given by the United States to El Salvador, the Armed Forces were plagued by corruption and incompetence. Commanders stole funds intended for salaries, and rank-and-file fighters were treated badly by their superiors. The military relied on forced recruitment in part because new recruits were paid a far lower wage than more experienced and more senior fighters (Gruson 1989). In addition, the elite of El Salvador were often able to avoid compulsory service, through bribes, by leaving the country, and by putting political pressure on the government not to forcibly recruit the children of the rich (Gruson 1989; Cabezas 1990). Strong class divisions separated officers and soldiers, who were deeply distrustful of the government (Peceny and Stanley 2010). A former soldier summed up the problem: "The lower classes were the ones sent to the front lines, so that the ones who were dying had little political power."[61]

Second, the training of the rank-and-file fighters was notable for its brevity and lack of quality. In an interview, a former rank-and-file member of the army stated this his training had been only twelve weeks long[62]: "After three months, I received an M-16 from the United States—it was left over from the Vietnam War." He described the training practices as humiliating: "We had to learn how to rappel down mountains. If you were afraid of heights, you were forced to dress as a woman and walk through the cafeteria while others yelled at you that you should leave the battalion because you were gay."[63] Once recruited, leaving the Armed Forces before the end of the required two-year period of service was impossible. "We were told we would face the death penalty if we tried to leave," said a former soldier.[64] The Armed Forces system of press-ganging meant that the military comprised units of "raw fighters," who rarely fought for longer than their enlistment required (Gruson 1989). Given their low cohesion and lack of loyalty to the military, along with their poor training, why wasn't rape by members of the Armed Forces much more widespread?

The answer to both puzzles illuminates the power of the intensive external and internal pressures to curb such violence that each group faced. In the case of the Armed Forces, we might expect the group to have engaged in large-scale rape of noncombatants in order to increase cohesion among its largely press-ganged fighting force. However, after the widespread and graphic civilian abuses of the earliest years of the war, the Armed Forces was under immense external pressure from the United States—its major military sponsor in the counterinsurgency campaign—to halt extreme and public abuse of civilians. Then-Vice President Bush traveled to El Salvador in December 1983 and demanded that the Salvadoran government "end the murders and human rights abuses . . . or the United States would instantly cut off aid." (Solomon 2011). This threat was perceived as credible, and the pressure—felt throughout the command structure—was such that it contributed to counteracting the drive to use group violence as a socialization tool. In addition, the infusion of US funding, along with its extensive advice on training the Armed Forces, helped professionalize the military and, in turn, decreased the need to create unit cohesion using violence. The United States also offered human rights training to the Salvadoran Armed Forces, but this has largely been seen as having proven ineffective in changing norms and beliefs (Hoover Green 2011, 182). Thus, the presence of an external sponsor with strong preferences against the use of public group violence, including gang rape, suggests one scope condition of the combatant socialization argument.

The case of the FMLN presents a second such condition: internal pressure. How did the FMLN cope with issues of decreased social cohesion during the period of abduction, if not through reliance on gang rape? The FMLN's deeply entrenched ideology and extensive training proved sufficient to overcome the challenges that other groups typically face when recruiting fighters. Interview evidence from a number of recent studies reveals that the FMLN indoctrinated recruits with strict rules governing both violence and sexuality (e.g., Hoover Green 2011; Viterna 2013). Viterna (2013, 267) notes that because "*not* raping was a critical aspect of their recruitment strategy" (emphasis added), FMLN members internalized this norm over time, obviating the need for strong command and control because of combatants' self-perception as the "good guys." These rules, combined with intensive political training and education, worked to instill combatants with a sense of respect for civilians (and especially women) both within and outside the armed group. However, this was a complicated form of respect, informed more by traditional views on gender roles rather than a belief in gender equality per se (Hoover Green 2011; Viterna 2013). How and why armed groups develop these types of strong institutions is still an open question; the ideology of the FMLN, and its deep-seated political commitment to progressive rights under a repressive regime, are likely key factors. But these variables have not yet been thoroughly analyzed in existing studies of how ideology, training, and recruitment affect violence.

Overall, rape in the El Salvador conflict was more limited than in the other two case studies. While scholars have found that other forms of sexual violence were common, particularly sexual violence in detention as a form of torture during interrogations, rape and gang rape were reportedly relatively rare. When rape did happen, evidence suggests that it may have occurred due to opportunism, while support also exists for the combatant socialization argument.

The case of El Salvador demonstrates that widespread rape in wartime is not inevitable—even when armed groups are committing a host of other forms of violence, and sometimes even when they are engaged in extreme forms of forced recruitment. An analysis of the armed groups in El Salvador reveals that the problems stemming from low cohesion—which many armed groups solve by perpetrating gang rape—can also be overcome through other external and internal forces, including training and ideology. These scope conditions offer some direction for policymakers looking to mitigate the problem of rape in wartime, to which I return in the conclusion.

Conclusion

UNDERSTANDING AND PREVENTING RAPE DURING CIVIL WAR

In this book I have demonstrated that dramatic variation exists in in the phenomenon of rape during civil war. Some wars are characterized by mass rape, while others never are. In addition, even within the context of the same war, some armed groups perpetrate rape on a large scale while others refrain entirely. This variation in and of itself presents strong evidence against older arguments that rape is ubiquitous, or that it is perpetrated by every armed group. This variation has become a part of the common discourse in policy circles, with activists such as Angelina Jolie repeatedly emphasizing that "rape in war is not inevitable" (Smith-Spark 2014).

How can we best explain the puzzle of why some armed groups perpetrate rape while others do not? I argue that one essential, but previously overlooked, factor is the level of internal cohesion within an armed group: groups that struggle with cohesion are more likely to perpetrate rape—and especially gang rape—than those that do not. Armed groups that engage in extreme and random forms of forced recruitment of strangers—particularly when such recruitment is done very quickly—often experience low morale and a lack of group loyalty among their members. Participation in group violence, and especially *sexualized* group violence, serves several functions: gang rape breaks social taboos, communicates norms of virility and masculinity, and increases mutual esteem among perpetrators. This argument resolves a number of key questions about the typical patterns of reported rape in conflict zones—namely, that rape commonly takes the form of gang rape, and it is frequently perpetrated by "ordinary" people who were not seemingly predisposed to brutal sexual violence. The combatant socialization argument suggests a testable hypothesis, with implications that are observable both in a cross-national comparison and on the micro level in individual detailed case studies.

Chapter 2 explores the macro-level implications of the book's central argument. The statistical tests demonstrate that both state and nonstate armed groups that randomly kidnap and press-gang their fighters are more likely to be reported as perpetrators of rape than are armed groups that use voluntary recruitment methods. The chapter also examines other, more common narratives about why rape happens during war, including arguments about opportunism and greed, ethnic hatred, and gender inequality. The results show that the evidence supports the predictions of several strands of the opportunism argument, but not the arguments of ethnic hatred or gender inequality. The findings suggest that the conventional wisdom about the roles played by ethnic tensions and gender inequality in wartime rape are incomplete or simply wrong.

In chapters 3, 4, and 5, I turn to individual conflicts and analyze detailed micro-level implications of the combatant socialization argument and plausible alternative theoretical explanations. Chapter 3 focuses on the case of Sierra Leone, where rape was widespread despite limited evidence that it was ordered by commanders as part of a military strategy. The evidence from this case strongly supports the combatant socialization argument: the main rebel group, the RUF, perpetrated the vast majority of the rape and forcibly abducted almost all of its fighters. In addition, another armed group, the CDF, changed its recruitment strategy over the course of the war from voluntary to forced, and, as predicted, reports of rape by the group increased dramatically. Data on perpetrators of rape from the RUF also provide surprising evidence about *who* perpetrates rape. A significant number of abducted female combatants reportedly participated in acts of gang rape alongside their male counterparts. While arguments about opportunism also find some support, the observed variation is best explained by combatant socialization. Interviews with ex-combatants in Sierra Leone demonstrate that groups that relied on abduction used rape as a means of creating more coherent fighting units.

Chapter 4 analyzes another mass-rape war, in Timor-Leste. The nearly twenty-five-year-long war was characterized throughout by low to moderate levels of numerous forms of sexual violence, but a dramatic increase in reports of gang rape occurred in 1999, the final year of the conflict. At the same time, the identities of the reported perpetrators also changed—from mostly Indonesian armed forces to mainly local East Timorese militias—as did those who were targeted. Where victims of rape had previously been primarily supporters of the insurgency, the rape shifted to a kind of random, indiscriminate violence. To explain the shifts that took place in 1999, I consider three arguments: opportunism/greed, revenge during secession (on the part of either the Indonesian military or the members of the local militias), and combatant socialization. Although the opportunism argument mostly fails to explain the patterns of violence in Timor-Leste, both the revenge/secessionist and the combatant socialization arguments resolve troubling puzzles. Violence in 1999 was encouraged and supported, both directly and indirectly, by the Indonesian military, but there is scant evidence that the military directly ordered violence, including rape. East Timorese members of the militias, in contrast to how they are often portrayed in histories of the conflict, were not merely thugs or mere puppets of the regime; instead, they articulated political and emotional grievances that motivated their violence. The combatant socialization argument clarifies why the perpetrators of the violence changed over time, from the foreign military to the local people, as well as why the targets and types of rape shifted.

Chapter 5, the final case study, looks to El Salvador, a war in which rape was more limited than in the other two cases. To explore the motivations for the rape that did occur, I consider two plausible arguments: opportunism/greed and combatant socialization. Although opportunism can help to clarify some of the patterns of reported rape, broad patterns of variation in both recruitment practices and rape largely support the combatant socialization argument. The FMLN guerrillas were a voluntary group that almost never used forced recruitment, and, as the argument predicts, committed very little rape. In contrast, the Salvadoran Armed Forces used press-ganging and perpetrated rape, including gang rape. Given the widespread nature of press-ganging by the Armed Forces—as well as the fact that the FMLN did turn to abduction for a brief period—why was rape not *more* common in this conflict? The answer lies in the constraints that each group faced. Internal pressures from within the FMLN and external pressures from the United States on the Armed Forces were factors in overcoming the predicted turn toward group violence for cohesion building. The case of El Salvador demonstrates that widespread rape is not inevitable, even when armed groups are engaged in such extreme forms of forced recruitment as abduction and press-ganging.

Theoretical Implications

The findings presented in this book have important implications for a number of subdisciplines in political science. First, there are broad implications for theories of *violence against civilians during wartime*. Research has established that mass killing by states may be a strategy of intentional targeting meant to reduce civilian support for insurgencies (e.g., Valentino, Huth, and Balch-Lindsay 2004; Downes 2008). Scholars have also argued that lethal violence by insurgents against civilians may also have a coercive function, designed to induce popular support in the fight against the state (e.g., Kalyvas 2006; Wood 2010) or to gain concessions from the state (Hultman 2012). However, much less is understood about the strategic and/or rational uses of nonlethal forms of violence. Wartime rape is not inexplicable, senseless, or irrational, but it also does not necessarily follow the logic that dictates lethal violence against civilians. Why do armed groups choose the particular range of violations that they perpetrate? How do these violations relate to the organization and structure of armed groups, and to their ideologies and political beliefs? These are essential questions for future research.

Explicating the foundations of *motivations for violence* is also possible using some of the results from this book. Because of the strongly gendered assumptions that scholars have often made about the composition of combatant groups, several prominent theories on the causes of wartime rape (and indeed, wartime violence more generally) can account only for male perpetrators. Yet as demonstrated by the findings in this study, women may be active combatants and perpetrators of atrocities, including sexual violence.[1] Are women's motivations for violence different or similar to those of men? Although scholars have considered this question mainly in terms of women's motivations for terrorist violence (e.g., Bloom 2011), promising lines of inquiry include examining both the demand for and supply of political violence perpetrated by women who are members of armed groups (e.g., Alison 2007; Bond and Thomas 2015; Coulter 2008).

Another set of implications is for scholars of *repression and human rights violations by states* (e.g., Davenport 2007). The patterns explored in chapter 2 show that rape by state actors was reported in over 75 percent of the major civil wars in the study period, and that the majority of these wars included at least some reports of the rape of detainees associated with the conflict. These patterns suggest alarming rates of sexualized torture as part of the regular repertoire of counterinsurgency violence—an issue at the forefront of US policy debates following the December 2014 release of the Senate Intelligence Committee report on the CIA's use of torture. At the very least, these patterns indicate that rape as torture is—perhaps unexpectedly—common. The combatant socialization argument may help to explain some of this violence, particularly when it is unordered and perpetrated by groups whose members may not know one another well. But the conditions under which states use rape and other forms of sexual violence as a regular part of detainee torture, carried out by specialists, are largely unexplored, and these present another area for future exploration.

The findings herein also have implications for *research on armed groups*, particularly their internal structures, rules, and regulations. Scholars are increasingly looking to the role of ideology and internal intuitions, such as intensive training and political education, as essential factors in explaining the forms and degrees of violence wielded by such groups (e.g., Hoover Green 2011; Oppenheim, Vargas, and Weintraub 2015). The example of the FMLN, in the El Salvador case, hints at the way strong internal rules may serve to redefine norms around violence and masculinity, ultimately restraining the rape of noncombatants. Future studies may examine how these institutions influence groups' decisions about the uses of violence and can analyze those groups that are not well explained by the central argument in this book. For example, some groups, such as the Lord's Resistance Army (LRA) in Uganda, abducted their fighters but generally did not rape civilians. The LRA, however, had strict regulations on sexual behavior and instituted a system of forced marriage that was intended, at least in part, to curb the rape of civilians (Annan et al. 2009). How and why some groups develop these norms and rules is still an open question in the literature, as is the question of why some armed groups abduct their fighters while others never do.

The findings presented in this book—one of the first systematic cross-national analyses of rape during recent civil wars—can provide new avenues of research and new ways of theorizing the conditions under which *sexual violence,* broadly defined, occurs during wartime. Wood (2016) has developed a typology of political violence that separates violence that is purposefully adopted as policy from violence that develops as a practice. While evidence suggests that rape ordered by commanders is relatively rare, future work can continue to explore the conditions under which strategic, directed, or institutionalized forms of rape and sexual violence, such as forced marriage and sexual slavery, are more common.

An emerging debate among scholars of wartime rape is whether and how sexual violence during wartime is connected to the violence that occurs before conflicts begin and after they end. It is a common contention that there is a "continuum" of violence (e.g., Boesten 2014; Swaine 2011; Wood 2015), but I argue that this is true only in the broadest sense: rape during wartime looks qualitatively different in many ways than rape during peacetime, with different forms, perpetrators, victims, and levels of brutality. Increasingly, however, scholars believe that widespread wartime rape may be predictive of increased rates of rape in the postconflict context. Citing Sierra Leone, Liberia, and the DRC as examples, Nicholas Kristof writes, "The pattern is that after peace arrives, men stop shooting each other but continue to rape women and girls at staggering rates—and often at staggeringly young ages."[2] However, no systematic, comparative studies have yet established these connections. Scholars are also starting to analyze whether baseline, preconflict rates of rape are predictive of rape in wartime (e.g., Butler and Jones 2014).

As more and better data become available, analysts will be able to examine more rigorously the connections between violence during different pre- and postconflict periods. Open questions remain on the general consequences of wartime rape, which are often assumed to be ruinous for societies and states. The effects of sexual violence on political and social outcomes for states is a promising avenue for future inquiry. Scholars are learning about an increasing number of victim groups, including men and boys and sexual and gender minorities. Puzzles for future research include whether the widespread rape of men may be explained by the combatant socialization argument (although, it should be noted, *widespread* wartime rape of men has not been reported in any conflicts), as well as whether the motivations for rape and sexual violence targeted at sexual and gender minorities are similar to the motivations for public gang rape of female victims, as explored in this study.

Finally, the cases in this book are limited to modern civil wars, but the findings may also have implications for other types of wars and other periods in history. While it is outside the scope of the current study to explore fully how its main argument applies to other infamous cases—such as the wave of rapes on the Eastern Front during World War II, rape by the Japanese during the siege of Nanking, and rape during the partition of India—the findings provide an alternative testable argument for future scholars interested in examining motivations for violence. Careful consideration of the quality of unit-level cohesion and its effects on violence may lead to new insights in these well-documented historical cases.

Policy Implications

Although there are no simple or direct policy solutions that follow from the results of this book, the results can offer valuable guidance for policymakers, advocates, and activists who are concerned with mitigating the terrible tragedy of widespread rape during war.

In recent years, through both formal channels and informal advocacy, the policy community has developed a strong and admirable political will to devise policies that prevent and mitigate the problem of conflict-related rape and other forms of sexual violence.[3] The UN Security Council passed a series of resolutions that, among other actions, formally recognized sexual violence as a problem of international security, called for increased awareness and data collection, and created the Special Representative on Sexual Violence in Armed Conflict, a new position within the UN that focuses exclusively on the issue. In addition, several prominent international campaigns are devoted to the issue, including the Stop Rape Now campaign of UN Action against Sexual Violence in Conflict, a joint project across thirteen separate UN programs and departments; the International Campaign to Stop Rape and Gender Violence in Conflict; the Sexual Violence in Conflict campaign of the Nobel Women's Initiative; and the Women Under Siege Project of the Women's Media Center, focused on rape and sexual violence during conflict. These are but a few examples of the enormous attention that the issue has received in recent years.

Perhaps the grandest policy gesture has been the June 2014 Global Summit to End Sexual Violence in Conflict. Hosted by Angelina Jolie and then-foreign secretary William Hague, the international conference was hailed as the largest meeting ever of its type, and was billed as bringing together "over 900 experts, NGOs, survivors, faith leaders, and international organizations from across the world."[4] But others (e.g., Hoover Green 2014) have pointed out that social scientists, and recent findings from social science research, were largely absent from the meeting. Academic researchers who were invited to present at the meeting included public health and legal academics, which provides insight into how policymakers view rape: first and foremost as a crime and a social problem. In contrast, the central argument of this book is that wartime rape is a form of *political violence* by armed groups, commonly perpetrated in groups. By viewing wartime rape as both political violence and group violence, policymakers can open up an array of possible avenues of intervention and can draw lessons from other forms of well-studied political and group violence, such as genocide and mass killing.

One of the most problematic aspects of the current public discourse is that it is still dominated by the narrative that *all* wartime rape is used as a "weapon of war," and that the root cause of wartime rape is impunity for the perpetrators. As Eriksson Baaz and Stern (2012) have argued, one of the appeals of the "rape as a weapon of war" narrative is that it suggests a relatively simple solution for the problem of wartime rape, namely, holding responsible the commanders that order rape. Because the narrative is so powerful, and has reached such widespread acceptance, many policy interventions are focused on prosecuting past perpetrators and closing the so-called impunity gap. The first priority of the Global Summit was to "shatter the culture of impunity," according to the summit website.

The focus on prosecution and deterrence has a number of problems, however. Trials are immensely costly, in terms of both time and resources. As a result, there have been only a small number of charges for crimes of sexual violence, and an even smaller number of convictions, in international war crimes courts. At the International Criminal Tribunal for the former Yugoslavia (ICTY), seventy-eight people have been charged with crimes of sexual violence and twenty-eight convicted since 1993. At the International Criminal Tribunal for Rwanda (ICTR), thirty-seven people have been charged and fourteen convicted since 1994. And since 2002, only sixteen people have been charged at the International Criminal

Court (ICC), with no convictions as of 2014 (Henry 2014). By one estimate, each conviction at the ICTY and ICTR was astonishingly expensive: $35 million and $39 million, respectively (Kirby 2015). Although the cases are costly in part because they are so complex, these figures raise significant questions about whether such trials are the best use of these large sums of funds. This is especially vexing in light of the fact that few victims and survivors of rape rank prosecution and accountability of their perpetrators as priorities.[5]

Beyond practical considerations of costs and benefits, a notable finding from the analysis presented in this book is that mass rape occurs even in the absence of direct orders from commanders. Indeed, this is what took place in the Sierra Leone war: despite very limited evidence of direct orders to rape, rape happened on a large scale. A corollary is that rape may be ordered but only occur in a very limited way. The rapes of the churchwomen in El Salvador were likely ordered by the command—but such rapes of nuns and church laypersons were rare. These two patterns suggest that policymakers should be careful not to conflate the frequency of rape with the motivations of its perpetrators. The phrase "widespread and systematic" has become overused in descriptions of conflict-related rape and has had the unfortunate consequence of implying equivalence: that *widespread* rape is *systematic* rape. The evidence presented in this book suggests that these are separable concepts; indeed, widespread rape—with respect to targeting victims—may be quite unsystematic and random.

Beyond policy changes, the combatant socialization argument has legal implications for impunity gap advocates. If it is indeed the case that rape is often organized from the bottom up rather than ordered from the top down, then the type of "smoking gun," chain-of-command evidence commonly sought by human rights advocates for war crimes prosecutions will likely be rare. Nonetheless, the doctrine of command responsibility still holds that commanders are accountable for failing to prevent or punish the atrocities of their subordinates. Kate Cronin-Furman (2013) conducted an analysis of the conditions under which international criminal trials might serve as a deterrent for future perpetrators of wartime atrocities. She concludes that deterrence is most likely when violence is tolerated—as in the combatant socialization argument—rather than directly ordered. Cronin-Furman advocates for interventions that incentivize commanders to restrain violence; she discusses increased prosecution and punishment, although the logic of creating incentives for commanders to restrain sexual violence may be applied to nonlegal policy interventions as well, such as withholding external support. However, she argues that the cases the ICC has chosen to pursue, along with the tepid punishments it often hands down, suggest that deterrence of future perpetrators is unlikely.

Other implications of the study include the possibility that forced recruiting by armed groups can serve as an early warning sign for wartime rape. Reports of rape may take months or even years to filter out of a conflict zone. Reports of forced recruitment, on the other hand, are less likely to be hidden because they do not carry the same stigma and shame for the victims. Paying close attention to where and how armed groups recruit their fighters may be of use in determining the types of hidden violence being perpetrated. According to the results presented here, it is common that abduction and press-ganging precede mass rape. Forced recruitment, then, could serve as a litmus test for disbursing foreign and military aid when policymakers are actively seeking to avoid supporting belligerents who engage in acts of wartime rape.

In addition, the fact that states are common perpetrators of wartime rape presents an opportunity for policymakers. Research has shown that states may respond to public campaigns intended to embarrass states as violators of human rights (Krain 2012; DeMeritt 2012). Scholars who have studied public information campaigns—such as ratings, rankings, and watch lists of violators—have found them to be effective tools for changing states' behaviors. For example, Kelley and Simmons (2015) have shown that appearing in the State Department's Trafficking in Persons Report had a discernible effect on the likelihood of states to criminalize trafficking (although whether criminalization then leads to measurable policy change has yet to be studied). Pressure through private or secretive channels may be effective as well. In El Salvador, a secret visit from the US vice president, with a credible threat to withdraw military aid, influenced the behavior of the Salvadoran Armed Forces. Altering the behavior of rebel groups—particularly those that aim to control the central state—through similar means is theoretically possible, but less understood; this is a promising avenue for future research.

The findings from this analysis suggest a number of ways that external parties can intervene to assist armed groups struggling with internal cohesion. Groups that are well resourced, and that use these resources to provide recruits with basic training and cohesion-building exercises, may be less likely to turn to violence as a tool of socialization. External parties, then, can assist armed groups by providing training that emphasizes group identity–building exercises, ultimately helping to professionalize armed groups. Organizations like Geneva Call and the International Committee of the Red Cross, which regularly engage with armed groups, are well placed to communicate the benefits of these types of training. In addition, external parties, such as diaspora organizations, as well as other states and major international organizations should place clear conditions on material aid to armed groups that perpetrate human rights violations, including rape. Strong, consistent external pressure may serve to foster norms and rules within an armed group that prioritize the protection—rather than the exploitation—of civilian populations.

Another implication of this work for policymakers are reforms of disarmament, demobilization, and rehabilitation (DDR) processes to more directly recognize the psychological effects of having served in armed groups that use violence—rape and other forms—as a means of building cohesion. Recent research shows that violent actions increase loyalty among the group and thus potentially contribute to the "longevity of the group's existence" (Littman and Paluck 2015, 94). Rather than DDR programming focused solely on incentives aimed at helping individuals leave such groups, such as cash transfers or job training, Littman and Paluck (2015) advocate for assisting ex-combatants in creating new social groups, or reestablishing old ones. These types of policies may serve to reduce some of the negative outcomes of combatants' exposure to violence, such as increased interpersonal violence in the postwar period.

Finally, gender inequality—and strong patriarchal norms—is an insufficient explanation for wartime rape (Cohen, Hoover Green, and Wood 2013). However, research has shown that the onset of war, both intrastate and international, is associated with various measures of gender inequality (e.g., Hudson et al. 2012). Thus, while policies aimed at increasing gender equality may not have a direct effect on mitigating wartime rape, they may decrease the likelihood of war in general. And given that rape seems to increase during periods of war, these policies may lower the incidence of rape through indirect pathways in the long term.

In my research for this book, I sought to resolve the puzzles of why rape is widespread in some conflicts and not in others, and why some armed groups perpetrate widespread rape while others never do—even in the context of the same war. Using new data, the argument presented here suggests that armed groups are the most important unit of analysis in understanding these puzzles. Examining in detail how armed groups use rape to build and to maintain social ties clarifies the logic of rape—a form of violence that for too long has been accepted as an inevitable and unavoidable consequence of war.

NOTES ON DATA COLLECTION ON WARTIME RAPE

This appendix provides a discussion of issues of bias that may arise when collecting data on wartime rape as well as a set of strategies that I used to mitigate some of these biases. It also includes further detail on the procedures used for coding wartime rape and explicates a number of coding decisions. In addition, it describes changes that have been made to the Cohen 2013a dataset since it was used in the article "Explaining Rape during Civil War: Cross-National Evidence (1980–2009)" (Cohen 2013a).

Biases in Research on Rape

Political scientists, with few exceptions (e.g., Wood 2003) and unlike their counterparts in such fields as anthropology, spend little time explicitly discussing the process of conducting research in postconflict zones (Fujii 2010). But bias is always a concern in conducting research, and particularly so when that research is focused on a sensitive topic like rape. Data gathered from perpetrators, victims, and even human rights organizations may be affected by different forms of bias, and here I consider them each in turn,

Broadly speaking, the dangers of simply taking what interviewees report at face value, especially in postconflict environments, are well documented. Interview subjects may lie about their roles in events, attempt to disguise their true intentions related to past actions, or exaggerate their stories for the researcher (Wood 2007; Fujii 2010). Less strategically, research on memory shows that interview subjects may misremember events in the aftermath of conflict, or that more recent events may obscure or alter older memories (Wood 2003). People in time-illiterate communities may not remember exact sequences of events from the past and may be unaware of basic facts about their own histories, such as their ages or dates of birth. Biases may also exist in memories of violence; extreme types of violence might be more salient and thus recalled more easily than more mundane types of violence. For instance, respondents whose families were killed may be less likely to report rape, whereas respondents whose only other experience with violence during a war had been looting may be more likely to report rape (Cohen and Hoover Green 2012).

Interviewing perpetrators can present obvious problems of veracity. Theidon (2007) found during her fieldwork in Peru that men would rarely report having perpetrated rape themselves, in a first-person narrative, instead describing acts that they said they had witnessed. Similarly, Eriksson Baaz and Stern (2009) conducted focus groups about sexual violence in their study of combatants in the Democratic Republic of the Congo, and the combatants never identified themselves as perpetrators. I generally found this to be the case during my fieldwork as well, although some of the ex-combatants I interviewed—both men and women—described their own participation in episodes of rape. Whether interviewees are forthcoming about their own culpability may not be especially problematic, provided that the central research question is about broad patterns of violence by an armed group or a military unit, as it is in this study, rather than the experience of specific individuals.

Various biases are also associated with interview data collected from victims and survivors. First, and most obviously, there is a potential for underreporting. Victims of rape may be unwilling or unable to share their stories. Indeed, researchers often treat any estimate of the number of victims as a conservative estimation, with the assumption that many victims were either unable or unwilling to report (e.g., Green 2006). Victims may not report rape due to a fear of stigmatization, shame, concerns about retributive violence, an inability to reach authorities due to damaged infrastructure, a lack of medical and social services, and the dispersion of social support groups (Green 2006; Wood 2006; Leiby 2009). In countries where abortion is illegal, rape victims who have had abortions may be particularly unlikely to report (Wood 2006). Victims may also be less likely to report their rapes in strongly patriarchal contexts in which virginity is highly prized (Green 2006). However, it is a mistake to assume that war itself necessarily decreases the reporting of rape and other forms of sexual violence. Wood (2006) argues that, in some contexts, human rights groups and medical service organizations may actually be more accessible to war-affected populations than they are during peacetime.

Finally, human rights advocates may face enormous pressures to exaggerate or dramatize the extent of human rights violations in order to secure media attention or donor funding from a largely apathetic and unresponsive public. The often-repeated, and likely inflated, statistic that 75 percent of women in Liberia were raped during the civil war is indicative of the pressure to dramatize humanitarian crises, sometimes at the cost of exaggerating the extent of the problem.[1] Human rights groups also typically limit their reporting to a particular event, and so their selection of stories to feature is commonly not representative of all violence; rather, such groups may highlight the worst cases and incidents and the most sympathetic victims.

Mitigation Strategies

Veracity

To mitigate the sources of potential bias around veracity, I employed several strategies during fieldwork. Successful interviewing about sensitive themes depends a great deal on trust. To create trust with ex-combatant interview subjects, I began by recruiting people through the network of local NGOs that advocate for the rights of ex-combatants, political prisoners, and/or victims of violence. Before each interview, I was careful to make clear that I was not affiliated with the NGOs, local or foreign governments, international bodies such as the Special Court in Sierra Leone or the Serious Crimes Unit of the UN in Timor-Leste, or the various TRCs. My introduction through a local network helped reassure interviewees that I could be trusted. I always interviewed people in a quiet, private setting. As a policy, I did not record the name of any interviewee, ensuring anonymity.

I took a different approach to create trust among the local populations where I hoped to conduct interviews with noncombatants. Rather than rely on introductions by NGOs, I traveled with a local interpreter and introduced myself as an independent researcher. I attempted to travel inconspicuously, which can be particularly important for safety in tense regions (Swiss et al. 1998). I dressed like a student, stayed in local guesthouses, shopped in the public markets, and took public transportation. I used pen and paper to take notes and avoided recording equipment, in order not to alienate interviewees. As other researchers have described in their work, these activities allowed me to establish that I was who I said I was (Fujii 2010), likely enabling my interviews.

Researching violence in postconflict settings involves listening carefully to what is being shared. Fujii (2010) advocates paying close attention to what she terms the "meta-data" of interviews in such settings: the exaggerations, silences, lies, or denials that an interview subject makes during data collection. Skjelsbæk (2011), in her research with Bosnian victims, also emphasizes the importance of noting silences when interviewing victims of wartime rape. Paying close attention to such meta-data helps to provide context to interviews. For example, in an interview in eastern Sierra Leone, one woman said that she had escaped from being raped because an uncle of hers had come to save her at the last minute, when the perpetrator was already on top of her.[2] In consultation after the interview concluded, both my interpreter and I agreed that her escape story was likely not true, based on the woman's body language and the difficulty she had in telling us about the attempted rape. The escape story may have represented the woman's attempt to assert agency into a description of a very painful moment in her life, while still relaying her experience of rape.

Other strategies to deal with truthfulness in interviews include doing repeat interviews with subjects that become more detailed over time. Pressing interviewees on details that do not make sense and being persistent in asking follow-up questions may also be useful. Whether challenging lies or inconsistencies presents an ethical dilemma will depend on situational factors and the researcher's own comfort (Wood 2006b).

Interpreters as Research Partners

The use of a local interpreter can also help to reduce biases and misunderstandings. Traditionally, researchers have seen interpreters as detrimental to the research process (Skjelsbæk 2011), and many scholars pride themselves on learning local languages and conducting interviews alone, without relying on the skills and patience of a translator. However, for reasons both practical and ethical, I chose to work with skilled local interpreters and research assistants when conducting the interviews that inform this study.

Typically, US universities do not teach the multiple local languages and dialects of Sierra Leone and Timor-Leste; this study involved several cross-national fieldwork sites, and investing time in learning several languages was not feasible. Beyond the necessity of breaking through language barriers, there were additional benefits to having an interpreter: ready assistance figuring out the complex systems of mini-buses that comprise local transportation, an advocate in the endless cycles of bargaining over prices, instruction as to how to greet village chiefs and community leaders and to maneuver through local bureaucracies, and advice on how to best explain the research and methods for local comprehension.[3] Having a local interpreter also helped to facilitate trust with the people I was interviewing. One interpreter decided that when we were traveling in the rural areas of Sierra Leone, she should introduce herself using her tribal name instead of the English name she used in the capital city, and that she should wear traditional skirts instead of her usual uniform of jeans; these insights proved valuable in creating trust with the rural interview subjects.

Most importantly, I found it essential to have a local perspective on the interview process, including visual cues and social mores that I as a foreign researcher may have overlooked or misunderstood. For example, my interpreter once suggested we stop an interview when she perceived that one informant was becoming uncomfortable. The informant had not asked to stop, nor did I think she looked visibly upset, but my interpreter had noticed subtle signs of discomfort that I would have likely missed.

In all three fieldwork sites, nearly all of the interpreters with whom I worked were female students and had some previous interest in or experience with human rights issues or gendered violence.[4] It was especially useful to have female translators when discussing the topic of rape. Both women and men seemed more willing to share their experiences in the presence of only women. On the occasions when I used a male interpreter to interview ex-combatants, I generally found that these interviews resulted in less-detailed information. Male subjects seemed less embarrassed overall when interviewed by women and were more likely to use proper anatomical terms and descriptions of sexual acts than when other men were present. Other researchers have confirmed this observation. Asher (2009) found that female enumerators, conducting a household survey on violence in Sierra Leone, were able to obtain more information regarding human rights violations than were male enumerators, regardless of the gender of the respondent.

Are Victim Interviews and Surveys Necessary for Research on Rape?

Some researchers interested in wartime rape and other forms of sexual violence have made the decision not to interview or survey rape victims (e.g., Swiss and Jennings 2006; Leiby 2012). These scholars believe that the risks to the victims, including the potential of retraumatization, are too high and without sufficient benefit, particularly given the proliferation of victim and witness testimonies in other sources, such as human rights organizations' reports or TRC statements. Shana Swiss and Peggy Jennings (2006) decided to halt a population-based randomized survey in a Sri Lankan IDP camp—intended to measure the effects of conflict on women—because the potential subjects faced such severe risks. They argue that in Sri Lankan culture, the shame and stigma of being identified as a rape victim, particularly for women in IDP camps, carried enormous potential risks to the victim and that the intangible benefits of participating in the survey were not sufficiently large to offset these costs.

Researchers have relied on a number of creative methods for garnering information about wartime rape and other forms of sexual violence that do not involve direct contact with victims, including analyzing transcripts of TRC focus groups, examining testimonies given to TRCs, and reviewing documents from international court proceedings (Houge 2008; Leiby 2009; Mullins 2009; Theidon 2007). While these sources can provide a rich description of human rights violations, they also feature a set of potential biases, such as a lack of representativeness. Finally, scholars have employed a sophisticated statistical triangulation method to estimate numbers of victims, based on sources of "found" data (for example, cemeteries, church lists of the dead, or lists of victims from NGOs). This method, called multiple systems estimation (MSE), has been used to provide prevalence estimations of human rights violations in a number of postconflict countries (e.g., Hoover Green 2013).[5]

Extension to 2012 Dataset and Revisions to Civil Wars List

The Cohen 2013a dataset covered the period from 1980 to 2009 and included eighty-six civil wars. The revised Cohen 2016 dataset, used in this book, extends this time period to 2012 and includes ninety-one civil wars. The source of the civil wars data is Fearon 2015, a list of civil wars updated from Fearon and Laitin 2003. The version used in this analysis is the beta version of Fearon 2015. Changes to the Cohen 2013a dataset are detailed below.

The following conflicts were added to the dataset:

- Iran (MEK) 1979–1982
- Nigeria (NVPDF, MEND) 2004–ongoing
- Nigeria (Boko Haram) 2009–ongoing
- Libya (NTC) 2011
- South Africa (Namibia) 1966–1988
- Syria (FSA) 2011–ongoing

The following conflict was deleted from the dataset:

- Djibouti 1991–1994 (insufficient number of deaths)

The following changes were made to start and end dates:

- Afghanistan (Mujahideen) start date was revised from 1979 to 1978
- India (NE rebels) start date was revised from 1956 to 1978
- India (Naxalites) start date was revised from 1988 to 1990
- Pakistan (MQM) start date was revised from 1993 to 1992

- Pakistan (Taliban) start date was revised from 2007 to 2004
- Peru (Sendero Luminoso) end date was extended from 1996 to 1999
- Uganda (LRA, West Nile) start date was revised from 1989 to 1987

The following wars are ongoing as of 2012:

- Afghanistan (Taliban II)
- Algeria (FIS)
- Burma /Myanmar (CPB, Karens)
- Chad (Frolinat)
- Colombia (FARC)
- DRC (RCD)
- Ethiopia (Oromo)
- India (Kashmir)
- India (NE rebels)
- India (Naxalites)
- Iran (PJAK)
- Iran (Sunni and Shia rebels)
- Israel (Palestinian insurgents)
- Pakistan (Baluchistan)
- Pakistan (Taliban)
- Philippines (MILF)
- Philippines (NPA)
- Russia (Chechnya II)
- Senegal (MFDC)
- Somalia (post-Barre war)
- Sudan (Darfur)
- Thailand (Pattani)
- Turkey (PKK)
- Uganda (LRA, West Nile)
- Yemen (al-Houthi)

Conflict-Years with a Coding of 3

As described in chapter 2, the rule used in the dataset in this book for a coding of 3 as the worst/highest level for reports of rape is slightly different than in Cohen 2013a. Previously, a code of 3 was assigned when rape during a conflict was described as "systematic" or "massive," or otherwise as a "weapon," "means of intimidation," or another synonymous term. These terms imply both the *intention* for the violence as well as the *scale* of the violence.

In order to avoid coding those conflicts where the source describes *only* the intention but not the scale, the revised dataset has an additional coding requirement: to be coded as 3, the description of the violence must contain an intention term *and* terms that would qualify for a 2 coding. The new coding rule resulted in three conflict-years that did not meet this new requirement but were nonetheless retained as a 3—based on additional research that confirmed the conflict's intensity, or on a similarity in language used to describe violence in other conflict-years that were coded as a 3: Burma/Myanmar (CPB, Karens), 2011; Iraq (KDP, PUK), 1993; and Bosnia (Rep. Srpska/Croats), 1994.

Finally, one additional coding change resulted from a probable error discovered in the source documentation. The 2010 State Department human rights report for Israel includes the following paragraph, which describes reports of rape of Palestinian children by Israeli state forces:

> The NGO Defense for Children International-Palestine Section (DCI-Palestine) claimed Israeli security authorities often tortured and abused minors in custody to coerce confessions during interrogation, employing tactics such as beatings, longterm handcuffing, threats, *rape*, and solitary confinement. In 40 affidavits collected by DCI-Palestine in the last six months of the year, 28 children arrested and detained by the IDF claimed they were beaten and kicked, 24 experienced some form of position abuse, seven were stripped naked, and three were subjected to electric shocks [emphasis added].

Because this is an unusual allegation of the rape of children—and because no other reports of conflict-related rape in Israel are coded in the dataset—a research assistant contacted the NGO to ask about the allegations. Representatives from the NGO reported that while all of the other forms of violence are accurate, they have no record of children reporting rape (albeit there are reports of *threats* of rape from this time period). A subsequent conversation with a foreign affairs officer at the State Department confirmed that this description of rape was likely an error in the report. As a result, I have coded a 0 for Israel in 2010.

Notes

INTRODUCTION

1. As described in more detail in chapter 2, the cross-national data indicate that 65% of the conflicts (fifty-nine of ninety-one conflicts) in the study period involved significant rape in at least one conflict-year (i.e., a code of 2 or 3, corresponding with reports of "numerous" incidents or reports of "massive" rape, respectively). The data used in this book are an expanded and updated version of the data used in Cohen 2013a and include an additional three years (extended from 2009 through 2012) and five more conflicts. A number of other changes to the dataset are described in chapter 2, with further details in the appendix.

2. Others have argued that rape is inevitable in war. For example, Catharine MacKinnon (1994, 188) writes, "Every time there is a war, there is rape. Of course rape does occur in all wars, both within and between all sides."

3. Of the seventy-four wars that had at least isolated reports of rape in the study period, 62% had reports of both state and insurgent perpetrators, 31% had reports of only state perpetrators, and 7% had reports of only insurgent perpetrators.

4. This alternative hypothesis is briefly outlined in the conclusion of Humphreys and Weinstein 2006, where the authors raise the possibility that "individuals [may] perform . . . violent acts to establish their position within the organization" (444).

5. Wood (2006, 308) defines sexual violence as "a broader category that includes rape, non-penetrating sexual assault and coerced undressing."

6. See Fisher 1996, for example, for an analysis of forced impregnation as a tool of genocide and as a war crime distinct from rape.

7. In her typology of political violence, Wood (2016) includes sexual slavery and forced marriage under the heading of rape as a "policy"; these have logics distinct from that of rape as a "practice" (described later in the introduction), the form of violence that is the center of the present analysis.

8. Human rights advocates sometimes use the term "gender-based violence" interchangeably with "sexual violence." Gender-based violence is generally defined as nonrandom violence whose victims are targeted because of their sex. The neutral application of the definition of gender-based violence includes many acts of violence that are not explicitly sexualized in nature. Under this definition, for example, violence that is mainly directed at military-aged men, such as the wartime killing of noncombatants, should be considered gender-based violence. In practice, however, gender-based violence programming is targeted at women and girls, and it tends to be focused particularly on rape and other forms of sexual violence (Carpenter 2006). Because of the imprecise application of the term, I avoid the use of "gender-based violence" in this book.

9. For a discussion of definitional issues regarding sexual violence, see Leiby 2009, 81–83.

10. The 2012 International Men and Gender Equality Survey in the DRC found that, "in qualitative interviews, men openly shared their opinions about the 'right to have sex' with their female partner even if she refuses; most men did not consider it to be rape to force their wives to have sex with them" ("Gender Relations, Sexual Violence and the Effects of Conflict on Women and Men in North Kivu, Eastern Democratic Republic of Congo," 10, http://resourcecentre.savethechildren.se/sites/default/files/documents/6945.pdf).

The 2013 survey by Fulu et al. did not ask specifically about rape, but included questions such as, "Have you ever had sex with your partner when you knew she didn't want to but you thought she should agree because she's your wife/partner?"

11. Although in most contexts gang rape (in public, by strangers) is not socially condoned, scholars have noted several examples where gang rape is used in some cultures as a punishment or a social sanction by family members or by a community (Dole 2009; Rozée 1993; Sanday 1981; Wood 2006). In addition, Jewkes et al. (2013) write that peacetime gang rape has achieved "cultural legitimacy" in several contexts, including in Papua New Guinea, Cambodia, and South Africa. In Papua New Guinea, for example, gang rape is a traditional punishment, approved by clan elders, used to sanction women for transgressions relating to sexuality or marriage (NSRRT and Jenkins 1994).

12. See Cohen, Hoover Green, and Wood 2013 for an overview of recent research findings as well as a discussion of the limitations of these findings. See also Wood 2015 for a review of how recent findings can better inform policy.

13. Aranburu (2012) also points to another possible source of underreporting: reluctance by advocacy groups to highlight male victims for fear that doing so may detract attention from violence against women.

14. Eight countries currently prescribe the death penalty for homosexual conduct: Brunei, Iran, Mauritania, Saudi Arabia, Sudan, and Yemen, as well as parts of Nigeria and Somalia (UN 2015, 13). In addition, at least seventy-six states retain legislation "used to criminalize and harass people on the basis of sexual orientation and gender identity or expression" (UN 2015, 12). Such discriminatory legal codes make it all the more difficult to collect data on male victims of sexual violence, who are unlikely to risk reporting assaults to authorities.

15. The Trial Chamber restricted its purview to sexual violence against women and girls, however, so no convictions were made for the rape of men (Sivakumaran 2010).

16. The definitional problem is limited neither to wartime violence nor to developing countries; a *New York Times* article (Rabin 2012) highlighted similar issues with studying the sexual assault of men in the United States (see also Cohen, Hoover Green, and Wood 2013 for a related discussion on challenges with sexual violence data).

17. Bourke (2007, 376–77) writes, "One of the startling differences between rape in peacetime and rape in wartime is the much greater prevalence of group rapes in war. A radically higher proportion of wartime rapes involve a group of men rather than a solitary offender."

18. A study of the prevalence of rape in six Asian countries—outside the context of wartime—found that gang rape was high in Cambodia, parts of Indonesia, and Papua New Guinea. Notably, Cambodia was the only country in the study in which reported gang rape exceeded reported single-perpetrator rape (Jewkes et al. 2013).

19. Indeed, Hoover Green (2011, 59) writes that UN staffers are concerned that "disclosure bias" has caused a systematic overreporting of public gang rape: "Essentially, rape victims whose assaults are already known to their communities have little to lose by reporting their status as victims, while disclosure may be exceptionally risky for those who were assaulted in private."

20. The ninety-one wars analyzed in this study are listed in Fearon and Laitin 2015, a beta version of an updated list of civil wars used in Fearon and Latin 2003 and described in more detail in the appendix. Their definition of a violent civil war includes three criteria (2003, 76): (1) The fighting is between agents of (or claimants to) a state and organized, nonstate groups who sought either to take control of a government, to take power in a region, or to use violence to change government policies; (2) The conflict killed at least one thousand over its course, with a yearly average of at least one hundred; (3) The conflict killed at least one hundred on both sides (including civilians attacked by rebels).

21. Another relevant study is the largest-scale survey on rape ever conducted, which included over ten thousand men in six Asian countries (Fulu et al. 2013; Jewkes et al. 2013). The authors examined the lifetime incidence of sexual violence and rape perpetration by the respondents, against both intimate partners and strangers. They found that between 25.4% and 80% of men reported perpetrating sexual or physical violence (or both) against their intimate partners across the various study sites. In contrast, between 2.5% and 26.6% of men reported single-perpetrator rape of nonpartners, and between 1.4% and 14.1% reported multiple-perpetrator rape of nonpartners. These figures confirm that rape of nonpartners is relatively infrequent, and the multiple-perpetrator rape of a nonpartner is especially rare. Surveys on war-related violence reveal that rates of multiple-perpetrator rape during wartime are much higher than in peacetime, often constituting the majority of the reported rape.

22. For an alternate view, see, for example, Swaine 2011, in which the author emphasizes the importance of "continuums theory," or analyzing violence in the pre- and postconflict phases, as well as during wartime.

23. Sometimes, perpetrators of wartime rape are portrayed literally as monsters. A video about wartime rape, released by the UK Foreign and Commonwealth Office in conjunction with the June 2014 Global Summit to End Sexual Violence in Conflict, featured cartoon "monsters"—complete with red eyes and sharp teeth—committing "the worst crimes you can imagine" and terrorizing women and children (see "Don't Believe the Thumbnail, This Video Is the Stuff of Nightmares," https://www.youtube.com/watch?v=1QFUD2Q6D8k).

24. UN documentation (UN Action 2011, 2) on conflict-related sexual violence notes that "sexual violence as a 'tactic of war' refers to acts of sexual violence that are linked with military/political objectives and that serve (or intend to serve) a strategic aim related to the conflict. *This will rarely be reflected in overt orders*" (emphasis added). Instead, the UN suggests several other observable factors that may suggest orders or direction from the top, including a strong chain of command, restraint in the use of other violations, failure to punish perpetrators of sexual violence, and, most importantly, evidence that "sexual violence is in line with the overall objectives of the group." This conceptualization is problematic because sexual violence is viewed as both costless and highly effective, two features that would appeal to any armed group. It is therefore very difficult to make the case that sexual violations are *not* in line with the overall objectives of an armed group.

25. Recent cases in which there is evidence that rape was ordered include Rwanda, where "militia directed . . . sexual violence to further their political goal: the destruction of the Tutsi as a group" (Nowrojee 1996, 2), and Sudan, where soldiers reported to Human Rights Watch that commanders had ordered them to rape (Loeb 2015).

26. See Eriksson Baaz and Stern (2013), who argue against viewing rape as a "weapon of war"—an explanation that, they maintain, is politically expedient and offers simpler policy interventions than does viewing rape as unordered or nonstrategic violence.

1. THE LOGIC OF WARTIME RAPE

1. Throughout the book, I use "gang rape" to mean rape by multiple perpetrators. Some scholars avoid this term because, among other reasons, they argue it implies lower status and/or nonwhite perpetrators. These scholars prefer the terms "group rape" or "multiple-perpetrator rape" (see Adams 2005 for a summary of the debate over terminology and, more generally, Horvath and Woodhams 2013).

2. I use "perpetrator" to mean members of armed groups who have committed or participated in rape or other forms of wartime violence, including selecting and restraining the victims. While imprecise, the term is widely used in both policy (e.g., UN, AI, HRW, USIP) and scholarly literature (e.g., Wood 2006) on wartime rape and is preferable

to alternatives, such as colloquial terms like "rapist" or "attacker" and legal terms such as "the accused."

3. One argument that I do not consider in detail in this book is the evolutionary psychology perspective (e.g., Thornhill and Palmer 2000), which views rape as motivated mainly by male sexual desire rather than by aggression or violence. Evolutionary psychologists argue, for example, that because most rape victims are young women, presumably at their peak sexual attractiveness, rape must be motivated by sexual desire. However, the other observed patterns of rape—that many men do not rape, that there is increasing evidence of male victims as well as female perpetrators of rape, and that the most common form of wartime rape (i.e., gang rape) occurs with greater frequency in wartime than in peacetime—all suggest that the argument is too simplistic. In short, evolutionary psychology does not sufficiently explain the documented variation in wartime rape. However, I do consider several related arguments throughout the book; Thornhill and Palmer (2000, 194) maintain, for example, that rape is more likely to occur during wartime because costs to perpetrators during such periods are especially low, an explanation I consider as part of the opportunism/greed argument.

4. This view of rape—as one of a variety of forms of group violence—contrasts with arguments by others that gender violence is different or worse than other forms of violence. See, for example, Sharlach 2000 on rape as a form of genocide.

5. Recent research suggests that intimate-partner sexual violence is the most common form of sexual violence experienced by women in both peacetime and wartime (Peterman, Palermo, and Bredenkamp 2011; HSRP 2012). In this book, I do not analyze intimate-partner violence, but instead examine rape perpetrated by armed actors in the context of conflict.

6. Exceptions include Rwanda and Sudan, as highlighted in the introduction, as well as historical cases such as the mass rape during the Soviet occupation of Germany in 1945. As Wood (2006b, 324) writes, a vivid example is the Soviet Army's formal order on the night before marching into East Prussia that included the following infamous passage, which is often interpreted as encouraging rape (and other forms of violence): "On German soil there is only one master—the Soviet soldier, that he is both the judge and the punisher for the torments of his fathers and mothers, for the destroyed cities and villages . . . 'remember your friends are not there, there is the next of kin of the killers and oppressors'" (Norman Naimark as quoted in Wood 2006b, 310).

7. Interviewees in Sierra Leone described the violent process of abduction; details are included in chapter 3.

8. Blattman (2009) uses the random nature of abduction in the Ugandan civil war as the basis for a natural experiment comparing ex-combatants and noncombatants.

9. I address the differences in social cohesion and task cohesion later in the chapter.

10. As explored in more detail in the case studies, interview evidence from Sierra Leone and Timor-Leste shows that some fighters could—and sometimes did—refuse to participate in acts of rape. These "resisters" reported suffering socially for not participating, but there is little evidence that the costs were more severe (or lethal). This is similar to findings from the peacetime context; Franklin (2004, 31) notes that costs for not participating in gang rape include "be[ing] branded as nonmasculine, . . . expulsion from the group, or, in extreme cases, becom[ing] victims themselves."

11. In developing her argument about rape as a practice, Wood (2012, 414–15; 2016) draws on earlier results from my research in the Sierra Leone civil war and cross-national statistical analyses as evidence. Although Wood stops short of arguing that the majority of cases of wartime rape are likely a practice rather than strategic or opportunistic, I argue that the evidence suggests strategic rape (or "rape as a weapon of war") is relatively rare.

12. In the cross-national analysis in chapter 3, I consider the issue of reverse causation—that is, if rape could be an outcome of a cohesive group rather than a cause of cohesion.

13. As shown in chapter 3, ethnic war is not associated with measures of forced recruitment by either insurgencies or states. This finding lends support to the argument that groups relying on ethnic ties to attract fighters are less likely to force their members to join—and are therefore less likely to perpetrate wartime rape.

14. The fact that, in some cases, forcibly recruited fighters might be children should also affect the desire of combatants to fit in with the group, because children are more likely than adults to be influenced by group pressures. See Checkel 2015 for a discussion on the role that youth may play in facilitating socialization; he argues that the effects of socialization are reduced when the targets are older.

15. This assumption contrasts with the social movements literature on overcoming collective-action problems. Oberschall (1993), for example, argues that bloc recruitment— the process by which a social movement stems from "an already existing set of groups and associations that have leaders, members, . . . social bonds, shared beliefs, . . . and a common language, cemented over a period of years" (24)—is the "rule rather than the exception" (74). In later work, Oberschall (2007, 19) cites the Serbian militia group Arkan's Tigers as an example where fighters were recruited by bloc, from a preexisting group—in this case, from the Belgrade Red Star football team's fan club. However, much recent evidence about combatants forced into armed groups suggests that fighters are *not* recruited by bloc, either by accident or by design, and that they are more likely to serve in an armed unit with strangers than with family or friends. I test this argument in chapter 3 and find that conscription (a less random process that is more likely to result in fighters knowing others in their unit) and press-ganging have dissimilar effects.

16. This survey is the only representative survey of ex-combatants known to the author that specifically questions former fighters about the nature of their ties with their peers.

17. In this previous literature, scholars typically trace the source of sexual violence perpetrated by armed factions to group norms and argue that a militarized sense of masculinity is imparted to combatants through the training process. Wood (2006) argues that these explanations cannot account for the observed patterns; military training is not sufficiently different across groups to account for the variation with which militaries commit sexual violence. Like these earlier scholars, I also argue that rape and socialization within the military unit are inextricably linked. My argument focuses not on norms of masculinity per se but rather on the practical needs of combatant groups and their strategies for responding to these needs. Masculinity plays an important role in the choice of sexualized violence to create social ties.

18. One of the main critiques of the former US military ban on gay service members was that, despite claims that unit cohesion was central to effectiveness, few military resources were allocated to the development of cohesion (e.g., Kier 1998). However, a renewed belief in the importance of cohesion among armed group units may be seen in the gradual evolution of policy in the US military. In both World War II and the Vietnam War, the military had systems of rapid replacement for lost troops, in which new additions to the group would be brought into an already-established military unit (Goldstein 2001, 197). More recently, the US Army experimented with an alternative to the practice of rapid replacement, namely, the use of the "unit manning initiative" or "unit-focused stability," in which entire units were kept together, through both training and fighting, for three-year periods (Loeb 2003; Brown 2004). This change, as well as the abandonment in late 2011 of the "don't ask, don't tell" policy, lends greater credibility to military arguments about the central importance of cohesion among units.

19. For example, social cohesion may lead to lower productivity on the job and less independent thought (MacCoun 1993). More specific to the military context, strong

social cohesion among dissatisfied combatants may lead to greater levels of desertion, the increased use of drugs, or acts of subversive group violence—such as "fragging" during the Vietnam War (the assassination of an officer in one's own unit by means of a fragmentation grenade) (MacCoun 1993; Kier 1998; Kenny 2011).

20. Although some previous research has shown that cohesion may form readily between members of groups (e.g., Horowitz 1985), caution is necessary when extrapolating from these findings; especially in long-term groups, the dynamics are arguably impossible to reconstruct in a laboratory setting. Unsurprisingly, real groups—especially enduring groups such as military units—have been found to behave quite differently than experimental groups (MacCoun 1993, 306). These concerns are particularly important in light of the finding that cohesion may form readily in laboratory experiments. After all, if cohesion develops as easily as these experiments suggest, why would gang rape be necessary to create cohesion? My research indicates that cohesion is not so readily formed among abducted combatants, who reported feeling frightened and isolated when first abducted.

21. Some do make such arguments. A Japanese mayor sparked a controversy in 2013 when he stated publicly that access to comfort women by the Japanese Army in World War II was "necessary at the time to maintain discipline in the army" and that the system of comfort women was needed to allow "emotionally charged soldiers a rest" (Giacomo 2013).

22. Calculations are based on the dataset in Bellows and Miguel 2006.

23. See Knouse 1998 for a description of ways in which the US military has developed task cohesion, including an event devised by the Marines called "The Crucible," a fifty-four-hour-long training exercise designed to increase coordination of group tasks and decision making.

24. Similar reasons are commonly offered as justifications for forcing child combatants to commit acts of violence in their home communities.

25. See Wood 2005 for a brief review of how anthropology has treated the issue of gang rape; she argues that that the research is generally divided into three topics: wartime violence, rituals in Amazonian societies, and street gang violence. Wood argues, however, that much of the anthropological research has been focused on the meaning of gang rape, rather than the "lived experience" (304).

26. Interviewee 17, RUF ex-combatant, June 1, 2007.

27. Specifically, the data from *The Lancet* study are as follows (single-perpetrator rape, gang rape, p-value of the difference): rape after drinking: 25.9%, 34%, 0.004; sexual entitlement: 75.9%, 72.2%, 0.191; rape for fun: 58.3%, 62.6%, 0.166; rape from anger or as punishment: 36.1%, 48.4%, <0.0001. All data from Rachel Jewkes, pers. comm., July 20, 2015.

28. See also Bosson et al. 2009; in addition, Eriksson Baaz and Stern (2009, 499) imply a similar argument about the "fragility . . . of militarized masculinity."

29. When presenting my research, I am frequently asked a version of the following question: "Why do combatants need to rape to create social bonds? Why can't they just play chess/play soccer/go out for ice cream?" This series of psychological studies offers an initial answer. An especially interesting finding (Vandello et al. 2008, 1335) is that in experimental settings, men who received a "gender-threatening" treatment were more likely to select an aggressive task (boxing) than a nonaggressive one (finishing a puzzle) to perform next.

30. William Hague, "Confronting Rape as a Weapon of War: A Challenge for Our Generation," speech delivered at the conference "Preventing Sexual Violence in Conflict and Post-Conflict Situations, Wilton Park, November 14, 2012, https://www.gov.uk/government/speeches/confronting-rape-as-a-weapon-of-war-a-challenge-for-our-generation.

31. Focus group, Northern Province chiefdom, April 29, 2007.

32. The 2003 HIV/AIDS adult prevalence rate in Sierra Leone was estimated to be 7% of the adult population (CIA 2003). One RUF ex-combatant reported that he did not believe AIDS exists because he had never seen anyone die of AIDS (Interviewee 4, RUF ex-combatant, July 10, 2006). NGO workers said that this reaction is typical of much of the population, who often mistake the advanced stages of AIDS for tuberculosis or who dismiss the severity of the disease because the symptoms of earlier stages of AIDS are more subtle than those of other STIs. Interview with Nurse-Patient Advocate, International Rescue Committee, Kailahun, July 25, 2006.

33. Interviewee 2, SLA ex-combatant, July 10, 2006.

34. Interviewee 3, RUF ex-combatant, July 10, 2006; Interviewee 5, RUF/AFRC ex-combatant, July 10, 2006.

35. The historical record, on the other hand, contains many examples of the scourge of STIs affecting fighters. There is evidence from World War II that "poor sexual hygiene" at its peak caused the US Army to lose the service of eighteen thousand combatants per day. The two most common STIs were gonorrhea and syphilis, which in 1943 required a hospital stay of thirty days and a six-month treatment, respectively ("Venereal Disease and Treatment during WW2," WW2 US Medical Research Centre website, https://www.med-dept.com/articles/venereal-disease-and-treatment-during-ww2/, accessed December 29, 2015). In fact, 41% of disease-related hospital admissions for the entire US Army between 1942 and 1945 were the result of three STIs: gonorrhea, syphilis, and chancroid, a bacterial infection (Smallman-Raynor and Cliff 2004, 537).

36. Interviewee 18, RUF ex-combatant, June 4, 2007; Interviewee 17, RUF ex-combatant, June 1, 2007.

37. Interviewee 10, RUF ex-combatant, May 28, 2007; Interviewee 16, RUF ex-combatant, June 1, 2007; Interviewee 9, RUF ex-combatant, August 2, 2006.

38. Interviewee 16, RUF ex-combatant, June 1, 2007.

39. Interviewee 10, RUF ex-combatant, May 28, 2007.

40. Interviewee 17, RUF ex-combatant, June 1, 2007.

41. Interviewee 11, RUF ex-combatant, May 28, 2007.

42. Centers for Disease Control, "Gonorrhea—CDC Fact Sheet (Detailed)," http://www.cdc.gov/std/gonorrhea/stdfact-gonorrhea-detailed.htm; "Syphilis—CDC Fact Sheet (Detailed), http://www.cdc.gov/std/syphilis/stdfact-syphilis-detailed.htm.

43. Interviewee 3, RUF ex-combatant, July 10, 2006.

44. For example, Interviewee 11, RUF ex-combatant, May 28, 2007.

45. I do not consider these additional costs in depth because they do not seem to present a substantial challenge for armed groups. While fear of future prosecution is a potential cost, the record shows that, even in cases of mass rape, very few named perpetrators are ever held responsible through a formal justice process. From an individual's perspective, then, future prosecution is (unfortunately) not a rational deterrent. (See Cronin-Furman 2013 for an examination of international criminal prosecutions as a deterrent for mass atrocities.) Reputational costs, on the other hand, might be a more immediate concern, but the types of groups that engage in civilian abuses are unlikely to care much about reputational costs.

46. Amir (1971, 38) defines group rape as rape involving three or more perpetrators and one victim.

47. See Littman and Paluck 2015 for a review of the psychological literature on the puzzle of ordinary people and collective violence.

48. As one example, scholars have estimated that only 388 battles took place over the entire decade-long conflict in Sierra Leone (Bellows and Miguel 2009).

49. Militia ex-combatant, interview with author, Atambua, West Timor, July 31, 2012. Members of the Saca militia described a similar blood-drinking swearing-in ceremony.

Two militia refugee camps leaders, interview with author, near Kupang, West Timor, August 3, 2012.

50. As noted earlier, one argument for why social cohesion was so poor during the Vietnam War despite intensive training is that combatants were separated from the groups with whom they had trained and then deployed individually (e.g., Kenny 2011). This process has important similarities to being randomly abducted into an armed group; the armed group units are comprised of members who do not know one another.

51. Specifically, Card (1996, 12) asks, "What is the likelihood that males would rape in war if they fought side by side with equally trained and armed females and under the command of even more powerful females, in a society in which this phenomenon was not exceptional? Gang rape is an unlikely instrument of heterosexual peer bonding."

52. Interviewee 10, RUF ex-combatant, May 29, 2007.

53. Brownmiller (1975, 5) writes that "rape has played a critical function . . . [as] a conscious process of intimidation by which *all men* keep *all women* in a state of fear" (emphasis in original).

54. See also Hoover Green 2011 on the role of political education in mediating violence.

55. In chapter 2, I test proxies for insurgents' lack of accountability to civilians (contraband funding and diaspora support) in a statistical analysis. However, it is difficult to operationalize the norms of combatant groups in order to test Wood's hypothesis more directly in a quantitative, cross-national analysis.

56. Interviewee 5, RUF/AFRC ex-combatant, July 10, 2006.

57. Wood (2012, 393) also defines opportunistic sexual violence as violence for "private reasons, not group objectives."

58. Interviewee 4, RUF ex-combatant, July 10, 2006.

59. Interviewee 2, SLA ex-combatant, July 10, 2006.

60. Interviewee 7, former Falintil commander, Dili, June 24, 2012.

61. Gender consultant, interview with author, Dili, July 4, 2012.

62. Timorese victim's rights advocate, interview with author, July 4, 2012.

63. Related arguments have been used to explain the absence of wartime rape against civilians in some contexts. Scholars have hypothesized that the presence of women fighters in an armed group may mitigate the incidence of rape against noncombatants because female fighters serve as rape substitutes for noncombatant victims (e.g., Gutiérrez 2008; Annan et al. 2011). These scholars argue that the availability of women within an armed group may allow men to form sexual relationships, whether coerced or consensual, with their female peers. Gutiérrez (2008) theorizes that the inclusion of a substantial number of women in the Revolutionary Armed Forces of Colombia (FARC)—who commonly experienced rape and other forms of sexual violence—may have prevented that group from committing acts of sexual violence against civilians. Annan et al. (2011) make a similar argument: that forced marriage within the Lord's Resistance Army (LRA) obviated the rape of civilian women. See Cohen 2013b for a detailed exploration of this idea in the context of Sierra Leone, where the presence of women in fighting factions was not correlated with the absence of rape.

64. See also Fujii (2013, 411), who examines the rationality of what she terms "extra-lethal violence," or those acts that breach norms about the "appropriate treatment of the living as well as the dead."

65. Weinstein (2007, 200) defines violence broadly—to include killing, rape, abduction, forced labor, forced displacement, looting, and destruction—but the data used in his case studies are mainly focused on killing, looting, and destruction (table 6.2) and are limited to killing in the cross-national analysis (table 8.1).

66. Contraband and diaspora funding are not the only types of material support that an insurgency might receive, but they are among the more commonly cited forms of external support. Weinstein (2005, 599) gives three examples of "economic endowments" that a rebel group might use: "natural resources, diaspora remittances, or the support of an external patron." Further, Weinstein (2005, 612) suggests that what matters most for his argument is not broad military support from an external sponsor, but rather those forms of support that can easily become a selective incentive used to entice recruits—such as money, food, and clothing. In chapter 2, I explicitly test the first two of these types of support, contraband and diaspora funding, which are arguably the most relevant to this argument.

67. One challenge of these types of arguments is that they tend to view the utility of rape as near-universally beneficial (and often costless) from the perspective of armed groups. If that were true, the incidence of rape should not vary significantly by conflict. Indeed, some scholars maintain that rape is a ubiquitous form of wartime violence, particularly in recent conflicts (Farr 2009). However, as I argue in chapter 2, the observed variation in reported wartime rape is dramatic; some conflicts experience mass rape while others experience very little.

68. Beyond terrorizing a particular ethnic group, it is possible that rape is used as a targeted form of violence against certain populations. For example, combatants may rape a specific class of victims during a conflict in order to punish those who disagree with the aims of the combatant group or to discourage those who are considering disagreeing. This argument is drawn from Kalyvas (1999), who shows that selective violence can be used as a tool of coercion to prevent civilians from supporting the opposition. Rape may also be ordered as a collective punishment. For example, in a February 2011 landmark verdict, a colonel in the Congolese army was found guilty of ordering his troops to rape and terrorize the village of Fizi in retaliation for the death of one of his soldiers. The number of rape victims was unclear, but sixty-two women sought medical treatment after the attack and forty-nine women testified at the trial, including against the commander himself (AP 2011). As with the ethnicity-specific argument, rape as a punishment—whether collective or more targeted—is necessarily directed from those at the top. If rape is targeting specific victims or types of victims, the orders concerning choice of victims and types of violence to inflict must be orchestrated by commanders.

69. Scholars also maintain that spreading HIV through wartime rape is also a form of rape as genocide, even though the victim who contracts HIV may live for many years (e.g., Sharlach 2000).

70. Valentino (2004), on the other hand, argues that mass killings—of which genocides are a subset—are rarely motivated by ethnic hatreds, occurring instead because of powerful leaders and apathetic publics.

71. Nitsan's master's thesis, "Controlled Occupation: The Rarity of Military Rape in the Israeli-Palestinian Conflict" (2007), is available only in Hebrew. However, she writes in English about the thesis—and the national controversy it provoked in Israel—in Nitsan 2012. See also Wood 2006.

72. For definitions of genocide and ethnic cleansing, see the *PITF Problem Set Codebook* (Vienna, VA: Political Instability Task Force, Center for Systematic Peace), accessed December 29, 2015, http://www.systemicpeace.org/inscr/PITFProbSetCodebook2014.pdf.

73. While ethnic cleansing may occur even in the absence of ethnic hatred (for example, when combatants seek to punish an ethnic group for supporting the opposition, rather than because of hatred per se), most arguments about rape during episodes of ethnic cleansing focus on hatred as the central motivation.

74. For this reason, when warring groups expect to live together following conflict, Hayden (2000) predicts that rape will not be used. However, this prediction raises the question of why rape occurs in many civil wars that do not involve secession.

2. RESEARCH STRATEGY, CROSS-NATIONAL EVIDENCE (1980–2009), AND STATISTICAL TESTS

1. This dataset is an extension and an updated version of the dataset used in Cohen 2013a. The changes are described in the appendix. The extension includes three additional years of data (extended from 2009 to 2012, the most recently available year at the time of writing) and five additional conflicts. The number of conflict-years increased from 963 to 1090.

2. While the temporal patterns of different forms of violence may appear similar, often the peaks of the different forms occur at different times. I consider this essential evidence to establish that different forms of violence require different explanations.

3. See the appendix for a discussion of possible sources of bias—including issues of veracity in the interview process—and several strategies I used to mitigate these biases.

4. Perhaps most frequently cited in the research on wartime rape are the statements from perpetrators in Bosnia-Herzegovina (e.g., Alexandra Stiglmayer, *Mass Rape: The War against Women in Bosnia-Herzegovina*, as cited in Henry, Ward, and Hirschberg 2003).

5. Speculating about perpetrators' motives and experiences may be necessary in the midst of conflict, when it can be unsafe, for both researchers and interviewees, to discuss war violence in detail. However, researchers have conducted successful studies of rape and sexual violence in the midst of ongoing conflict in some cases (e.g., Eriksson Baaz and Stern 2009; Swiss et al. 1998).

6. Particularly challenging are cases where rape is authorized, not directly ordered (Wood 2016); tangible evidence of authorization may be difficult to find.

7. Besides evidence of direct orders, Wood (2012, 418) lists other potential indicators that could imply rape was directed by the command, including punishment of combatants who refused to participate. I find almost no evidence of this in the cases included in this book, besides social costs (see especially the interview evidence from Sierra Leone in chapter 3).

8. Other scholars have implemented surveys of ex-combatants, including in Sierra Leone (Humphreys and Weinstein 2004), Liberia (Pugel 2007), and Uganda (Annan et al. 2008). However, because of both practical and ethical considerations, such surveys do not always inquire about the violence to which a combatant was a witness or a participant. In addition, even the best surveys are limited, because they are not able to capture the details and nuance of individual experiences. For this reason, interviews with ex-combatants are perhaps the best method for gathering useful and detailed data on the process of perpetrating violence.

9. Non-combatant interviewees are generally described as they themselves chose (i.e. State Department official; gender consultant). Ex-combatants are described in terms of their faction and—because it would otherwise be difficult to tell individuals from the same faction apart—are each assigned a unique number (e.g. Interviewee 2, RUF ex-combatant). The numbering starts at 1 in each fieldwork site. (Ex-combatant interviewees are largely but not exclusively men. When I have interviewed a woman ex-combatant, I note it explicitly in the citation.)

10. Data collection on rape was conducted only on those years that overlap with the period of study. Thus, if a war began before 1980, the data reflect only that part of it starting in 1980. One reason for this decision is that the State Department's human rights reports began in 1975, and reliable reporting on violence, sexual or otherwise, is least likely in its first few years. The potential problems posed by this collection strategy are mitigated in part by controls for the duration of the war. See the *Human Security Report 2012* for a critique of this approach; specifically, the authors write of the earlier years in these data, "We believe that there is a strong possibility that the low levels of reported sexual violence in this period were almost certainly a function of low levels of reporting,

not low levels of sexual violence" (HSRP 2012, 115n34). To address this concern, in the robustness checks described at the end of this chapter, I subdivide the dataset into decade-long periods and test each period separately.

11. The US State Department Country Reports on Human Rights Practices are submitted on an annual basis to the US Congress and include information on "internationally recognized individual, civil, political, and worker rights" for all UN member states. More information can be found at http://www.state.gov/j/drl/rls/hrrpt/.

12. While the specific armed group, rather than aggregated group type, may be the ideal unit of analysis, there are two main concerns with such disaggregated data. First, a complete dataset of *all* armed groups during *all* civil conflicts does not exist. UCDP/PRIO armed group data includes armed groups that reach the twenty-five-deaths threshold, but because of this coding rule, these data include only the most lethal groups. Second, even given a complete set of all armed groups, accurate conflict-year data on the perpetration of wartime rape by individual armed groups on the cross-national level are challenging to code, because reports are not always specific about who the perpetrators were. For example, there may be reports that "rebels" committed widespread rape, but in cases with more than one active rebel group, it is not clear which particular group or groups were perpetrators. If disaggregated data are collected on level of the armed group, reports of "rebels" perpetrating rape in cases with more than one rebel group are not codeable and thus would be missing from the dataset. More aggregated data of the sort employed in this analysis avoids missing these highly relevant, but less specific, details as reported in the original source.

13. This is a revised coding rule from Cohen 2013a, in which descriptions of strategic intention were coded as 3. The revision to the coding rules resulted in a handful of coding changes to conflict-years in the dataset. However, several well-documented conflict-years that are widely recognized to have had mass rape but that did not meet this rule were retained as a 3 coding, including Bosnia in 1994. A description of the changes that were made is provided in the appendix.

14. As presented in chapter 3, 1999 was a peak year for rape in the Sierra Leone civil war, confirming that the revised coding rule captures those cases that are known to be the most severe.

15. Gang rape was specifically reported in twelve of the twenty-one wars in which at least one conflict-year was coded as 3, and incidents of conflict-related gang rape were reported in ten of the thirty-eight wars that were coded as a 2 as the highest level. There were no other reports of conflict-related gang rape. As additional supporting evidence of the correlation between gang rape and widespread rape, available detailed survey data on conflict-related sexual violence in the DRC, Sierra Leone, and Liberia indicate that gang rape was quite frequent in each of these conflicts—in some cases constituting the vast majority of the reported rape. All three of these cases are coded as 3 in my data.

16. In her study of gang rape in US college fraternities, Sanday (2007, 83) writes that perpetrators "brag about the act among their male friends and revel in a sense of enhanced masculinity that comes from a feeling of sexual power and dominance over women."

17. In preparing to collect information for its annual human rights reports, the State Department issues detailed instructions to each field office on what data to gather and report. The instructions might require, for instance, that the number of prosecutions for domestic violence be cited. The content of the instructions change annually and are vetted in a clearance process each year. Over time, as congressional interest in certain forms of violence has evolved, reflecting the changing interests of the human rights advocacy community, the instructions have required reporting on previously ignored forms of violence. For example, the instructions for the 2010 report required that field offices gather data on child marriage practices for the first time, due to congressional demands for this

information. Ideally, an analysis of these annual instructions would determine whether wartime rape was consistently on the agenda during the study period. According to interviews with State Department officials, although the instructions are not classified, they are considered "proprietary," and are not publicly accessible. A FOIA request for these instructions is ongoing at the time of this writing. As is displayed in figure 2.4, the data reveal reports of wartime rape as early as 1981, suggesting an awareness of the problem even in those early years.

18. Mala Htun and S. Laurel Weldon, "Civic Origins of Progressive Policy Change: Combating Violence against Women in Global Perspective, 1975–2005—CORRIGENDUM," *American Political Science Review* 109, no. 1 (February 2015): 201, doi:10.1017/S0003055415000015.

19. For a detailed argument against the claim that the global trend of wartime rape is getting better over time, see Hoover Green, Cohen, and Wood 2012.

20. One scholar who worked with Sierra Leonean refugees in Liberia noted that all of the women he interviewed self-identified as victims of rape; he reasons that these admissions are an effort by the women to "[establish] themselves as 'legitimate recipients' of humanitarian aid" (Utas 2005, 409).

21. Fionnuala Ní Aoláin (2012) writes, "feminist scholars have consistently decried State Department reports, citing the reports' systematic failure to address and note violations of women's rights–including women's right to sexual autonomy."

22. State Department officials themselves admit that the reports were "politicized in the earlier years." State Department officials, interview with author, June 10, 2009.

23. This is what happened with the 1999 report on Indonesia, according to a former State Department official: "The 1999 Indonesia report is the longest, most detailed human rights report that year. . . . [The author] had an 'end justifies the means' sort of approach . . . and took all the stuff that the NGOs were saying and threw it in there. . . . The bottom line is that the 1999 report is a compilation of what was in the activist literature at that time." However, the official admitted that this kind of report-writing was unusual and, indeed, "sins of omission might be a bigger problem than reporting on stuff that actually never happened." Former State Department official, interview with author, July 12, 2012.

24. A former State Department official who had drafted human rights reports for numerous countries where he was stationed over the course of his career explained, "The quality and reliability of the reports vary, though more than one person is involved in the writing of every report. But sometimes it comes down to a judgment call. I might include a report of a massacre, but it has to be based on how credible the source is. The ICRC [International Committee of the Red Cross], for example, is an extremely solid source, and they never, ever exaggerate. But sometimes I had to agree not to cite them directly, so if I got information from them, I'd need to look for another open source that I could cite." Former State Department official, Dili, Timor-Leste, July 12, 2012.

25. A previous version of this comparison, analyzing only the subset of African conflicts, appeared in Hoover Green, Cohen, and Wood 2012. The Sexual Violence in Armed Conflict (SVAC) dataset, created by the author and colleagues at the Peace Research Institute Olso (PRIO), codes information on reports of conflict-related sexual violence by specific armed actors for a different universe of cases (civil and interstate wars and small-scale conflicts, as defined by UCDP/PRIO conflict data). See Cohen and Nordås 2014 for an analysis of the differences between the two datasets.

26. The UCDP/PRIO Armed Conflict Dataset, which has become the most widely used conflict dataset in the field, includes information on all conflicts between 1946 and 2014. More information is available here: http://www.pcr.uu.se/research/ucdp/datasets/ucdp_prio_armed_conflict_dataset/.

27. Of the seventy-five conflicts that appear in both datasets, 44% of the wars had identical codes for the highest levels of reported sexual violence/rape. Of the cases in which coding differed, all cases of disagreement resulted from either differences in the unit of analysis or differences in the coding rules between the two projects. For example, in the State Department reports, massive rape in Rwanda is described as being committed by "both combatant forces," resulting in both state and rebel actors being coded as perpetrators in my data. However, because these groups were not specifically named, the SVAC project—which uses the armed group-conflict-year as the unit of analysis—did not utilize this information for a coding decision. Even given these differences, there was perfect agreement for the highest level of sexual violence/rape for state actors (33% of the conflicts) and for rebel actors (53% of the conflicts).

28. See Miller 2013 for an analysis of the global reactions to the public sexual assaults in Egypt since the revolution of 2011.

29. I indicate a parenthetical case name from Fearon and Laitin 2015 for countries where there was more than one major civil war during the study period.

30. Of the ninety-one total wars in the study period, 59% (fifty-four wars) were ethnic, 19% (seventeen wars) were not ethnic, and 22% (twenty wars) were ambiguous or mixed.

31. While other scholars have noted that violence is typically committed in escalating cycles in which fighters mimic the brutality of their foes, it is interesting to note that rape was reported to be asymmetric—that is, committed by only one side—in more than one-third (38%) of the cases.

32. U.S. Department of State, *Country Reports on Human Rights Practices for 1991*, 861, available at http://onlinebooks.library.upenn.edu/webbin/serial?id=crhrp.

33. There was also variation by region in perpetrator type (not shown). Wars with only insurgent perpetrators occurred mostly in Eastern Europe and Sub-Saharan Africa, while wars with only state perpetrators were most frequent in Sub-Saharan Africa and the North Africa/Middle East region.

34. Percentage of Muslim adherents was determined using the variable *Muslim* from Fearon and Laitin 2003.

35. In the statistical analyses, I test the effect of *Muslim* and find that it is negative and statistically significant for insurgent-perpetrated rape and otherwise not significant (not shown).

36. However, the WomanStats Project (2011) ranks rape—not limited to periods of war—as either "prevalent" or "endemic" in much of the region.

37. The ideal measure of recruitment would vary by conflict-year, on a scale similar to how wartime rape is measured. However, due to the amount of missing data on the armed group-conflict-year level when coding these data from State Department reports, I instead use a conflict-level dummy variable in the analysis. In addition, as with the rape variables, these measures are not disaggregated by armed group, but are aggregated to the level of the group type.

38. For Uganda, see U.S. Department of State, *Country Reports on Human Rights Practices for 1996*, 301; for Guatemala, see U.S. Department of State, *Country Reports on Human Rights Practices for 1991*, 613. Both are available at http://onlinebooks.library. upenn.edu/webbin/serial?id=crhrp.

39. I code abduction and forced recruitment separately; by contrast, Eck (2014) argues that they are part of a continuum, ranging from social pressure to threats of force to outright force.

40. Mulligan and Shleifer (2005, 88) define conscription as the "legal and regulated form of forced labor for the state."

41. For Nicaragua, U.S. Department of State, *Country Reports on Human Rights Practices for 1985*, 616; for El Salvador, U.S. Department of State, *Country Reports on Human Rights*

Practices for 1991, 598; for Ethiopa, U.S. Department of State, *Country Reports on Human Rights Practices for 1983*, 119. All available at http://onlinebooks.library.upenn.edu/webbin/serial?id=crhrp.

42. I used multiple sources for conscription data in order to cover as long a time period as possible and to include all of the conflicts. For the study period, data from Pickering 2010 are available until 2001; from Horowitz 2014, until 2005; and from Karim 2015, until 2012 and alphabetically through Papua New Guinea, at the time of writing. Missing values for the Syria (FSA) conflict were coded from The Military Balance (2012) to avoid losing that entire conflict in the cross-sectional analysis.

43. Two alternative measures of state weakness are described in the robustness checks, at the end of the chapter.

44. The correlation between *Troop Quality* and the level of rape perpetrated by states is -.05. A correlation matrix is displayed in table 2.13.

45. Two alternative measures of gender inequality—women's rights and female labor force participation—are described in the robustness checks at the end of the chapter.

46. Despite the utility of fertility rates as a proxy for gender inequality, it may be argued that fertility rates will be influenced by excess birth caused by mass wartime rape. However, medical research indicates that the rate of pregnancy is only 5% per rape (Holmes et al. 1996), so even in cases where rape was widespread, it is unlikely that so many pregnancies would result as to affect the national fertility rate.

47. The fertility variable was missing in a few conflict-years; I used the Croatian fertility rate for the 1991 Yugoslavian conflict-year and interpolated values using the Serbian fertility rates for the 1998–1999 Yugoslavian conflict-years.

48. A value for *Drugs* was missing in four conflicts in Fearon and Laitin 2015: Iran (MEK), Thailand (Hill Tribes, CPT), Nigeria (NVPDF), and Nigeria (Boko Haram). For these wars, I coded *Drugs* as 0 to avoid losing observations.

49. Data and brief narratives of each event are listed in "Table A-1: Political Instability Task Force (PITF) Consolidated Problem Set, Historical State Armed Conflicts and Regime Crises, 1955–2013," available at http://www.systemicpeace.org/inscr/PITF%20Consolidated%20Case%20List%202013.pdf. The narratives in the table provide short descriptions of the specific perpetrators of each event along with the month and year that each event occurred. Of the nineteen conflicts in the study period coded as experiencing genocide/politicide, seventeen conflicts have only state perpetrators and two conflicts have both state and nonstate perpetrators (Angola [UNITA] and Burundi).

50. Although both variables have a mixed/ambiguous category, I use the most conservative coding (a clearly secessionist aim and a clearly ethnic war) to create the ethnic cleansing variable.

51. The battle deaths data are based on the UCDP/PRIO Armed Conflict dataset (Pettersson and Wallensteen 2015), which has different coding rules than the Fearon and Laitin 2015 data, resulting in the large number of missing data points.

52. Two additional measures of deaths in conflict—mass killing and conflict intensity—are described in the robustness checks at the end of the chapter.

53. *Duration* is a constant for each conflict. I also created an incremental duration variable that varies by each conflict-year as a robustness check (not shown); the main results do not change with the incremental duration variable.

54. I do not perform a fixed effects analysis for two reasons. First, because the data includes only active conflict-years, the panels are both unbalanced (ranging from one to several dozen observations) and relatively small. Second, several challenges are associated with using fixed effects for nonlinear models with smaller panels that produce biased beta coefficients and standard errors. Thus the favored approach is utilized here: namely, an ordered probit model with clustered standard errors.

55. The cut points displayed in tables of regression results provide information about the probability of falling into each category of wartime rape, conditional on explanatory variables being zero. While the cut points provide little substantive information about how the combatant socialization argument fares in predicting wartime rape, the statistical significance of the cut points provides additional assurance that the categories of the dependent variable are indeed distinct from one another.

56. Another reason for the lack of significance of state failure in the case of state-perpetrated rape may be the variable used for state weakness. The *Magfail* variable is a conservative measure capturing various degrees of total state collapse. Under such conditions, when the state no longer exists per se, state forces may join other active armed groups to commit violence—in which case the violence would be coded as insurgent-perpetrated violence.

57. The negative association of genocide with wartime rape may also be an artifact of reporting bias—women may be killed after being raped, resulting in rape being underreported.

58. The broader question of why insurgencies commit seemingly counterproductive violence against civilians is beyond the scope of this analysis, but has inspired numerous recent studies (e.g., Hovil and Werker 2005; Wood 2010). See also the discussion in chapter 1.

59. Despite the lack of evidence for a more systematic association, there are cases where experts believe that rape has been used as a tool of ethnic cleansing, in order to force the births of babies with different ethnic identities than their mothers, including the rape by Serb forces in Bosnia in the 1990s and the rape by Pakistani forces in Bangladesh in 1971 (Smith-Spark 2004).

60. I used CLARIFY software (Tomz, Wittenberg and King 2003) to calculate the predicted probabilities.

61. Replications files for all of the analyses in this chapter, including the robustness checks, are available from the author.

62. To reduce the amount of missing data, I aggregated battle deaths of different insurgent groups when it was possible to match several UCDP/PRIO wars to one Fearon and Laitin war, and I used the aggregated battle deaths to code intensity based on the UCDP/PRIO coding rules. Altogether, 214 conflict-years are missing and six conflicts are without any intensity data.

63. I considered two other measures of violence, but neither was appropriate for the present analysis. The Correlates of War intrastate dataset v.4.0 (Sarkees and Wayman 2010) codes conflict—rather than the conflict-year—as the unit of analysis. Thus, although there are data on aggregate battle deaths, it is not possible to determine year-to-year variation. The UCDP One-Sided Violence dataset (Eck and Hultman 2007) codes perpetrator-year as the unit of analysis, so deaths by conflict-year are not readily available. Further, for countries with overlapping conflicts, it is difficult to determine the number of victims of one-sided violence when the perpetrator is the state actor.

64. Much of the data is taken from the World Bank 2009 female labor force participation series (World Bank 2009), which measured the proportion of the female population, ages fifteen and above, that participates in the labor force. Since this series has not been updated, I filled in missing values using the International Labour Organization estimate (World Bank 2015b). Finally, for any remaining missing values, I used the national estimate (World Bank 2015c).

65. Each of the rights variables is coded on a four-point scale. Zero indicates that these rights are not encoded in laws, 1 means there are some legal rights but they are not enforced, 2 indicates that there are some rights that are enforced, but discrimination against women still exists in practice, and 3 signifies that all or almost all rights are guaranteed by law

and that the government fully enforces these laws. The CIRI data (2014) covers the years from 1981 to 2011 and are missing for periods of interruption or interregnum; these observations are dropped from analyses.

66. None of the women's rights variables is significant, with the exception of social rights in one specification—but not in the hypothesized direction.

3. MASS RAPE BY REBEL ACTORS

1. The history provided draws largely from Smith, Gambette, and Longley 2004 and Humphreys and Weinstein 2004.

2. I do not rely on data from the Sierra Leone Special Court (SLSC), mainly because testimonies given in the court are likely to be biased for a number of reasons that make them less useful for the present study. For example, court lawyers selected witnesses for the SLSC for particular purposes, and their experiences may not be representative of a more random sample. In addition, individuals—especially perpetrators of violence— may have strong incentives to relate a selective version of the truth in a courtroom setting. Another challenge is the sheer number of court documents that have yet to be aggregated into a quantitative dataset: the RUF trial alone contains 171 testimonies that comprise 18,000 pages of documents (ten Bensel 2014). Because of these challenges, I use information collected from my own fieldwork interviews for perpetrators' perspectives, instead of relying on the SLSC transcripts.

3. Additional information on patterns of rape and other forms of violence is available in a number of other sources. For example, the Human Rights Watch report *"We'll Kill You If You Cry": Sexual Violence in the Sierra Leone Conflict* (Taylor 2003) provides richly detailed excerpts from many interviews with victims.

4. These categories include amputation, physical assault, property violations, forced displacement, drugging, arrest and detention, forced recruitment, sexual slavery, forced labor, sexual violence, and forced consumption; the dataset includes subcategories for numerous more specific forms of violence, including rape, which is the category I use in this chapter. See Asher (2009) for more detail on why and how these categories were determined. Note that, for various reasons, killing was not itself a category of violence; I rely on TRC data for information on reported deaths.

5. See Gohdes 2010 for an analysis of the differences between the SLWCD survey and the TRC data. Gohdes argues that it is critical to rely on more than a single source when examining patterns of violence; to the extent possible, I discuss the patterns and differences between sources throughout the chapter.

6. As per the user agreement for the TRC dataset (Gohdes and Ball 2010), I note the following: "These are convenience sample data, and as such they are not a statistically representative sample of events in this conflict. These data do not support conclusions about patterns, trends, or other substantive comparisons (such as over time, space, ethnicity, age, etc.)." See https://hrdag.org/sierra-leone-data. I do use these data—combined with other sources—to draw such conclusions.

7. I ultimately visited eighteen villages in six chiefdoms in the three main provinces and the Western Area in Sierra Leone. See Cohen 2010 for a description of how the sample of interview sites was chosen. Random selection of interview sites in Sierra Leone presented a variety of challenges. Logistically, traveling in the rural areas of Sierra Leone can be extremely challenging. My translator and I were generally based in larger towns, and we hired motorcycles (with drivers) to drive us to the selected villages each day. We traveled on the backs of motorcycles between 1½ and 8 hours round-trip each day. Some of the villages were located near fairly good dirt roads, but many of the villages were accessible only by a very rocky bush path—a six-inch wide lane in the middle of the dense jungle. The travel conditions, particularly once the rainy season had started, were treacherous. Parts

of Sierra Leone are swampy; we had to use a canoe to get the motorcycles across a river in one case and wade through a river in another case. Several times on our journeys, there was no road; we had to drive though grass that was taller than the bikes. Our motorcycle drivers would not take us to some of the villages I had selected because of the distance and poor road conditions; in these cases, we skipped the village I had initially chosen and visited the next randomly selected place.

8. Although rape was widespread, women were not the main victims of war violence. According to the TRC data, across all violation types, men suffered an average of two violations to every one that women did; exceptions include rape and sexual slavery, which reportedly affected only women.

9. Specifically, the SLWCD survey contains a total of 229 incidents of rape, reported by 179 of the surveyed households (household heads could report incidents of rape for multiple household members). The initial sampling design for the SLWCD survey was based on the 1985 census, the most recently available at the time; updated 2004 census data became available after the survey was conducted. Due to updated census data, as well as to an error overestimating the population of the Port Loko district, sampling weights—calculated by the survey author—must be employed when interpreting the raw response data. For all estimates of the incidents of violence presented in this chapter, including in all of the figures, I use these weighted estimates. An explanation of the development of the weights is available in Asher 2009.

10. Although the two sources agree on the peak years, they differ on the percentage of all reported wartime rape that occurred during these years. The SLWCD survey indicates that 68% of all reported rape was committed in 1998 and 1999, while the TRC data indicate that 37% of the total occurred in these years.

11. The SLWCD survey instrument did not inquire about the exact number of perpetrators, but it did distinguish between single perpetrators and a group of perpetrators.

12. Although later I argue that committing rape in a public manner was part of the process of enabling perpetrators to perform for each other, messaging a willingness and prowess for violence, an alternative argument was offered by an interviewee: ambush by opponents was less likely when the rape was in an open space (Interviewee 16, RUF ex-combatant, Freetown, June 1, 2007). This alternative, however, cannot account for why gang rape was more common than single-perpetrator rape.

13. Interviewee 6, RUF ex-combatant, August 1, 2006.

14. Interviewee 13, RUF ex-combatant, May 30, 2007.

15. Interviewee 8, female RUF ex-combatant, August 2, 2006.

16. Interviewee 17, RUF ex-combatant, June 1, 2007.

17. Interviewee 9, RUF ex-combatant, August 2, 2006.

18. Interviewee 24, female RUF ex-combatant, March 28, 2008.

19. This finding is echoed in an analysis of the victims of RUF violence, where no ethnic group was disproportionately represented (Conibere et al. 2004).

20. Focus group respondent, Northern Province, Sierra Leone, April 2007.

21. I attempted a more systematic analysis of the ethnicity of victims and perpetrators of rape, but findings should be interpreted with caution due to poor data quality on reported ethnicity. Using data from the SLWCD survey, rape victims reported they were from a total of fourteen different ethnicities, with 28.7% of rape victims reporting Temne (9,122 of 31,759) and 18% of rape victims reporting Mende (5,723 of 31,759). Mende and Temne each make up about 30% of the population (CIA 2003); thus, Mende women are underrepresented in the sample. In addition, I calculated how often rape victims identified at least one member of the group that attacked them as a co-ethnic. This measure is rough, as 30% of the raw data on ethnicity of the perpetrator are missing, as is one case

of the ethnicity of the victim (these missing cases are 69 of the 229 reports in the dataset). However, in the available data, rape victims identified at least one of their attackers as co-ethnics in about 7% of the reported cases (2,195 of 31,759).

22. I did find rare exceptions. In one village, a woman described the first attack on her village, during which she perceived that the rebels seemed to be seeking out the wealthier inhabitants. This woman owned a large store in the town, with an inventory of "two hundred bushels of rice," and she has gold caps on her front teeth, making her obviously wealthier than many of her neighbors. She stated that she was chosen to be raped because she was rich, although her perception was not echoed by others in the group, who thought that the rebels had not sought out particular people to harm (Focus group, Malal Mara chiefdom, April 30, 2007).

23. The Human Development Index is a composite measure that was created by the UNDP to measure relative levels of development—including health, education and living standards—in each country. More information is available here: http://hdr.undp.org/en/content/human-development-index-hdi.

24. Interviewee 17, RUF ex-combatant, June 1, 2007.

25. Interviewee 2, SLA ex-combatant, July 10, 2006; see also Keen (2005, 242).

26. In contrast, evidence shows that the armed groups used *collective* punishment—through the use of killing, torture, and other terrible violence—of entire villages believed to be harboring enemy factions (e.g., Smith, Gambette, and Longley 2004).

27. An additional fifty cases of rape by "rebels" were reported; if these are included as violations by the RUF, the percentage of reported rape perpetrated by the RUF increases to 78%.

28. Interviewee 20, SLA ex-combatant, June 19, 2007. These soldier-rebels are sometimes called "sobels," or "soldiers by day, rebels by night" (Keen 2005, 109). The TRC report also noted that the word "sobel" was used by civilians to describe "government soldiers who were suspected of joining or collaborating with the RUF rebels during the course of the conflict" (TRC 2004, vol. 3B, 170). According to the TRC report, the term "sobel" came to symbolize the mistrust of the SLA and the perceived collusion of the SLA with the rebel fighters (vol. 3A, 197).

29. To underscore the complexity of the war, two of the other main sources used in this analysis (NPJW and SLWCD) sometimes lump together as a reported perpetrator the AFRC with the RUF and/or the SLA (and the SLA with the RUF and/or "rebels"). To avoid confusion, I report data disaggregated by reported perpetrator whenever possible and note cases when I include more than one faction in a statistic or figure. Although aggregating these factions (and other small factions, like the West Side Boys) into the RUF is a simplification that masks some differences in ideology and structure, all of these groups used similar forced-recruitment methods, did not generally offer basic training, and comprised largely the same types of people.

30. However, not included in these numbers are seventy-nine additional incidents in which the AFRC is reported as a co-perpetrator of rape with the RUF, beginning in 1997.

31. These data include all reports in which the SLA or AFRC was cited as a perpetrator, but other groups were often cited for the same incident. For example, of the fifty-six incidents in the SLWCD survey that included the AFRC, the RUF was also reported as a perpetrator in thirty-four of them; with the sampling weights, the RUF co-perpetrated about 67% of the incidents.

32. Even very violent armed groups do not always view rape as a payment. According to Weinstein (2007, 111–16), Renamo in Mozambique began to rely on abduction to garner recruits after paying fighters became impossible; the "payoff" to the fighters, in lieu of monetary compensation, was permitting combatants to loot and steal from civilians. However, it is notable that rape was not considered a type of payment akin to looting—Renamo considered rape a "serious crime" (147).

33. This assumes a nontrivial percentage of men who want to rape; as discussed in chapter 1, some research supports the idea that ordinary or typical men may have an inherent desire to rape (Malamuth 1981; Mezey 1994).

34. The TRC data are similar, with the youngest reported victim six years old, and the oldest sixty-nine. However, age data are missing is 40% of reported cases.

35. Exact ages of victims were available in most cases in the SLWCD survey (205 of 229). In nineteen cases where exact age was missing, the maximum estimated age value was used. In five cases, all age information was missing—these cases are excluded from these calculations. Population percentages are calculated from the 1995 population estimates for females in Sierra Leone from the UN Population Division, *World Population Prospects: The 2008 Revision*.

36. See Marks (2013a) for an analysis of forced marriage and the regulation of sexuality within the RUF.

37. In the Humphreys and Weinstein (2004) data, only one of the AFRC informants reported being offered access to women, and no combatants from other factions reported that women were offered to them as an incentive.

38. John Bellows and Edward Miguel, "War and Local Collective Action in Sierra Leone," working paper, University of California Berkeley Institutions and Governance Program, 2007, http://www.igovberkeley.com/sites/default/files/miguel_endo2007.pdf.

39. Kalyvas (2007) raises vexing questions about the RUF and its use of abduction; for example, given that the RUF was reportedly so well funded, its reliance on kidnapping, as opposed to paying, recruits was a curious decision. Keen (2005, 137) reports that rebels complained of their low pay—which was estimated at less than 50 cents per day—even in the early years of the war (e.g., 1994 and 1995) .

40. The data are unclear as to the role material incentives may have played in individuals' motivations to join the RUF, and how material incentives may correlate with violence. Humphreys and Weinstein (2006) find that, across combatant groups, units composed of people who joined because they were offered money or diamonds were more violent toward noncombatants than those who were not offered such incentives. However, according to the survey data, only 5% of RUF members reported being offered diamonds and only 16% reported being offered money to join the faction. In addition, RUF *volunteers*, who made up a small proportion of the group, were not generally motivated to join by material gains, while some RUF *abductees* reported being offered diamonds or money (Humphreys and Weinstein 2008, 13). Thanks to Jeremy Weinstein for assistance on this point.

41. As described later, in 1991, "only" 78% of RUF fighters reported having been abducted (Humphrey and Weinstein 2004).

42. Some scholars claim that volunteers made up a larger proportion of the RUF than is shown by the survey data used here. See, for example, Peters and Richards (1998, 187), who write that "many" of the child soldiers they interviewed had joined voluntarily.

43. Detailed analyses of the female propensity to rape in peacetime are not readily available; however, existing evidence indicates that few perpetrators of rape are women. In a study of 223 cases of gang rape collected from news reports, legal sources, books, and articles, researchers found a total of 739 perpetrators, of which only 17 were female. Moreover, these women were mainly involved in securing the victim of the attack rather than actively participating in the rape (Porter and Alison 2006).

44. Interviewee 4, RUF ex-combatant, July 10, 2006.

45. Interviewee 13, RUF ex-combatant, May 30, 2007.

46. Interviewee 12, RUF ex-combatant, May 29, 2007.

47. The RUF was a party to 376 of 392 total battles; of those 376 battles, the RUF lost 186. (All values calculated from the Bellows and Miguel 2006 dataset.)

48. See Hoffman (2007), who argues that the CDF was less a military organization than a militarized social network based on preexisting relationships.

49. Arguably, this general pattern of violence by the CDF may also support a simple hypothesis that the more armed groups rely on civilian support, the less they perpetrate abuse. However, this simple hypothesis does not explain the forms of violence that the group chooses to perform, nor the fact that several sources report that new recruits to the CDF seemed qualitatively different than the old ones.

50. Interviewee 7, RUF ex-combatant, August 1, 2006.

51. Interviewee 33, female SLA ex-combatant, March 31, 2008; Interviewee 20, SLA ex-combatant, June 19, 2007.

52. Interviewee 12, RUF ex-combatant, May 29, 2007.

53. Interviewee 10, RUF ex-combatant, May 29, 2007; Interviewee 12, RUF ex-combatant, May 29, 2007.

54. Interviewee 14, RUF ex-combatant, May 31, 2007.

55. Interviewee 11, RUF ex-combatant, May 28, 2007.

56. Interviewee 14, RUF ex-combatant, May 31, 2007.

57. Interviewee 6, RUF ex-combatant, August 1, 2006.

58. See Wood (2016) on strategic rape, which includes rape that is authorized, not directly ordered. Authorization to rape is different than violence perpetrated as a practice, which is what I am arguing in this case.

59. Interviewee 18, RUF ex-combatant, June 4, 2007.

60. While ex-combatants may have an incentive to lie about their involvement in violence, there are several reasons to believe that respondents were truthful on this point. First, as per the Lomé peace accord, only the twenty-one individuals indicted by the Special Court process can ever be charged with crimes for the wartime atrocities—a fact well known to the ex-combatants. Second, the vast majority of ex-combatants I interviewed said they had been given no orders to rape. Third, ex-combatants have an incentive to claim they were ordered to rape—to displace responsibility onto their superiors—rather than pointing out, as they did, that they had committed rape of their own volition. See the appendix for a longer discussion of the issue of veracity in interviews.

61. Interviewee 7, RUF ex-combatant, August 1, 2006. Wood (2010) argues that the participation in sexual violence by commanders, as well as reports that sexual violence was perpetrated on state property, may serve as "indirect indicators" of effective command and control. But commanders' co-perpetration of rape is not the same as their giving orders to commit rape, which typically implies more than just the peer pressure to emulate commanders and cannot be easily refused absent punishment.

62. Interviewee 17, RUF ex-combatant, June 1, 2007. See also Marks (2013a), who notes that, while rape was officially punishable by death, this was rarely enforced, especially at the front lines.

63. Interviewee 16, RUF ex-combatant, June 1, 2007.

64. Interviewee 6, RUF ex-combatant, August 1, 2006.

65. Indeed, the premise of the SLSC process would seem to require that rape was ordered from the top down. The prosecution of a small number of people for the atrocities of the war implies a strict chain of command, with responsible actors at the top ordering their fighters—who presumably had no choice but to act and are thus deemed comparatively blameless, at least legally—to behave in particular ways. Humphreys and Weinstein (2006) make a similar argument about this fundamental assumption of the justice process in Sierra Leone.

66. David Keen (2005, 242) locates motivation for the rape in the desire to humiliate; however, he also recognizes that the rapes were not simply random, particularly because some were organized events.

67. Interviewee 10, RUF ex-combatant, May 28, 2007.

68. Interviewee 4, RUF ex-combatant, July 10, 2006.

69. Interviewee 12, RUF ex-combatant, May 29, 2007.

70. As described in chapter 2, the cross-national data showed no association between broad measures of gender inequality and wartime rape. The micro-level evidence from Sierra Leone offers additional support. If gender inequality helped to predict wartime rape, we would expect that armed groups with greater gender equality would be the least likely to commit rape. A plausible proxy for gender equality in an armed group is the proportion of female combatants; the recruitment, training, and arming of women all suggest that the group values the contributions of women as fighters. Of all the factions in the Sierra Leone war, the RUF had the largest percentage of female combatants; thus we might expect that the RUF would perpetrate the fewest acts of rape. However, evidence demonstrates that the proportion of women in an armed group in Sierra Leone is *positively* associated with the perpetration of rape; that is, despite having by far the most female fighters, the RUF or "rebels" perpetrated the vast majority of the rape. In contrast, the SLA/AFRC was about 9% female and was implicated in about 8% of the rape reported in the SLWCD survey, while the CDF, about 2% female, perpetrated less than 1% of the rape (Cohen 2013b).

71. Women were reported as perpetrators *only* in acts of group rape; men were reported as perpetrators in both single-perpetrator rape and gang rape. Women in the RUF participated in many types of group violence, including amputation, beating, looting, and forced cannibalism; see Cohen (2013b, 405–6).

72. Members of the RUF were the only ex-combatants interviewed who had seen or heard about women in their respective factions participating in rape. The female members of the SLA, for instance, said that rape was a punishable offense in their unit. One woman said, "The SLA had strong rules about not raping women. I saw an SLA soldier get tied up and beaten after he got caught raping a woman in a house outside of Freetown." Interviewee 21, female SLA ex-combatant, March 25, 2008.

73. Interviewee 28, female RUF ex-combatant, March 29, 2008.

74. Similar observations have been made about the phenomenon of gang rape in college fraternities: providing a victim to be raped is a method used to increase cohesion and solidarity among perpetrators (O'Sullivan 1991, 146).

75. Interviewee 24, female RUF ex-combatant, March 28, 2008.

76. Interviewee 24, female RUF ex-combatant, March 28, 2008.

77. Interviewee 26, AFRC ex-combatant, March 29, 2008. Statements such as these cast doubt on arguments about a "sisterhood," in which women do not inflict certain types of pain on other women (Sharlach 1999).

78. See Cohen (2013b) for a more detailed examination of female perpetrators of rape in Sierra Leone. See also Mackenzie (2012) for a study of female fighters in the Sierra Leone civil war and their reintegration in the postwar period.

4. MASS RAPE BY STATE ACTORS

1. Although Timor-Leste is still called East Timor in some circles, I use "Timor-Leste" to refer to the country officially known as the Democratic Republic of Timor-Leste, and I use "East Timorese" or "Timorese" as the demonym to refer to the people of Timor-Leste. The exception is in direct quotes from a source or interviewee who uses "East Timor."

2. While this analysis is focused on rape during the war in Timor-Leste, the Indonesian military perpetrated many other documented forms of sexual violence, including sexual slavery and forced prostitution, reportedly holding East Timorese women as captives, sometimes in makeshift brothels, for long periods (see Mason 2005; CAVR, chap. 7.7).

3. Some scholars argue that the violence in 1999 was targeted rather than random (see, e.g., Robinson 2006; Boyle 2009). I discuss these arguments later in the chapter.

4. Many scholars have debated the reasons for the incredible violence of the 1999 crisis. In addition to the two arguments highlighted in the chapter, some maintain that the violence was intended to purge the country of foreigners, while others argue that there is a connection between the forms of violence and traditional methods of East Timorese warfare.

5. The history in this section draws from numerous sources, including the CAVR report (2005, chaps. 3 and 4), Rees 2004, Myrttinen 2009, and timelines from CNN ("Timeline: East Timor's Long Path to Nationhood," May 16, 2002) and the BBC ("East Timor Profile—Timeline," February 17, 2015). The relatively small size of Timor-Leste was itself used as a justification for the Indonesian occupation. However, Timor-Leste is larger in land mass than over three dozen of the world's countries, including Lebanon and Qatar, and comparable in population to Gambia (Durand 2006).

6. For a detailed history of this period, including the rise of Gusmão as the leader of Falintil, see Rees 2004.

7. While Falintil had relatively few armed women fighters, women were heavily involved in the clandestine movement as couriers, cooks, and nurses and in a myriad other roles that provided support to the fighters. Recognition of these efforts has become a major political issue in postconflict Timor-Leste. For more on women's roles in the resistance, see, for example, Franks 1996; Cristalis and Scott 2005; and Loney 2012.

8. This sustained development marked a departure from the Portuguese efforts to develop Timor-Leste during the previous four centuries. The Portuguese had created a highly segregated class system, with Portuguese at the top, then *mesticos*, or mixed-race Timorese, then *assimilados*, or Timorese who spoke Portuguese and were of the Catholic faith. Only children of the ruling classes, and some of the *mesticos*, were allowed to attend the state-run schools. The remainder of the Timorese, who spoke no Portuguese—the vast majority of the population—could attend only one of a very small number of schools that were run by Catholic missionaries (Cristalis 2009, 76).

9. Religious dissimilarity with Muslim-majority Indonesia became an important expression of the desire for a separate identity from Indonesia. Over the course of the occupation, Timorese converted to Catholicism in large numbers. In 1975, Cristalis (2009, 61) estimates, only 30% of Timorese were Catholic; over subsequent decades, the vast majority of Timorese converted.

10. By one estimate, 90% of the weaponry used in the initial invasion of Timor-Leste was supplied by the United States, and a substantial proportion of military supplies, training, and support was provided to Indonesia by the United States, the United Kingdom, and Australia throughout the period of the occupation (Nevins 2002, 630–31).

11. Former CAVR researcher, interview with author, Dili, Timor-Leste, July 10, 2012.

12. More broadly, see Mack (1975) and Lyall and Wilson (2009) for two arguments—one political, one tactical—about why asymmetric wars so often result in the stronger state losing the conflict.

13. Irian Jaya, East Timor, and Aceh were collectively called *daerah rawan,* or troubled provinces, and scholars argue that the Indonesian response to rebellions in each province was marked by similarities in the use of torture, rape, and murder (Widjajanto and Kammen 2000). For an opposing view—specifically, that the militias in East Timor and Aceh differed fundamentally—see Barter (2013).

14. Former State Department official, interview with author, Dili, July 11 and 12, 2012.

15. Walter (2009, 154–55) hypothesizes that another reason for the referendum decision was that the war in Timor-Leste had become too costly in terms of military causalities and economic expenses.

16. Suharto's regime, with its focus on the *Pancasila* ideology, had a strict policy of not negotiating with separatist groups that threatened the notion of a unitary Indonesian state (Stanton 2009).

17. Stanton (2009, 336) argues that these changes were spurred by concern about international audiences and the desire to democratize. However, the worst sexual violence of the conflict (and among the worst of other forms of violence) occurred at the very end of this period, when Indonesia was well on its way to democratization.

18. The fact that the TNI (Indonesian National Army) was both withdrawing troops in response to political directives *and* organizing militias in Timor-Leste is puzzling. It is a matter of some debate as to whether the militias were organized by the TNI acting on its own initiative, or whether there were orders from Habibie to do so in order to allow Indonesia a degree of plausible deniability. Stanton (2009) maintains that the 1999 violence was a result of Habibie's inability to control the security forces, not part of a carefully planned campaign. Walter (2009) offers a different argument, suggesting that Habibie directed the violence in order to signal to other potential secessionists across Indonesia that independence would be very costly. Nevins (2005, 5) makes a similar, more general argument: that the violence was intended to send a message to Indonesia's pro-democracy and human rights movements about the costs of challenging the military.

19. For a critique of this approach, see Drexler (2013, 85), who writes, "Militias have different names and histories but . . . they have become one group frozen into an abstract conflict narrative."

20. See Robinson 2010 for a personal account of working in the UN mission during the 1999 crisis.

21. The current situation in Timor-Leste is characterized by low-level sporadic violence attributed to various martial and ritual arts groups that comprise former militia, ex-combatants, and disenfranchised youth (Myrttinen 2009).

22. Uppsala Conflict Data Program, *UCDP Conflict Encyclopedia*, Uppsala University, Department of Peace and Conflict Research, www.ucdp.uu.se/database.

23. As discussed in chapter 2, Timor-Leste is included in several recent cross-national studies that include what is believed to be the worst instances of wartime rape and other forms of sexual violence (e.g., Bastick, Grimm, and Kunz 2007; UN 2001; Farr 2009).

24. Swaine (2011, 51) acknowledges that Timor-Leste is a case in which "women's experiences with violence are . . . widely acknowledged but are by no means fully understood or explored." Harris-Rimmer (2009, 2) also writes of "inadequate documentation," and states "there are no accurate statistics on the scale and distribution of sexual violence during the occupation until 1999."

25. Falintil ex-combatant, interview with author, Dili, January 28, 2008.

26. NGO worker/former director of Fokupers, interview with author, Dili, August 6, 2012. Fokupers is an East Timorese women's NGO.

27. NGO worker/former Fokupers activist, interview with author, Dili, August 6, 2012.

28. NGO worker/former director of Fokupers, interview with author, Dili, August 6, 2012.

29. NGO worker/former director of Fokupers, interview with author, Dili, August 6, 2012.

30. NGO worker/former director of Fokupers, interview with author, Dili, August 6, 2012.

31. Best practices included female statement-takers, private interviews with female enumerators, a public hearing focused on women, and gender-segregated counseling workshops (CAVR 2005, chap. 7.7, 4).

32. Note that the CAVR (2005, chap. 7.7, 6) cites three male victims, but Silva and Ball (2006, 66) write that there were no male rape victims.

33. Without estimates of the numbers of victims in Sierra Leone and Timor-Leste, it is difficult to state with certainty that rape in Sierra Leone was more or less prevalent than in Timor-Leste. However, both cases are classified as mass-rape wars, the most severe of the categories in this study.

34. A former Fokupers volunteer described the organization's data-gathering process as follows: "We gathered the victims and we would have activities and would provide ritual counseling, including praying and singing. They did not want Fokupers workers to take notes, or even to be holding a pen. We would have to remember the stories and then scribble them down in the bathroom." NGO worker/former director of Fokupers, interview with author, Dili, August 6, 2012.

35. Studies on related topics in Timor-Leste, such as a household survey on torture of about one thousand households, published in the *Lancet*, found that 5% of respondents reported "rape or sexual abuse" (one of six specific types of torture included in the survey); reports of children raped by Timorese militias were also made (Modvig et al. 2000, 1763).

36. The Timor-Leste Gender-Based Violence Survey (Hynes et al. 2003, 301) defines sexual violence as "improper sexual comments, [being] stripped of clothing, internal body cavity searches, unnecessary medical exam of private areas, unwanted kissing, [being] touched on sexual parts of body, [being] beaten on sexual parts of body, and [being] forced to give/receive oral/vaginal/anal sex, or rape."

37. The survey was not conducted in the border districts, where the worst violence of the 1999 period was reported. Absent data from these districts, it is not possible to determine whether rape is, in fact, underreported or simply occurred less frequently in the two districts where the survey was conducted. However, Dili was one of the two districts surveyed, and—based on other sources—rape was frequently reported in Dili.

38. Former Australian diplomat/researcher, interview with author, Dili, July 15, 2012.

39. Other forms of indirect evidence can been used to estimate rates of rape, such as the rate of cervical cancer in the years following conflict (Ghobarah, Huth, and Russett 2003); these rates are not available for Timor-Leste. The lowest level of aggregation of rates of cervical cancer reported by the World Health Organization is the Southeast Asia region.

40. Two local feminist researchers/heads of a local NGO, interview with author, Dili, August 5, 2012.

41. Falintil ex-combatant, interview with author, Dili, June 19, 2012.

42. NGO worker/former director of women's organization, interview with author, Dili, August 6, 2012.

43. Two human rights researchers, interview with author, Dili, August 6, 2012.

44. Timorese historian/Falintil ex-combatant, interview with author, Dili, July 7, 2012.

45. My fieldwork was cut short by the February 2008 assassination attempt on President José Ramos-Horta, the Nobel Peace Prize winner, who was shot in the stomach near his home in Dili. A notorious rebel leader and former commander of the military police, Alfredo Reinado, was killed in the attack. After the shootings, a state of emergency was declared; a strict curfew was imposed in Dili, and travel outside of the capital city was restricted. Thus, it became impossible to conduct interviews, particularly about a previous conflict.

46. Timorese historian/Falintil ex-combatant, interview with author, Dili, July 7, 2012.

47. See also Drexler 2013 on this point.

48. One researcher from the International Crisis Group who has done extensive interviews with ex-militia, including the leadership, in West Timor, said that it was "surreal how easy it was to find the militia leaders" (ICG researcher, Skype interview with author, July 11, 2012). On the issue of impunity for the militia in West Timor, a lawyer who works with the UN in Timor-Leste said, "Most of the men being investigated [by the UN currently] are in West Timor. The UN unit is investigating crimes by the TNI and the militias, but the TNI

will never return to Timor-Leste to be prosecuted, and Indonesia will not send back the militias who are in West Timor. Timor-Leste will not press the issue. They are sensitive about their relationship with Indonesia. In fact, it is likely that no one who is indicted will ever face trial. And even if they did, the sentences are so minor—perpetrators will face only two to eight years for murders. What is the point [of the UN Serious Crimes Unit]? Honestly, I ask myself that. . . . The truth is that I came to do law, but now I realize that I am here to do politics." UN lawyer, interview with author, Dili, July 7, 2012.

49. Recent studies of the militia tend to rely on secondary sources rather than interviews (e.g., Barter 2013). Exceptions include Myrttinen 2009 and Satki 2012, on the relationships among East Timorese residing in West Timor.

50. During this second period of consolidation, the goals of the guerrillas reportedly shifted to a war of attrition. One local researcher described the change as follows: "From 1980 to 1999, the objective of the resistance shifted from national liberation—the idea of liberating a people and a nation—to defeating the Indonesian military."

51. Some observers have an alternate view of the patterns of violence. One researcher hypothesized that 1999 only seemed more violent because there were more international witnesses: "One reason that it may look like there was a spike of violence in 1999 is that there were more reporters here then. There were peaks of violence throughout the occupation." Gender consultant, 2012.

52. Some scholars argue that the violence in 1999 was targeted against Falintil supporters (e.g., Boyle 2009). However, most analysts maintain that the 1999 violence was indiscriminate, or at least much more so than in previous stages of the conflict.

53. The Indonesian armed forces, which included the army, the navy, and the air force, were known as the ABRI (Angkatan Bersenjata Republik Indonesia, or the Armed Forces of the Republic of Indonesia) for the majority of the study period. The armed forces were renamed the TNI (Tentara Nasional Indonesia, or the Indonesian National Army) in April 1999, when the police force and armed forces were separated. The police force became known as the Polri (Polisi Republik Indonesia, or the Police of the Republic of Indonesia). To avoid confusion, and because the precise faction that perpetrated acts of violence is often not identified in sources, I refer to all of these groups simply as the Indonesian military.

54. One form of sexual violence that was sometimes reported, although not explored in depth in this analysis, is forced sterilization. A number of studies have noted that forced sterilization and forced contraception by the Indonesian government was common. The government would reportedly perform surgeries or deliver injections without informing women and girls what they were receiving—or claiming that they were being vaccinated when instead they were injected with the contraceptive Depo-Provera (Sissons 1997; Mason 2005). However, a former State Department official, tasked with leading an investigation of these charges during the occupation, said that he remains unconvinced of the accuracy of these reports: "There were also rumors of forced and coerced family planning. But we could not come up with conclusive evidence for this. There were probably some overly enthusiastic family planners—and in a Catholic province, people were especially sensitive to this. But there was no evidence of a campaign of forced sterilization." Former State Department official, interview with author, Dili, July 11, 2012.

55. One exception includes a news story about rape in Timor-Leste, published prior to the 1999 crisis, which quoted Bishop Belo emphasizing in a public discussion in Jakarta that women in Timor-Leste had been raped by the Indonesian military since 1975 (Williams 1998).

56. While these two patterns appear to be the most common, they were not the only forms of rape. Dunn (2003, 246–47) describes Indonesian troops "demanding women and girls to help them celebrate their victory," which was "said to have been a daily occurrence."

57. For an analysis that places the use of sexual torture in the Timorese and global contexts, see Stanley (2009).

58. Falintil ex-combatant, interview with the author, Dili, June 19, 2012.

59. NGO worker/former Fokupers activist, interview with the author, Dili, August 6, 2012.

60. Falintil ex-combatant, interview with the author, Dili, June 20, 2012.

61. Former CAVR researcher, interview with author, Dili, July 5, 2012.

62. Indonesian human rights lawyer, interview with author, Dili, June 29, 2012; Falintil ex-combatant, interview with author, Dili, June 26, 2012.

63. Female former MP, interview with author, Dili, July 13, 2012. A strong advocate for women's rights in Timor-Leste, the MP told of how the women who engaged in more voluntary sexual relations are now shunned by other East Timorese in present-day Timor-Leste: "The women who were involved with Indonesians—this is not seen as a sacrifice. These women were called 'Indonesian whores' by a female MP. But these women did not ask for it; whether willing or unwilling, they are now all victims. They are called *autonomistas*—essentially, traitors. Even their children are called this."

64. Former Timorese high-level official for the Indonesian government, interview with author, Dili, August 6, 2012.

65. The integration of local Timorese into the fighting of the conflict extended over the period of the occupation and allowed Indonesia both plausible deniability and a justification for its continued occupation of the territory (Robinson 2001; Thaler 2012; Drexler 2013). A variety of means by which to Timorize the conflict were employed, including the use of local informants, civil defense groups, and militias. Some Timorese combined their roles as informants or pro-Indonesia fighters with efforts to advance the cause of the resistance, serving as double agents. This created what Drexler (2013, 75) calls "gray zones of collaboration and betrayal" for many of the Timorese involved on both sides of the conflict, with devastating consequences for the fabric of social trust. A Falintil ex-combatant who had served as a self-described "involuntary helper" to the Indonesian military in his youth described how he would attempt to support the resistance by stealing from the military: "[As an involuntary worker] I was still allowed to go to mass, so I would deliver stolen weapons, uniforms, and food from the Indonesians. I would leave them in a particular place so that they could be picked up. . . . I would take the ammunition and give it to Falintil. I would wait until they were showering and then steal their uniforms from the door [laughing]." Falintil ex-combatant, interview with author, Dili, June 22, 2012.

66. UN worker, interview with author, Dili, January 29, 2008.

67. Local academic, interview with author, Dili, January 30, 2008.

68. However, the CAVR data are not disaggregated by the number of perpetrators; thus, the specific incidence of gang rape is impossible to discern.

69. Director of local NGO, interview with author, Kupang, West Timor, August 2, 2012.

70. Falintil ex-combatant, interview with author, Dili, February 4, 2008.

71. Falintil ex-combatant, interview with author, Dili, January 28, 2008.

72. Former CAVR researcher, interview with author, Dili, July 5, 2012.

73. Falintil ex-combatant, interview with author, Dili, January 28, 2008.

74. Timorese historian/Falintil ex-combatant, interview with author, Dili, July 7, 2012.

75. Former CAVR researcher, interview with author, Dili, July 10, 2012. He traced the history of women in the movement as follows: "In 1977, there was a decision by the Fretilin central command to involve women as a female detachment, and the women were to be trained with guns. But because of the counterattacks by the Indonesians, this idea was never developed. After the destruction of the liberated zones, civilians had to surrender, but fighters stayed in the jungle, including women. After 1979, all women were unarmed. Even though they lived with Falintil, they were not considered part of Falintil, but rather

civilians who lived in the jungle with the fighters. The women considered themselves part of Falintil, however."

76. Former *clandestina*, interview with author, Dili, July 24, 2012.

77. Female former MP, interview with author, Dili, July 13, 2012.

78. Similar competing arguments—whether the militia violence was directed from the top down or innovated from the bottom up—are described briefly in Nevins 2002 (where he terms the opportunism argument "the rogue element" school of thought) and compared in depth in Robinson 2001.

79. Stanton (2009) argues that Habibie withdrew his candidacy for the presidency in 1999 as a result of his inability to control the violence.

80. Militia ex-combatant, interview with author, Atambua, West Timor, July 30, 2012.

81. Former pro-integration activist, interview with author, Atambua, West Timor, July 31, 2012.

82. Former Falintil commander, interview with author, Dili, June 24, 2012.

83. Timorese victims' rights advocate, interview with author, Dili, July 4, 2012.

84. Former Apodeti/militia leader, interview with author, Dili, July 15, 2012.

85. Former State Department official, interview with author, Dili, July 11, 2012.

86. Former State Department official, interview with author, Dili, July 11, 2012.

87. Former CAVR researcher, interview with author, Dili, July 5, 2012.

88. Indonesian human rights lawyer, interview with author, Dili, June 29, 2012.

89. Former Falintil commander, interview with the author, Dili, June 24, 2012.

90. Falintil ex-combatant, interview with author, Dili, June 26, 2012.

91. Two local feminist researchers/heads of a local NGO, interview with author, Dili, August 5, 2012.

92. Former State Department official, interview with author, Dili, July 11, 2012.

93. Timorese former high-level official for Indonesia, interview with author, Dili, August 6, 2012. Indonesia had long promoted migration to Timor-Leste, however, so it is uncertain whether these people were Indonesians brought in to serve as militia fighters, as the interviewee suggests; they might have been residing in Timor-Leste as part of the migration program.

94. Former Apodeti/militia leader, interview with the author, Dili, July 15, 2012.

95. Female former MP, interview with author, Dili, July 13, 2012.

96. Timorese victims' rights advocate, interview with author, Dili, July 4, 2012.

97. Militia ex-combatant, interview with the author, Atambua, West Timor, July 31, 2012.

98. Militia ex-combatant, interview with the author, Atambua, West Timor, July 31, 2012.

99. Two local feminist researchers/heads of a local NGO, interview with author, Dili, August 5, 2012.

100. Former CAVR researcher, interview with author, Dili, July 5, 2012.

101. Militia refugee camps leader, interview with the author, outside Kupang, West Timor, August 3, 2012.

102. Falintil ex-combatant, interview with author, Dili, June 26, 2012.

103. Militia ex-combatant, interview with author, Atambua, West Timor, August 1, 2012.

104. Militia ex-combatant, interview with author, Atambua, West Timor, July 30, 2012.

105. Militia ex-combatant, interview with author, Atambua, West Timor, July 31, 2012.

106. Timorese former high-level official for the Indonesians, interview with author, Dili, August 6, 2012.

107. Aitarak militia ex-combatant, interview with the author, Atambua, West Timor, July 30, 2012.

108. Militia ex-combatant, interview with the author, Atambua, West Timor, August 1, 2012.

109. Militia ex-combatant, interview with the author, Atambua, West Timor, July 31, 2012.

110. Robinson (2006, 40) also writes that most of the victims of human rights violations in 1999 were not "prominent local or national figures," but rather "ordinary people living in villages thought to be pro-independence strongholds." At least part of the debate over whether violence was targeted may stem from differing definitions of indiscriminate violence. I consider violence against entire villages to be indiscriminate, but others, such as Robinson, may consider this to be targeted violence when directed against residents of areas thought to be supportive of independence.

111. An alternative argument might be that, in the Falintil strongholds, militias would have lower capacity and stronger organized resistance from Falintil forces. Thus, it may have been easier to commit violence in the border areas, where militias were stronger and more familiar with the communities. (Thanks to Kai Thaler for this point.) However, even if this were true, it does not follow from a revenge logic but instead would support an opportunism argument.

112. Robinson (2006, 53–54), however, interprets the consistency of the chaotic, frenzied nature of the militia violence as additional evidence that the militia were directed to behave in this manner in order to inflict maximum psychological fear.

113. Earlier incidents of violence, including the 1989 attacks on protestors during Pope John II's visit and the 1991 Santa Cruz cemetery massacre, are cited by Walter (2009) as examples of violence intentionally publicized to increase Suharto's reputational power. Yet this interpretation neglects the fact that Timor-Leste was essentially—and successfully—sealed off from outsiders for nearly twenty-five years. In addition, the 1989 papal-visit violence was orchestrated by Timorese, not the Indonesian security forces, in order to embarrass the Indonesian government. The Santa Cruz massacre was captured on camera purely by chance, by an undercover cameraman, and—counter to Walter's expectation—was met with denials from the Indonesian government regarding the extent of the violence, including the number killed.

114. Although most were press-ganged, not all East Timorese fighters were; for example, some East Timorese volunteered to fight with the Indonesians, including the UDT members who had fled to West Timor in 1974.

115. An exception is the creation of the *Tombak* troops, a small group of East Timorese who were armed only with spears (CAVR 2005, chap. 7.5, 37–39).

116. Director of local NGO, interview with the author, Kupang, August 2, 2012.

117. Timorese victims' rights advocate, interview with the author, Dili, July 4, 2012.

118. Timorese victims' rights advocate, interview with the author, Dili, July 4, 2012.

119. Militia ex-combatant, interview with the author, Atambua, West Timor, July 30, 2012.

120. Former CAVR researcher, interview with the author, Dili, July 5, 2012.

121. Gender consultant, interview with the author, Dili, July 4, 2012.

122. Falintil ex-combatant, interview with author, Dili, January 28, 2008.

123. Falintil ex-combatant, interview with author, Dili, February 4, 2008.

124. Indonesian human rights researcher, interview with the author, Dili, June 30, 2012.

125. Aitarak militia ex-combatant, interview with the author, Atambua, West Timor, July 30, 2012.

126. Militia ex-combatant, interview with the author, Atambua, West Timor, July 31, 2012.

127. Militia ex-combatant, interview with the author, Atambua, West Timor, August 1, 2012.

128. Former militia leaders, interview with the author, near Kupang, West Timor, August 3, 2012.

129. Militia ex-combatant, interview with the author, Atambua, West Timor, August 1, 2012.

5. LESS FREQUENT RAPE IN WARTIME

1. This estimate of deaths is the most widely accepted and frequently cited, although scholars' estimates have ranged from thirty thousand to eighty-two thousand (Hoover Green 2011, 237). Hoover Green (2011), using a sophisticated statistical triangulation method called Multiple Systems Estimation, also finds that about eighty thousand conflict-related deaths occurred in El Salvador, with the most deadly year being 1982.

2. Although the Armed Forces contain numerous subgroups—the army; a number of specialized security forces, including the National Guard and the Treasury Police; and paramilitary groups—for simplicity, I refer to all of these state-affiliated groups as the Armed Forces throughout this chapter. The one exception is when I briefly compare patterns of violence and recruitment by several subgroups (i.e., the army, the National Guard, and the National Police) later in the chapter.

3. The FMLN was an umbrella organization made up of five different rebel groups; however, I follow Viterna (2013) and treat the group as a unitary actor in this chapter. This decision is justified in part by the strong central command that controlled the activities of the subgroups; for example, evidence shows that the central command was able to rein in the violent activities of a subgroup when it did not believe the violence was justified or warranted (e.g., Wood 2009, 153).

4. The frequency of wartime rape in the El Salvador conflict is contested, and no consensus exists among scholars, activists, and experts on its true extent (Leiby 2011). Typically, experts on the case briefly mention that rape occurred, but provide little additional detail on frequency or patterns. Leiby (2011, 196) notes that human rights activists have argued that rape "occurred regularly" during the Salvadoran conflict. Viterna (2013, 31, 113) writes that nearly all of her interviewees experienced the "torture, rape and death of their family, friends and neighbors" and that "rapes in the war zone were . . . tragically common." Stanley (1996, 1) states that female victims of security forces were "often raped; so, less frequently, were men"—but rape is mentioned nowhere else in the book, except for the churchwomen case (described later in the chapter). Finally, Isikozlu and Millard (2010, 10) argue that El Salvador is an example of a conflict where "rape was extensively perpetrated by at least one group during the civil war"; using this criterion, they pair the case with Bosnia-Herzegovina in a comparative study. However, the authors base this claim on a small number of interviews with local activists and ex-combatants in El Salvador. As I discuss later, while it is possible that rape is severely underreported in available data sources, many experts agree that it is unlikely that rape in El Salvador occurred on a massive scale—and certainly not on a scale comparable to the rape in Bosnia-Herzegovina. Wood (2008, 332), for example, writes that sexual violence in El Salvador was "very low in comparison to Bosnia-Herzegovina and Sierra Leone." While reports of other forms of sexual violence, such as harm to the genitals of male detainees, appear commonly in source documents, *rape* is reported far less frequently (again, as compared to other cases considered in this book).

5. This history draws mainly from Bracamonte and Spencer (1995), Wood (2000, 2003), Peceny and Stanley (2010), and two documentary films that aired on PBS (and their corresponding websites): *Enemies of War* (2001, produced by Esther Cassidy and Rob Kuhns, New Day Films) and *Justice and the Generals: El Salvador* (2002, produced by Gail Pellett, Icarus Films).

6. Former FMLN commander, interview with author, San Salvador, March 30, 2009.

7. Armed Forces ex-combatant, interview with author, San Salvador, March 31, 2009.

8. Scholars disagree somewhat about the major cause of the reduction in violence by the state. Wood (2003) argues the change occurred because of external pressure from the United States, while Stanley (1996) argues that internal pressures caused the change, in that the Salvadoran government had become alienated and had created sufficient enemies as to almost cause its own defeat.

9. The two women were shot at close range in their genital areas—a fact not reported by the CVES. One scholar interprets this violence as evidence that the women were raped, arguing that the Armed Forces soldiers were hiding their sexual crimes by destroying the evidence (Tombs 2006).

10. Hayner (1994) notes that Salvadorans were explicitly excluded from taking part in the CVES, due to concerns about neutrality in a tense political postwar environment. The truth commission was staffed entirely by foreigners. The CVES was later critiqued for this decision, and for potentially silencing local perspectives.

11. The CVES, as compared to other major truth commissions—including those that took place in the other two cases in this book—was much smaller in scale, with a small staff and a short timeline of about nine months. Unlike the truth commissions in Sierra Leone and Timor-Leste, the CVES held no public hearings (Hayner 2006), an unfortunate loss of an opportunity to gain more detailed data on the violence.

12. Although the CVES report indicates a total of 22,000 incidents of violence, a dataset coded from the CVES data annex by researchers at the University of North Texas (UNT) includes a total of 20,929 incidents.

13. Tombs (2006) maintains that the CVES was silent around issues of rape due in part to its attempt to hold *individuals* rather than *institutions* responsible.

14. The annex uses the term *violaciones*, the Spanish word for "sexual violence." Although the specific form(s) of sexual violence is not explicitly defined, Leiby (2011) infers that the CVES used a very narrow definition of sexual violence: rape against mostly female victims (she notes only one male name of a *violacion* in the annex lists). In 2012, the annex became available, in Spanish, at the UNT Digital Library; see http://digital.library. unt.edu/ark:/67531/metadc268920. Hereafter, I refer to this annex as the "UNT data."

15. The CVES annex displays its own summary statistics of reports of rape received, in a brief section at the beginning; these reports include 270 direct reports and 180 indirect reports of rape (CVES 1993, 24). However, the UNT data include only 99 cases of *violaciones*. In the following analysis, I use data from Hoover Green (2014), who combined the UNT data (although her dataset includes 96 cases of sexual violence from the CVES) with an additional 313 cases reported to two other NGOs (El Rescate and CDHES). The inconsistencies in frequencies likely arise from the difficulty of accurately coding the data in the annex—several hundred pages of blurry photocopied text in very small type.

16. According to the mandate, the recommendations of the CVES were supposed to be legally binding, which is unusual for a truth commission mandate. Ultimately, some of the recommendations were implemented (e.g., the dismissal/retirement of about two hundred senior army officers), while others were never acted upon (e.g., the payment of reparations to the victims) (USIP, http://www.usip.org/publications/truth-commission-el-salvador>). The amnesty remains controversial in El Salvador, and calls to overturn the law—in order to hold perpetrators accountable—persist.

17. Documents from both organizations, which were smuggled out of El Salvador during the war, are archived at the University of Colorado, Boulder. However, the cache of documents that Leiby reviewed is not the full set of all such documents; a larger number of documents is held at the Tutela Legal offices in San Salvador, and the percentage of overlap between the Boulder archive and the Tutela Legal archive is unknown (Michele Leiby, pers. comm., January 5, 2015).

18. Leiby (2012, 358) reports that the category of "rape and gang rape" comprises 24% of the 123 total acts of sexual violence coded from these documents, which I calculated to be 29 reports; of these, Leiby reports that 10% were men, which I calculated to be 3 reports. In addition, using a broad definition of sexual violence, Leiby finds in the dataset coded from these documents that men comprise the majority of sexual-violence victims and that sexual humiliation—which includes forced undressing (a type of violence not included in the ICC definition)—is the most frequently reported category of sexual violence. Hoover Green (2011, 126) also uses data coded from official reports of these same legal aid organizations (originally gathered together by the Los Angeles–based NGO El Rescate and ultimately included in the 2014 dataset) and finds 111 reports of sexual violence (these are not disaggregated by type, so the proportion of rape is unclear); I use the Hoover Green 2014 data in the tables later in this chapter.

19. Human rights NGO president, interview with author, San Salvador, March 31, 2009.

20. Human rights activist, interview with author, San Salvador, April 3, 2009.

21. Former FMLN combatant, interview with author, San Salvador, April 2, 2009.

22. Scholars have argued that another source of bias could arise due to victims being killed after being raped. If, as Leiby (2011) and others have argued, there was a pattern of mass rape prior to executions—as in the El Mozote massacre and the murders of the churchwomen—then there may be few survivors or witnesses to report the violence. In addition, we cannot know what violence was suffered by the many people who were disappeared; it is possible—but unknown and unknowable—that they too were raped. However, patterns of violence as in the El Mozote massacre—which included mass rape and then large-scale killing—appear to be rare; evidence suggests that numerous such incidents of mass killing preceded by large-scale rape are unlikely (the CVES lists only three major massacres, including El Mozote, Sumpul River, and El Calabozo).

23. See Danner (1994) for a detailed examination of the El Mozote massacre. The massacre at El Mozote and the rape and murder of the churchwomen are both included in the findings of the CVES, but information on the rapes is conspicuously absent in the report. Specifically, rape is not included in descriptions of El Mozote and is mentioned only once in the churchwomen case (CVES 1993, 22); instead, the murders are the central focus (Tombs 2006).

24. Former FMLN commander, interview with the author, San Salvador, March 30, 2009.

25. The data used in chapter 2 of this book—coded from the State Department's Country Reports on Human Rights Practices—indicate only limited wartime rape by the state, and then only in the context of prison torture; indeed, I selected El Salvador as a case for this book based on these data. However, several infamous cases of sexualized violence by the Salvadoran government are not captured in the State Department reporting, including the massacre at El Mozote (which the US government dismissed as exaggeration for years) and the rape and murder of the four US churchwomen. See Valencia-Weber and Weber (1986) for a critique of the State Department's human rights reports for El Salvador and, particularly, its reporting on lethal violence. The authors write that the data on deaths and disappearances in the official weekly cables and annual reports were based exclusively on newspaper reports, even when other data sources were available; they note an instance in which an embassy official visited a site commonly used for dumping bodies and reported seeing six corpses, but these deaths were not recorded in the official cable traffic (745). Nonetheless, the authors show similar basic temporal trends in reports of deaths between the State Department and Tutela Legal, the Christian legal aid organization, despite their different organizational ideologies, which suggests that the State Department data on lethal violence, while underreported, may not be strongly biased.

26. Although some scholars have found that the sexual torture of men was common (e.g., Leiby 2012), Viterna (2013, 113) writes that no such violence was ever reported in any of the major human rights reports, or in her two hundred interviews or the many testimonies she had analyzed.

27. I return to these patterns across subgroups in the subsequent analysis. All three of these Armed Forces groups recruited their members through forcible means, though probably to varying degrees.

28. Isikozlu and Millard (2010, 33) write, "In the case of rape as a torture tool, most female detainees, if not all, were raped; in some, perhaps all, cases men were also raped while in detention." However, this claim is supported only by citations to two interviews.

29. U.S. Department of State, *Country Reports on Human Rights Practices for 1984*, 517, available at http://onlinebooks.library.upenn.edu/webbin/serial?id=crhrp.

30. Human rights activist, interview with author, San Salvador, March 31, 2009.

31. Human rights activist, interview with author, San Salvador, March 31, 2009.

32. Human rights activist, interview with author, San Salvador, March 31, 2009.

33. Interestingly, El Mozote was not thought to be an FMLN village. By many accounts, the massacre occurred after the FMLN had tried to encourage the villagers to leave, but the villagers had not trusted the guerrillas.

34. Human rights activist, interview with author, San Salvador, March 31, 2009.

35. Although not the focus of this analysis, there is some evidence of sexual harassment of female fighters, who comprised about 30% of the FMLN cadre (Rubio 2007). Some former fighters report that women in the FMLN faced sexual harassment and pressure to have sex by the men in the organization, but rape was rarely, if ever, reported. "Some women in the FMLN felt obligated to have sex with the commanders, but there was no overt violence involved," said a representative from one human rights organization (San Salvador, April 7, 2009). See also Viterna (2013) for a discussion of the complexities of "respect" for women within the FMLN; she argues that the focus was on respecting a man's exclusive sexual right to a woman rather than on respecting the rights of the woman.

36. Former FMLN commander, interview with author, San Salvador, March 30, 2009.

37. Female FMLN commander, interview with author, San Salvador, April 2, 2009.

38. See Viterna (2013) for an analysis of how sexuality was regulated with the ranks of the FMLN.

39. Viterna (2013, 113) notes that her interviewees commonly cited the fear of being raped in refugee camps in neighboring countries, and she includes the story of an eleven-year-old girl who was impelled to join the FMLN while a refugee in Honduras, after Honduran soldiers had threatened to rape the young women in her camp. However, Viterna notes that she was unable to find evidence that rape occurred in Honduran refugee camps.

40. Viterna (2013) also argues that the FMLN used these narratives of protecting women's sexuality because they served the group's goals of upholding a conservative or traditional gender arrangement.

41. One of Viterna's interviewees illustrates this point. While rumors of rape were rampant, evidence from primary witnesses or survivors is sparse. "Norma" reports to Viterna (2013, 113), "I never saw it, but I heard a lot of things about other places. . . . There were young girls that they would rape and after raping them, they would kill them."

42. A third alternative, which is not considered here in depth, is the simple hypothesis that groups that require civilian support will abuse the population less frequently. While that is strictly true—for instance, the FMLN relied heavily on civilian support and committed far less abuse than did the Armed Forces of noncombatants—the hypothesis explains neither the changes in the types of violence nor the temporal variation.

43. Armed Forces ex-combatant, interview with the author, San Salvador, March 31, 2009.

44. The single FMLN property crime report, from 1988, is not displayed in figure 5.1.

45. Others have argued that rape was directed from the top down as part of an Armed Forces military strategy. For instance, Isikozlu and Millard (2010, 32) write, "The Salvadoran army had a clear command structure and a clear war strategy. While there are no documents which state that rape was committed by order, the characteristics of some of the types of rape witnessed in El Salvador, at the hands of the armed forces or police structures, indicate that the events were *masterminded at high levels of command* within the perpetrating group" (emphasis added). However, few scholars argue that rape was commonly directly ordered, with the exception of a few high-profile cases, as previously discussed. For example, Tombs (2006) concurs that no clear orders were given to commit rape in El Salvador. Others argue that the very fact that the churchwomen from the United States were raped and murdered strongly indicates that these acts were ordered from above; such violence against foreigners was highly unusual (Aron et al. 1991). Another version of the strategic rape argument would be that violence was aimed at a particular class of victims—insurgents and their supporters—which is suggestive of orders to target certain people. However, being a "supporter" of the insurgency was often broadly defined to the point of meaninglessness, and claims that people had such affiliations were likely abused by state forces seeking an excuse for violence. For instance, Aron et al. (1991) find evidence that women who were desired as sexual objects were also accused of being guerrilla collaborators, and thus legitimate targets for rape by state forces.

46. In an interview, however, a military officer dismissed reports of widespread press-ganging as overblown: "Military service was compulsory during the war for both men and women, so kidnapping stories are likely related to this" (San Salvador, March 25, 2009).

47. U.S. Department of State, *Country Reports on Human Rights Practices for 1991*, section on El Salvador, available at http://onlinebooks.library.upenn.edu/webbin/serial?id=crhrp.

48. Former "cabo" in Armed Forces, interview with author, San Salvador, March 31, 2009.

49. Former FMLN leader, interview with author, San Salvador, April 1, 2009.

50. U.S. Department of State, *Country Reports on Human Rights Practices for 1985*, 516, available at http://onlinebooks.library.upenn.edu/webbin/serial?id=crhrp. The State Department reports first indicate forced recruitment by the FMLN guerrillas, including the recruitment of children, in 1984, and then again in each subsequent year (except for 1985) until 1992, when the peace accords were signed. This likely exaggerates the length of the practice, which most experts agree was fairly short-lived. The United States provided substantial military aid to the Salvadoran counterinsurgency; it is possible that political pressures biased the reporting on recruitment practices by the guerrillas. Additionally, in contrast to the State Department reports, Viterna (2013, 72) explicitly notes that women were never forcibly recruited during this period.

51. Former FMLN leader, interview with the author, San Salvador, April 7, 2009.

52. Former FMLN leader, interview with the author, San Salvador, April 1, 2009.

53. Military officer, interview with author, San Salvador, March 25, 2009.

54. Former FMLN commander, interview with the author, San Salvador, March 30, 2009.

55. Of course, leaving the country was another alternative for civilians. Many did leave, rather than joining the FMLN or being conscripted by the state, in a wave of mass migration to the United States and Mexico.

56. Although the CVES (1993, 37) notes that more than half of the complaints against the FMLN concerned "enforced disappearances and forcible recruitment," the formal

report makes only a few brief mentions of these, and the unpublished annexes include no such category of violation. Related violations in the annexes include disappearances and *secuestros* (kidnapping, usually for extortion). However, only one report of a kidnapping by the FMLN appears in the UNT data, making it unlikely that this category includes forced recruitment.

57. An additional forty-five incidents of kidnapping by the FMLN were reported, but these are likely cases of *secuetros*, or kidnapping for extortion, not abduction into the armed group.

58. Leiby (2011) interprets these patterns as evidence against the opportunism argument because, she argues, elite groups like the National Guard had the greatest independence from the central government (that is, the greatest opportunity) yet were not the worst perpetrators of rape. However, these elite groups were also the most highly trained and were specialists in "disappearances," resulting in two implications. First, in contrast to Leiby's argument, the elite forces might actually have had very little discretion in their choice of targets or forms of violence. And second, most of their victims were disappeared, meaning there is no way to know—no witnesses, no forensic evidence—if they were raped.

59. A better test would be to consider the patterns of perpetrators of rape in detention settings and whether perpetrators of prison torture had themselves been abducted. (That is, was rape being used as a cohesion-building exercise in detention?) However, after conducting extensive research and contacting a number of El Salvador experts (including some who had worked in the prisons at the time), I was able to uncover few definitive details about either the identity of the perpetrators of torture or the processes by which they ended up there. Several of these experts suggested that violence in detention was perpetrated by more elite or specialized units, or by long-serving enlisted members of the intelligence branches, who were less likely to have been recruited with force. Thus, rape in detention—including gang rape—may have followed a different logic than rape by the regular Armed Forces. One exception to the dearth of information on perpetrator identity is a declassified State Department cable, dated June 10, 1982, which described the torture of a suspected guerrilla sympathizer by a *comandante* (a noncommissioned offer ranked above a sergeant) in the National Police. The victim got to know his torturer over the three days he was imprisoned in a soundproofed torture chamber, and he later provided details to the US embassy. The victim reported myriad abuses, including torture to his testicles, but not rape or gang rape. The *comandante* was described as being in his mid-forties, without family, and having a fifth-grade education. The cable notes that he had "spent his life conducting torture and was rewarded for his efficiency in extracting information" (Digital National Security Archive [DNSA], El Salvador, 1980–1994 Collection, Cable number EL00757, June 10, 1982). These details suggest that the *comandante* was a specialist in torture, but whether that is true of many or most of the individuals in similar positions remains unclear.

60. Armed Forces ex-combatant, interview with the author, San Salvador, March 31, 2009.

61. Armed Forces ex-combatant, interview with the author, San Salvador, March 31, 2009.

62. Hoover Green (2011) writes that the standard three-months-long army training, which focused only on using weapons and tactics, was offered only toward the end of the war; earlier, there had often been no training at all. Other reports confirm that army training might last six months, at most (Chavez 1983).

63. Armed Forces ex-combatant, interview with the author, San Salvador, March 31, 2009. Hoover Green (2011, 197–98) also found evidence of sexual humiliation during the army's training process.

64. Armed Forces ex-combatant, interview with the author, San Salvador, March 31, 2009.

CONCLUSION

1. See Sjoberg (forthcoming) for a study on women as perpetrators of rape during wars and genocides.

2. Nicholas Kristof, "In This Rape Center, the Patient Was 3," *New York Times*, October 8, 2011, http://www.nytimes.com/2011/10/09/opinion/sunday/kristof-In-This-Rape-Center-the-Patient-Was-3.html?_r=0.

3. Although many welcome attention to the long-hidden problem of wartime rape, there is a vocal backlash against what some see as an overfocus on the issue. See, for example, Henry (2014) for an analysis of the feminist legal community's increasing concerns about a "fixation" on wartime sexual violence. Some scholars have expressed concern over creating a "hierarchy of crimes" (Henry 2014, 101) or perverse incentives to identify as a rape victim in order to better access services (e.g., Utas 2005). In addition, there have been a host of thoughtful critiques of the Global Summit and the advocacy campaigns focused so heavily on sexual violence; see Kirby 2015 for an examination of the politics of the Global Summit.

4. UK Foreign Commonwealth Office and the Rt. Hon. William Hague, "Global Summit to End Sexual Violence—The Aims," June 9, 2014, available at https://www.gov.uk/government/news/global-summit-to-end-sexual-violence-in-conflict-the-aims.

5. Liz Ford, "Sexual Violence in War: Women Must Get Reparations, Says Head of UN Women," *Guardian*, June 11, 2014, available at http://www.theguardian.com/global-development/2014/jun/11/ending-sexual-violence-conflict-summit-reparations-un-women-mlambo-ngcuka.

APPENDIX

1. The statistic that 75% of the women in Liberia were raped during the war has been repeated frequently in media and policy circles (e.g., Kristof 2009). See Cohen and Hoover Green 2012 for an analysis of the statistic's source and a discussion of its potential consequences.

2. Female villager, eastern chiefdom, Sierra Leone, July 18, 2006.

3. Once in Sierra Leone, when asked by a village chief how I had decided to visit a particularly remote village, I explained that a computer had randomly selected the location. Knowing that the notion of computers and random selection would not be well understood, my interpreter instead demonstrated the process by drawing slips of paper out of the chief's hat.

4. In her research on victims of sexual violence in Bosnia, Skjelsbæk (2011) also used female interpreters who had previous experience working with victims of violence.

5. For an excellent series of blog posts on the mechanics and utility of MSE for social science researchers, see Hoover Green 2013.

Adams, Sarah. 2005. "Straight Talk: Could 'Group Rape' Lessen the Perception of the Crime?" *Guardian*, September 20. http://www.theguardian.com/society/2005/sep/21/crime.penal.

Advocates for Human Rights. 2009. *A House with Two Rooms: Final Report of the Liberia Truth and Reconciliation Commission Diaspora Project*. Saint Paul, MN: Dispute Resolution Institute. http://www.theadvocatesforhumanrights.org/final_report.

African Rights. 1995. *Rwanda—Not So Innocent: When Women Become Killers*. Kigali: African Rights.

Alison, Miranda. 2007. "Wartime Sexual Violence: Women's Human Rights and Questions of Masculinity." *Review of International Studies* 33 (1): 75–90.

Allen, Beverly. 1996. *Rape Warfare: The Hidden Genocide in Bosnia-Herzegovina and Croatia*. Minneapolis: University of Minnesota Press.

Amir, Menachem. 1971. *Patterns in Forcible Rape*. Chicago: University of Chicago Press.

Annan, Jeannie, Christopher Blattman, Khristopher Carlson, and Dyan Mazurana. 2008. *The State of Female Youth in Northern Uganda: Findings from the Survey of War-Affected Youth*. Phase 2. http://chrisblattman.com/documents/policy/sway/SWAY.Phase2.FinalReport.pdf.

——. 2009. "Women and Girls at War: 'Wives,' Mothers, and Fighters in Uganda's Lord's Resistance Army." Unpublished manuscript. https://www.prio.org/utility/Download.ashx?x=146.

Annan, Jeannie, Christopher Blattman, Dyan Mazurana, and Khristopher Carlson. 2011. "Civil War, Reintegration, and Gender in Northern Uganda." *Journal of Conflict Resolution* 55 (6): 877–908.

Aoláin, Fionnuala Ní. 2012. "Some Caution in Reading Human Security Report." *IntLawGrrls* (blog), October 15. http://www.intlawgrrls.com/2012/10/some-caution-in-reading-new-human.html.

AP (Associated Press). 2011. "Congo Army Colonel Guilty of Ordering Mass Rape on New Year's Day." *Guardian*, February 21. http://www.theguardian.com/society/2011/feb/21/congo-rape-trial.

Aranburu, Xabier Agirre. 2010. "Sexual Violence beyond Reasonable Doubt: Using Pattern Evidence and Analysis for International Cases." *Law and Social Inquiry* 35 (4): 855–79.

——. 2012. "Beyond Dogma and Taboo: Criteria for the Effective Investigation of Sexual Violence." In Bergsmo, Skre, and Wood 2012, 267–94.

Arendt, Hannah. 1963. *Eichmann in Jerusalem: A Report on the Banality of Evil*. New York: Viking Press.

Aron, Adrianne, Shawn Corne, Anthea Fursland, and Barbara Zelwer. 1991. "The Gender-Specific Terror of El Salvador and Guatemala: Post-Traumatic Stress Disorder in Central American Refugee Women." *Women's Studies International Forum* 14 (1): 37–47.

Asher, Jana. 2009. "Methodological Innovations in the Collection and Analysis of Human Rights Violations Data." PhD diss. (draft), Carnegie Mellon University.

Asher, Jana, ed. 2004. *Sierra Leone War Crimes Documentation Survey Database*. Version 2. American Bar Association and Human Rights Data Analysis Group of Benetech. Available by request from Jana Asher.

Baron, Larry, and Murray Straus. 1989. *Four Theories of Rape in American Society: A State-Level Analysis*. New Haven: Yale University Press.

Barry, Lyndal. 2001. *East Timorese Children Involved in Armed Conflict, Case Studies Report: October 2000–February 2001*. Dili: UNICEF East Asia and Pacific Regional Office. http://www.etan.org/etanpdf/pdf2/unicef_childsoldiers.pdf.

Barter, Shane Joshua. 2013. "State Proxy or Security Dilemma? Understanding Anti-Rebel Militias in Civil War." *Asian Security* 9 (2): 75–92.

Bartone, Paul, Bjorn Helge Johnsen, Jarle Eid, Wibecke Brun, and Jon Laberg. 2002. "Factors Influencing Small-Unit Cohesion in Norwegian Navy Officer Cadets." *Military Psychology* 14 (1): 1–22.

Bastick, Megan, Karin Grimm, and Rahel Kunz. 2007. *Sexual Violence in Armed Conflict: Global Overview and Implications for the Security Sector*. Geneva: Geneva Centre for the Democratic Control of Armed Forces.

BBC News. 2010. "UN Official Calls DR Congo 'Rape Capital of the World.'" *BBC News,* April 28. http://news.bbc.co.uk/2/hi/8650112.stm.

Beber, Bernd, and Christopher Blattman. 2013. "The Logic of Child Soldiering and Coercion." *International Organization* 67 (1): 65–104.

Bellows, John, and Edward Miguel. 2006. "War and Institutions: New Evidence from Sierra Leone." *American Economic Review* 96 (2): 394–99.

———. 2009. "War and Local Collective Action in Sierra Leone." *Journal of Public Economics* 93 (11): 1144–57.

Benard, Cheryl. 1994. "Rape as Terror: The Case of Bosnia." *Terrorism and Political Violence* 6 (1): 29–43.

Bergsmo, Morten, Alf B. Skre, and Elisabeth J. Wood, eds. 2012. *Understanding and Proving International Sex Crimes*. Beijing: Torkel Opsahl Academic Epublisher.

Berman, Eli. 2003. "Hamas, Taliban and the Jewish Underground: An Economist's View of Radical Religious Militias." NBER Working Paper 10004, National Bureau of Economic Research, Cambridge, MA. http://www.nber.org/papers/w10004.

Bijleveld, Catrien, and Jan Hendriks. 2003. "Juvenile Sex Offenders: Differences between Group and Solo Offenders." *Psychology, Crime and Law* 9 (3): 237–45.

Bijleveld, Catrien, Frank Weerman, Daphne Looije, and Jan Hendriks. 2007. "Group Sex Offending by Juveniles: Coercive Sex as a Group Activity." *European Journal of Criminology* 4 (1): 5–31.

Blanchard, William. 1959. "The Group Process in Gang Rape." *Journal of Social Psychology* 49 (2): 259–66.

Blattman, Christopher. 2009. "From Violence to Voting: War and Political Participation in Uganda." *American Political Science Review* 103 (2): 231–47.

Blattman, Christopher, and Edward Miguel. 2010. "Civil War." *Journal of Economic Literature* 48 (1): 3–57.

Bloom, Mia. 1999. "War and the Politics of Rape: Ethnic versus Non-Ethnic Conflicts?" Unpublished manuscript. Microsoft Word file.

Bloom, Mia. 2011. *Bombshell: Women and Terrorism*. Philadelphia: University of Pennsylvania Press.

Boesten, Jelke. 2014. *Sexual Violence During War and Peace: Gender, Power and Post-Conflict Justice in Peru*. New York: Palgrave Macmillan.

Boesten, Jelke, and Melissa Fisher. 2012. "Sexual Violence and Justice in Postconflict Peru." USIP Special Report 310, United States Institute of Peace, Washington, DC. http://www.usip.org/sites/default/files/SR310.pdf.

Bond, Kanisha, and Jakana Thomas. 2015. "Women's Participation in Violent Political Organizations. *American Political Science Review* 109 (3): 488–506.

Bosson, Jennifer, Joseph Vandello, Rochelle Burnaford, Jonathan Weaver, and S. Azru Wasti. 2009. "Precarious Manhood and Displays of Physical Aggression." *Personality and Social Psychology Bulletin* 35 (5): 623–34.

Bourgois, Phillippe. 1996. *In Search of Respect: Selling Crack in El Barrio*. Cambridge: Cambridge University Press.

Bourke, Joanna. 2007. *Rape: Sex, Violence, History*. London: Virago.

Boyle, Michael. 2009. "Explaining Strategic Violence after Wars." *Studies in Conflict and Terrorism* 32 (3): 209–36.

Bracamonte, José Angel Moroni, and David Spencer. 1995. *Strategy and Tactics of the Salvadoran FMLN Guerrillas: Last Battle of The Cold War, Blueprint for Future Conflicts*. Westport, CT: Praeger.

Brown, Reginald J. 2004. "Statement on Active and Reserve Military Issues." Second Session, 108th Congress, Washington, DC, March 2. http://www.globalsecurity.org/military/library/congress/2004_hr/040302-reginald_brown.pdf.

Browning, Christopher. 1992. *Ordinary Men: Reserve Policy Battalion 101 and the Final Solution in Poland*. New York: HarperCollins.

Brownmiller, Susan. 1975. *Against Our Will: Men, Women, and Rape*. New York: Simon & Schuster.

Butler, Christopher, Tali Gluch, and Neil Mitchell. 2007. "Security Forces and Sexual Violence: A Cross-National Analysis of a Principal-Agent Argument." *Journal of Peace Research* 44 (6): 669–86.

Butler, Christopher, and Jessica Jones. 2014. "Establishing a Baseline: Can Peacetime Levels of Sexual Violence Predict Levels of Sexual Violence in Civil Conflict?" Unpublished manuscript. http://www.unm.edu/~ckbutler/workingpapers/ButlerJones2014SVACWorkshop.pdf.

Cabezas, Mary. 1990. "Where the Press Gang Reigns." *Guardian*, August 1.

Call, Charles. 2003. "Democratisation, War, and State-Building: Constructing the Rule of Law in El Salvador." *Journal of Latin American Studies* 35 (4): 827–62.

Caprioli, Mary. 2005. "Primed for Violence: The Role of Gender Inequality in Predicting Internal Conflict." *International Studies Quarterly* 49 (2): 161–78.

Caprioli, Mary, Valerie Hudson, Rose McDermott, Bonnie Ballif-Spanvill, Chad Emmett, and S. Matthew Stearmer. 2009. "The WomanStats Project Database: Advancing an Empirical Research Agenda." *Journal of Peace Research* 46 (6): 839–51.

Card, Claudia. 1996. "Rape as a Weapon of War." *Hypatia* 11 (4): 5–18.

Carey, Peter. 2003. "Third-World Colonialism, the Geração Foun, and the Birth of a New Nation: Indonesia through East Timorese Eyes, 1975–99." *Indonesia*, no. 76: 23–67.

Carpenter, R. Charli. 2006. "Recognizing Gender-Based Violence against Civilian Men and Boys in Conflict Situations." *Security Dialogue* 37 (1): 83–103.

CAVR (Commission for Reception, Truth, and Reconciliation in Timor Leste). 2005. *Chega! The Report of the Commission for Reception, Truth, and Reconciliation in Timor-Leste*. http://www.etan.org/news/2006/cavr.htm.

CDHES (Comisión de los Derechos Humanos de El Salvador [Human Rights Commission of El Salvador]). 1986. *La Tortura Actual en El Salvador (Current Use of Torture in El Salvador)*. San Salvador, El Salvador: CDHES.

Chang, Iris. 1997. *The Rape of Nanking.* New York: Basic Books.

Chavez, Lydia. 1983. "GIs in Salvador: Busy behind Battle Scenes." *New York Times,* May 26.

Checkel, Jeffrey. 2015. *Socialization and Violence: Introduction and Framework.* Simons Papers in Security and Development, no. 48. Vancouver: School of International Studies, Simon Fraser University.

CIA (Central Intelligence Agency). 2003. *The World Factbook 2003.* https://www.cia. gov/library/publications/download/download-2003/index.html.

Cingranelli, David, David Richards, and K. Chad Clay. 2014. *The CIRI Human Rights Dataset.* Version 2014.04.14. http://www.humanrightsdata.com/p/data-documentation.html.

Clark, Ann Marie, and Kathryn Sikkink. 2013. "Information Effects and Human Rights Data: Is the Good News about Increased Human Rights Information Bad News for Human Rights Measures?" *Human Rights Quarterly* 35 (3): 539–68.

Cohen, Dara Kay. 2010. "Explaining Sexual Violence during Civil War." PhD diss., Stanford University.

——. 2013a. "Explaining Rape during Civil War: Cross-National Evidence." *American Political Science Review* 107 (3): 461–77.

——. 2013b. "Female Combatants and the Perpetration of Violence: Wartime Rape in the Sierra Leone Civil War." *World Politics* 65 (3): 383–415.

Cohen, Dara Kay, and Amelia Hoover Green. 2012. "Dueling Incentives: Sexual Violence in Liberia and the Politics of Human Rights Advocacy." *Journal of Peace Research* 49 (3): 445–58.

Cohen, Dara Kay, Amelia Hoover Green, and Elisabeth Wood. 2013. "Wartime Sexual Violence: Misconceptions, Implications, and Ways Forward." USIP Special Report 323, United States Institute of Peace, Washington, DC. http://www.usip. org/sites/default/files/wartime%20sexual%20violence.pdf.

Cohen, Dara Kay, and Ragnhild Nordås. 2014. "Sexual Violence in Armed Conflict: Introducing the SVAC Dataset, 1989–2009." *Journal of Peace Research* 51 (3): 418–28.

Collier, Paul, and Anke Hoeffler. 2007. "Civil War." In *Defense in a Globalized World.* Vol. 2 of *Handbook of Defense Economics,* edited by Todd Sandler and Keith Hartley, 711–40. Amsterdam: Elsevier.

Conibere, Richard, Jana Asher, Kristen Cibelli, Jana Dudukovich, Rafe Kaplan, and Patrick Ball. 2004. *Statistical Appendix to the Report of the Truth and Reconciliation Commission of Sierra Leone.* Palo Alto, CA: Benetech Human Rights Data Analysis Group. https://hrdag.org/content/sierraleone/SL-TRC-statistics-chapter-final.pdf.

Coulter, Chris. 2008. "Female Fighters in the Sierra Leone War: Challenging the Assumptions?" *Feminist Review* 88 (1): 54–73.

Cristalis, Irena. 2009. *East Timor: A Nation's Bitter Dawn.* London: Zed Books.

Cristalis, Irena, and Catherine Scott. 2005. *Independent Women: The Story of Women's Activism in East Timor.* London: Catholic Institute for International Relations.

Cronin-Furman, Kate. 2013. "Managing Expectations: International Criminal Trials and the Prospects for Deterrence of Mass Atrocity." *International Journal of Transitional Justice* 7 (3): 434–54.

CVES (Comisión de la Verdad para El Salvador [Commission on the Truth for El Salvador]). 1993. *From Madness to Hope: The 12-Year War in El Salvador: Report of the Commission on the Truth for El Salvador.* Washington, DC: United States Institute of Peace. http://www.usip.org/files/file/ElSalvador-Report.pdf.

Danner, Mark. 1994. *The Massacre at El Mozote.* New York: Vintage.

Davenport, Christian. 2007. "State Repression and Political Order." *Annual Review of Political Science* 10: 1–23.

DeMeritt, Jacqueline H. R. 2012. "International Organizations and Government Killing: Does Naming and Shaming Save Lives?" *International Interactions* 38 (5): 1–25.

De Soysa, Indra, and Hanne Fjelde. 2010. "Is the Hidden Hand an Iron Fist? Capitalism and Civil Peace, 1970–2005." *Journal of Peace Research* 47 (3): 287–98.

Dole, Gertrude. 2009. "Anarchy without Chaos: Alternatives to Political Authority among the Kuikuru." In *Political Anthropology,* edited by Marc Swartz, Victor Turner, and Arthur Tuden, 73–88. New Brunswick: Transaction.

Dow, Thomas. 1971. "Fertility and Family Planning in Sierra Leone." *Studies in Family Planning* 2 (8): 153–65.

Downes, Alexander. 2008. *Targeting Civilians in War.* Ithaca, NY: Cornell University Press.

Drexler, Elizabeth. 2013. "Fatal Knowledges: The Social and Political Legacies of Collaboration and Betrayal in Timor-Leste." *International Journal of Transitional Justice* 7 (1): 74–94.

Dunn, James. 2001. "Crimes against Humanity in East Timor, January to October 1999: Their Nature and Causes." Report to the United Nations. *East Timor Action Network.* http://www.etan.org/news/2001a/dunn1.htm.

Dunn, James. 2003. *East Timor: A Rough Passage to Independence.* New South Wales: Longueville Books.

Durand, Frederic. 2006. *East Timor: A Country at the Crossroads of Asia and the Pacific: A Geo-Historical Atlas.* Bangkok: Research Institute on Contemporary Southeast Asia.

Eck, Kristine. 2014. "Coercion in Rebel Recruitment." *Security Studies* 23 (2): 364–98.

Eck, Kristine, and Lisa Hultman. 2007. "Violence against Civilians in War." *Journal of Peace Research* 44 (2): 233–46.

Eriksson Baaz, Maria, and Maria Stern. 2009. "Why Do Soldiers Rape? Masculinity, Violence, and Sexuality in the Armed Forces in the Congo (DRC)." *International Studies Quarterly* 53 (2): 495–518.

——. 2013. *Sexual Violence as a Weapon of War? Perceptions, Prescriptions, Problems in the Congo and Beyond.* London: Zed Books.

Evans, Robert. 2007. "UN Says Violence against Women 'Beyond Rape' in Congo." *Reuters,* July 30. http://uk.reuters.com/article/2007/07/30/uk-congo-women-idUKL3047166820070730.

Faedi Duramy, Benedetta. 2014. *Gender and Violence in Haiti: Women's Path from Victims to Agents.* New Brunswick: Rutgers University Press.

Farr, Kathryn. 2009. "Extreme War Rape in Today's Civil-War-Torn States: A Contextual and Comparative Analysis." *Gender Issues* 26 (1): 1–41.

Fearon, James. 1995. "Ethnic War as a Commitment Problem." Paper presented at the 1994 annual meeting of the American Political Science Association, New York, August 30–September 2. Posted online August 1995. https://web.stanford.edu/group/fearon-research/cgi-bin/wordpress/wp-content/uploads/2013/10/Ethnic-War-as-a-Commitment-Problem.pdf.

——. 2006. "Ethnic Mobilization and Ethnic Violence." In *The Oxford Handbook of Political Economy,* edited by Barry Weingast and Donald Wittman, 852–68. Oxford: Oxford University Press.

——. 2010. "Governance and Civil War Onset." World Development Report Background Paper 62009, The World Bank, Washington, DC. http://documents.worldbank.org/curated/en/2010/08/14266244/governance-civil-war-onset.

Fearon, James, and David Laitin. 2003. "Ethnicity, Insurgency, and Civil War." *American Political Science Review* 97 (1): 75–90.

———. 2015. "A List of Civil Wars, 1945–2012." Unpublished list (revised and updated version of list in Fearon and Laitin 2003). Stanford University. Available by request from authors.

Fisher, Siobhan. 1996. "Occupation of the Womb: Forced Impregnation as Genocide." *Duke Law Journal* 46 (1): 91–133.

Forney, Jonathan. 2015. "Who Can We Trust with a Gun? Information Networks and Adverse Selection in Militia Recruitment." *Journal of Conflict Resolution* 59 (5): 824–49.

Franklin, Karen. 2004. "Enacting Masculinity: Antigay Violence and Group Rape as Participatory Theater." *Sexuality Research and Social Policy* 1 (2): 25–40.

Franks, Emma. 1996. "Women and the Resistance in East Timor: 'The Centre, As They Say, Knows Itself by the Margins.'" *Women's Studies International Forum* 19 (1/2): 155–68.

Fujii, Lee Ann. 2009. *Killing Neighbors: Webs of Violence in Rwanda.* Ithaca, NY: Cornell University Press.

———. 2010. "Shades of Truth and Lies: Interpreting Testimonies of War and Violence." *Journal of Peace Research* 47 (2): 231–41.

———. 2013. "The Puzzle of Extra-Lethal Violence." *Perspectives on Politics* 11 (2): 410–26.

Fulu, Emma, Rachel Jewkes, Tim Roselli, and Claudia Garcia-Moreno. 2013. "Prevalence of and Factors Associated with Male Perpetration of Intimate Partner Violence: Findings from the UN Multi-Country Cross-Sectional Study on Men and Violence in Asia and the Pacific." *Lancet Global Health* 1 (4): 187–207.

Gates, Scott. 2002. "Recruitment and Allegiance: The Microfoundations of Rebellion." *Journal of Conflict Resolution* 46 (1): 111–30.

Ghobarah, Hazem Adam, Paul Huth, and Bruce Russett. 2003. "Civil Wars Kill and Maim People—Long after the Shooting Stops." *American Political Science Review* 97 (2): 189–202.

Giacomo, Carol. 2013. "Did Japan 'Need' Comfort Women?" *Taking Note* (blog), *New York Times*, May 15. http://takingnote.blogs.nytimes.com/2013/05/15/did-japan-need-comfort-women.

Gibney, Mark, Linda Cornett, and Reed Wood. 2015. "The Political Terror Scale 1976–2006." *Political Terror Scale.* http://www.politicalterrorscale.org.

Gidycz, Christine A., and Mary P. Koss. 1990. "A Comparison of Group and Individual Sexual Assault Victims." *Psychology of Women Quarterly* 14 (3): 325–42.

Gohdes, Anita. 2010. "Different Convenience Samples, Different Stories: The Case of Sierra Leone." *Human Rights Data Analysis Group.* https://hrdag.org/content/sierraleone/Gohdes_Convenience%20Samples-1.pdf.

Gohdes, Anita, and Patrick Ball. 2010. "Benetech/ABA-CEELI/Human Rights Data Analysis Group Database of Violations Reported by the Sierra Leone Truth and Reconciliation Commission." *Human Rights Data Analysis Group.* https://hrdag.org/sierra-leone-data.

Goldstein, Joshua. 2001. *War and Gender: How Gender Shapes the War System and Vice Versa.* Cambridge: Cambridge University Press.

Gottschall, Jonathan. 2004. "Explaining Wartime Rape." *Journal of Sex Research* 41 (2): 129–36.

Gourevitch, Philip, and Errol Morris. 2008. "Exposure: The Woman behind the Camera at Abu Ghraib." *New Yorker*, March 24.

Green, Jennifer Lynn. 2006. "Collective Rape: A Cross-National Study of the Incidence and Perpetrators of Mass Political Sexual Violence, 1980–2003." PhD diss., Ohio State University.

Groth, A. Nicholas, and H. Jean Birnbaum. 1979. *Men Who Rape: The Psychology of the Offender.* New York: Plenum.

Gruson, Lindsey. 1989. "Salvador Army Fills Ranks by Force." *New York Times*, April 21. http://www.nytimes.com/1989/04/21/world/salvador-army-fills-ranks-by-force.html.

Gusmão, Kirsty Sword. 2003. *A Woman of Independence.* Sydney: Macmillan.

Gutiérrez, Francisco Sanín. 2008. "Repertoires of Violence: Colombia 1930–2006." Unpublished manuscript. Microsoft Word file.

Hague, William. 2012. "Rape Is a Weapon of War. We Must Confront It." *Times* (London), October 15. http://www.thetimes.co.uk/tto/opinion/columnists/article3568124.ece.

Hansen, Lene. 2001. "Gender, Nation, Rape: Bosnia and the Construction of Security." *International Feminist Journal of Politics* 3 (1): 55–75.

Harff, Barbara. 2003. "No Lessons Learned from the Holocaust? Assessing Risks of Genocide and Political Mass Murder since 1955." *American Political Science Review* 9 (1): 57–73.

Harris-Rimmer, Susan. 2007. "'Orphans' or Veterans? Justice for Children Born of War in East Timor." *Texas International Law Journal* 42 (2): 323–44.

——. 2009. "After the Guns Fall Silent: Sexual and Gender-Based Violence in Timor-Leste." TLAVA Issue Brief No. 5, Timor-Leste Armed Violence Assessment. http://www.timor-leste-violence.org/pdfs/Timor-Leste-Violence-IB5-ENGLISH.pdf.

Hauffe, Sarah, and Louise Porter. 2009. "An Interpersonal Comparison of Lone and Group Rape Offences." *Psychology, Crime and Law* 15 (5): 469–91.

Hayden, Robert. 2000. "Rape and Rape Avoidance in Ethno-National Conflicts: Sexual Violence in Liminalized States." *American Anthropologist* 102 (1): 27–41.

Hayner, Priscilla. 1994. "Fifteen Truth Commissions—1974–1994: A Comparative Study." *Human Rights Quarterly* 16 (4): 597–655.

——. 2006. "Truth Commission: A Schematic Overview." *International Review of the Red Cross* 88 (862): 295–310.

Hedgepeth, Sonja, and Rochelle Saidel, eds. 2010. *Sexual Violence against Jewish Women during the Holocaust.* Waltham, MA: Brandeis University Press.

Heise, Lori, Mary Ellsberg, and Megan Gottemoeller. 2002. "A Global Overview of Gender-Based Violence." *International Journal of Gynecology and Obstetrics* 78 (supp. 1): S5–S14.

Henry, Nicola. 2014. "The Fixation on Wartime Rape: Feminist Critique and International Criminal Law." *Social and Legal Studies* 23 (1): 93–111.

Henry, Nicola, Tony Ward, and Matt Hirshberg. 2003. "A Multifactorial Model of Wartime Rape." *Aggression and Violent Behavior* 9 (5): 535–62.

HHI (Harvard Humanitarian Initiative). 2009. "Characterizing Sexual Violence in the Democratic Republic of the Congo." Final report for the Open Society Institute. http://hhi.harvard.edu/publications/characterizing-sexual-violence-democratic-republic-congo-profiles-violence-community.

Hoeffler, Anke, and Marta Reynal-Querol. 2003. "Measuring the Costs of Conflict." Unpublished manuscript. http://www.conflictrecovery.org/bin/2003_Hoeffler_Reynal-Measuring_the_Costs_of_Conflict.pdf.

Hoffman, Danny, 2007. "The Meaning of a Militia: Understanding the Civil Defence Forces of Sierra Leone." *African Affairs* 106 (425): 639–62.

Högbladh, Stina, Therése Pettersson, and Lotta Themnér. 2011. "External Support in Armed Conflict 1975–2009: Presenting New Data." Paper presented at the 52nd Annual International Studies Association Convention, Montreal, March 16–19.

Holmes, Melisa, Heidi Resnick, Dean Kilpatrick, and Connie Best. 1996. "Rape-related Pregnancy: Estimates and Descriptive Characteristics from a National Sample of Women." *American Journal of Obstetrics and Gynecology* 175 (2): 320–25.

Holmstrom, Lynda Lytle, and Ann Wolbert Burgess. 1980. "Sexual Behavior of Assailants during Reported Rapes." *Archives of Sexual Behavior* 9 (5): 427–39.

Hoover Green, Amelia. 2011. "Repertoires of Violence against Noncombatants: The Role of Armed Group Institutions and Ideologies." PhD diss., Yale University.

——. 2013. "Multiple Systems Estimation: Does It Really Work?" *Human Rights Data Analysis Group* (blog), March 26. https://hrdag.org/mse-does-it-really-work.

——. 2014. "El Salvador Violence Dataset." Unpublished dataset (updated version of dataset used in Hoover Green 2011). Available by request from author.

Hoover Green, Amelia, Dara Kay Cohen, and Elisabeth Jean Wood. 2012. "Is Wartime Rape Declining on a Global Scale? We Don't Know—And It Doesn't Matter." *Political Violence @ a Glance* (blog), November 1. http://politicalviolenceataglance.org/2012/11/01/is-wartime-rape-declining-on-a-global-scale-we-dont-know-and-it-doesnt-matter.

Horowitz, Donald. 1985. *Ethnic Groups in Conflict.* Berkeley: University of California Press.

Horowitz, Michael C., and Allan C. Stam. 2014. "How Prior Military Experience Influences the Future Militarized Behavior of Leaders." *International Organization* 68 (3): 527–59.

Horvath, Miranda, and Jessica Woodhams, eds. 2013. *Handbook on the Study of Multiple Perpetrator Rape: A Multidisciplinary Response to an International Problem.* New York: Routledge.

Houge, Anette Bringedal. 2008. "Wartime Rape and Sexual Violence: A Qualitative Analysis of Perpetrators of Sexual Violence during the War in Bosnia and Herzegovina." Master's thesis, University of Oslo.

Hovil, Lucy, and Eric Werker. 2005. "Portrait of a Failed Rebellion: An Account of Rational, Sub-Optimal Violence in Western Uganda." *Rationality and Society* 17 (1): 5–34.

Hudson, Valerie, Bonnie Ballif-Spanvill, Mary Caprioli, and Chad Emmett. 2012. *Sex and World Peace.* New York: Columbia University Press.

Hultman, Lisa. 2012. "Attacks on Civilians in Civil War: Tageting the Achilles Heel of Democratic Governments." *International Interactions* 38 (2): 164–81.

HSRP (Human Security Report Project). 2008. *Human Security Brief 2007.* Vancouver: Human Security Press.

——. 2012. *Human Security Report 2012: Sexual Violence, Education, and War: Beyond the Mainstream Narrative.* Vancouver: Human Security Press.

Humphreys, Macartan, and Jeremy Weinstein. 2004. *What the Fighters Say: A Survey of Ex-Combatants in Sierra Leone, June–August 2003.* New York: Center on Globalization and Sustainable Development, Columbia University.

——. 2006. "Handling and Manhandling Civilians in Civil War." *American Political Science Review* 100 (3): 429–47.

——. 2008. "Who Fights? The Determinants of Participation in Civil War." *American Journal of Political Science* 52 (2): 436–55.

Hynes, Michelle, Jeanne Ward, Kathryn Robertson, and Chadd Crouse. 2004. "A Determination of the Prevalence of Gender-Based Violence among Conflict-Affected Populations in East Timor." *Disasters* 28 (3): 294–321.

Hynes, Michelle, Jeanne Ward, Kathryn Robertson, and Mary Koss. 2004. "A Determination of the Prevalence of Gender-Based Violence among Conflict-Affected Populations in East Timor." *Disasters* 28 (3): 294–321.

Iannaccone, Laurence. 1992. "Sacrifice and Stigma: Reducing Free-Riding in Cults, Communes, and Other Collectives." *Journal of Political Economy* 100 (2): 271–91.

Ibanez, Ana Christina, 2001. "El Salvador: War and Untold Stories, 2001." In *Victims, Perpetrators or Actors? Gender, Armed Conflict and Political Violence*, ed. Caroline O. N. Moser and Fiona C. Clark. New York: Zed.

International Institute of Strategic Studies. 2012. "Middle East and North Africa." *The Military Balance* 112 (2): 303–60.

ICG (International Crisis Group). 2011. "Timor-Leste: Reconciliation and Return from Indonesia." Asia Briefing No. 122, April 18. http://www.crisisgroup.org/en/regions/asia/south-east-asia/timor-leste/B122-timor-leste-reconciliation-and-return-from-indonesia.aspx.

IRIN. 1999. "Sierra Leone: IRIN Special Report on Demobilisation." *IRIN News,* July 9. Reprinted on University of Pennsylvania website. http://www.africa.upenn.edu/Newsletters/irinw_71399e.html.

Isikozlu, Elvan, and Ananda Millard. 2010. "Towards a Typology of Wartime Rape." BiCC Brief 43, Bonn International Center for Conversion. http://www.bicc.de/uploads/tx_bicctools/brief43.pdf.

Jankowski, Martin Sanchez. 1991. *Islands in the Street: Gangs and American Urban Society*. Berkeley: University of California Press.

Jefferson, LaShawn R. 2004. "In War as in Peace: Sexual Violence and Women's Status." In *World Report 2004: Human Rights and Armed Conflict*, by Human Rights Watch, 325–50. https://www.hrw.org/legacy/wr2k4/15.htm.

Jewkes, Rachel, and Yandisa Sikweyiya. 2013. "Streamlining: Understanding Gang Rape in South Africa." In Horvath and Woodhams 2013, 116–31.

Jewkes, Rachel, Emma Fulu, Tim Roselli, and Claudia Garcia-Moreno. 2013. "Prevalence of and Factors Associated with Non-Partner Rape Perpetration: Findings from the UN Multi-Country Cross-Sectional Study on Men and Violence in Asia and the Pacific." *Lancet Global Health* 1 (4): 208–18.

Johnson, Kirsten, Jana Asher, Stephanie Rosborough, Amisha Raja, Rajesh Panjabi, Charles Beadling, and Lynn Lawry. 2008. "Association of Combatant Status and Sexual Violence with Health and Mental Health Outcomes in Postconflict Liberia." *Journal of the American Medical Association* 300 (6): 676–90.

Johnson, Kristin, Jennifer Scott, Bigy Rughita, Michael Kisielewski, Jana Asher, Ricardo Ong, and Lynn Lawry. 2010. "Association of Sexual Violence and Human Rights Violations with Physical and Mental Health in Territories of the Eastern Democratic Republic of the Congo." *Journal of the American Medical Association* 304 (5): 553–62.

Jones, Adam. 2002. "Gender and Genocide in Rwanda." *Journal of Genocide Research* 4 (1): 65–94.

Kalyvas, Stathis. 1999. "Wanton and Senseless? The Logic of Massacres in Algeria." *Rationality and Society* 11 (3): 243–85.

——. 2001. "'New' and 'Old' Civil Wars: A Valid Distinction?" *World Politics* 54 (1): 99–118.

——. 2006. *The Logic of Violence in Civil War*. Cambridge: Cambridge University Press.

——. 2007. Review of *Inside Rebellion: The Politics of Insurgent Violence*, by J.M. Weinstein. *Comparative Political Studies* 40 (9): 1146–51.

Kaminski, Marek. 2003. "Games Prisoners Play: Allocation of Social Roles in a Total Institution." *Rationality and Society* 15 (2): 189–218.

Karim, Sabrina. 2015. "Finding the Right Security Sector Strategy: How Do Post-Conflict

States Reform Their Domestic Security Sectors?" Paper presented at the Folke Bernadotte Academy UNSC 1325 Workshop, Stockholm, June 8–10.

Keen, David. 2005. *Conflict and Collusion in Sierra Leone.* New York: Palgrave.

Kelley, Judith and Beth Simmons. 2015. Politics by Number: Indicators as Social Pressure in International Relations." American Journal of Political Science 59 (1): 55–70.

Kelly, Jocelyn, Theresa Betancourt, Denis Mukwege, Robert Lipton, and Michael VanRooyen. 2011. "Experiences of Female Survivors of Sexual Violence in Eastern Democratic Republic of the Congo: A Mixed-Methods Study." *Conflict and Health* 5 (25): 1–8.

Kelman, Herbert, and V. Lee Hamilton. 1989. *Crimes of Obedience: Toward a Social Psychology of Authority and Responsibility.* New Haven: Yale University Press.

Kenny, Paul. 2011. "Organizational Weapons: Explaining Cohesion in the Military." HiCN Working Paper 107, Institute of Development Studies, Households in Conflict Network, University of Sussex, Brighton, UK.

Kier, Elizabeth. 1998. "Homosexuals in the US Military: Open Integration and Combat Effectiveness." *International Security* 23 (2): 5–39.

Kirby, Paul. 2015. "Ending Sexual Violence in Conflict: The Preventing Sexual Violence Initiative and Its Critics." *International Affairs* 91 (3): 457–72.

Knouse, Stephen. 1998. "Keeping 'On Task': An Exploration of Task Cohesion in Diverse Military Teams." DEOMI Research Series Pamphlet 98–1, Defense Equal Opportunity Management Institute, Office of Naval Research.

Koo, Katrina Lee. 2002. "Confronting a Disciplinary Blindness: Women, War, and Rape in the International Politics of Security." *Australian Journal of Political Science* 37 (3): 525–36.

Krain, Matthew. 2012. "J'accuse! Does Naming and Shaming Perpetrators Reduce the Severity of Genocides or Politicides?" *International Studies Quarterly* 56 (3): 574–89.

Lacina, Bethany, and Nils Petter Gleditsch. 2005. "Monitoring Trends in Global Combat: A New Dataset of Battle Deaths." *European Journal of Population* 21 (2–3): 145–66.

Landesman, Peter. 2002. "A Woman's Work." *New York Times Magazine,* September 15. http://www.nytimes.com/2002/09/15/magazine/a-woman-s-work.html.

Leiby, Michele. 2009. "Digging in the Archives: The Promise and Perils of Primary Documents." *Politics and Society* 37 (1): 75–99.

——. 2011. "State-Perpetrated Wartime Sexual Violence in Latin America." PhD diss., University of New Mexico.

——. 2012. "The Promise and Peril of Primary Documents: Documenting Wartime Sexual Violence in El Salvador and Peru." In Bergsmo, Skre, and Wood 2012, 315–66.

Littman, Rebecca, and Elizabeth Levy Paluck. 2015. "The Cycle of Violence: Understanding Individual Participation in Collective Violence." *Political Psychology* 36 (supp. S1): 79–99.

Loeb, Jonathan. 2015. "Mass Rape in North Darfur: Sudanese Army Attacks against Civilians in Tabit." *Human Rights Watch,* February 11. https://www.hrw.org/report/2015/02/11/mass-rape-north-darfur-sudanese-army-attacks-against-civilians-tabit.

Loeb, Vernon. 2003. "From the Front Lines to the Home Front; For Key Army Colonel, Transition is Abrupt." *The Washington Post,* November 4. https://www.highbeam.com/doc/1P2-303202.html.

Loney, Hannah. 2012. "Women's Activism in Timor-Leste: A Case Study on Fighting Women." In *New Research on Timor-Leste: Proceedings of the Third Timor-Leste Studies Association Conference,* edited by Michael Leach, Nuno Canas Mendes,

Antero da Silva, Alarico da Costa Ximenes and Bob Boughton, 265–69. Hawthorne: Swinburne.

——. 2015. "Women's Experiences of the Indonesian Occupation of East Timor, 1975–1999." PhD diss. (draft), University of Melbourne.

Lutz, Brenda, and James Lutz. 2013. "Indonesian Terror against East Timorese Separatists and the International Response." In *State Terrorism and Human Rights: International Responses since the End of the Cold War*, edited by Gillian Duncan, Orla Lynch, Gilbert Ramsay, and Alison M. S. Watson, 102–13. New York: Routledge.

Lyall, Jason, and Isaiah Wilson. 2009. "Rage against the Machines: Explaining Outcomes in Counterinsurgency Wars." *International Organization* 63 (1): 67–106.

MacCoun, Robert. 1993. "What Is Known about Unit Cohesion and Military Performance." In *Sexual Orientation and US Military Personnel Policy: Options and Assessment,* edited by Bernard Rostker and Scott A. Harris, 283–331. Santa Monica: RAND.

MacCoun, Robert, Elizabeth Kier, and Aaron Belkin. 2006. "Does Social Cohesion Determine Motivation in Combat? An Old Question with an Old Answer." *Armed Forces and Society* 32 (4): 646–54.

Mack, Andrew. 1975. "Why Big Nations Lose Small Wars: The Politics of Asymmetric Conflict." *World Politics* 27 (2): 175–200.

MacKenzie, Megan. 2012. *Female Soldiers in Sierra Leone: Sex, Security, and Post-Conflict Development.* New York: New York University Press.

MacKinnon, Catharine. 1994. "Rape, Genocide, and Women's Human Rights." In *Mass Rape: The War against Women in Bosnia-Herzegovina,* edited by Alexandra Stiglmayer, 73–81. Lincoln: University of Nebraska Press.

——. 2006. *Are Women Human? And Other International Dialogues.* Cambridge, MA: Belknap Press of Harvard University Press.

Malamuth, Neil. 1981. "Rape Proclivity among Males." *Journal of Social Issues* 37 (4): 138–57.

——. 1996. "The Confluence Model of Sexual Aggression: Feminist and Evolutionary Perspectives." In *Sex, Power, Conflict: Evolutionary and Feminist Perspectives*, edited by David Buss and Neil Malamuth, 269–95. Oxford: Oxford University Press.

Marks, Zoe. 2013a. "Sexual Violence inside Rebellion: Policies and Perspectives of the Revolutionary United Front of Sierra Leone." *Civil Wars* 15 (3): 359–79.

Marks, Zoe. 2013b. "Sexual Violence in Sierra Leone's Civil War: 'Virgination,' Rape, and Marriage." *African Affairs* 113 (450): 67–87.

Marrus, Michael. 1987. "Jewish Leaders and the Holocaust." *French Historical Studies* 15 (2): 316–31.

Marshall, Monty G., Ted Robert Gurr, and Barbara Harff. 2015. "Genocide/Politicide" spreadsheet. *PITF State Failure Problem Set, 1955–2014.* Center for Systemic Peace. http://www.systemicpeace.org/inscrdata.html.

Marshall, Monty G., Ted Robert Gurr, and Keith Jaggers. 2014. *Political Regime Characteristics and Transitions, 1800–2013.* Center for Systemic Peace, Polity IV Project. http://www.systemicpeace.org/inscrdata.html.

Martin, Patricia Yancey, and Robert Hummer. 1989. "Fraternities and Rape on Campus." *Gender and Society* 3 (4): 457–73.

Mason, Christine. 2005. "Women, Violence, and Nonviolent Resistance in East Timor." *Journal of Peace Research* 42 (6): 737–49.

McKelvey, Tara, ed. 2007. *One of the Guys: Women as Aggressors and Torturers.* Emeryville, CA: Seal Press.

Mezey, Gillian. 1994. "Rape in War." *Journal of Forensic Psychiatry* 5 (3): 583–97.

Miller, Anna Lekas. 2013. "Exploiting Egypt's Rape Culture for Political Gain." *The Nation*, August 8. http://www.thenation.com/article/175669/exploiting-egypts-rape-culture-political-gain.

Mitchell, Neil. 2004. *Agents of Atrocity: Leaders, Followers, and the Violation of Human Rights in Civil War.* New York: Palgrave Macmillan.

Modvig, Jens, June Pagaduan-Lopez, Janet Rodenburg, Charissa Mia D. Salud, Rowena V. Cabigon, and Carlo Irwin A. Panelo. 2000. "Torture and Trauma in Post-Conflict East Timor." *Lancet* 356 (9243): 1763.

Montgomery, Tommie Sue. 1992. *Revolution in El Salvador: From Civil Strife to Civil Peace.* Boulder: Westview.

Morris, Madeline. 1996. "By Force of Arms: Rape, War, and Military Culture." *Duke Law Journal* 45 (4): 651–781.

Mueller, John. 2000. "The Banality of 'Ethnic War.'" *International Security* 25 (1): 42–70.

Mukwege, Denis, and Eve Ensler. 2009. "Group Fights Rape in Democratic Republic of the Congo." Interview by Scott Simon. *Weekend Edition Saturday*. NPR, January 24. http://www.npr.org/templates/transcript/transcript.php?storyId=99838343.

Mulligan, Casey, and Andrei Shleifer. 2005. "Conscription as Regulation." *American Law and Economics Review* 7 (1): 85–111.

Mullins, Christopher. 2009. "'He Would Kill Me with His Penis': Genocidal Rape in Rwanda as a State Crime." *Critical Criminology* 17 (1): 15–33.

Murdock, Heather. 2011. "Domestic Rape in Congo a Rapidly Growing Problem." *Voice of America*, May 29. http://www.voanews.com/content/domestic-rape-in-congo-a-rapidly-growing-problem-122826644/140086.html.

Myrttinen, Henri. 2009. "Histories of Violence, States of Denial: Militias, Martial Arts, and Masculinity in East Timor." PhD diss., University of Kwazulu-Natal.

Nevins, Joseph. 2002. "The Making of 'Ground Zero' in Timor-Leste in 1999: An Analysis of International Complicity in Indonesia's Crimes." *Asian Survey* 42 (4): 623–41.

——. 2005. *A Not-So-Distant Horror: Mass Violence in East Timor.* Ithaca, NY: Cornell University Press.

Newby, John, Robert Ursano, James McCarroll, Xian Liu, Carol Fullerton, and Ann Norwood. 2005. "Postdeployment Domestic Violence by US Army Soldiers." *Military Medicine* 170 (8): 643–47.

Nitsan, Tal. 2012. "The Body that Writes: Reflections on the Process of Writing about Wartime Rape Avoidance in the Israeli-Palestinian Conflict." In *Rape in Wartime*, edited by Raphaelle Branche and Fabrice Virgili, 153–68. London: Macmillan.

Nowrojee, Binaifer. 1996. *Shattered Lives: Sexual Violence during the Rwandan Genocide and Its Aftermath.* New York: Human Rights Watch.

NSRRT (National Sex and Reproduction Research Team) and Carol Jenkins. 1994. *National Study of Sexual and Reproductive Knowledge and Behavior in Papua New Guinea.* Goroka: Papua New Guinea Institute of Medical Research.

Oberschall, Anthony. 1993. *Social Movements: Ideologies, Interests, and Identities.* New Brunswick: Transaction.

——. 2007. *Conflict and Peace Building in Divided Societies: Responses to Ethnic Violence.* New York: Routledge.

O'Neill, Bard. 2001. *Insurgency and Terrorism: Inside Modern Revolutionary Warfare.* Dulles, VA: Brassey's.

Oppenheim, Ben, Juan Vargas, and Michael Weintraub. 2015. "Learning How Not to Fire a Gun: The Impact of Combatant Training on Civilian Killings." Unpublished manuscript, last updated February 21. http://papers.ssrn.com/sol3/papers.cfm?abstract_id=1962400.

Osiel, Mark. 1999. *Obeying Orders: Atrocity, Military Discipline, and the Law of War*. New Brunswick: Transaction.

O'Sullivan, Chris. 1991. "Acquaintance Gang Rape on Campus." In *Acquaintance Rape: The Hidden Crime*, edited by Andrea Parrot and Laurie Bechhofer, 140–56. New York: John Wiley & Sons.

Ouédraogo, Emile. 2014. "Advancing Military Professionalism in Africa." Research Paper No. 6, Africa Center for Strategic Studies, Washington, DC. http://africacenter.org/wp-content/uploads/2014/07/ARP-6-EN.pdf.

Peceny, Mark, and William D. Stanley. 2010. "Counterinsurgency in El Salvador." *Politics and Society* 38 (1): 67–94.

Peterman, Amber, Tia Palermo, and Caryn Bredenkamp. 2011. "Estimates and Determinants of Sexual Violence against Women in the Democratic Republic of Congo." *American Journal of Public Health* 101 (6): 1060–67.

Peters, Krijn, and Paul Richards. 1998. "'Why We Fight': Voices of Youth Combatants in Sierra Leone." *Journal of the International African Institute* 68 (2): 183–210.

Pettersson, Therese and Peter Wallensteen. 2015. "Armed Conflicts, 1946–2014." *Journal of Peace Research* 52 (4): 536–50.

Pickering, Jeffrey. 2010. "Dangerous Drafts? A Time-Series, Cross-National Analysis of Conscription and the Use of Military Force, 1946–2001." *Armed Forces and Society* 36 (2): 1–22.

Plümper, Thomas, and Eric Neumayer. 2006. "The Unequal Burden of War: The Effect of Armed Conflict on the Gender Gap in Life Expectancy." *International Organization* 60 (3): 723–54.

Poe, Steven, and C. Neal Tate. 1994. "Repression of Human Rights to Personal Integrity in the 1980s: A Global Analysis." *American Political Science Review* 88 (4): 853–72.

Porter, Louise, and Laurence Alison. 2001. "A Partially Ordered Scale of Influence in Violent Group Behavior: An Example from Gang Rape." *Small Group Research* 32 (4): 475–97.

———. 2006. "Examining Group Rape: A Descriptive Analysis of Offender and Victim Behavior." *European Journal of Criminology* 3 (3): 357–81.

Powell, Sian. 2001. "Rape: Just Another Weapon of War." *Weekend Australian*, March 10. http://www.etan.org/et2006/january/28/30rape.htm.

Pugel, James. 2007. "What the Fighters Say: A Survey of Ex-Combatants in Liberia." Monrovia: Joint Implementation Unit, UN Development Program. http://www.operationspaix.net/DATA/DOCUMENT/904~v~What_the_Fighters_Say__A_Survey_of_Ex-combatants_in_Liberia.pdf.

Rabin, Roni Caryn. 2012. "Men Struggle for Rape Awareness." *New York Times*, January 23. http://www.nytimes.com/2012/01/24/health/as-victims-men-struggle-for-rape-awareness.html.

Reed, Elizabeth, Jay Silverman, Anita Raj, Emily Rothman, Michele Decker, Barbara Gottlieb, Beth Molnar, and Elizabeth Miller. 2008. "Social and Environmental Contexts of Adolescent and Young Adult Male Perpetrators of Intimate Partner Violence: A Qualitative Study." *American Journal of Men's Health* 2 (3): 260–71.

Rees, Edward. 2004. "Under Pressure: Falintil: Three Decades of Defense Force Development in Timor Leste, 1975–2004." Working Paper 139, Geneva Centre for the Democratic Control of Armed Forces, Geneva.

Reis, Chen, Lynn Amowitz, Kristina Hare Lyons, and Vincent Iacopino. 2002. *War-Related Sexual Violence in Sierra Leone: A Population-Based Assessment.* Boston: Physicians for Human Rights. https://s3.amazonaws.com/PHR_Reports/sierra-leone-sexual-violence-2002.pdf.

Replogle, Elaine. 2011. "Reference Groups, Mob Mentality, and Bystander Intervention: A Sociological Analysis of the Lara Logan Case." *Sociological Forum* 26 (4): 796–805.

Rittner, Carol, and John Roth. 2012. *Rape: Weapon of War and Genocide.* Saint Paul, MN: Paragon House.

Robben, Antonius. 2006. "Combat Motivation, Fear, and Terror in Twentieth-Century Argentinian Warfare." *Journal of Contemporary History* 41 (2): 357–77.

Robinson, Geoffrey. 1995. *The Dark Side of Paradise: Political Violence in Bali.* Ithaca, NY: Cornell University Press.

——. 2001. "People's War: Militias in East Timor and Indonesia." *South East Asia Research* 9 (3): 271–318.

——. 2006. *East Timor 1999: Crimes against Humanity.* Report commissioned by the United Nations Office of the High Commissioner for Human Rights. Dili: HAK Association

——. 2010. *"If You Leave Us Here, We Will Die": How Genocide Was Stopped in East Timor.* Princeton: Princeton University Press.

Ross, Michael. 2004. "How Do Natural Resources Influence Civil War? Evidence from Thirteen Cases." *International Organization* 58 (1): 35–67.

Rozée, Patricia. 1993. "Forbidden or Forgiven? Rape in Cross-Cultural Perspective." *Psychology of Women Quarterly* 17 (1): 499–514.

Rubio, Noemy Anaya. 2007. "Mujeres y Situaciones de Conflicto Armado y Post Conflicto en El Salvador [Women and situations of conflict and post-conflict in El Salvador]." In *Monitoreo Sobre Violencia Sexual en Conflicto Armado,* 61–88. Lima: CLADEM. http://bd.cdmujeres.net/documentos/monitoreo-violencia-sexual-conflicto-armado-colombia-salvador-guatemala-honduras-nicargua.

Samset, Ingrid. 2011. "Sexual Violence: The Case of Eastern Congo." In *The Peace in Between: Post-War Violence and Peacebuilding,* edited by Mats Berdal and Astri Suhrke, 229–47. New York: Routledge.

Sanday, Peggy Reeves. 1981. "The Socio-Cultural Context of Rape: A Cross-Cultural Study." *Journal of Social Issues* 37 (4): 5–27.

——. 2007. *Fraternity Gang Rape: Sex, Brotherhood, and Privilege on Campus.* 2nd ed. New York: New York University Press.

Sarkees, Meredith Reid and Frank Wayman. 2010. *Resort to War: 1816–2007.* Washington DC: CQ Press.

Satki, Victoria Kumala. 2012. *Remaking a World beyond State Demarcation: Emotion, Violence and Memory in Post-Conflict Oecussi, East Timor.* Paper presented at the International SIT Symposium, Kigali, January 10–13. http://digitalcollections.sit.edu/cgi/viewcontent.cgi?article=1120&context=conflict_reconcilation_symposium.

Saul, Ben. 2001. "Was the Conflict in East Timor 'Genocide' and Why Does It Matter?" *Melbourne Journal of International Law* 2 (2): 477–522.

Scully, Diana. 1990. *Understanding Sexual Violence: A Study of Convicted Rapists.* 2nd ed. New York: Routledge.

Seifert, Ruth. 1996. "The Second Front: The Logic of Sexual Violence in Wars." *Women's Studies International Forum* 19 (1/2): 35–43.

Sharlach, Lisa. 1999. "Gender and Genocide in Rwanda: Women as Agents and Objects of Genocide." *Journal of Genocide Research* 1 (3): 387–99.

——. 2000. "Rape as Genocide: Bangladesh, the Former Yugoslavia, and Rwanda." *New Political Science* 22 (1): 89–102.

———. 2009. States of Emergency, State of Terror: Sexual Violence in the South African and Peruvian Counterinsurgencies." *Journal of Power* 2 (3): 441–60.

Shils, Edward, and Morris Janowitz. 1948. "Cohesion and Disintegration in the Wehrmacht in World War II." *Public Opinion Quarterly* 12 (2): 280–315.

Silva, Romesh, and Patrick Ball. 2006. "The Profile of Human Rights Violations in Timor-Leste, 1974–1999." A report by the Benetech Human Rights Data Analysis Group to the Commission on Reception, Truth and Reconciliation of Timor-Leste, February 9. https://hrdag.org/content/timorleste/Benetech-Report-to-CAVR.pdf

Sissons, Miranda. 1997. *From One Day to Another: Violations of Women's Reproductive and Sexual Rights in East Timor.* Melbourne: East Timor Human Rights Centre.

Sivakumaran, Sandesh. 2007. "Sexual Violence against Men in Armed Conflict." *European Journal of International Law* 18 (2): 253–76.

———. 2010. "Lost in Translation: UN Responses to Sexual Violence against Men and Boys in Situations of Armed Conflict." *International Review of the Red Cross* 92 (877): 259–77.

Sjoberg, Laura. Forthcoming. *Women as Wartime Rapists: Beyond Sensation and Stereotyping.* New York: New York University Press.

Skjelsbæk, Inger. 2011. *The Political Psychology of War Rape: Studies from Bosnia and Herzegovina.* New York: Routledge.

Slegh, Henry, Gary Barker, Benoit Ruratotoye, and Tim Shand. 2012. *Gender Relations, Sexual Violence, and the Effects of Conflict on Women and Men in North Kivu, Eastern Democratic Republic of Congo: Preliminary Results from the International Men and Gender Equality Survey.* Cape Town: Sonke Gender Justice Network and Promundo. http://resourcecentre.savethechildren.se/sites/default/files/documents/6945.pdf.

Smallman-Raynor, Matthew, and Andrew Cliff. 2004. *War Epidemics: An Historical Geography of Infectious Diseases in Military Conflict and Civil Strife, 1850–2000.* Oxford: Oxford University Press.

Smillie, Ian, Lansana Gberie, and Ralph Hazleton. 2000. "The Heart of the Matter: Sierra Leone, Diamonds, and Human Security." *Partnership Africa Coalition.* http://www.pacweb.org/Documents/diamonds_KP/heart_of_the_matter-full-2000-01-eng.pdf.

Smith-Spark, Laura. 2004. "How Did Rape Become a Weapon of War?" *BBC News,* December 8. http://news.bbc.co.uk/2/hi/4078677.stm.

———. 2014. "Angelina Jolie: Rape in War Is Not Inevitable: Shame Is on the Aggressor." *CNN,* June 11. http://www.cnn.com/2014/06/10/world/violence-against-women-summit/.

Smith, Alison, Catherine Gambette, and Thomas Longley. 2004. "Conflict Mapping in Sierra Leone: Violations of International Humanitarian Law from 1991 to 2002." *No Peace without Justice.* http://www.npwj.org/ICC/Conflict-Mapping-Sierra-Leone-Violations-International-Humanitarian-Law-1991-2002.html.

Solomon, John. 2011. "George H. W. Bush—Revisited: The Bush Americans Didn't Know but Now Celebrate." *Center for Public Integrity,* March 21. http://www.publicintegrity.org/2011/03/21/3695/george-hw-bush-revisited.

Specht, Irma. 2006. *Red Shoes: Experiences of Girl-Combatants in Liberia.* Geneva: International Labour Office.

Stanley, Elizabeth. 2009. *Torture, Truth, and Justice: The Case of Timor-Leste.* New York: Routledge.

Stanley, William. 1996. *The Protection Racket State: Elite Politics, Military Extortion, and Civil War in El Salvador.* Philadelphia: Temple University Press.

Stanton, Jessica. 2009. "Strategies of Violence and Restraint in Civil War." PhD diss., Columbia University.

Stemple, Lara. 2011. "The Hidden Victims of Wartime Rape." *New York Times*, March 1. http://www.nytimes.com/2011/03/02/opinion/02stemple.html.

Straus, Scott. 2006. *The Order of Genocide: Race, Power, and War in Rwanda*. Ithaca, NY: Cornell University Press.

Sundberg, Ralph. 2009. "Revisiting One-sided Violence—A Global and Regional Analysis." In *States in Armed Conflict 2008*, ed. Lotta Harbom and Ralph Sundberg. Uppsala: Universitetstryckeriet.

Swaine, Aisling. 2011. "Transition or Transformation: An Analysis of Before, During, and Post-Conflict Violence against Women in Northern Ireland, Liberia, and Timor-Leste." PhD diss., University of Ulster.

Swiss, Shana, and Peggy J. Jennings. 2006. "Documenting the Impact of Conflict on Women Living in Internally Displaced Persons Camps in Sri Lanka: Some Ethical Considerations." *Women's Rights International*. http://womens-rights.org/Publications/Ethics_IDPSurvey.pdf.

Swiss, Shana, Peggy J. Jennings, Gladys V. Aryee, Grace H. Brown, Ruth M. Jappah-Samukai, Mary S. Kamara, Rosana D. H. Schaack, and Rojatu S. Turay-Kanneh. 1998. "Violence against Women during the Liberian Civil Conflict." *Journal of the American Medical Association* 279 (8): 625–29.

Tanaka, Yuki. 1997. *Hidden Horrors: Japanese War Crimes in World War II*. Boulder: Westview.

Taylor, Louise. 2003. *"We'll Kill You If You Cry": Sexual Violence in the Sierra Leone Conflict*. New York: Human Rights Watch. http://hrw.org/reports/2003/sierraleone.

ten Bensel, Tusty. 2014. "Framing in the Making: The Evolution of Sex Offender Motivation in Sierra Leone." *International Criminal Justice Review* 24 (1): 590–81.

Thaler, Kai. 2012. "Foreshadowing Future Slaughter: From the Indonesian Killings of 1965–1966 to the 1974–1999 Genocide in East Timor." *Genocide Studies and Prevention* 7 (2/3): 204–22.

Theidon, Kimberly. 2007. "Gender in Transition: Common Sense, Women, and War." *Journal of Human Rights* 6 (4): 453–78.

Thornhill, Randy, and Craig T. Palmer. 2000. *A Natural History of Rape: Biological Bases of Sexual Coercion*. Cambridge, MA: MIT Press.

Timor Information Service (newsletter). 1978. Number 25. https://chartperiodicals.files.wordpress.com/2010/09/tis_25_p.pdf.

Tombs, David. 2006. "Unspeakable Violence: The UN Truth Commissions in El Salvador and Guatemala." In *Reconciliation, Nations, and Churches in Latin America*, edited by Ian Maclean, 57–84. Burlington, VT: Ashgate.

Tomz, Michael, Jason Wittenberg, and Gary King. 2003. CLARIFY: Software for Interpreting and Presenting Statistical Results. Version 2.1. http://j.mp/k3k0rx.

TRC (Truth and Reconciliation Commission) of Sierra Leone. 2004. *Witness to Truth: The Final Report of the Truth and Reconciliation Commission of Sierra Leone*. Washington, DC: United States Institute of Peace. http://www.usip.org/publications/truth-commission-sierra-leone.

UCDP (Uppsala Conflict Data Program). 2015. *UCDP Battle-Related Deaths Dataset*. Version 5, *1989–2014*. Uppsala University. Last updated June 22. http://www.pcr.uu.se/research/ucdp/datasets/ucdp_battle-related_deaths_dataset.

Ullman, Sarah. 2007. "A 10-Year Update of 'Review and Critique of Empirical Studies of Rape Avoidance.'" *Criminal Justice and Behavior* 34 (3): 411–29.

UN (United Nations). 2001. *Violence against Women Perpetrated and/or Condoned by the State during Times of Armed Conflict (1997–2000): Report of the Special Rapporteur on Violence against Women, Its Causes and Consequences.* E/CN.4/2001/73, January 23. http://undocs.org/E/CN.4/2001/73.

———. 2015. *Discrimination and Violence against Individuals Based on Their Sexual Orientation and Gender Identity: Report of the Office of the UN High Commissioner for Human Rights.* A/HRC/29/23, 4 May. http://undocs.org/A/HRC/29/23.

UN Action (UN Action against Sexual Violence in Conflict). 2011. "Analytical and Conceptual Framing of Conflict-Related Sexual Violence." *Stop Rape Now.* http://www.stoprapenow.org/uploads/advocacyresources/1321456915.pdf.

UN Human Rights. 2009. "Violence against Women and Sexual Violence." UN Mapping Report Info Note 3: Democratic Republic of the Congo 1993–2003, United Nations Office of the High Commissioner for Human Rights, Geneva. http://www.ohchr.org/Documents/Countries/CD/FS-3_Sexual_Violence_FINAL.pdf.

UNICEF. 2002. *Adult Wars, Child Soldiers: Voices of Children Involved in Armed Conflict in the East Asia and Pacific Region.* Bangkok: UNICEF East Asia and Pacific Regional Office. http://www.unicef.org/sowc06/pdfs/pub_adultwars_en.pdf.

USIP (United States Institute of Peace). "Truth Commission: El Salvador." http://www.usip.org/publications/truth-commission-el-salvador. Accessed January 2, 2016.

Utas, Mats. 2005. "Victimcy, Girlfriending, Soldiering: Tactic Agency in a Young Woman's Social Navigation of the Liberian War Zone." *Anthropological Quarterly* 78 (2): 403–30.

Valencia-Weber, Gloria, and Robert Weber. 1986. "El Salvador: Methods Used to Document Human Rights Violations." *Human Rights Quarterly* 8 (4): 731–70.

Valentino, Benjamin. 2004. *Final Solutions: Mass Killing and Genocide in the 20th Century.* Ithaca, NY: Cornell University Press.

Valentino, Benjamin, Paul Huth, and Dylan Balch-Lindsay. 2004. "Draining the Sea: Mass Killing, Guerrilla Warfare." *International Organization* 58 (2): 375–407.

Vandello, Joseph, Jennifer Bosson, Dov Cohen, Rochelle Burnaford, and Jonathan Weaver. 2008. "Precarious Manhood." *Journal of Personality and Social Psychology* 95 (6): 1325–39.

Vermeij, Lotte. 2009. "Children of Rebellion: Socialization of Child Soldiers within the Lord's Resistance Army." Master's thesis, University of Oslo.

Viterna, Jocelyn. 2013. *Women in War: The Micro-Processes of Mobilization in El Salvador.* Oxford: Oxford University Press.

Walter, Barbara. 2009. *Reputation and Civil War: Why Separatist Conflicts Are So Violent.* Cambridge: Cambridge University Press.

Wax, Emily. 2003. "Soldiers with Dolls and Blue Hair Gel: Rape and Despair Turn Liberian Girls into Armed Fighters." *Washington Post*, August 29.

Weinstein, Jeremy. 2005. "Resources and the Information Problem in Rebel Recruitment." *Journal of Conflict Resolution* 49 (4): 598–624.

———. 2007. *Inside Rebellion: The Politics of Insurgent Violence.* New York: Cambridge University Press.

Widjajanto, Bambang, and Douglas Kammen. 2000. "The Structure of Military Abuse." *Inside Indonesia*, no. 62 (April–June). http://www.insideindonesia.org/weekly-articles/the-structure-of-military-abuse.

Wilkinson, David John, Luke Samuel Bearup, and Tong Soprach. 2005. "Youth Gang Rape in Phnom Penh." In *Sex without Consent: Young People in Developing Countries*, edited by Shireen J. Jejeebhoy, Iqbal Shah, and Shyam Thapa, 158–68. New York: Zed Press.

Williams, Lethia, and Daniel Masters. 2011. "Assessing Military Intervention and Democratization: Supportive versus Oppositional Military Interventions." *Democracy and Security* 7 (1): 18–37.

Williams, Louise. 1998. "Bishop Deplores Rape of East Timor Women." *The Age*, July 17.

Williams, Louise, and Leonie Lamont. 1999. "Shame of Wartime Orphans: East Timor: A People Betrayed." *Sydney Morning Herald*, September 13.

Winslow, Donna. 1999. "Rites of Passage and Group Bonding in the Canadian Airborne." *Armed Forces and Society* 25 (3): 429–57.

WomanStats Project. 2011. "Combined Scale of the Prevalence and Sanction of Rape and Sexual Assault of Women." LRW Scale 7. *WomanStats.* http://womanstats.org/laststatics/combinedscaleandsanctionofrape20113.png.

Wood, Elisabeth Jean. 2000. *Forging Democracy from Below: Insurgent Transitions in South Africa and El Salvador.* Cambridge: Cambridge University Press.

——. 2003. *Insurgent Collective Action and Civil War in El Salvador.* Cambridge: Cambridge University Press.

——. 2006a. "The Ethical Challenges of Field Research in Conflict Zones." *Qualitative Sociology* 29 (3): 373–86.

——. 2006b. "Variation in Sexual Violence during War." *Politics and Society* 34 (3): 307–42.

——. 2007. "Field Research during War: Ethical Dilemmas." In *New Perspectives in Political Ethnography,* edited by Lauren Joseph, Matthew Mahler, and Javier Auyero, 205–23. New York: Springer.

——. 2008a. "Sexual Violence during War: Toward an Understanding of Variation." In *Order, Conflict, and Violence,* edited by Stathis N. Kalyvas, Ian Shapiro, and Tarek Masoud, 321–51. Cambridge: Cambridge University Press.

——. 2008b. "The Social Processes of Civil War: The Wartime Transformation of Social Networks." *Annual Review of Political Science,* no. 11: 539–61.

——. 2009. "Armed Groups and Sexual Violence: When Is Wartime Rape Rare?" *Politics and Society* 37 (1): 131–62.

——. 2012. "Rape during War Is Not Inevitable: Variation in Wartime Sexual Violence." In Bergsmo, Skre, and Wood 2012, 389–419.

——. 2013. "Multiple Perpetrator Rape during War." In Horvath and Woodhams 2013, 132–59.

——. 2015. "Conflict-Related Sexual Violence and the Policy Implications of Recent Research." *International Review of the Red Cross,* no. 894: 1–22.

——. 2016. "Rape as a Practice of War: Towards a Typology of Political Violence." Unpublished manuscript, last updated March 13. Microsoft Word file.

Wood, Kate. 2005. "Contextualizing Group Rape in Post-Apartheid South Africa." *Culture, Health and Sexuality* 7 (4): 303–17.

Wood, Reed 2010. "Rebel Capability and Strategic Violence against Civilians." *Journal of Peace Research* 47 (5): 601–14.

Woodhams, Jessica, Claire Cooke, Leigh Harkins, and Teresa da Silva. 2012. "Leadership in Multiple Perpetrator Stranger Rape." *Journal of Interpersonal Violence* 27 (4): 728–52.

The World Bank. 2009. *Labor Force Participation Rate, Females (% of Female Population Ages 15+).* World Development Indicators.

——. 2015a. *Fertility rate, Total (Births per Woman).* World Development Indicators. http://data.worldbank.org/indicator/SP.DYN.TFRT.IN.

———. 2015b. *Labor Force Participation Rate, Females (% of Female Population Ages 15+) (modeled ILO estimate).* World Development Indicators. http://data.world bank.org/indicator/SL.TLF.CACT.FE.ZS.

———. 2015c. *Labor Force Participation Rate, Females (% of Female Population Ages 15+) (national estimate).* World Development Indicators. http://data.world bank.org/indicator/SL.TLF.CACT.FE.NE.ZS.

WWII US Medical Research Center. "Venereal Disease and Treatment during WW2." http://med-dept.com/articles/venereal-disease-and-treatment-during-ww2. Accessed January 2, 2016.

Index

abduction, 3, 14–15, 22–25, 31, 54, 77–80, 85–87, 90–95, 99, 116–26, 161–62, 164, 166–67, 170, 185–86, 188, 190, 192, 193, 195
abortion, 4, 50
Abu Ghraib prison, 8, 65
Aceh (Indonesia), 62, 74, 132, 155
Afghanistan, 62, 64, 78, 80
Aileu (Timor-Leste), 140
Aitarak, 42, 163, 166
Algeria, 62, 64, 78, 80
Alison, Miranda, 31, 50
All People's Congress (APC), 99–100. *See also* Sierra Leone
Amaya, Rufina, 179
Ambon (Indonesia), 155
Amir, Menachem, 32, 37–38
Amnesty International (AI), 50, 67, 69–70, 139–40
amputations, 45, 98, 104
Angola, 62, 64, 78, 80
Annan, Jeannie, 34
Apodeti, 130
Arab Spring, 71
Arendt, Hannah, 40
Argentina, 8, 27, 64
Armed Forces for the National Liberation of East Timor. *See* Falintil
Armed Forces Revolutionary Council (AFRC), 100, 102, 105, 110–11, 120–21. *See also* Sierra Leone
Atambua (Indonesia), 142–43
Australia, 129–31, 133, 135, 140–42, 155
Azerbaijan, 62, 64, 80

Bali, 132
Ball, Patrick, 144
Bangladesh, 30, 61–62, 64
Beber, Bernd, 24
Bellows, John, 117
Belo, Bishop Carlos, 132
Berman, Eli, 36
biru, 150
Blattman, Christopher, 24
Bloom, Mia, 32

Bo district (Sierra Leone), 106
Bobonaro district (Timor-Leste), 134
Bombali district (Sierra Leone), 106–7
Bonthe district (Sierra Leone), 106
Bosnia-Herzegovina, 2, 8, 39, 50, 58, 61–62, 64, 67, 72–73, 78, 80, 148
Bourgois, Phillippe, 38
Bourke, Joanna, 8, 10
Boyle, Michael, 157, 160
Brana Plan, 58
Browning, Christopher, 27, 39
Burkina Faso, 48
Burma/Myanmar, 62, 64–65, 72–73, 78, 80
Burundi, 62, 64, 72–73, 78, 80
Bush, George H. W., 171, 189
Butler, Christopher, 6, 61, 63

Cambodia, 29–30, 62, 64, 78, 80
Canada, 22–23, 43
Canadian Airborne Regiment (CAR), 22–23
Caprioli, Mary, 81
Card, Claudia, 44
Carnation Revolution, 129–30
Carpenter, R. Charli, 35
Carter, Jimmy, 171
Central African Republic, 64
Central Intelligence Agency (CIA), 194
Chad, 62, 64, 78, 80
Chechnya, 64–65, 80
Checkel, Jeffrey, 21
Chile, 8, 64
China, 30, 62, 80, 130
CIRI Human Rights Dataset, 69, 83, 94
Civil Defense Forces (CDF) (Sierra Leone)
    abductions, 24, 122
    child soldiers, 46
    civilian support, 117
    combatant socialization hypothesis, 23–24, 120–23, 192
    demographic composition, 99–100, 108–9
    funding, 100
    interview subjects, 102
    Kamajors, 112
    opportunism/greed hypothesis, 46–47, 117
    origins, 100

62153379R00173

Made in the USA
Lexington, KY
30 March 2017